SECOND EDITION

Concise Introduction
to Tonal Harmony
WORKBOOK

SECOND EDITION

Concise Introduction to Tonal Harmony
WORKBOOK

L. POUNDIE BURSTEIN
Graduate Center and Hunter College
City University of New York

JOSEPH N. STRAUS
Graduate Center
City University of New York

W. W. NORTON & COMPANY
NEW YORK • LONDON

W. W. Norton & Company has been independent since its founding in 1923, when William Warder Norton and Mary D. Herter Norton first published lectures delivered at the People's Institute, the adult education division of New York City's Cooper Union. The firm soon expanded its program beyond the Institute, publishing books by celebrated academics from America and abroad. By midcentury, the two major pillars of Norton's publishing program—trade books and college texts—were firmly established. In the 1950s, the Norton family transferred control of the company to its employees, and today—with a staff of five hundred and hundreds of trade, college, and professional titles published each year—W. W. Norton & Company stands as the largest and oldest publishing house owned wholly by its employees.

....

Editor: Justin Hoffman
Project Editor: David Bradley
Assistant Editor: Julie Kocsis
Manuscript Editor: Jodi Beder
Managing Editor, College: Marian Johnson
Managing Editor, College Digital Media: Kim Yi
Production Manager: Elizabeth Marotta
Media Editor: Steve Hoge
Media Project Editor: Meg Wilhoite
Media Editorial Assistant: Ellie Shirocky
Marketing Manager, Music: Trevor Penland
Design Director: Rubina Yeh
Art Direction: Jillian Burr
Design: Wendy Lai
Permissions Manager: Bethany Salminen
Composition: Six Red Marbles
Music Engraving: David Botwinik, Willow Graphics, London N3 2BN
Manufacturing: Sheridan Books, Inc.

Permission to use copyrighted material is included in the credits section of this book, which begins on page C-1.

ISBN: 978-0-393-41703-6

W. W. Norton & Company, Inc., 500 Fifth Avenue, New York, NY 10110-0017
wwnorton.com
W. W. Norton & Company, Ltd., 15 Carlisle Street, London WID 3BS

3 4 5 6 7 8 9 0

Contents in Brief

Contents

Preface

This workbook contains thousands of exercises to help students master music theory. There are far more than could be used by any one class, enabling instructors to choose from a wide array of possibilities in constructing assignments that best suit the needs of their classes. The exercises are suitable both for homework and in-class activities.

Nearly every chapter includes the following types of exercises, which are pedagogically graded from easiest to most challenging:

- **Questions for Review** ask students to summarize the main points in each chapter in their own words.

- **Preliminary Exercises** make sure students can spell each harmony correctly.

- In **Realizing Roman Numerals** and **Realizing Figured Bass**, students compose harmonic progressions of varying length and difficulty in keyboard or SATB format. The second edition includes additional extended chord progressions and opportunities to realize figured basses from musical literature.

- **Harmonizing Melodies** includes a variety of melodies, long and short, simple and complex, all using harmonies from the chapter.

- Structured **Composition** activities include guidelines to help students compose works using techniques discussed in each chapter. The composition exercises are designed for a variety of instruments and ensembles. With the second edition, we've expanded the number of composition exercises throughout the workbook.

- **Analysis** exercises feature numerous passages from the literature and include diverse composers and works. They provide clear and beautiful illustrations of each theoretical concept. Each analysis exercise tests students' recognition of the concepts explored in the chapter; discussion questions offer opportunities to go deeper; and the exercises can easily be extended to explore some of the more advanced concepts in class. Recordings of these excerpts are available online. The second edition features dozens of additional analysis exercises, including longer excerpts and examples that ask students to identify the harmonic rhythm. Additional open-ended questions offer more opportunities than ever for in-class discussion or writing assignments.

In addition to the print workbook, students and instructors can download assignment templates in Finale and MusicXML formats that can be completed with notation software. Whether completed in print or with notation software, this workbook matches the flexibility of *Concise Introduction to Tonal Harmony*. It gives instructors the resources to organize courses their way, and it gives students the tools to achieve and demonstrate mastery of music theory.

SECOND EDITION

Concise Introduction to Tonal Harmony

WORKBOOK

part
one

Fundamentals

chapter 0 Notation of Pitch and Rhythm

A. QUESTIONS FOR REVIEW

1. What is a clef and what does it tell you? How do you write a treble clef and what does it indicate? A bass clef?

2. What is the effect of the sharp sign? The flat sign? The natural sign? The double-sharp sign? The double-flat sign?

3. What are the relationships among whole notes, half notes, quarter notes, eighth notes, and sixteenth notes?

4. What is an augmentation dot? A tie?

5. What is a time signature? How do you interpret the top and bottom numbers of a time signature?

6. What is simple meter? What is compound meter?

B. IDENTIFYING NOTE NAMES

1. Provide a letter name for each note in treble clef.

c.

d.

2. Provide a letter name for each note in bass clef.

a.

C

b.

c.

d.

C. WRITING NOTES

Using no more than one ledger line, write as many pitches as you can for each note name. (There will be two or three correct items for each note name.)

1. Treble clef

a.

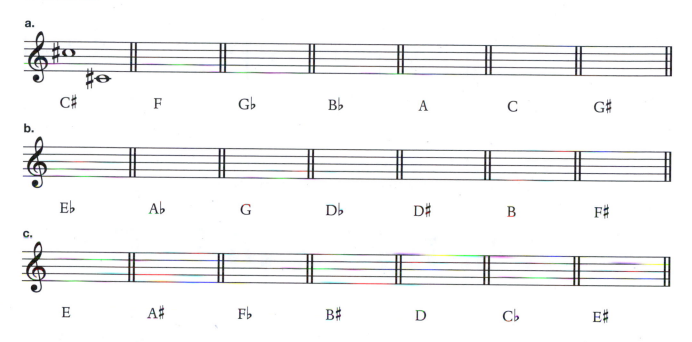

| C# | F | G♭ | B♭ | A | C | G# |

b.

| E♭ | A♭ | G | D♭ | D# | B | F# |

c.

| E | A# | F♭ | B# | D | C♭ | E# |

2. Bass clef

a.

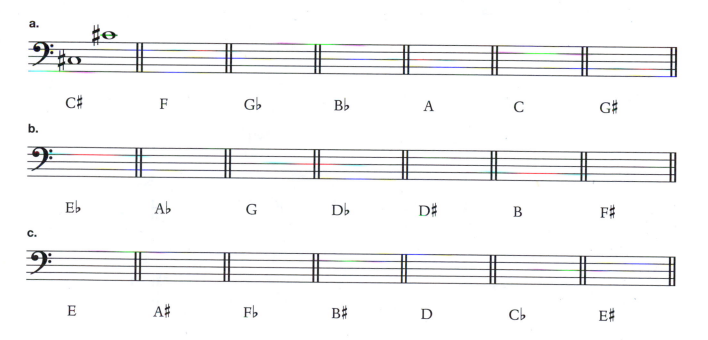

| C# | F | G♭ | B♭ | A | C | G# |

b.

| E♭ | A♭ | G | D♭ | D# | B | F# |

c.

| E | A# | F♭ | B# | D | C♭ | E# |

D. PITCH AND KEYBOARD

1. For each indicated key on the keyboard, write the corresponding note on the grand staff.

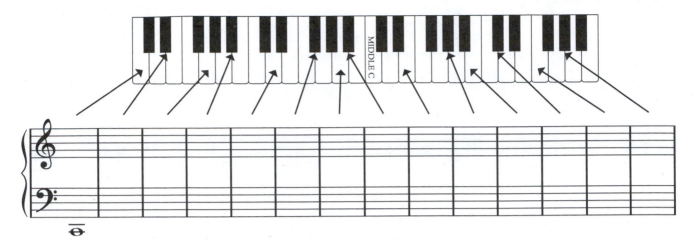

2. For each note on the grand staff, draw an arrow to the corresponding key on the keyboard.

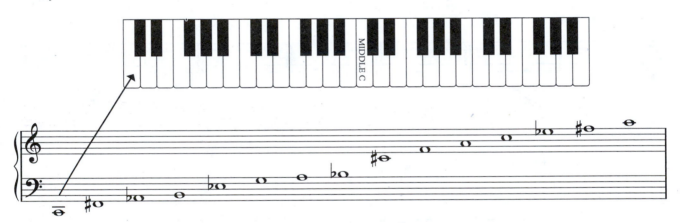

E. ENHARMONIC NOTES

Write a note enharmonically equivalent to each given note using only sharps or flats (not double sharps or double flats).

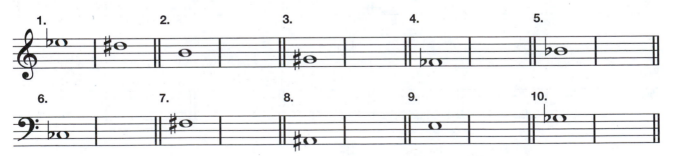

NAME: ....

F. BARLINES

Insert barlines to create complete measures in the indicated meter.

G. WRITING TIME SIGNATURES

For the following rhythms write in the correct time signature.

H. BEAMS

Rewrite these rhythms using beams that span the duration of one beat in the given time signature.

I. WRITING RHYTHMS

1. Insert one note of the proper duration to fill in each blank indicated with an arrow.

NAME: ....

2. Complete each four-measure rhythmic composition, using whatever rhythmic values you prefer in the meter indicated.

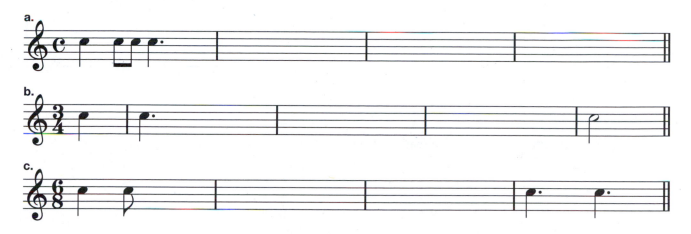

J. ANALYSIS

Identify the notes by writing the letter name (with sharp or flat sign, if needed) directly above or below the note.

1. Hildegard von Bingen, "O ignee Spiritus" ("O Fiery Spirit")

In - de vo - lún - tas a - scén - dit et gu - stum á - ni - mae trí - bu - it,

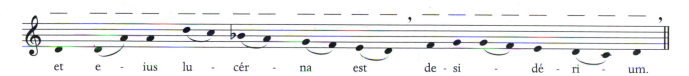

et e - ius lu - cér - na est de - si - dé - ri - um.

Translation: So mounts the will and grants the soul to taste—desire is its lamp.

- What are some ways that the melodies of the two lines are similar to each other, and what are some ways in which they differ?

2. Navajo folk song

A

- What is the meter? _____

- Is this a simple or compound meter? _____

- Measure 1 repeats exactly in m. 3. What other measures are repeated exactly?

  _____

3. "Rocky Road to Dublin" (Irish reel)

Remember that an accidental (flat or sharp) remains in force throughout a measure unless explicitly canceled by a natural sign, and that the barline cancels any accidentals (i.e., they do not continue in force beyond the barline).

- What is the time signature? _____

- Is this a simple or compound meter? _____

4. Ignatius Sancho, "Ruffs and Rhees"

Label the treble clef notes above the grand staff, and the bass clef notes below the grand staff.

- What is the time signature? _____

- Is this a simple or compound meter? _____

- Compare mm. 1–2 to mm. 3–4: in what ways are they similar, and in what ways do they differ?

5. Scott Joplin, "The Entertainer"

Identify the note immediately above or below each blank (ignore the notes in the middle of the chords). Remember that an accidental (flat or sharp) remains in force throughout a measure unless explicitly canceled by a natural sign, and that the barline cancels any accidentals (i.e., they do not continue in force beyond the barline).

- What is the time signature? _____

- Is this a simple or compound meter? _____

- There are lots of ties. Where in the measure do they tend to occur? What is their effect on the sound of the music?

6. Maria Szymanowska, Etude in D Minor

Identify every note in the melody and bass. Remember that an accidental (flat or sharp) remains in force throughout a measure unless explicitly canceled by a natural sign, and that the barline cancels any accidentals (i.e., they do not continue in force beyond the barline).

Risoluto

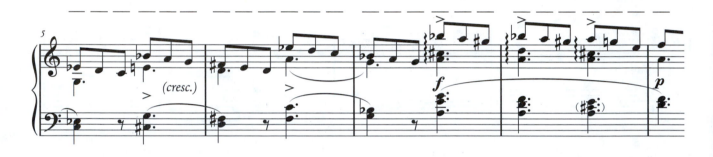

- What is the time signature? _____

- Is this a simple or compound meter? _____

- What is the time value of the beat? _____

- How many beats are there per measure? _____

chapter

1

Scales

A. QUESTIONS FOR REVIEW

1. What is the order of whole tones and semitones in a major scale? In a natural minor scale? In a harmonic minor scale? In an ascending melodic minor scale?

2. What are the traditional names for the scale degrees? (Remember that $\hat{7}$ has two different names in minor keys, depending on whether or not it is raised from its natural position.)

3. Which scale degrees are raised in the harmonic minor scale? In the ascending melodic minor scale?

4. What is a key signature?

5. What is the circle of fifths?

6. What are relative keys? Parallel keys?

B. WRITING MAJOR SCALES

Write the ascending major scales indicated, using accidentals rather than key signatures.

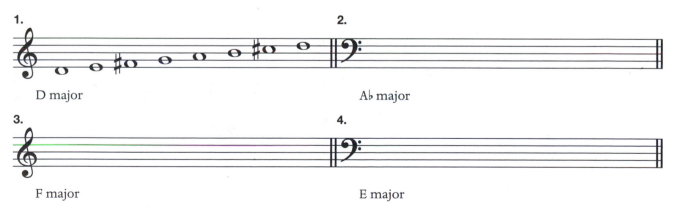

1.

D major

2.

A♭ major

3.

F major

4.

E major

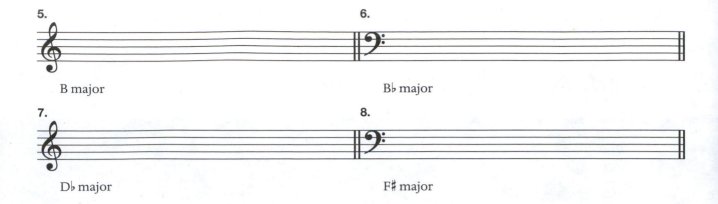

5.

B major

6.

B♭ major

7.

D♭ major

8.

F♯ major

C. WRITING MINOR SCALES

Write the ascending minor scales indicated, using accidentals rather than a key signature.

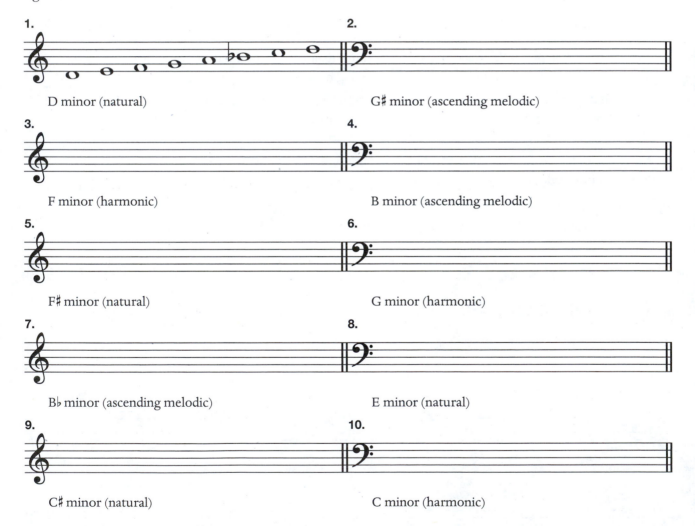

1.

D minor (natural)

2.

G♯ minor (ascending melodic)

3.

F minor (harmonic)

4.

B minor (ascending melodic)

5.

F♯ minor (natural)

6.

G minor (harmonic)

7.

B♭ minor (ascending melodic)

8.

E minor (natural)

9.

C♯ minor (natural)

10.

C minor (harmonic)

D. IDENTIFYING MAJOR KEYS FROM SCALE DEGREES

Each note below is the indicated scale degree in a major scale. Identify the key.

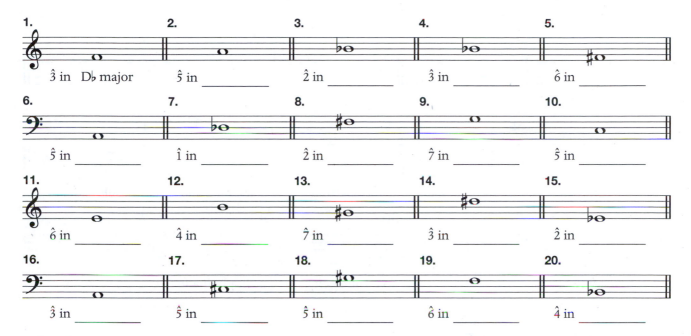

1. $\hat{3}$ in   D♭ major
2. $\hat{5}$ in _____
3. $\hat{2}$ in _____
4. $\hat{3}$ in _____
5. $\hat{6}$ in _____

6. $\hat{5}$ in _____
7. $\hat{1}$ in _____
8. $\hat{2}$ in _____
9. $\hat{7}$ in _____
10. $\hat{5}$ in _____

11. $\hat{6}$ in _____
12. $\hat{4}$ in _____
13. $\hat{7}$ in _____
14. $\hat{3}$ in _____
15. $\hat{2}$ in _____

16. $\hat{3}$ in _____
17. $\hat{5}$ in _____
18. $\hat{5}$ in _____
19. $\hat{6}$ in _____
20. $\hat{4}$ in _____

E. IDENTIFYING MINOR KEYS FROM SCALE DEGREES

Each note below is the indicated scale degree in a minor scale. Identify the key.

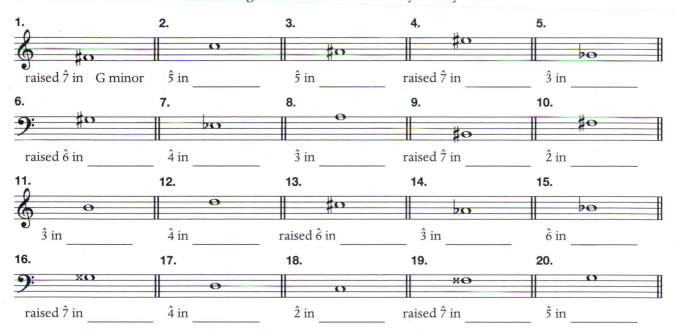

1. raised $\hat{7}$ in   G minor
2. $\hat{5}$ in _____
3. $\hat{5}$ in _____
4. raised $\hat{7}$ in _____
5. $\hat{3}$ in _____

6. raised $\hat{6}$ in _____
7. $\hat{4}$ in _____
8. $\hat{3}$ in _____
9. raised $\hat{7}$ in _____
10. $\hat{2}$ in _____

11. $\hat{3}$ in _____
12. $\hat{4}$ in _____
13. raised $\hat{6}$ in _____
14. $\hat{3}$ in _____
15. $\hat{6}$ in _____

16. raised $\hat{7}$ in _____
17. $\hat{4}$ in _____
18. $\hat{2}$ in _____
19. raised $\hat{7}$ in _____
20. $\hat{5}$ in _____

F. WRITING MAJOR SCALE DEGREES

Given the major scale and scale-degree name or number, write the note.

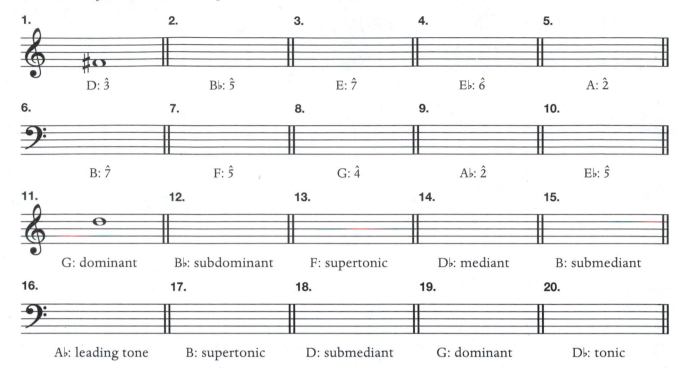

1. D: $\hat{3}$ 2. Bb: $\hat{5}$ 3. E: $\hat{7}$ 4. Eb: $\hat{6}$ 5. A: $\hat{2}$

6. B: $\hat{7}$ 7. F: $\hat{5}$ 8. G: $\hat{4}$ 9. Ab: $\hat{2}$ 10. Eb: $\hat{5}$

11. G: dominant   12. Bb: subdominant   13. F: supertonic   14. Db: mediant   15. B: submediant

16. Ab: leading tone   17. B: supertonic   18. D: submediant   19. G: dominant   20. Db: tonic

G. WRITING MINOR SCALE DEGREES

Given the minor scale and scale-degree name or number, write the note. Minor scales are assumed to be in their natural form unless "harmonic minor" (H) or "ascending melodic minor" (MA) is indicated.

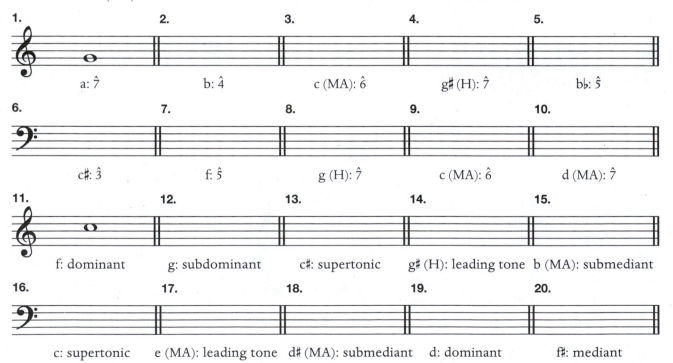

1. a: $\hat{7}$ 2. b: $\hat{4}$ 3. c (MA): $\hat{6}$ 4. g# (H): $\hat{7}$ 5. bb: $\hat{5}$

6. c#: $\hat{3}$ 7. f: $\hat{5}$ 8. g (H): $\hat{7}$ 9. c (MA): $\hat{6}$ 10. d (MA): $\hat{7}$

11. f: dominant   12. g: subdominant   13. c#: supertonic   14. g# (H): leading tone   15. b (MA): submediant

16. c: supertonic   17. e (MA): leading tone   18. d# (MA): submediant   19. d: dominant   20. f#: mediant

H. IDENTIFYING MAJOR KEY SIGNATURES

Identify the major key represented by each key signature.

1. G major

I. IDENTIFYING MINOR KEY SIGNATURES

Identify the minor key represented by each key signature.

1. E minor

J. WRITING MAJOR KEY SIGNATURES

Write the key signature for each major key.

1. F major   2. Db major   3. D major   4. F# major   5. Gb major

6. Bb major   7. A major   8. Eb major   9. Ab major   10. B major

K. WRITING MINOR KEY SIGNATURES

Write the key signature for each minor key.

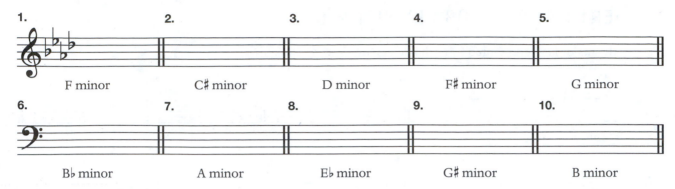

1. F minor   2. C♯ minor   3. D minor   4. F♯ minor   5. G minor

6. B♭ minor   7. A minor   8. E♭ minor   9. G♯ minor   10. B minor

L. IDENTIFYING RELATIVE KEYS

1. Name the two keys represented by each key signature. Give the major key first,
   using an uppercase letter, and then the relative minor, using lowercase.

a. B♭, g   b. _____   c. _____   d. _____   e. _____

f. _____   g. _____   h. _____   i. _____   j. _____

2. For each key (major or minor), name its relative key (minor or major) and write
   the shared key signature.

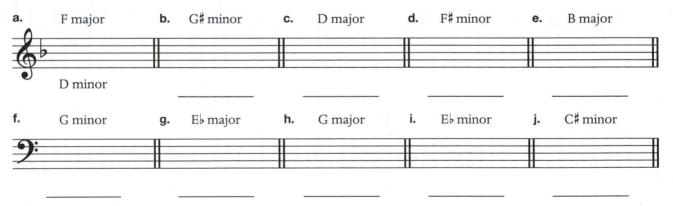

a. F major   b. G♯ minor   c. D major   d. F♯ minor   e. B major

D minor   _____   _____   _____   _____

f. G minor   g. E♭ major   h. G major   i. E♭ minor   j. C♯ minor

_____   _____   _____   _____   _____

M. PARALLEL KEYS

For each key (major or minor), name its parallel key (minor or major) and write the
key signatures for both keys.

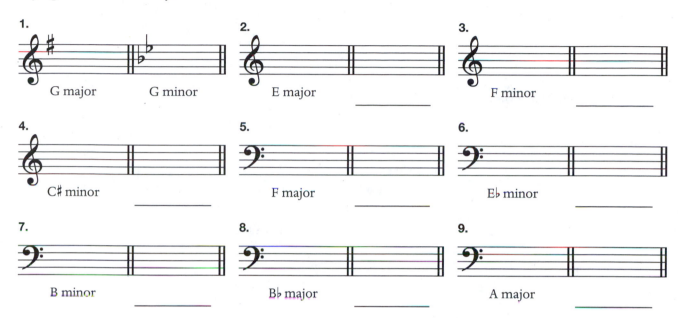

1. G major — G minor

2. E major — _____

3. F minor — _____

4. C♯ minor — _____

5. F major — _____

6. E♭ minor — _____

7. B minor — _____

8. B♭ major — _____

9. A major — _____

N. ANALYSIS

1. Figure out whether the following melodies are in major or minor keys. (Hint: In
minor keys, you will see $\hat{7}$ raised by an accidental—either natural or sharp—to
become the leading tone; $\hat{6}$ may also be raised by an accidental). Then identify the
keys and write the scale degree number of each note.

   a. Queen Lili'uokalani, "Oh Kou Aloha No"

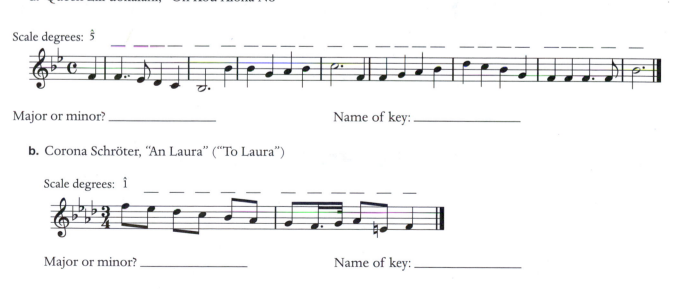

Scale degrees: $\hat{5}$ __ __ __ __ __ __ ...

Major or minor? _____   Name of key: _____

   b. Corona Schröter, "An Laura" ("To Laura")

Scale degrees: $\hat{1}$ __ __ __ __ __ __ ...

Major or minor? _____   Name of key: _____

c. Traditional Russian melody

Scale degrees: $\hat{1}$

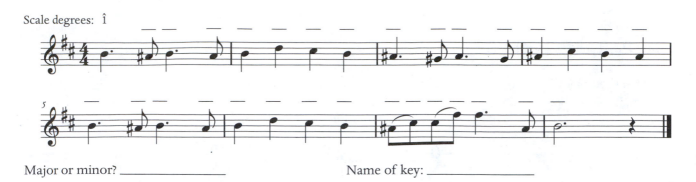

Major or minor? _____   Name of key: _____

d. Edvard Grieg, "Folkevise," Lyric Pieces, Op. 12, No. 5

Scale degrees: $\hat{5}$

Major or minor? _____   Name of key: _____

2. The key signatures for the following melodies are not given. For each, figure out whether the melody is in a major or minor key. Then identify the key and write the scale degrees numbers of each note.

a. Christoph Willibald Gluck, *Orfeo ed Euridice*

Scale degrees: $\hat{5}$

Major or minor? _____   Name of key: _____

b. Ludwig van Beethoven, Cello Sonata, Op. 69, i

Scale degrees: $\hat{1}$

Major or minor? _____   Name of key: _____

c. Fanny Mendelssohn Hensel, "Schwanenlied"

Scale degrees: $\hat{5}$

Major or minor? _____   Name of key: _____

d. Johann Christoph Pepusch, *The Beggar's Opera*

Write scale-degree numbers for the melody above the treble staff and for the bass below the bass staff.

Scale degrees
(treble clef): $\hat{1}$

Scale degrees
(bass clef): $\hat{3}$

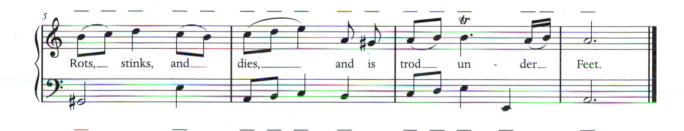

Major or minor? _____   Name of key: _____

3. For each of these passages, identify the key and write out the scale starting and ending on $\hat{1}$.

a. James Scott, "Quality (A High-Class Rag)"

Key: _____

Scale: _____

b. James Scott, "Frog Legs Rag"

Key: _____

Scale: _____

4. Ludwig van Beethoven, Trio for Piano, Violin, and Cello in B♭ major, Op. 97 ("Archduke")

For each boxed passage, name the key, then write out the scale, starting and ending with 1̂.

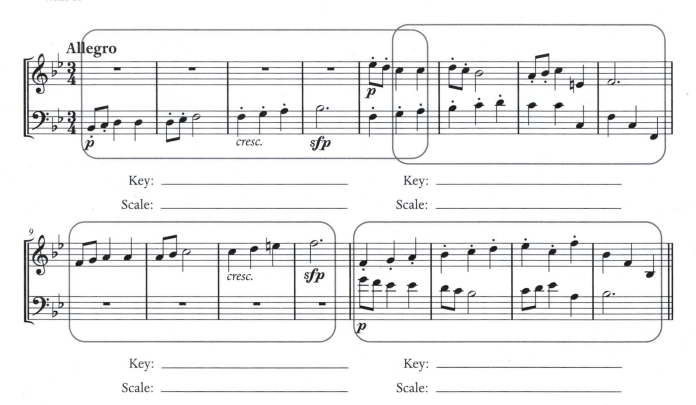

Key: _____   Key: _____

Scale: _____   Scale: _____

Key: _____   Key: _____

Scale: _____   Scale: _____

- What notes do these scales have in common?

  _____

- Which scale degree in the first scale becomes the tonic in the second?

  _____

- Which scale degree in the third scale becomes the tonic in the fourth?

  _____

5. J. S. Bach, Two-Part Invention in D minor

Answer the questions after each excerpt.

a. What key is this passage in? _____

b. If the key is major, write out its major scale, starting and ending on î. If the key
is minor, write out its harmonic minor scale, starting and ending on î.

_____

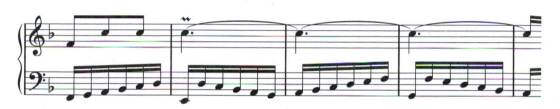

c. What key is this passage in? _____

d. If the key is major, write out its major scale, starting and ending on î. If the key
is minor, write out its harmonic minor scale, starting and ending on î.

_____

e. What is the relationship between this major scale and the minor scale in the
first passage?

_____

f. What key is this passage in? _____

g. If the key is major, write out its major scale, starting and ending on î. If the key
is minor, write out its harmonic minor scale, starting and ending on î.

_____

6. Élisabeth Jacquet de la Guerre, Suite in F, Allemande

Identify the key for these two passages and write out the scale starting and ending on 1̂.

Key: _____
Scale: _____

Key: _____
Scale: _____

    a. Which notes do these scales share in common?

_____

    b. Which scale degree in the first scale becomes the tonic of the second scale?

_____

chapter 2

Intervals

A. QUESTIONS FOR REVIEW

1. How do you determine the size of an interval?

2. What is a melodic interval? A harmonic interval?

3. What is the difference between simple and compound intervals?

4. Which intervals can be major or minor? Which intervals can be perfect?

5. What is interval inversion? What is the inversion of a second? A third? A fourth? A fifth? A sixth? A seventh?

6. What happens to the quality of perfect intervals when they are inverted? What happens to diminished intervals? Minor intervals? Major intervals? Augmented intervals?

7. What are the qualities of the natural (white-key) intervals?

8. What are enharmonic intervals?

9. What are the qualities of the intervals formed between the tonic and the other scale degrees in major? In minor?

B. IDENTIFYING INTERVAL SIZE

1. Identify the numerical size of each interval (ignore accidentals, which do not affect interval size).

2. *Identifying compound and simple intervals (numerical size only):* For each of these compound intervals, identify the numerical size of the simple interval to which it is equivalent.

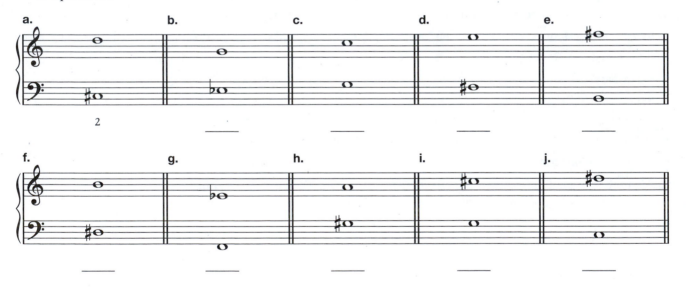

3. *Identifying natural intervals*: Identify each natural interval with its numerical size and quality (d = diminished; m = minor; M = major; P = perfect; A = augmented).

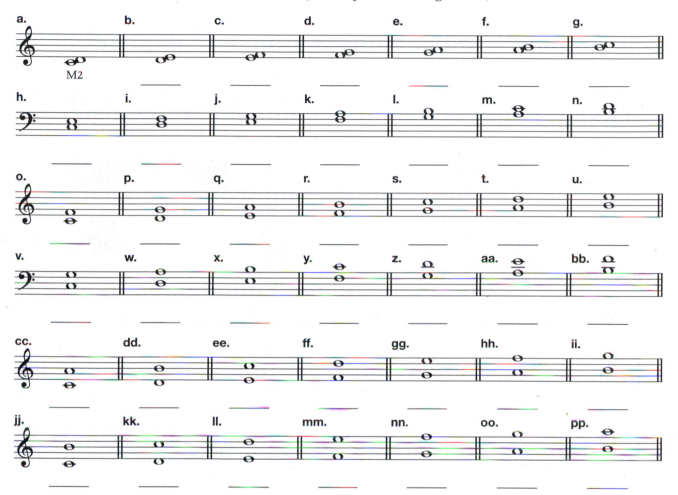

4. *Identifying seconds and thirds*: Identify each interval with its numerical size and quality (d = diminished; m = minor; M = major; A = augmented).

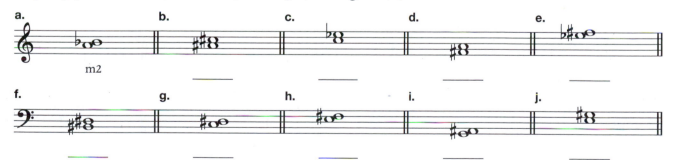

5. *Identifying fourths and fifths:* Identify each interval with its numerical size and quality (d = diminished; P = perfect; A = augmented).

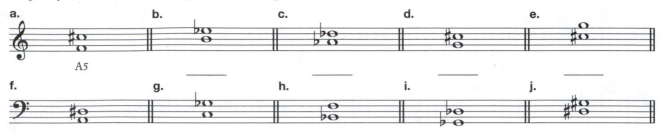

6. *Identifying sixths and sevenths:* Identify each interval with its numerical size and quality (d = diminished; m = minor; M = major; A = augmented).

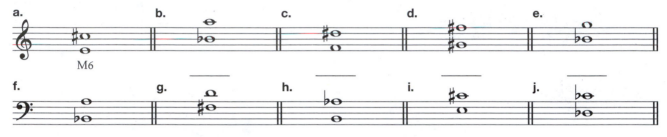

7. *Identifying all intervals:* Identify each interval with its numerical size and quality (d = diminished; m = minor; M = major; P = perfect; A = augmented).

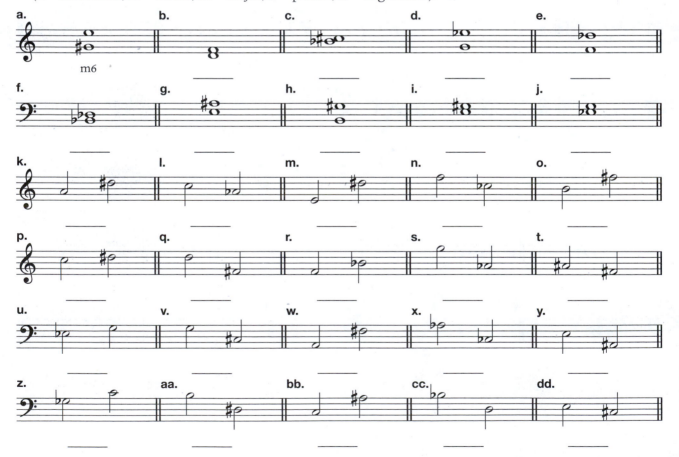

C. WRITING INTERVALS

1. Write each interval *above* the given note.

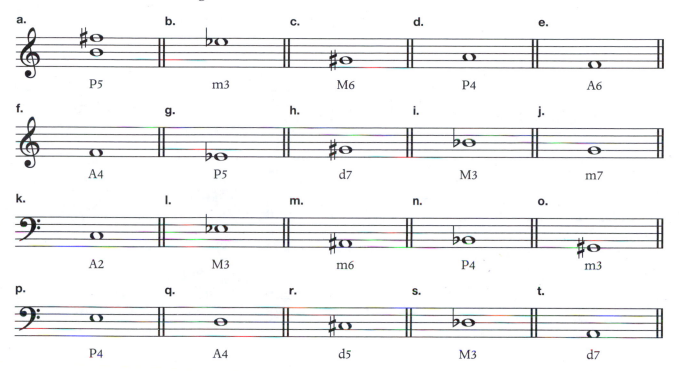

a. P5   b. m3   c. M6   d. P4   e. A6

f. A4   g. P5   h. d7   i. M3   j. m7

k. A2   l. M3   m. m6   n. P4   o. m3

p. P4   q. A4   r. d5   s. M3   t. d7

2. Write each interval *below* the given note.

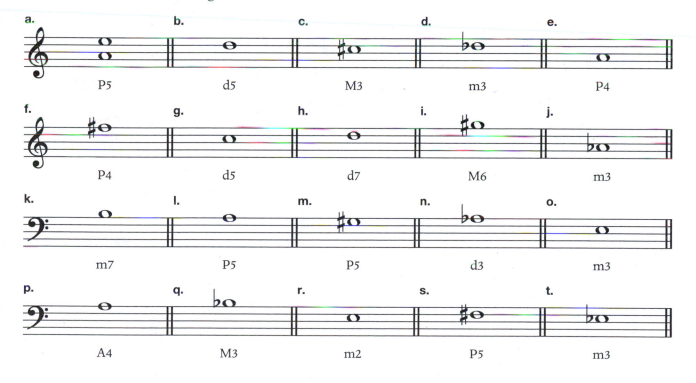

a. P5   b. d5   c. M3   d. m3   e. P4

f. P4   g. d5   h. d7   i. M6   j. m3

k. m7   l. P5   m. P5   n. d3   o. m3

p. A4   q. M3   r. m2   s. P5   t. m3

D. INVERTING INTERVALS

Identify each interval by size and quality, write its inversion, and identify the size and quality of the inversion.

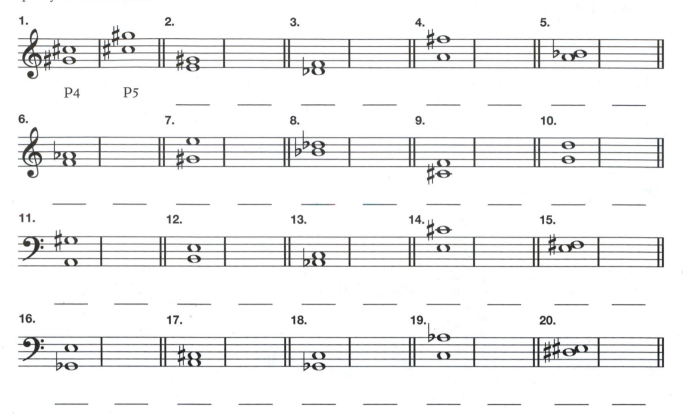

E. IDENTIFYING ENHARMONIC INTERVALS

For each interval, write one interval that is enharmonically equivalent (there may be several possibilities), and give the size and quality of both intervals.

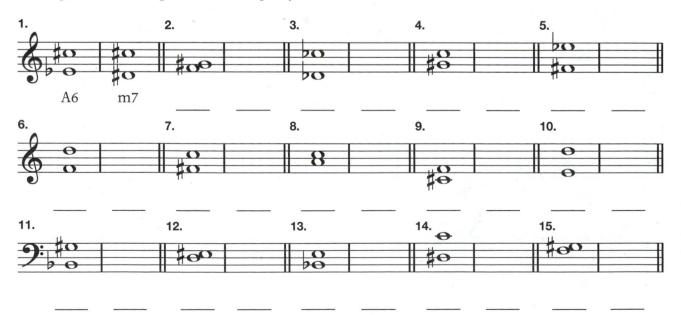

F. IDENTIFYING INTERVALS IN A KEY

1. Write the intervals (the scales are given for reference).

a. The three major thirds in G major

b. The six perfect fifths in D minor (natural)

c. The augmented second in C♯ minor (harmonic)

d. The diminished fifth in A♭ major

e. The four minor thirds in D major

f. The five major seconds in A major

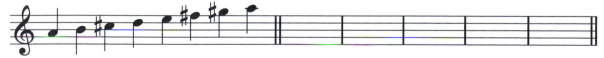

G. ANALYSIS

1. Mikalojus Čiurlionis, Fughetta in D minor

Identify the melodic intervals.

2. Nadia Boulanger, "J'ai frappé" ("I knocked")

Identify the melodic intervals. Remember that the key signature is in force throughout, and that any accidental remains in force through the whole measure.

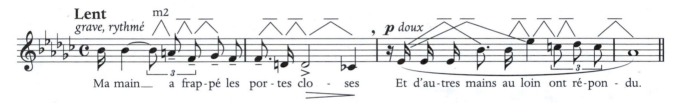

Translation: My hand knocked at the closed door. And other hands responded from a distance.

3. Richard Wagner, *Tristan und Isolde*, Act I

Identify the melodic intervals. Remember that the key signature remains in force throughout the passage (unless explicitly changed by an accidental) and that accidentals remain in force throughout a measure (unless explicitly canceled).

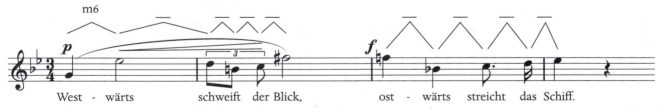

Translation: Westward the gaze wanders; eastward skims the ship.

4. Jelly Roll Morton, "Jelly Roll Blues"

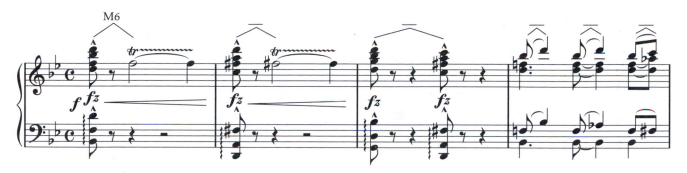

5. Gioachino Rossini, Duet No. 2 for Horns

Identify the harmonic intervals. Circle any dissonant interval.

6. Maddalena Cassulana, "Adio Lidia mia bella"

Identify the harmonic intervals.

Translation: Farewell, Lidia, my love.

7. J. S. Bach, Chorale 80

Identify the harmonic intervals between each pair of adjacent voices and write them in the table beneath the staff. Circle the dissonant intervals. If a fourth occurs between the bass and another voice, it is dissonant. Otherwise, it is consonant.

Interval between top two voices: M3 __ __ __ __ __ __ __ __ __ __

Interval between middle two voices: __ __ __ __ __ __ __ __ __ __ __

Interval between bottom two voices: __ __ __ __ __ __ __ __ __ __ __

8. Fanny Mendelssohn Hensel, Piano Trio Op. 11

Identify the harmonic intervals between each pair of adjacent voices and write them in the table beneath the staff. Circle the dissonant intervals. If a fourth occurs between the bass and another voice, it is dissonant. Otherwise, it is consonant.

Interval between top two voices: m3 __ __ __ __ __

Interval between middle two voices: __ __ __ __ __ __

Interval between bottom two voices: __ __ __ __ __ __

chapter

3

Triads and Seventh Chords

A. QUESTIONS FOR REVIEW

1. Name each of the triad qualities. What are the qualities of the thirds and fifths they contain?

2. What note of the chord (root, third, or fifth) is in the bass of a root-position triad? A first-inversion triad? A second-inversion triad? What are the figures for each of these inversions? What are common abbreviations for these symbols?

3. What is the quality of a triad identified by an uppercase Roman numeral? An uppercase Roman numeral with a plus sign (+)? A lowercase Roman numeral? A lowercase Roman numeral with a degree symbol (°)?

4. How does raising $\hat{7}$ in minor keys affect the triad whose root is $\hat{5}$? The triad whose root is $\hat{7}$?

5. Name each of the seventh-chord qualities. What are the qualities of the triads and sevenths they contain?

6. In major keys, what is the quality of the seventh chord built on $\hat{2}$? $\hat{4}$? $\hat{5}$? $\hat{7}$?

7. What note of the chord (root, third, fifth, or seventh) is in the bass of a root-position seventh chord? A first-inversion seventh chord? A second-inversion seventh chord? A third-inversion seventh chord? What are the figures for each of these inversions?

8. In minor keys, assuming the harmonic minor scale, what is the quality of the seventh chord built on $\hat{2}$? $\hat{4}$? $\hat{5}$? $\hat{7}$?

B. IDENTIFYING TRIAD QUALITY

1. *Identifying natural triads:* Identify the quality of each triad (d = diminished; m = minor; M = major; A = augmented).

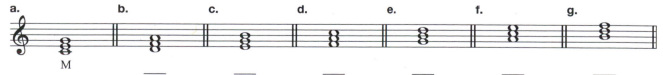

2. *Identifying triad quality for all triads:* Identify the quality of each triad (d = diminished; m = minor; M = major; A = augmented).

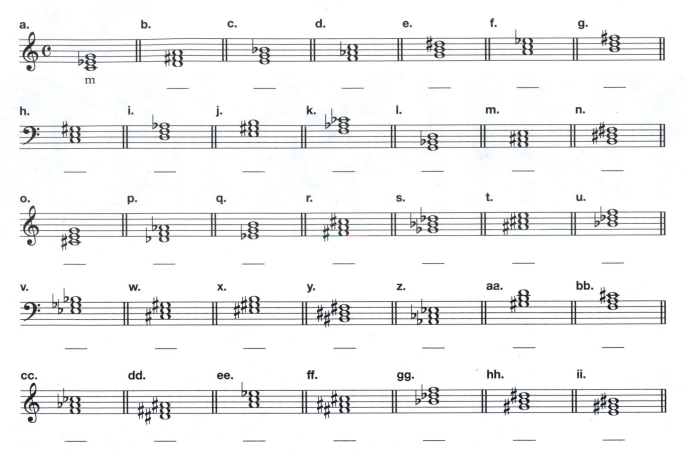

C. WRITING TRIADS

1. Add accidentals to the upper note(s) of each natural triad to produce the chord quality indicated. Do not alter the root.

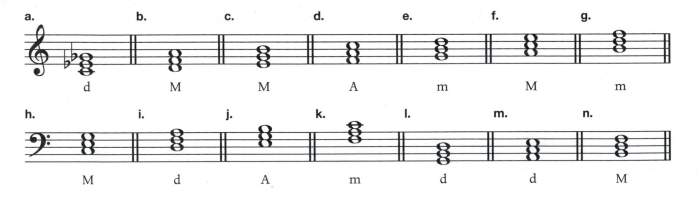

2. Write each triad in root position.

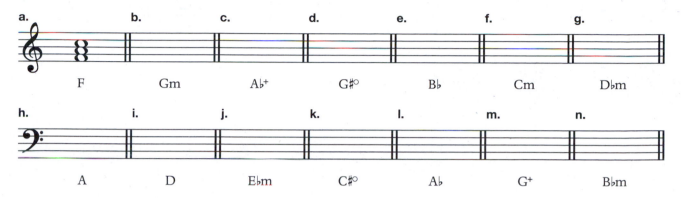

3. Given the root, third, or fifth, add two notes to complete the triad. Do not alter the given note.

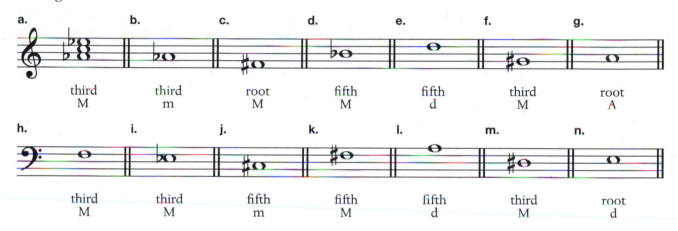

D. TRIAD INVERSIONS

1. *Identifying inversions:* Identify the position of each triad (root position = $\frac{5}{3}$; first inversion = $\frac{6}{3}$; second inversion = $\frac{6}{4}$).

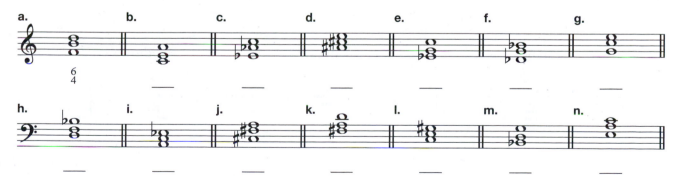

2. Complete the table to identify the position of each triad.

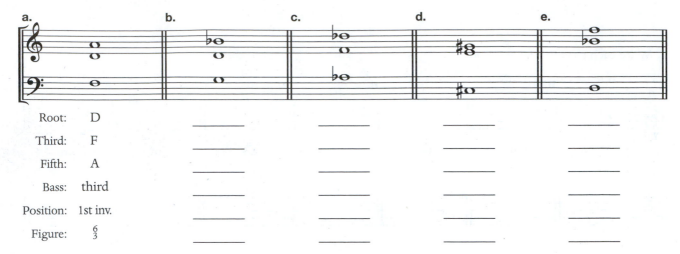

	a.	b.	c.	d.	e.
Root:	D				
Third:	F				
Fifth:	A				
Bass:	third				
Position:	1st inv.				
Figure:	6 3				

3. Complete the table to identify the position of each triad.

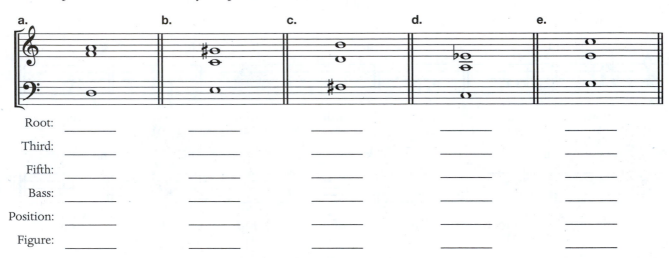

	a.	b.	c.	d.	e.
Root:					
Third:					
Fifth:					
Bass:					
Position:					
Figure:					

4. *Writing triad inversions*: Write each triad in all three positions.

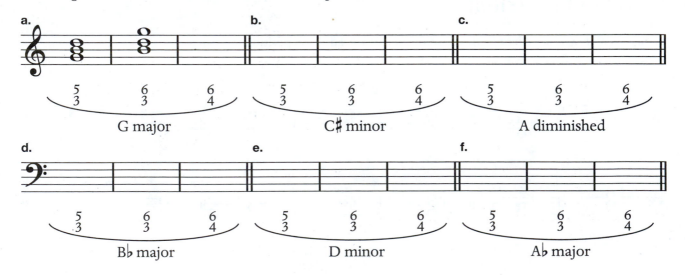

G major   C♯ minor   A diminished

B♭ major   D minor   A♭ major

5. *Writing triad inversions*: Write each triad (keep the spacing between the pitches as close as possible).

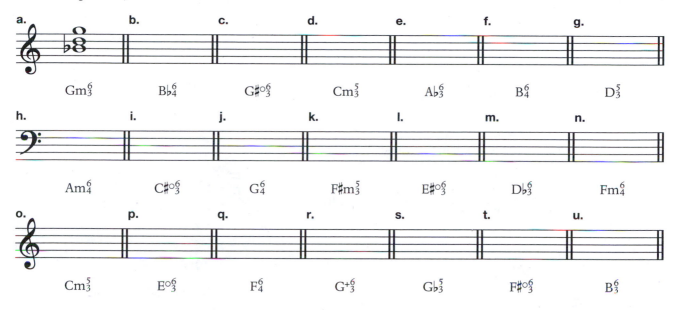

a. Gm$_3^6$ b. B♭$_4^6$ c. G♯°$_3^6$ d. Cm$_3^5$ e. A♭$_3^6$ f. B$_4^6$ g. D$_3^5$

h. Am$_4^6$ i. C♯°$_3^6$ j. G$_4^6$ k. F♯m$_3^5$ l. E♯°$_3^6$ m. D♭$_3^6$ n. Fm$_4^6$

o. Cm$_3^5$ p. E°$_3^6$ q. F$_4^6$ r. G+$_3^6$ s. G♭$_3^5$ t. F♯°$_3^6$ u. B$_3^6$

E. TRIADS IN MAJOR AND MINOR KEYS

1. *Writing triads in a key*: Write the key signature and the scale. Then write the seven triads in that scale, and identify the quality of each. (Note: The leading tone should not be raised in building the III triad.)

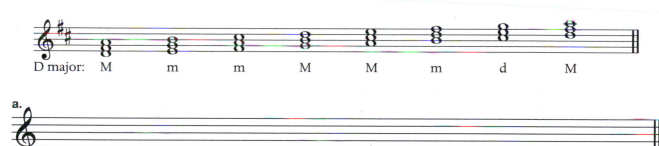

D major: M   m   m   M   M   m   d   M

a.

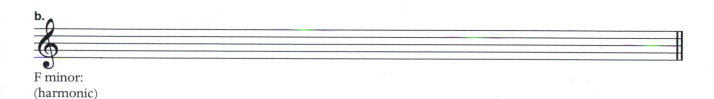

E♭ major:

b.

F minor:
(harmonic)

2. *Identifying triads in a major key:* Fill in the blanks to identify each triad.

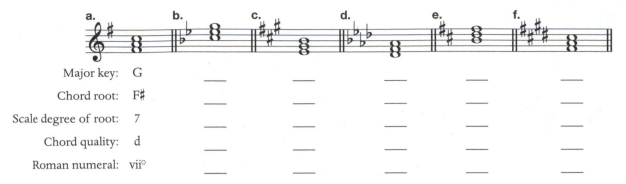

	a.	b.	c.	d.	e.	f.
Major key:	G	___	___	___	___	___
Chord root:	F♯	___	___	___	___	___
Scale degree of root:	7	___	___	___	___	___
Chord quality:	d	___	___	___	___	___
Roman numeral:	vii°	___	___	___	___	___

3. *Identifying triads in a minor key:* Fill in the blanks to identify each triad.

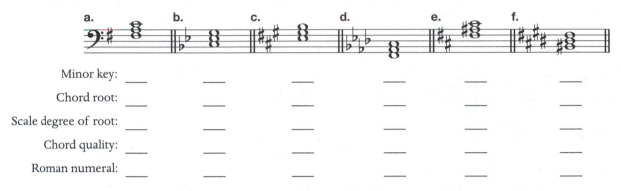

	a.	b.	c.	d.	e.	f.
Minor key:	___	___	___	___	___	___
Chord root:	___	___	___	___	___	___
Scale degree of root:	___	___	___	___	___	___
Chord quality:	___	___	___	___	___	___
Roman numeral:	___	___	___	___	___	___

4. *Identifying triads in major and minor keys:* Identify each triad in the key indicated with a Roman numeral and figures (uppercase letters = major keys; lowercase letters = minor keys).

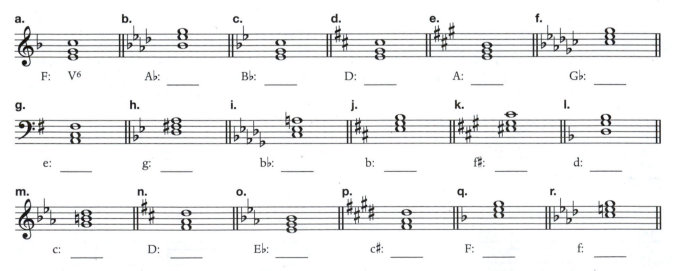

a.   F: V⁶   b.   A♭: ___   c.   B♭: ___   d.   D: ___   e.   A: ___   f.   G♭: ___

g.   e: ___   h.   g: ___   i.   b♭: ___   j.   b: ___   k.   f♯: ___   l.   d: ___

m.   c: ___   n.   D: ___   o.   E♭: ___   p.   c♯: ___   q.   F: ___   r.   f: ___

5. *Writing triads in major and minor keys:* Write each triad in the key indicated.

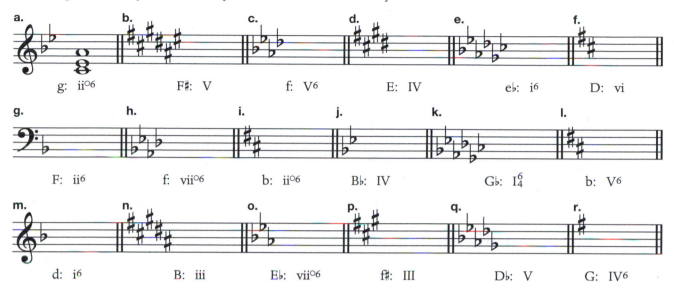

a.   b.   c.   d.   e.   f.

g: ii°6   F♯: V   f: V6   E: IV   e♭: i6   D: vi

g.   h.   i.   j.   k.   l.

F: ii6   f: vii°6   b: ii°6   B♭: IV   G♭: I$^6_4$ b: V6

m.   n.   o.   p.   q.   r.

d: i6   B: iii   E♭: vii°6   f♯: III   D♭: V   G: IV6

F. IDENTIFYING SEVENTH-CHORD QUALITIES

1. *Natural seventh-chord qualities:* Identify the quality of each seventh chord (°7 = fully diminished; ∅7 = half-diminished; m7 = minor; dom7 = dominant; maj7 = major).

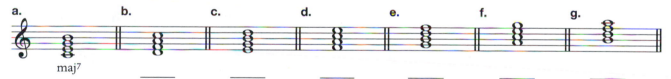

a.   b.   c.   d.   e.   f.   g.

maj7   _____   _____   _____   _____   _____   _____

2. *All seventh-chord qualities:* Identify the quality of each seventh chord (°7 = fully diminished; ∅7 = half-diminished; m7 = minor; dom7 = dominant; maj7 = major).

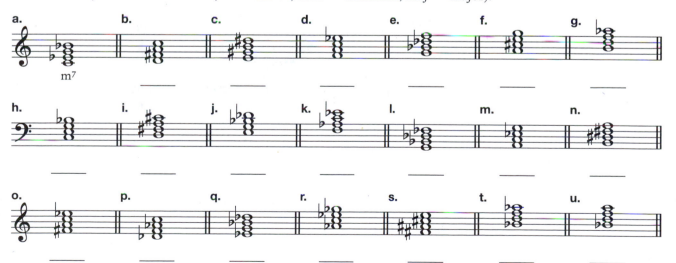

a.   b.   c.   d.   e.   f.   g.

m7   _____   _____   _____   _____   _____   _____

h.   i.   j.   k.   l.   m.   n.

_____   _____   _____   _____   _____   _____   _____

o.   p.   q.   r.   s.   t.   u.

_____   _____   _____   _____   _____   _____   _____

G. SEVENTH CHORDS BY ROOT AND QUALITY

1. *Writing seventh chords:* Write each seventh chord in root position, with the correct quality: maj7 (major seventh); m7 (minor seventh); 7 (dominant seventh); ∅7 (half-diminished seventh); o7 (diminished seventh).

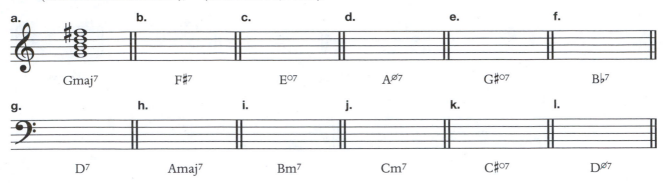

H. SEVENTH-CHORD INVERSIONS

1. *Identifying seventh-chord inversions:* Complete the table to identify the position of each seventh chord.

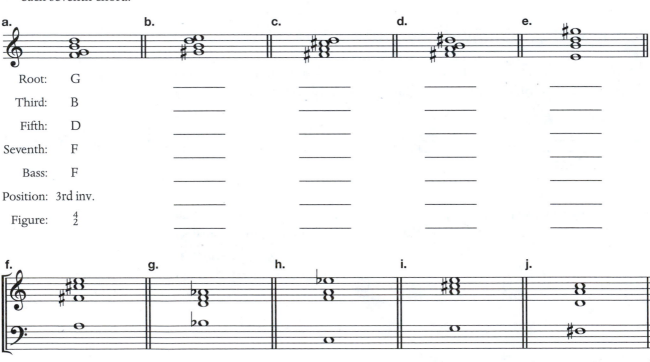

NAME: ....

2. *Writing seventh chords in inversion*: Write each seventh chord in all four positions.

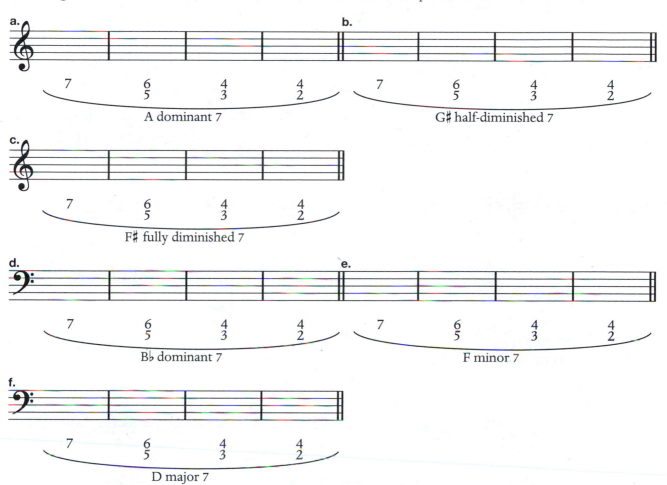

3. *Identifying seventh-chord inversions*: Use a Roman numeral and figure to identify each seventh chord in the major (uppercase) or minor (lowercase) key indicated.

4. *Writing seventh chords in inversion:* Write each seventh chord in the major (uppercase) or minor (lowercase) key indicated.

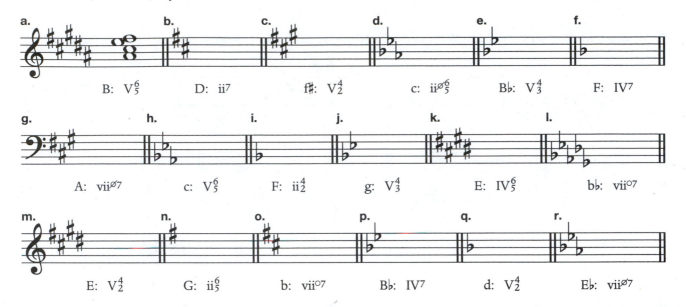

B: V$^6_5$ D: ii7   f♯: V$^4_2$ c: ii$^{ø6}_5$ B♭: V$^4_3$ F: IV7

A: vii^{ø}7   c: V$^6_5$ F: ii$^4_2$ g: V$^4_3$ E: IV$^6_5$ b♭: vii^{o}7

E: V$^4_2$ G: ii$^6_5$ b: vii^{o}7   B♭: IV7   d: V$^4_2$ E♭: vii^{ø}7

I. ANALYSIS

1. J. S. Bach, Chorale 80

Identify the chords by filling in the chart. Ignore any notes in triangles, which are not part of the prevailing chord.

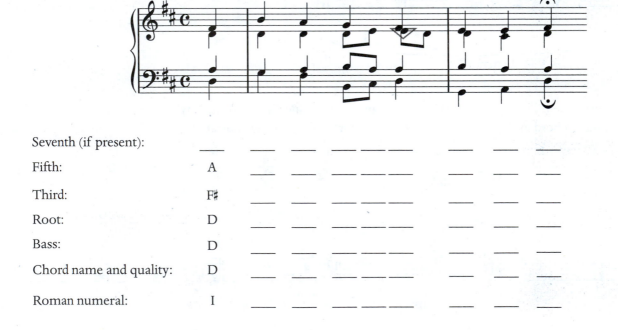

Seventh (if present):	—	— — — — — —	—	— — — — —
Fifth:	A			
Third:	F♯			
Root:	D			
Bass:	D			
Chord name and quality:	D			
Roman numeral:	I			

2. Josephine Lang, "Ich liebe dich" ("I Love You")

Identify the chord in each measure. The third is missing from one of these chords.
Ignore any notes in triangles, which are not part of the prevailing chord.

Seventh
(if present): _____   _____   _____   _____   _____

Fifth: _____   _____   _____   _____   _____

Third: _____   _____   _____   _____   _____

Root: _____   _____   _____   _____   _____

Bass: _____   _____   _____   _____   _____

Chord
name and
quality: _____   _____   _____   _____   _____

Roman
numeral: _____   _____   _____   _____   _____

3. Queen Lili'uokalani, "Aloha Oe"

Identify the chord in each measure. The lowest note in each measure is the bass of the chord. Ignore any notes in triangles, which are not part of the prevailing chord.

Seventh (if
present):   ___ ___   ___   ___   ___

Fifth: ___ ___   ___   ___   ___

Third: ___ ___   ___   ___   ___

Root: ___ ___   ___   ___   ___

Bass: ___ ___   ___   ___   ___

Chord name
and quality: ___ ___   ___   ___   ___

Roman
numeral: ___ ___   ___   ___   ___

Translation: Farewell to thee, farewell to thee, Thou charming one who dwells among the bowers.

4. Louise Reichardt, "Die Blume der Blumen" ("The Flower of Flowers")

Identify the chords. Each measure contains two chords, except for measures 2, 6, and 10, which contain only one chord. The lowest note should be regarded as the bass of the chord. The fifth is omitted in one chord. Ignore any notes in triangles, which are not part of the prevailing chord.

Seventh (if present):

Fifth:

Third:

Root:

Bass:

Chord name and quality:

Roman numeral:

Seventh (if present):

Fifth:

Third:

Root:

Bass:

Chord name and quality:

Roman numeral:

Translation: A beautiful flower blooms in a distant land; It is such a heavenly creation known only to a few.

5. Alex Rogers, "I May Be Crazy, but I Ain't No Fool"

Identify the chords by filling in the chart. Ignore any notes in triangles, which are not part of the prevailing The fifth is omitted in one chord.

Seventh (if
present): ___ ___ ___ ___ ___ ___ ___ ___ ___ ___ ___ ___ ___ ___

Fifth: ___ ___ ___ ___ ___ ___ ___ ___ ___ ___ ___ ___ ___ ___

Third: ___ ___ ___ ___ ___ ___ ___ ___ ___ ___ ___ ___ ___ ___

Root: ___ ___ ___ ___ ___ ___ ___ ___ ___ ___ ___ ___ ___ ___

Bass: ___ ___ ___ ___ ___ ___ ___ ___ ___ ___ ___ ___ ___ ___

Chord name
and quality: ___ ___ ___ ___ ___ ___ ___ ___ ___ ___ ___ ___ ___

Roman numeral: ___ ___ ___ ___ ___ ___ ___

6. Bert Williams, "Believe Me"

Identify the chords by filling in the chart. Ignore any notes in triangles, which are not part of the prevailing chord.

Seventh (if
present): ___ ___ ___ ___ ___

Fifth: ___ ___ ___ ___ ___

Third: ___ ___ ___ ___ ___

Root: ___ ___ ___ ___ ___

Bass: ___ ___ ___ ___ ___

Chord name
and quality: ___ ___ ___ ___ ___

Roman numeral: ___ ___ ___ ___ ___

Overview of Harmony and Voice Leading

chapter 4

Four-Part Harmony

A. QUESTIONS FOR REVIEW

1. In SATB format, which voices are written in treble clef? Which voices are in bass clef? Which voices are stemmed upward? Which voices are stemmed downward?

2. What is the proper range for each of the voices in SATB format?

3. Which pairs of voices should be within an octave of each other in SATB format?

4. When writing in keyboard format, which voices are in treble clef? How are they stemmed?

5. Which voices should be within an octave of one another in keyboard format?

6. What scale degree must typically be raised by a half step in a minor key?

7. Which notes should *not* be doubled in four-part harmony?

8. What do the numbers in figured bass indicate?

9. When realizing a figured bass, what intervals do you write if there are no numbers below the bass? If there is a 6? If there is a 7? If there is a ♯ or ♮ without a number?

B. IDENTIFYING CHORDS AND DOUBLINGS

1. Give the Roman numeral of each chord in the given key, and add figures to indicate inversions. Then place a square around the notes that are doubled.

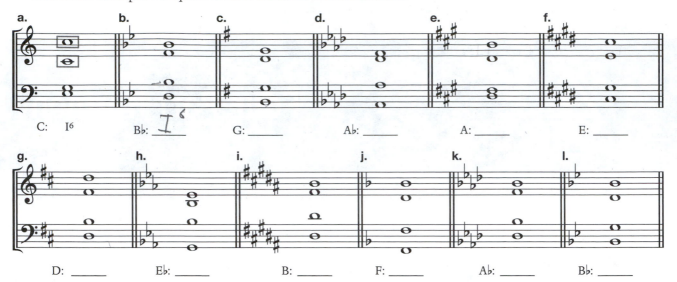

a.   b.   c.   d.   e.   f.

C: I⁶   Bb: I⁶   G: _____   Ab: _____   A: _____   E: _____

g.   h.   i.   j.   k.   l.

D: _____   Eb: _____   B: _____   F: _____   Ab: _____   Bb: _____

2. For each of the following chords, follow the steps below to identify the errors:

- Look at the Roman numeral, and write the correct note names of the chords in the blanks beneath the staff. Circle the letter name of the note that belongs in the bass.

- Check the notation; if any note does not belong in the chord, write a slash through it. Then write the correct note beside the incorrect note.

- If there are no problems with the chord, place a check above it.

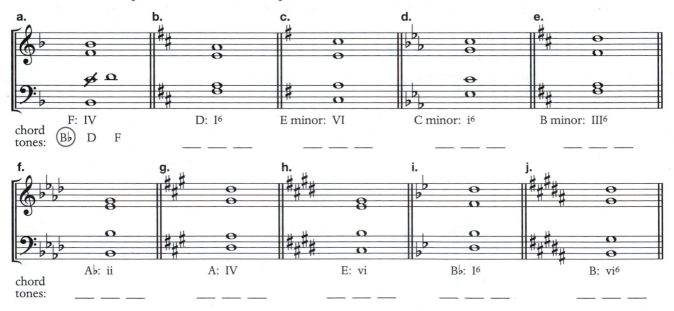

a.   b.   c.   d.   e.

F: IV   D: I⁶   E minor: VI   C minor: i⁶   B minor: III⁶

chord tones: (Bb)   D   F   ___ ___ ___   ___ ___ ___   ___ ___ ___   ___ ___ ___

f.   g.   h.   i.   j.

Ab: ii   A: IV   E: vi   Bb: I⁶   B: vi⁶

chord tones: ___ ___ ___   ___ ___ ___   ___ ___ ___   ___ ___ ___

3. Look at the following chords in SATB format.

   - Identify any notes that are too high or too low for the vocal range by writing a slash through the note.

   - Check the spacing and circle any pair of notes that are too far apart.

   - If there are no problems, place a check above the chord.

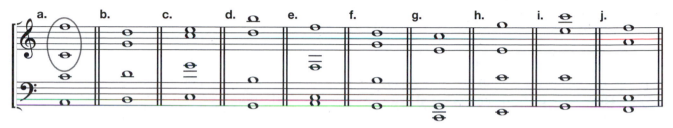

Rewrite any chord with errors in the staff below, using proper spacing and range.

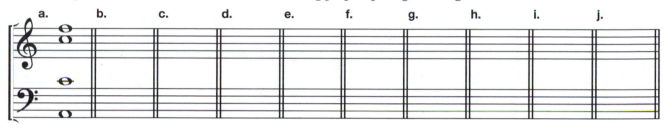

4. Look at the following chords in keyboard format. If the spacing between the top three notes is too wide, place an X above the chord. If there are no spacing problems, place a check above the chord.

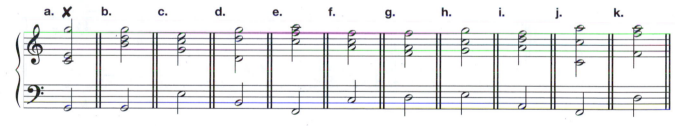

5. Label each chord and inversion below using Roman numerals; then place a box around the notes that are doubled.

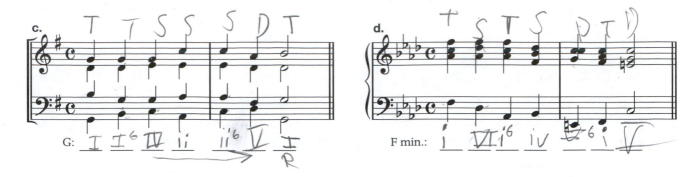

C. LEADING TONES AND CHORDAL SEVENTHS

1. Each of the following is a V^7 chord in root position or inversion; the key is indicated for each. Provide the Roman numeral and figures for each (either V^7, V^6_5, V^4_3, or V^4_2). Then circle each leading tone and place an inverted triangle around every chordal seventh.

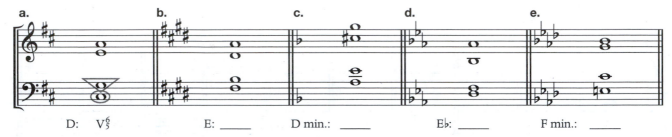

D: V^6_5 E: _____   D min.: _____   E♭: _____   F min.: _____

2. Each of the following exercises is in a major key and includes either a V or V^7, in root position or inversion. Label the major key, and add the necessary figures to the Roman numeral for each. Also, circle each leading tone and place an inverted triangle around every chordal seventh.

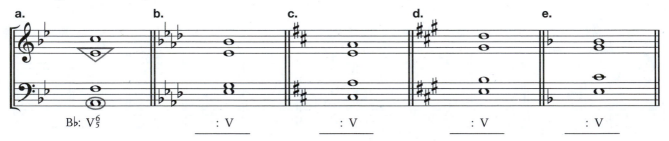

B♭: V^6_5 _____ : V   _____ : V   _____ : V   _____ : V

3. The following exercises each provide the seventh scale degree of a minor key. Turn each into a leading tone by using a sharp, natural, or double sharp to raise the note by a half step.

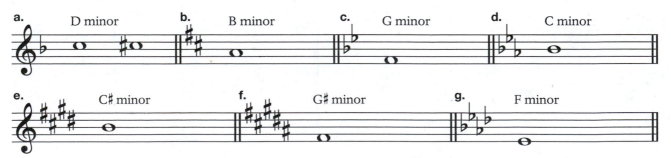

NAME: ....

4. In the following V chords in minor, the subtonic $\hat{7}$ should be raised to form the leading tone.

- Write the note name of the leading tone for each minor key in the blank below the staff.
- Add the correct accidental to the chord.

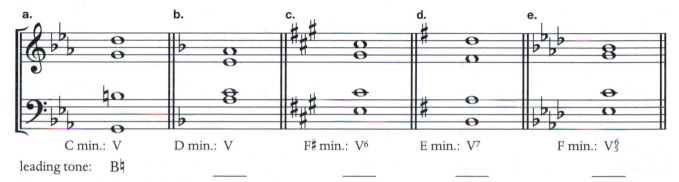

C min.: V   D min.: V   F♯ min.: V⁶   E min.: V⁷   F min.: V⁶₅

leading tone: B♮   ___   ___   ___   ___

In f–j, also provide the Roman numeral, making sure to indicate the inversion when necessary.

G min.: ___   B min.: ___   C♯ min.: ___   B♭ min.: ___   G♯ min.: ___

leading tone: ___   ___   ___   ___   ___

5. In the passages below:

- Use circles to mark leading tones and inverted triangles to mark chordal sevenths.
- If there is an incorrectly doubled leading tone or chordal seventh, place an X on the blank line in the appropriate row under each chord.

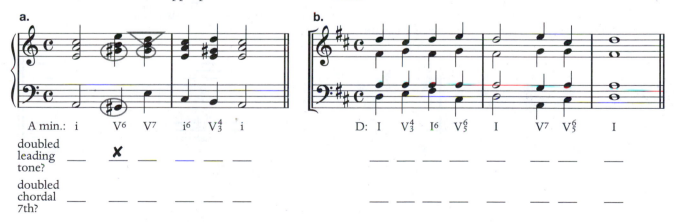

A min.: i   V⁶   V⁷   i⁶   V⁴₃   i   D: I   V⁴₃   I⁶   V⁶₅   I   V⁷   V⁶₅   I

doubled leading tone?   ___   **X**   ___   ___   ___   ___   ___   ___   ___   ___   ___   ___   ___   ___

doubled chordal 7th?   ___   ___   ___   ___   ___   ___   ___   ___   ___   ___   ___   ___   ___   ___

D. NOTATION IN SATB AND KEYBOARD FORMATS

1. In the blank measure that follows each chord or passage, rewrite in SATB format using proper notation.

2. In the blank measure (or measures) following each chord or passage below, rewrite in keyboard format using proper notation.

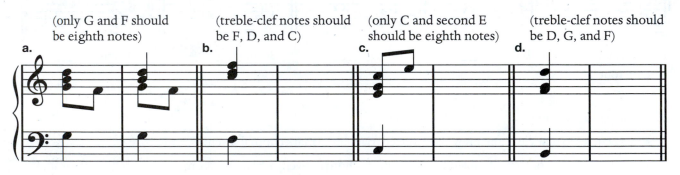

(only G and F should be eighth notes)
(treble-clef notes should be F, D, and C)
(only C and second E should be eighth notes)
(treble-clef notes should be D, G, and F)

(the only eighth notes should be A-G♯, A-C♯ on the last two beats of measure 1, and E-D on the second beat of measure 2)

3. *Rewriting keyboard and SATB notation:* Exercises (a) and (b) are written in keyboard format; rewrite them below as SATB. Exercise (c) and (d) are written in SATB format; rewrite in keyboard format.

E. REALIZING ROMAN NUMERALS

For each key and chord indicated below:

- Write the key signatures.
- Write the names of the notes of the chord in the blanks beneath the Roman numeral and circle the note that should be in the bass.

• On the staves, write the chord in SATB format in two different ways, using proper range, spacing, and notation. Double the bass.

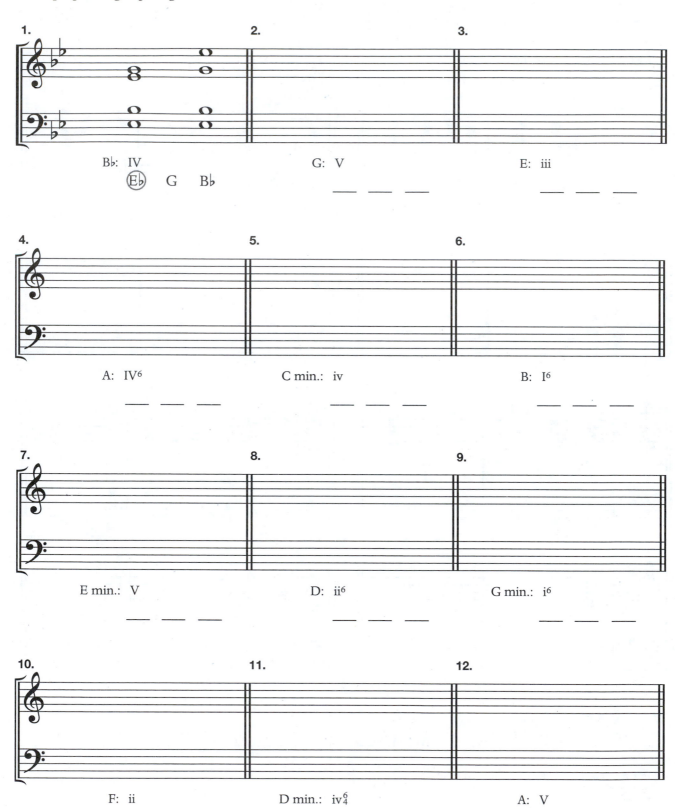

1.

Bb: IV

(Eb) G Bb

2.

G: V

___ ___ ___

3.

E: iii

___ ___ ___

4.

A: IV⁶

___ ___ ___

5.

C min.: iv

___ ___ ___

6.

B: I⁶

___ ___ ___

7.

E min.: V

___ ___ ___

8.

D: ii⁶

___ ___ ___

9.

G min.: i⁶

___ ___ ___

10.

F: ii

___ ___ ___

11.

D min.: iv⁶₄

___ ___ ___

12.

A: V

___ ___ ___

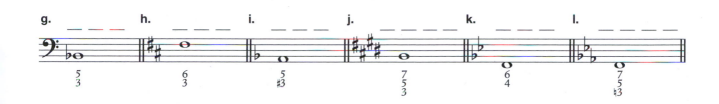

F. REALIZING FIGURED BASS

1. In the blanks above each chord, write the note names of the chord, as indicated by the figured bass.

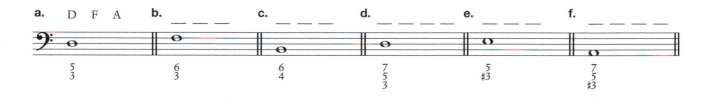

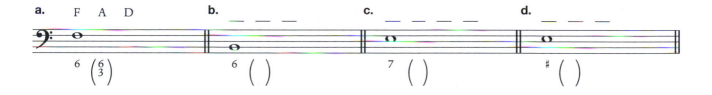

2. The following exercises provide abbreviated figured bass symbols. In the parentheses next to each symbol, provide the unabbreviated form of the figured bass. In the blanks above each chord, write the note names of the chord.

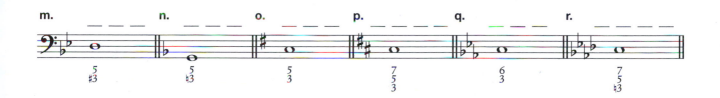

3. Write each chord as indicated by the figured bass in two different ways, using the correct notes with proper range, spacing, and notation. Exercises a–d are in keyboard format, e–h are SATB.

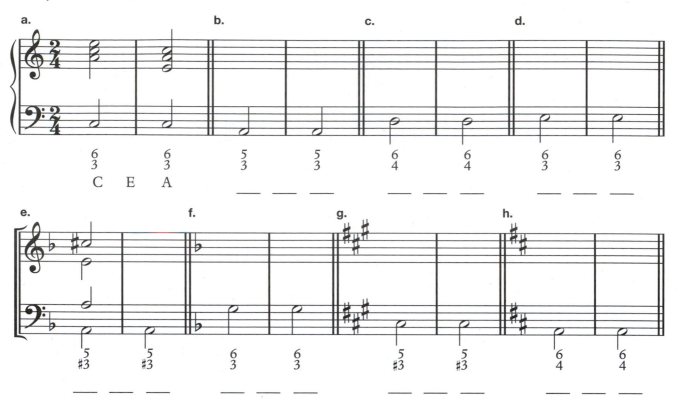

4. Write each chord as indicated by the abbreviated figured bass in two different ways, using the correct notes with proper range, spacing, and notation. In each chord, double the bass. For a–d, use SATB format; for e–h, use keyboard format.

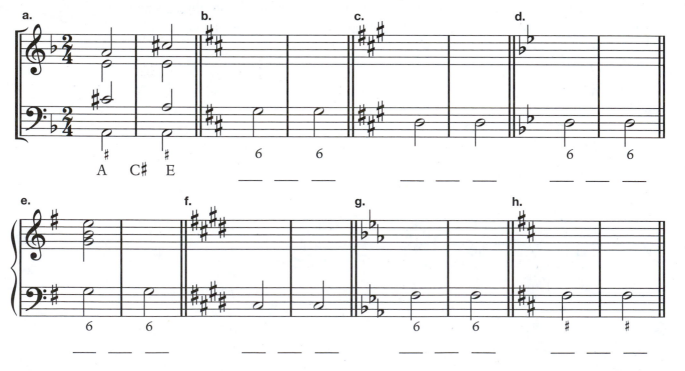

5

Voice Leading

A. QUESTIONS FOR REVIEW

1. What melodic intervals are most common in upper voices? What is the largest melodic interval allowed (occasionally) in an upper voice? What melodic intervals should be avoided in any voice, including the bass?

2. What are the types of motion used to approach intervals?

3. In four-part harmony, what intervals may not be approached in parallel motion?

4. Does a leading tone tend to resolve up or down? Does it resolve by step or leap? In which situations does the leading tone not need to resolve?

5. Does a chordal seventh tend to resolve up or down? Does it resolve by step or leap? Does a chordal seventh need to resolve if it appears in an inner voice?

6. Which is allowed, motion from a perfect fifth to a diminished fifth, or from a diminished fifth to a perfect fifth? Why?

7. In what situations is an approach to a perfect fifth or octave by similar motion incorrect in four-part harmony?

B. MOTION BETWEEN INTERVALS

1. On the blank lines below each staff, label the interval numbers. On the blank lines above each staff, label whether the second of each pair of intervals in each measure is approached in contrary motion (C), parallel motion (P), similar motion (SIM), oblique motion (O), or stationary motion (STA).

Note: G held for four beats

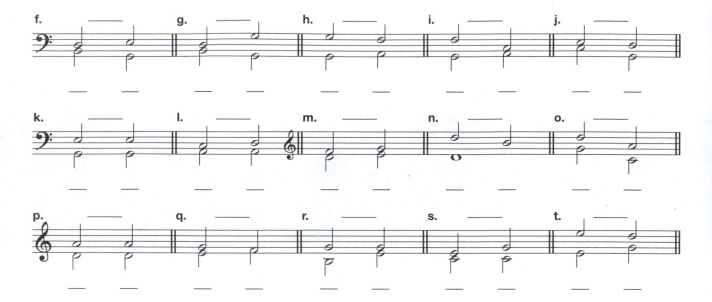

2. In each of the following passages, label the size of each interval. Then, label how each interval is approached with the abbreviations P (parallel), C (contrary), O (oblique), SIM (similar), and STA (stationary).

a.

interval size: 3 _____ _____ _____ _____ _____ _____ _____ _____ _____ _____ _____

motion type: P _____ _____ _____ _____ _____ _____ _____ _____ _____ _____ _____

b. Vittoria Alleoti, "Dicesti anima mia"

Di - ce - sti a - ni - ma mia_____

interval size: 5 _____ _____ _____ _____ _____ _____

motion type: _____ _____ _____ _____ _____ _____

Translation: [Did you] tell, my soul

c. Franz Schubert, "Lützows wilde Jagd" ("Lützow's Wild Hunt")

interval size: 1 _____ _____ _____ _____ _____ _____

motion type: _____ _____ _____ _____ _____ _____

d. Giovanni Pierluigi da Palestrina, *Missa L'homme armé*, Credo

interval
size: 8 ___ ___ ___ ___ ___ ___ ___ ___ ___

motion type: ___ ___ ___ ___ ___ ___ ___ ___ ___

e. Isabella Leonarda, "Sic ergo anima animae"

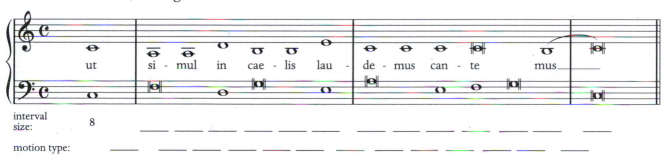

ut   si - mul   in   cae - lis   lau - de - mus   can - te   mus

interval
size: 8 ___ ___ ___ ___ ___ ___ ___ ___ ___ ___ ___

motion type: ___ ___ ___ ___ ___ ___ ___ ___ ___ ___ ___

Translation: Together, let us sing praises to heaven.

f. Ignatius Sancho, Minuet 1 in C (horn parts)

interval
size: 6 ___ ___ ___ ___ ___ ___ ___ ___

motion type: ___ ___ ___ ___ ___ ___ ___ ___

___ ___ ___ ___ ___ ___ ___ ___ ___

___ ___ ___ ___ ___ ___ ___ ___ ___

C. LOCATING PERFECT OCTAVES AND FIFTHS WITHIN CHORDS

1. In each chord below, locate the perfect octaves and fifths. Mark the octaves with a square bracket and fifths with a curved bracket. Note that either of these intervals may appear between more than one pair of voices (or they may not appear at all), and that the intervals may be simple or compound.

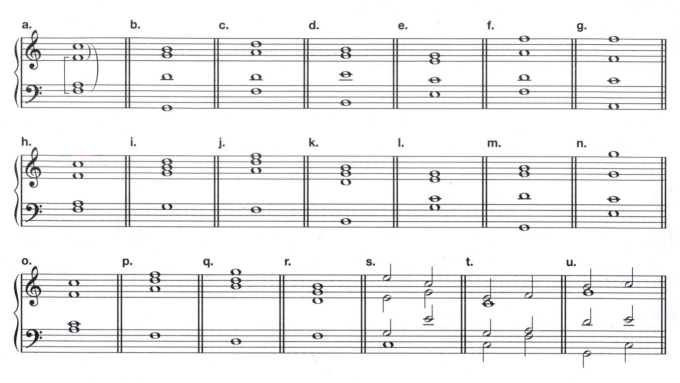

2. Below are a series of chords notated in keyboard format. Label the octaves with a square bracket and fifths with a curved bracket.

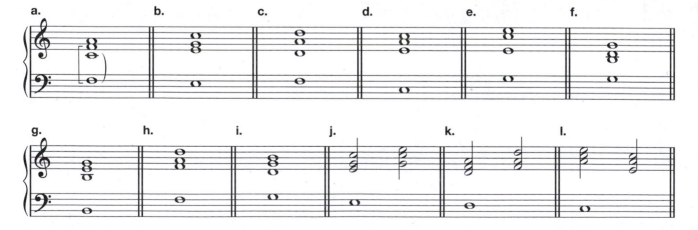

3. For each chord in the following passages, label octaves with square brackets and fifths with curved brackets. Then, label each chord with a Roman numeral and inversion.

a.

C: I   IV   I⁶

b.

D min.:   i

c.

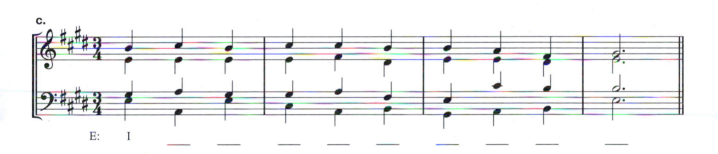

E: I

d.

E♭:   I

D. APPROACHING PERFECT OCTAVES AND FIFTHS

1. Determine how the octaves and fifths are approached in each of the following pairs of chords. Use the abbreviations P (parallel), C (contrary), O (oblique), SIM (similar), and STA (stationary).

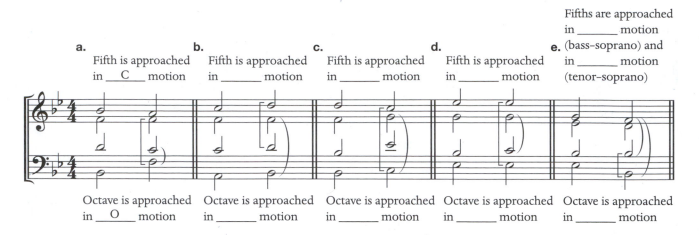

a. Fifth is approached in __C__ motion

b. Fifth is approached in _____ motion

c. Fifth is approached in _____ motion

d. Fifth is approached in _____ motion

Fifths are approached in _____ motion

e. (bass–soprano) and in _____ motion (tenor–soprano)

a. Octave is approached in __O__ motion

b. Octave is approached in _____ motion

c. Octave is approached in _____ motion

d. Octave is approached in _____ motion

e. Octave is approached in _____ motion

2. In each of the following chords, label fifths with curved brackets, and octaves or unisons with square brackets. Then check for parallel fifths or octaves (if there are any); mark parallel fifths and parallel octaves by drawing lines between the noteheads; write 5 or 8 above the staff to label the parallel interval.

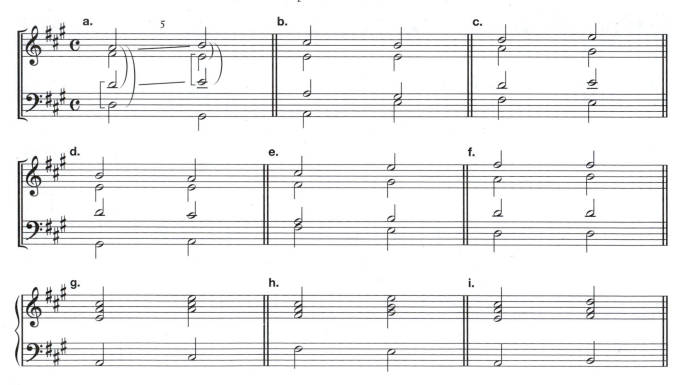

3. In each chord below, indicate the fifths with curved brackets and the octaves with square brackets. Label each chord with a Roman numeral. Then check for parallel fifths and octaves, marking them with lines between the noteheads; write 5 or 8 above the staff to label the parallel interval.

a.

b.

E. SMOOTH VOICE LEADING

1. In the excerpt below, mark with a squiggly line each leap of a fourth or larger. Then circle any leap that occurs when the chord changes.

2. Which voice contains the most melodic leaps between two different chords?

_____

F. RESOLVING THE LEADING TONE AND CHORDAL SEVENTHS

1. Identify the leading tone of each of the following major keys, then find and circle it within each excerpt. Finally, mark the resolution with a ✔ (for proper resolution) or ✘ (poor resolution).

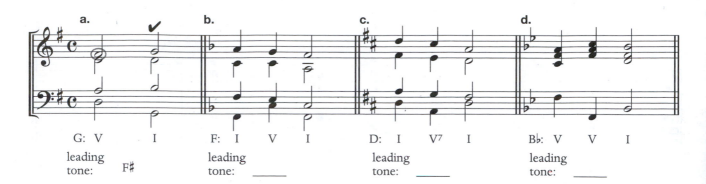

G: V   I
leading tone: F♯

F: I   V   I
leading tone: _____

D: I   V⁷   I
leading tone: _____

B♭: V   V   I
leading tone: _____

2. In each of the following, spell the V⁷ chord. Place an inverted triangle around the chordal seventh (both in the spelled chord and in the music itself). Then mark the resolution of the chordal seventh with a ✔ (for proper resolution) or ✘ (poor resolution).

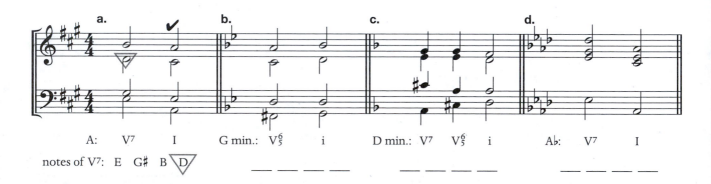

A: V⁷   I
notes of V⁷: E   G♯   B   ▽D▽

G min.: V⁶₅   i
__ __ __ __

D min.: V⁷   V⁶₅   i
__ __ __ __

A♭: V⁷   I
__ __ __ __

3. For each of the passages below:
- Spell the V⁷ chord in the given key, then identify the leading tone (circle) and chordal seventh (inverted triangle).
- Label the chords in each passage with Roman numerals.
- In the music, indicate leading tones with circles and chordal sevenths with inverted triangles.
- Place a ✔ for correctly resolving leading tones and chordal sevenths, an ✘ for incorrect resolutions.

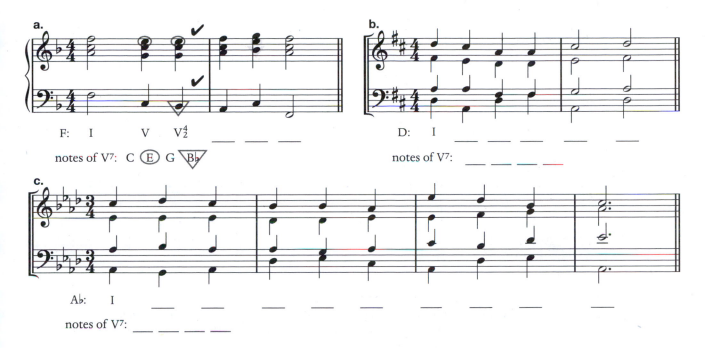

a.

F: I   V   V$^4_2$ ___   ___   ___

notes of V⁷: C Ⓔ G ▽B♭

b.

D: I   ___   ___   ___   ___

notes of V⁷: ___ ___ ___ ___

c.

A♭:   I   ___   ___   ___   ___   ___   ___

notes of V⁷: ___ ___ ___ ___

4. Below are short chord progressions in which the final note of the soprano is missing.

- Write the note names of each chord in the blanks below the staff.
- Place a circle around each leading tone and a triangle around each chordal seventh (in both the music and the spelled chords).
- Complete each excerpt by filling in the final note of the soprano, making sure to resolve the leading tone or chordal seventh correctly.

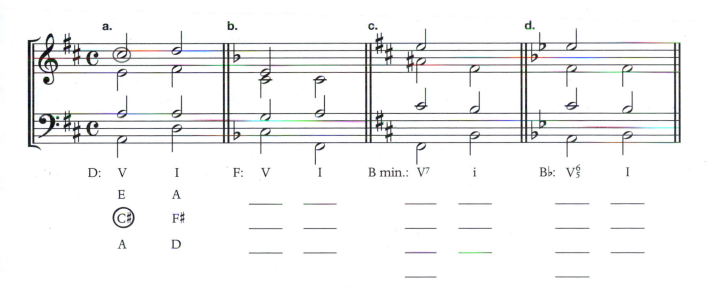

a.

D: V   I

E   A

Ⓒ#   F#

A   D

b.

F: V   I

___ ___

___ ___

___ ___

___ ___

c.

B min.: V⁷   i

___ ___

___ ___

___ ___

___ ___

d.

B♭: V$^6_5$ I

___ ___

___ ___

___ ___

G. RECOGNIZING ERRORS APPROACHING PERFECT INTERVALS

1. In each of the following exercises, a perfect interval is approached in similar motion, a diminished fifth is followed by a perfect fifth, or a perfect fifth is followed by a diminished fifth. Which of these are acceptable, and which involve improper voice leading?

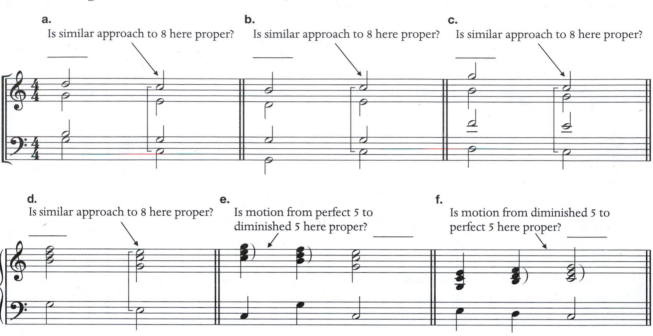

a. Is similar approach to 8 here proper?

b. Is similar approach to 8 here proper?

c. Is similar approach to 8 here proper?

d. Is similar approach to 8 here proper?

e. Is motion from perfect 5 to diminished 5 here proper?

f. Is motion from diminished 5 to perfect 5 here proper?

2. In the passage below:

   • Use squiggly lines to indicate each melodic leap of a fourth or larger.

   • Indicate fifths and octaves within each chord with curved and square brackets.

   • Mark with an ✗ any instance in which an octave is improperly approached.

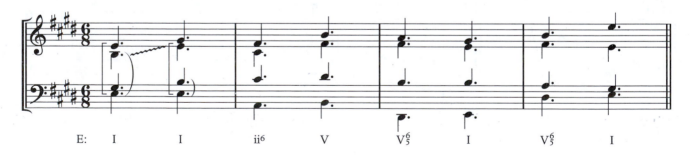

E: I   I   ii⁶   V   V⁶₅   I   V⁶₅   I

3. In the above passage, what is wrong with the bass line in the last two measures?

_____

_____

H. ERROR DETECTION

The following fragments each have one or more errors of chord construction (as discussed in Chapter 4) or voice leading. In the spaces above the staff, use these letters to indicate errors:

(a) Wrong notes or missing notes in a chord.

(b) Improper range or spacing.

(c) A leading tone or chordal seventh is doubled.

(d) A leading tone or chordal seventh resolves improperly.

(e) The seventh scale degree is not raised in a minor key.

(f) The upper voices leap too much.

(g) There is a faulty parallel octave or fifth.

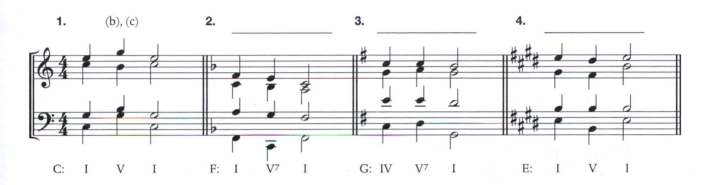

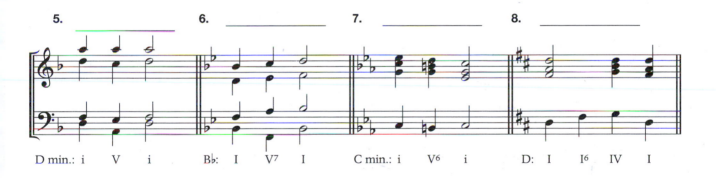

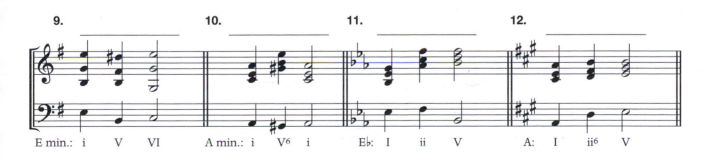

chapter

6

Harmonic Progression

A. QUESTIONS FOR REVIEW

1. What is a musical phrase?

2. With what chord does a phrase normally begin? With what chords does a phrase usually end?

3. What is a half cadence (HC)? What is an authentic cadence (AC)?

4. What is the difference between a perfect authentic cadence (PAC) and an imperfect authentic cadence (IAC)?

5. What are the two most conventional harmonic patterns involving the functional categories Tonic, Subdominant, and Dominant?

6. Can a Tonic chord follow another Tonic chord? Can a Dominant chord follow another Dominant chord? Can a Subdominant chord follow another Subdominant chord?

7. What are some of the chords that can serve as a Subdominant harmony?

8. What problems might arise when harmonizing a melody?

B. BEGINNING AND ENDING A PHRASE

1. In each of the following chorale excerpts:

- Identify the key, and write the note names of the I, V, and V^7 chords in the blanks.
- Label the two chords of the cadences (indicated by boxes) by Roman numeral.
- Label each boxed cadence as HC, PAC, or IAC.

a. key: B♭ major

I: B♭ D F   V: F A C V^7: F A C E♭

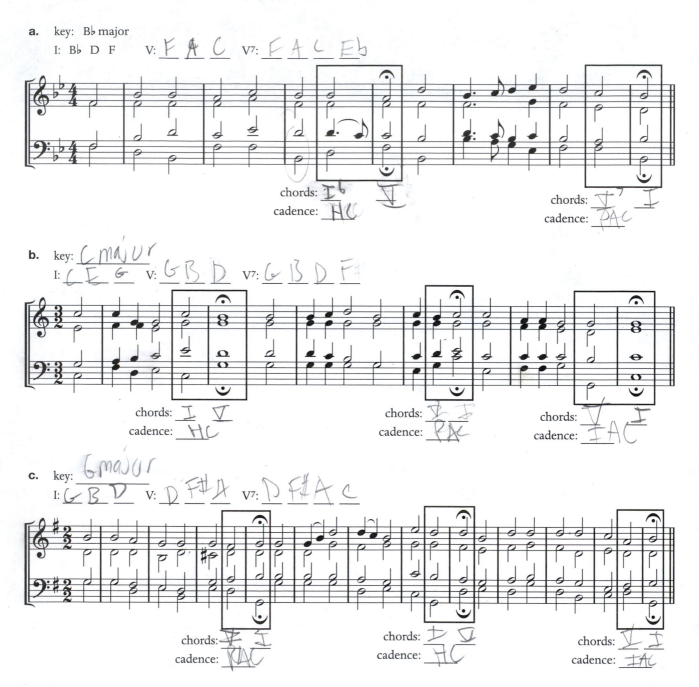

chords: I⁶ V
cadence: HC

chords: V⁷ I
cadence: PAC

b. key: C major

I: C E G   V: G B D V^7: G B D F♯

chords: I V
cadence: HC

chords: V I
cadence: PAC

chords: V I
cadence: IAC

c. key: G major

I: G B D   V: D F♯ A V^7: D F♯ A C

chords: V I
cadence: PAC

chords: D V
cadence: HC

chords: V I
cadence: IAC

2. Spell the I, V, and V⁷ chords and identify the boxed cadences of the following chorales. Also identify the first chord of each phrase (circled).

a. J. S. Bach, Chorale 1

I: G B D   V: D F♯ A   V⁷: D F♯ A C

G: I

cadence: IAC

cadence: PAC

b. J. S. Bach, Chorale 5

I: G B D   V: D F♯ A   V⁷: D F♯ A C

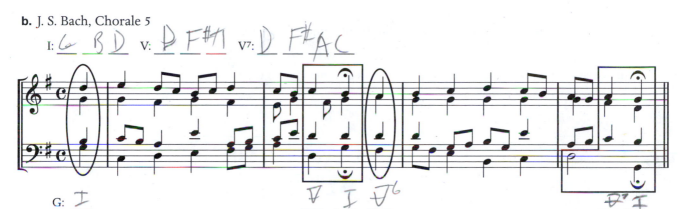

G: I

cadence: IAC

cadence: PAC

3. Answer the following questions about the excerpts above.

a. Taking the five chorale excerpts of (1a–c) and (2a–b) as a group, which voice includes the most melodic leaps of a fourth or larger: the soprano, alto, tenor, or bass? _____ Bass _____

b. In which of these five chorale excerpts (1a–c, 2a–b) is the spacing between the alto and soprano larger than an octave? _____ None _____

c. In which of these excerpts is the spacing between the tenor and alto ever larger than an octave? _____ None _____

d. In which of these excerpts is the spacing between the bass and tenor ever larger than an octave? _____ All Five _____

C. HARMONIZING MELODIES: PREPARATORY EXERCISES

1. In the key of D major, write the note names of the chords in the blanks below.

I: __D__ __F#__ __A__   V: ____ ____ ____

V7: ____ ____ ____ ____   IV: ____ ____ ____

Which of the chords above could be used to harmonize the notes below?

Possible chords: V or V7   ____   ____   ____   ____

(Neither IV nor I in
D major include a C#)

2. Underneath each melody below, Roman numerals suggest a possible harmonization. For each melody:

- Write the note names of the chords on the blanks underneath the Roman numerals.

- Check the harmonizations. If the melody note is not included in the indicated harmonization, mark it with an ✗.

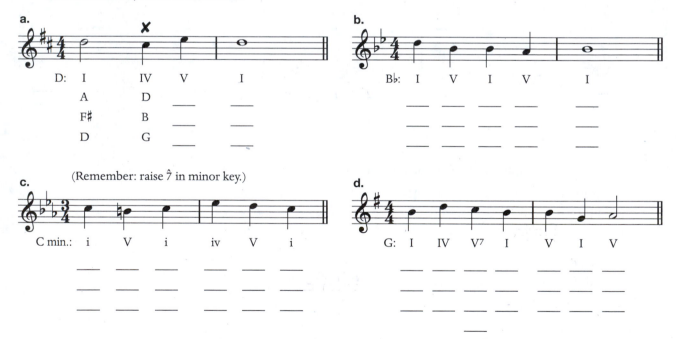

76 | CHAPTER 6 | Harmonic Progression

3. Underneath each melody below, Roman numerals suggest a possible harmonization. For each melody:

- Below each Roman numeral, write the note names of the chord. Circle the note that belongs in the bass.

- On the bass-clef staff, complete the bass line for each chord as indicated by the Roman numeral and figure (do not write the tenor or alto voices).

- Check the harmonizations. If the melody note is not included in the indicated harmonization, mark it with an ✗.

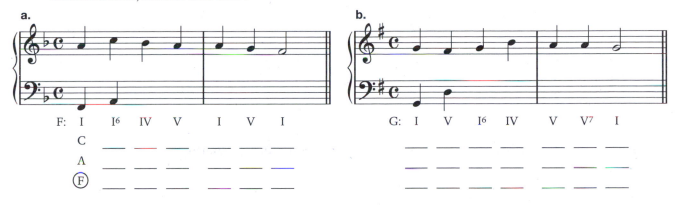

4. Below are two melodies, one in F major and one in A major, with three possible harmonizations indicated by Roman numerals and a bass line. In each case (a–c and d–f), one of the harmonizations is acceptable, and the other two have problems.

- Mark an ✗ below any chord that does not match the melody.

- Check for faulty intervals between the bass and the melody: mark parallel fifths and parallel octaves by drawing lines between the noteheads; write 5 or 8 above the staff to label the parallel interval.

- Circle every leading tone. Mark with an ✗ any *doubled* leading tones.

- If the proposed harmonization has no serious errors, write a ✔ above the staff.

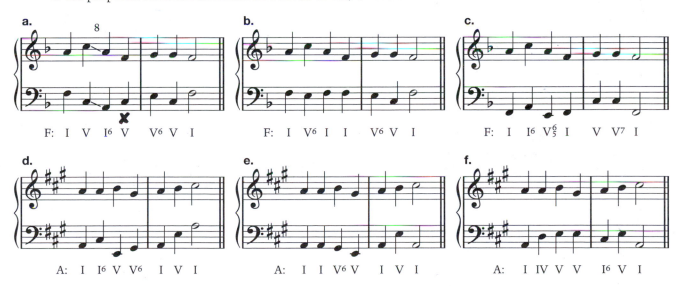

D. HARMONIC FUNCTIONAL CATEGORIES: **T, S, D**

For the following chord progressions, write the function of each chord—**T** (Tonic),
D (Dominant), or **S** (Subdominant)—in the blank below the Roman numeral. Then
identify the progression as **T–D–T**, **T–S–D–T**, or faulty **T–D–S–T** by circling the correct
choice.

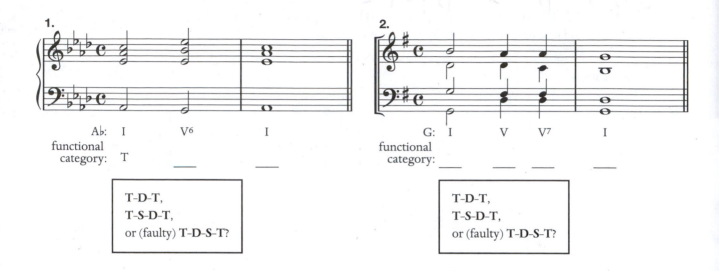

1.

Ab: I   V⁶   I

functional
category: T   _____   _____

T–D–T,
T–S–D–T,
or (faulty) **T–D–S–T**?

2.

G: I   V   V⁷   I

functional
category: _____ _____ _____ _____

T–D–T,
T–S–D–T,
or (faulty) **T–D–S–T**?

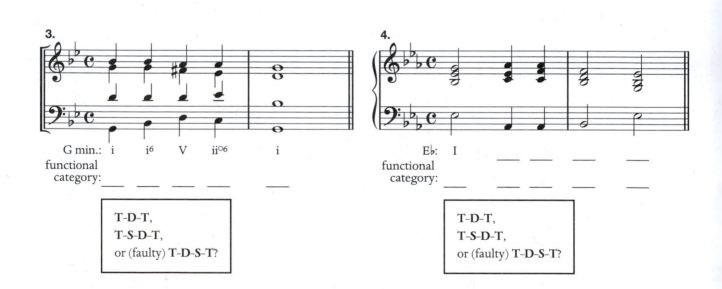

3.

G min.: i   i⁶   V   ii°⁶   i

functional
category: _____ _____ _____ _____

T–D–T,
T–S–D–T,
or (faulty) **T–D–S–T**?

4.

Eb: I   _____   _____   _____

functional
category: _____ _____ _____ _____

T–D–T,
T–S–D–T,
or (faulty) **T–D–S–T**?

chapter

7

Melodic Elaboration

A. QUESTIONS FOR REVIEW

1. What is an arpeggiation?

2. What is octave doubling? Does it create forbidden parallel octaves?

3. In what three ways may an embellishing tone be approached or left?

4. What is a passing tone? A neighbor tone? A suspension?

5. What is an incomplete neighbor tone? An anticipation? A retardation?

6. Which embellishing tones are most common?

B. ARPEGGIATION

- In the blanks beneath each measure, list the note names of the arpeggiated chord. (Some chords are triads, and others are seventh chords.)

- Circle the note name that is the root.

- Then in the boxes below the chords, provide the Roman numeral for each chord.

1. Mauro Giuliani, Etude for Guitar, Op. 100, No. 2

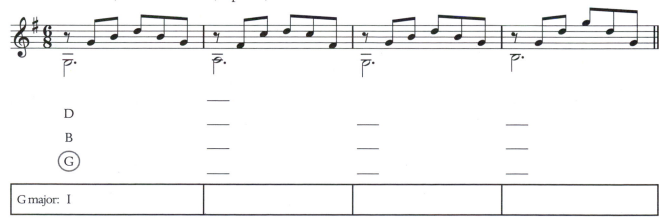

2. André Grétry, Serenade from *L'amant jaloux*

Ah! cou - ron - nez____ l'es - poir.____

E minor:

Translation: Ah! wreathed hope.

3. Louise Ferrenc, Étude Op. 30, No.1

C major:

4. Antonín Dvořák, Waltz, Op. 54, No. 4

Treat the note on each downbeat as the bass of the chord. Notes in triangles are embellishing tones.

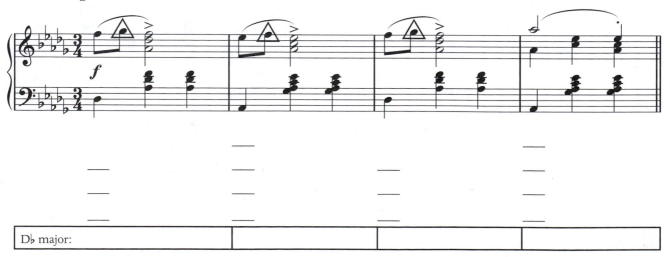

D♭ major:

5. Ludwig van Beethoven, Duet for Clarinet and Bassoon No. 1

Note: Each chord lasts for two quarter notes except for the final chord, which lasts for a whole measure. For each chord, the lowest note is to be understood as the bass note for the entire length of the chord.

C. IDENTIFYING EMBELLISHING TONES

1. In the excerpt below, a triangle appears around each embellishing tone. Label each as a passing tone (PT), neighbor tone (NT), or suspension (SUS).

William Byrd, "The March before the Battle"

2. The embellishing tones below are each indicated with a triangle. Label each as either a passing tone (PT) or neighbor tone (NT).

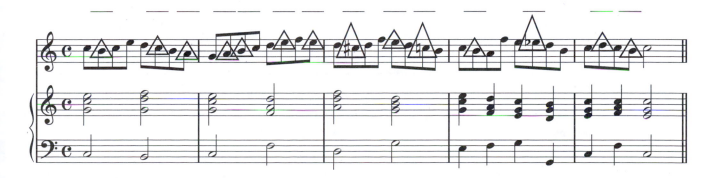

3. The embellishing tones below are each indicated with a triangle. Label each as either a passing tone (PT), neighbor tone (NT), suspension (SUS), incomplete neighbor tone (INT), retardation (RET), or anticipation (ANT).

D. ANALYSIS

For each example:

- List the note names of each chord in the blanks beneath the measure. Circle the note name that is the root.

- Place a triangle around each embellishing tone in the melody in the top staff, and label it as either a passing tone (PT) or neighbor tone (NT).

- Label the key, figuring out whether the key is major or minor. Then in the boxes below the staves, label the Roman numeral and figures for each chord.

1. Louise Reichardt, "Der Spinnerin Nachtlied"

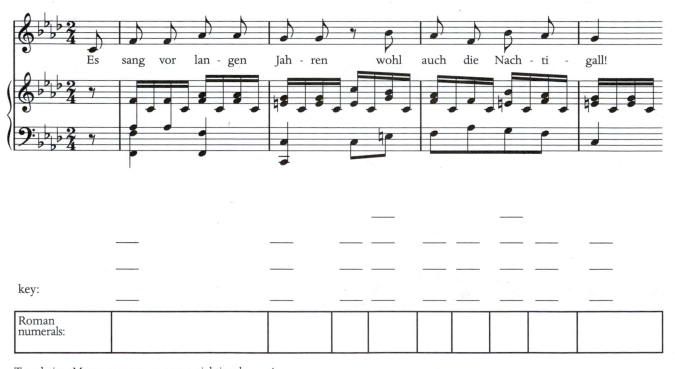

Translation: Many years ago, as now, a nightingale sang!

2. Franz Schubert, "Andenken" ("Remembrance")

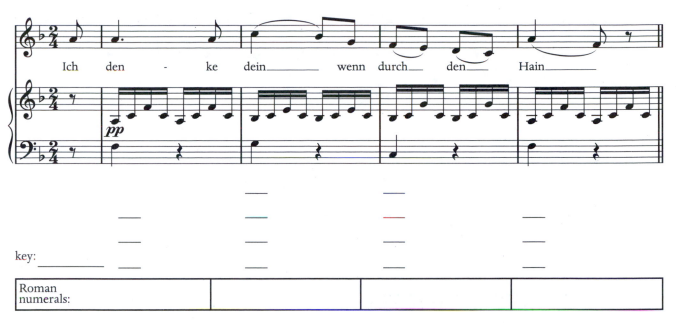

key: _____

Roman numerals:			

Translation: I think of you when in the grove.

3. Franz Schubert, "Andenken" ("Remembrance")

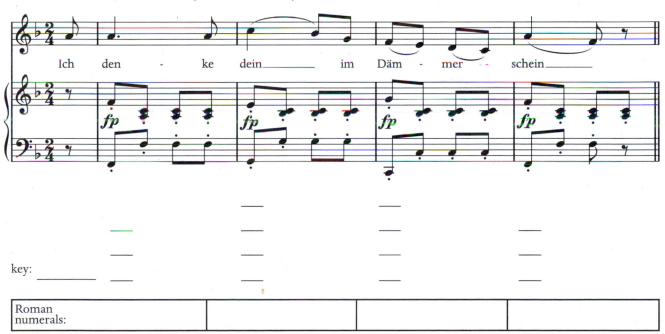

key: _____

Roman numerals:			

Translation: I think of you at twilight.

How do the harmonies in the two excerpts by Schubert, (2) and (3), compare?

4. Mauro Giuliani, *Pièces faciles et agréables*, Op. 74, No. 4

key: _____ ___

Roman numerals:		

E. ACCOMPANIMENT PATTERNS

1. Below are two chord progressions, each followed by the beginning of two accompaniment patterns. Complete the accompaniment patterns using the pitches of the progression.

b.

2. Below is a passage for keyboard with arpeggiations in the right hand.

* Rewrite the passage in four-part harmony keyboard format so that the notes of each chord appear simultaneously.
* There is a voice-leading problem in this passage. Circle and identify the voice-leading error.

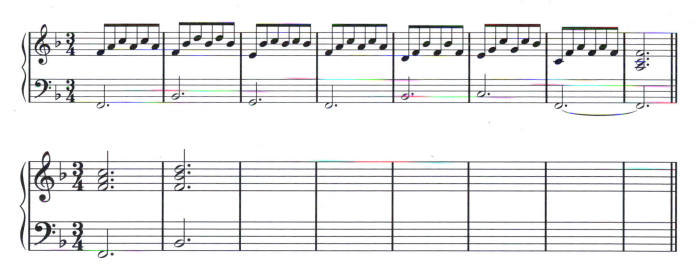

3. Below is an excerpt from the song "Poesie von Tieck" ("Poem by Tieck") by Louise Reichardt. The dissonant embellishing tones in the melody are marked by triangles. Label each embellishing tone as either NT (neighbor tone), PT (passing tone), or SUS (suspension).

Translation: Rest, sweet love, in the shade of the green twilight. The grass rustles in the meadow . . .

- On the bottom two staves below, write a simplified harmonic model of the piano accompaniment of this excerpt, removing the octave doublings and arpeggios so that the four notes of the chords all appear simultaneously.

- On the top staff, write a simplified version of the vocal melody by removing all the embellishing tones and chords skips.

- This model should use all dotted-half notes, except in measures 1 and 3, which should use dotted-quarter notes.

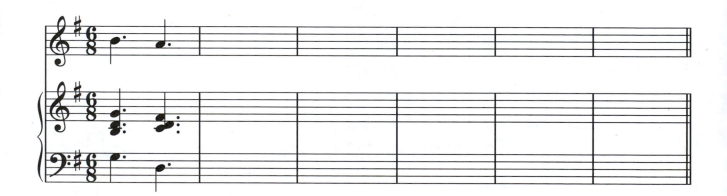

- At some points in this excerpt, the vocal line and one of the voices in the right hand of the keyboard part are doubled in parallel octaves. In which measures do these octave doublings occur?

chapter 8 Species Counterpoint

A. QUESTIONS FOR REVIEW

1. What is species counterpoint? What is first species? What is second species? What is fourth species?

2. In first species, what harmonic intervals are allowed between the two voices? What harmonic intervals are forbidden?

3. In second species, where can dissonances appear? How must they be approached and left?

4. In fourth species, where can dissonances appear? How must they be prepared? How must they be resolved?

5. In all species, which sorts of motion can be used to approach a perfect consonance (octave or fifth)? Which sorts of motion are forbidden in approaching a perfect octave or fifth?

6. In all species, which melodic intervals predominate? Which melodic intervals are forbidden?

B. FIRST SPECIES

1. *Ending: Labeling intervals and voice leading.* Label the intervals between the staves (perfect intervals go in boxes, dissonances in triangles). Find the voice-leading errors. Write your answer(s) above the staves using the following abbreviations: DISS (impermissible or improperly treated dissonance between the voices); MEL (impermissible melodic interval); PAR or SIM (forbidden parallel or similar motion to a fifth or octave); CHR (impermissible chromaticism); CAD (incorrect cadence).

a.

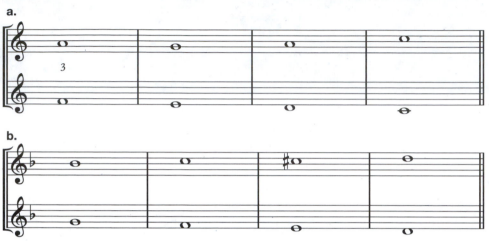

b.

2. *Ending: Completing the counterpoint.* Below are the last four notes of two cantus firmi. For each, write the ending of a first-species counterpoint on the upper staff. Label the intervals between the staves (perfect intervals go in boxes, dissonances in triangles).

a.

b.

3. *Beginning: Labeling the intervals and voice leading.* Label the intervals between the staves (perfect intervals go in boxes, dissonances in triangles). Find the errors in these first-species beginnings. Write your answer(s) above the staves: DISS (impermissible or improperly treated dissonance between the voices); MEL (impermissible melodic interval); PAR or SIM (forbidden parallel or similar motion to a fifth or octave); CHR (incorrect chromaticism); CROSS (voice crossing); START (wrong way to begin).

a.

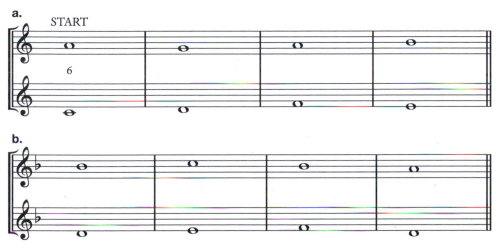

b.

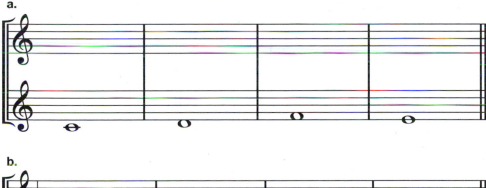

4. *Beginning: Completing the counterpoint.* Below are the first four notes of two cantus firmi. Write the beginning of a first-species counterpoint above each. Label the intervals between the staves.

a.

b.

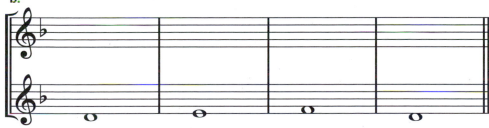

5. *Middle: Labeling the intervals and voice leading.* The examples below represent a middle portion: not including the beginning or the ending. Label the intervals between the staves. Then find the errors. Write your answer(s) above the staves: DISS (impermissible or improperly treated dissonance between the voices); MEL (impermissible melodic interval); PAR or SIM (forbidden parallel or similar motion to a fifth or octave); CHR (incorrect chromaticism); CROSS (voice crossing); START (wrong way to begin); CAD (incorrect cadence).

a.

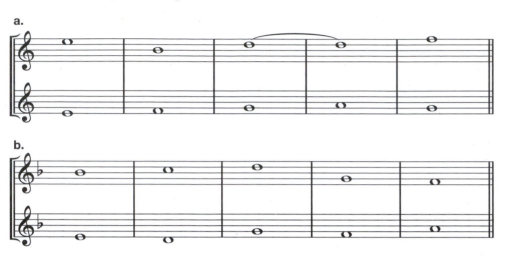

b.

6. *Middle: Completing the counterpoint.* Below are five notes from the middle of four cantus firmi. Write first-species counterpoint for each, following any instructions written above the staff. Label the intervals between the staves.

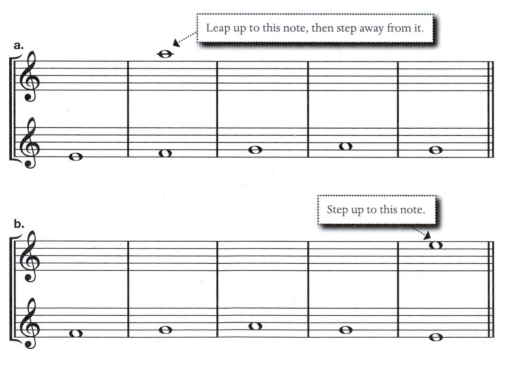

Leap up to this note, then step away from it.

a.

Step up to this note.

b.

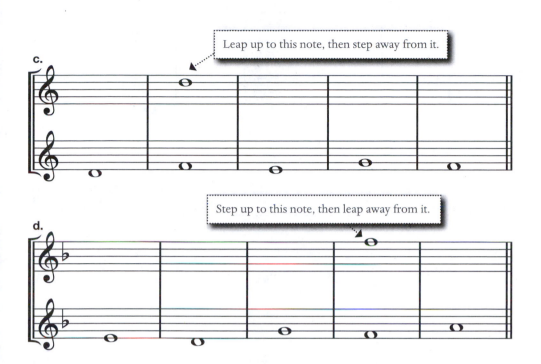

7. *First species, full counterpoint.* Write a complete first-species counterpoint above each cantus firmus. Label the intervals between the staves (perfect intervals go in boxes, dissonances in triangles). These cantus firmi were composed by important figures in the history of counterpoint. Strategies for composing counterpoint appear in A Closer Look in the ebook.

a. Johann Fux

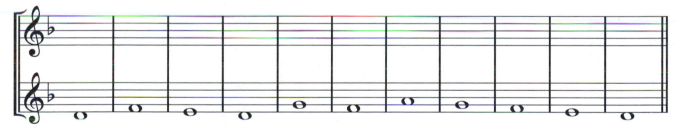

b. Knud Jeppesen

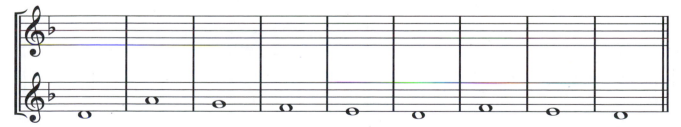

c. Johann Fux

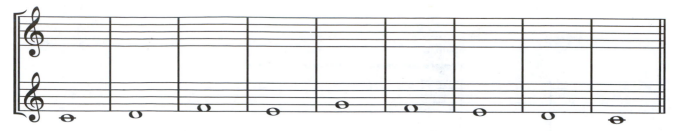

d. Johannes Brahms

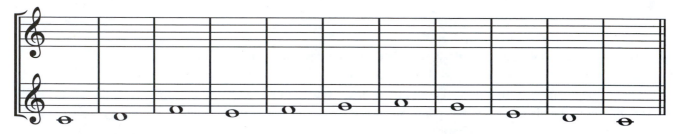

e. Heinrich Schenker

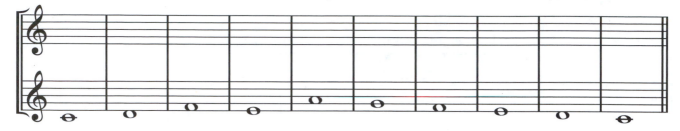

f. Johann Fux

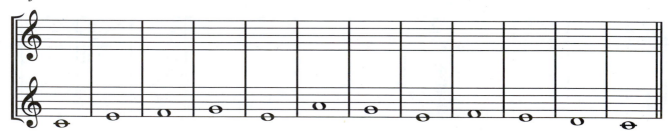

g. Johann Kirnberger

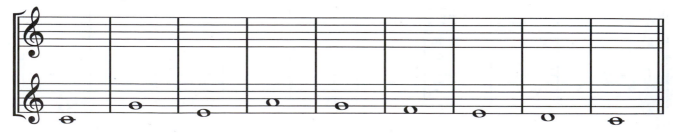

C. SECOND SPECIES

1. *Ending: Labeling intervals and voice leading.* Label the intervals between the staves (perfect intervals in boxes; dissonances in triangles). Then find the errors in these second-species endings. Write your answer(s) above the staves: DISS (impermissible or improperly treated dissonance between the voices); MEL (impermissible melodic interval); PAR or SIM (forbidden parallel or similar motion to a fifth or octave); CHR (incorrect chromaticism); CROSS (voice crossing); CAD (incorrect cadence).

a.

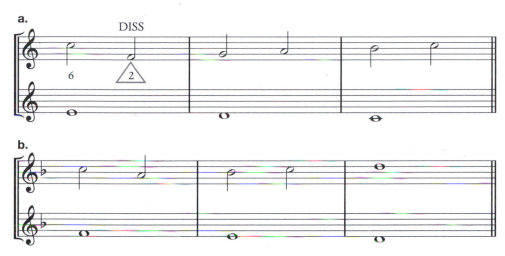

b.

2. *Ending: Completing the counterpoint.* Below are the last three notes of two cantus firmi. Write the end of a second-species counterpoint above each. Label the intervals between the staves.

a.

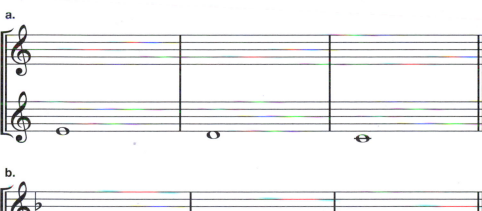

b.

3. *Beginning: Labeling intervals and voice leading.* Label the intervals between the staves of these second-species beginnings. Then find and label the errors: DISS (impermissible or improperly treated dissonance between the voices); MEL (impermissible melodic interval); PAR or SIM (forbidden parallel or similar motion to a fifth or octave); CHR (incorrect chromaticism); CROSS (voice crossing); START (wrong way to begin).

a.

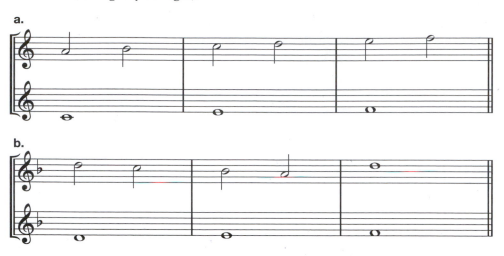

b.

4. *Beginning: Completing the counterpoint.* Below are the first three notes of two cantus firmi. Write the beginning of a second-species counterpoint above each. Label the intervals between the staves.

a.

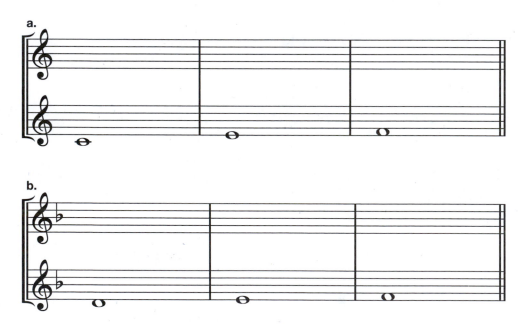

b.

5. *Middle: Labeling intervals and voice leading.* Label the intervals between the staves. Then find and label the errors: DISS (impermissible or improperly treated dissonance between the voices); MEL (impermissible melodic interval); PAR or SIM (forbidden parallel or similar motion to a fifth or octave); CHR (incorrect chromaticism); CROSS (voice crossing).

6. *Middle: Completing the counterpoint.* Below are four notes from the middle of two cantus firmi. Some notes are provided in the upper voice; fill in the rest using second-species counterpoint. Label the intervals between the staves.

a.

b.

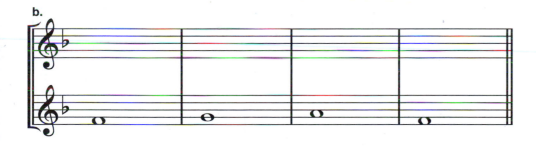

7. *Second species, short full counterpoint.* Below are short cantus firmi. Write a second-species counterpoint to each with a good beginning, middle, and end. Label the intervals between the staves.

a.

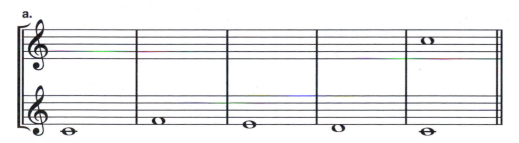

b.

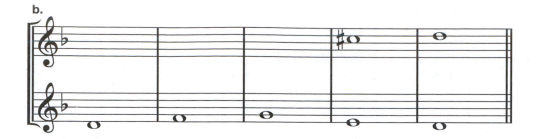

8. *Second species, long full counterpoint.* Write a complete second-species counterpoint for each cantus firmus. Label the intervals between the staves (perfect intervals in boxes; dissonances in triangles). Strategies for composing counterpoint appear in A Closer Look in the ebook.

a. Johann Fux

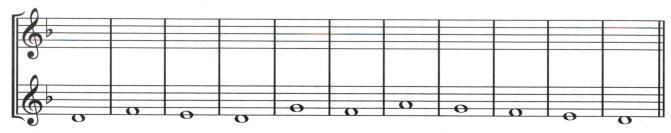

b. Knud Jeppesen

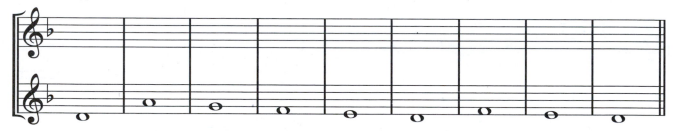

c. Johann Fux

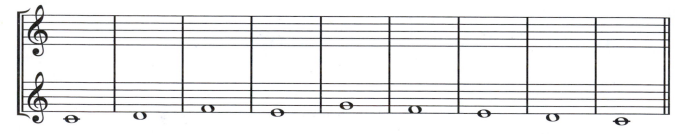

d. Johannes Brahms

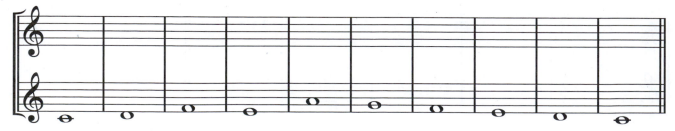

e. Heinrich Schenker

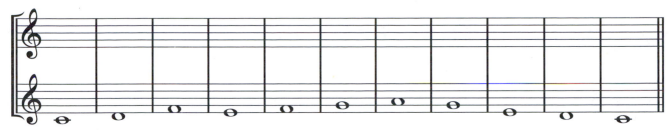

f. Johann Fux

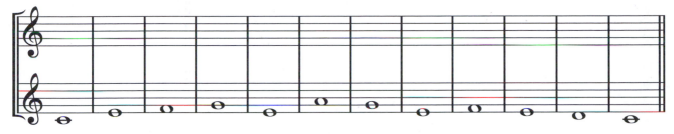

g. Johann Kirnberger

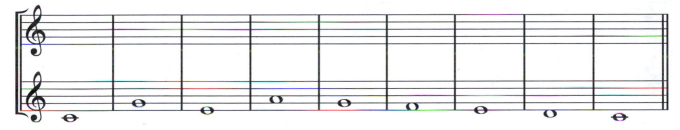

D. FOURTH SPECIES

1. *Ending: Labeling intervals and voice leading.* Label the intervals between the staves (perfect intervals in boxes; dissonances in triangles). Then find the errors, writing your answers above the staves: DISS (impermissible or improperly treated dissonance between the voices); MEL (impermissible melodic interval); PAR or SIM (forbidden parallel or similar motion to a fifth or octave); CHR (incorrect chromaticism); CROSS (voice crossing); CAD (incorrect cadence).

a.

b.

2. *Ending: Completing the counterpoint.* Below are the last four notes of two cantus firmi. Write the end of a fourth-species counterpoint above each. Label the intervals between the staves.

a.

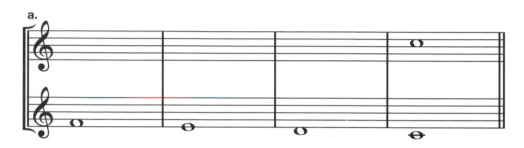

b.

3. *Beginning: Labeling intervals and voice leading.* Label the intervals between the staves (perfect intervals go in boxes, dissonances in triangles). Find the errors, writing your answers above the staves: DISS (impermissible or improperly treated dissonance between the voices); MEL (impermissible melodic interval); PAR or SIM (forbidden parallel or similar motion to a fifth or octave); CHR (incorrect chromaticism); CROSS (voice crossing); START (wrong way to begin).

a.

b.

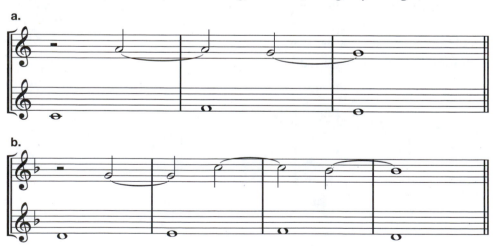

4. *Beginning: Completing the counterpoint.* Below are the first notes of two cantus firmi. Begin a fourth-species counterpoint above each. Label the intervals between the staves.

a.

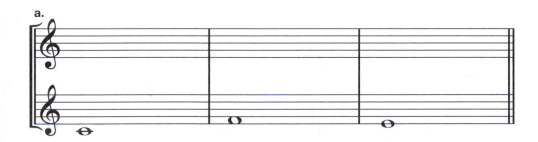

b.

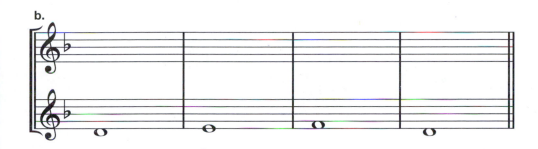

5. *Middle: Labeling intervals and voice leading.* Label the intervals between the staves (perfect intervals go in boxes, dissonances in triangles). Then find the errors, writing your answers above the staves: DISS (impermissible or improperly treated dissonance between the voices); MEL (impermissible melodic interval); PAR or SIM (forbidden parallel or similar motion to a fifth or octave); CHR (incorrect chromaticism); CROSS (voice crossing).

6. *Middle: Completing the counterpoint.* Below are five notes from the middle of two cantus firmi. Write fourth-species counterpoint above each, following the instructions. Label the intervals between the staves.

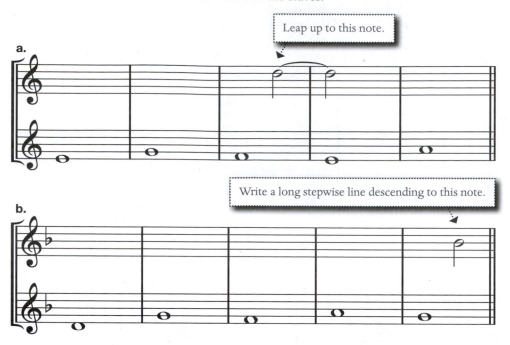

Leap up to this note.

a.

Write a long stepwise line descending to this note.

b.

7. *Fourth-species, complete short counterpoint.* Below are short cantus firmi. Write a fourth-species counterpoint to each with a good beginning, middle, and end. Label the intervals between the staves.

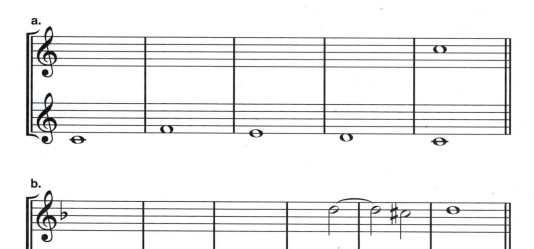

a.

b.

8. *Fourth species, complete long counterpoint.* Write a complete fourth-species counterpoint for each cantus firmus. Label the intervals between the staves (perfect intervals go in boxes, dissonances in triangles). Strategies for composing counterpoint appear in A Closer Look in the ebook.

a. Johann Fux

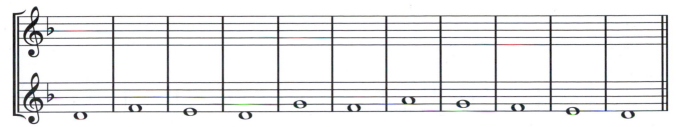

b. Knud Jeppesen

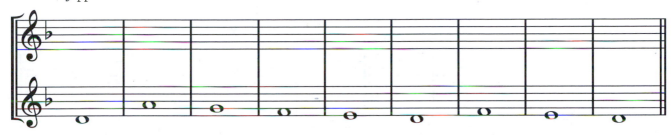

c. Johann Fux

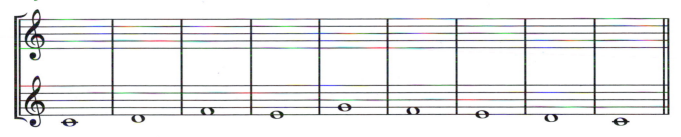

d. Johannes Brahms

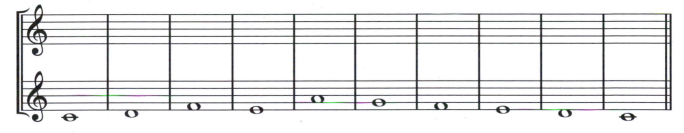

e. Heinrich Schenker

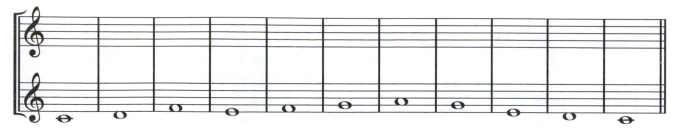

f. Johann Fux

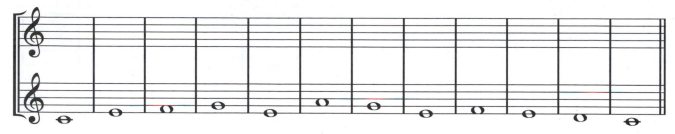

g. Johann Kirnberger

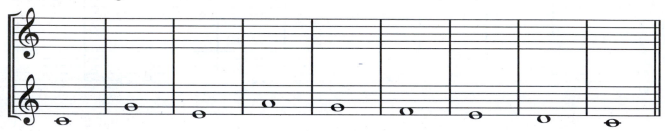

part three

Diatonic Harmony

chapter

9

I and V

A. QUESTIONS FOR REVIEW

1. In voice leading between I and V, how should you handle the upper voices?

2. When is it typical for the upper voices to move by leap?

3. What note is preferable to double in the I triad? What note is best to double in V? What note may never be doubled in V?

4. What is different about the tonic chord in major and minor keys? How should you alter the dominant chord in minor keys?

5. When moving from dominant to tonic, how should you handle the leading tone?

B. SPELLING I AND V

1. For each of the following major keys, write the key signature and the I and V chords. You need not worry about voice leading between the chords.

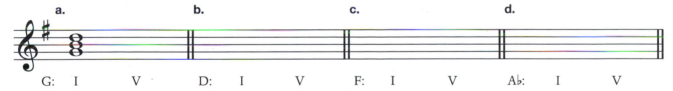

      G: I   V   D: I   V   F: I   V   A♭: I   V

2. For each of the following minor keys, write the key signature and the i and V chords. Remember to raise $\hat{7}$ to form a leading tone. You need not worry about voice leading between the chords.

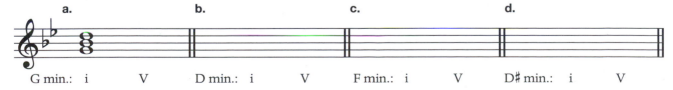

    G min.: i   V   D min.: i   V   F min.: i   V   D♯ min.: i   V

3. On the blank lines below the staff, write the names of the notes in each chord as indicated by the figured bass. Remember to include an accidental when necessary.

- No figures $= \frac{5}{3}$.
- A natural sign $= \natural\frac{5}{3}$.
- A sharp sign $= \sharp\frac{5}{3}$.

```
G   __   __   __   __   __   __   __
E   __   __   __   __   __   __   __
C   __   __   __   __   __   __   __
```

C. REALIZING ROMAN NUMERALS

1. *SATB format.* For the chords below, square brackets indicate octaves; curved brackets indicate fifths.

- On the lines below the staff, write the note names of the chords.
- Then complete the Roman numeral realization, using good voice leading and adding brackets as needed.
- Remember: since the chords are in root position, their roots should be in the bass!
- Circle the leading tones throughout.

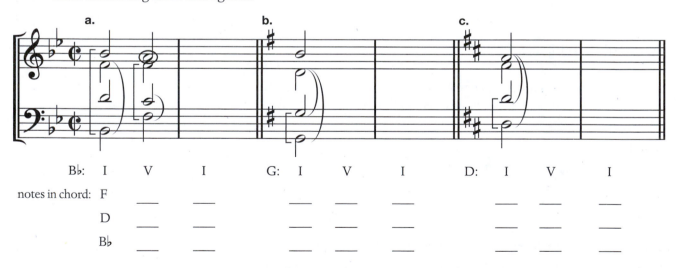

Bb: I   V   I   G: I   V   I   D: I   V   I

```
notes in chord:  F   __   __          __   __          __   __
                 D   __   __          __   __          __   __
                 Bb  __   __          __   __          __   __
```

Remember to add an accidental for the leading tone in minor keys.

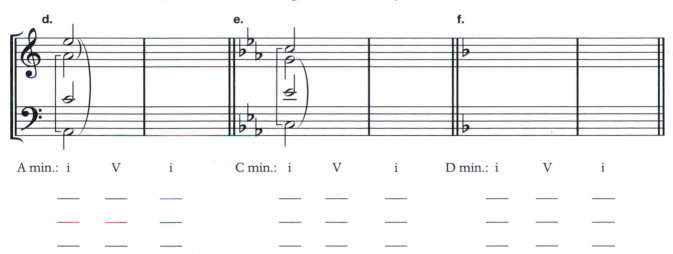

A min.: i   V   i   C min.: i   V   i   D min.: i   V   i

In both (g) and (h), revoice (use different notes in different voices and octaves) at least one of the chords that repeats.

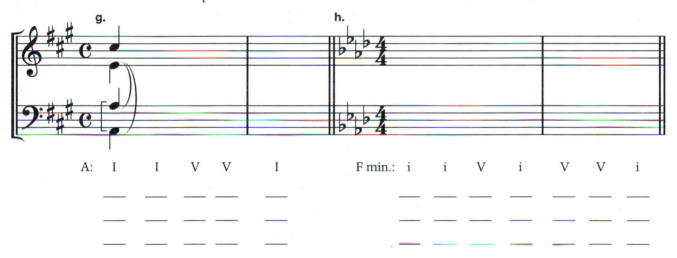

A: I   I   V   V   I   F min.: i   i   V   i   V   V   i

2. *Keyboard format.* On the lines below the staff, write the note names of the chords. Then complete the Roman numeral realization, using good voice leading. Remember: since the chords are in root position, their roots should be in the bass! Circle the leading tones throughout.

In both (d) and (e), revoice chords that repeat.

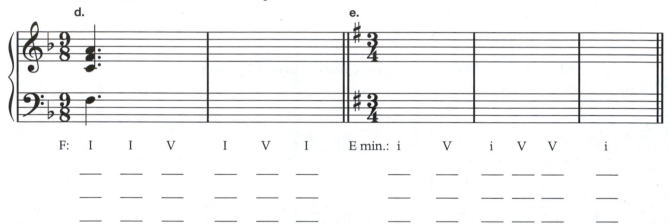

D. REALIZING FIGURED BASS

1. *Keyboard format.* On the blank lines below the staff, write the note names of the chords indicated by each figured bass symbol. Then complete the figured bass realizations, label the Roman numerals, and circle the leading tones.

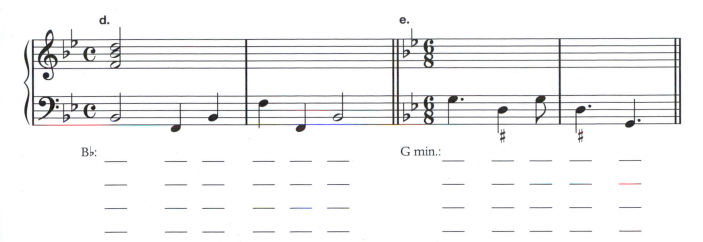

2. *SATB format.* On the blank lines below the staff, write the note names of the chords indicated by each figured bass symbol. Then complete the figured bass realizations, label the Roman numerals, and circle the leading tones.

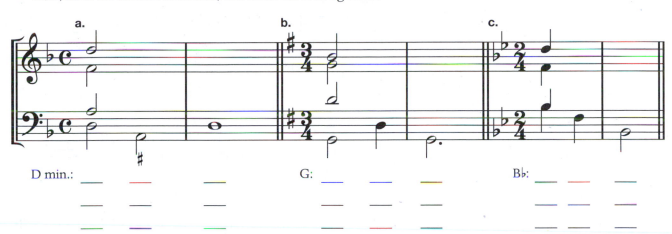

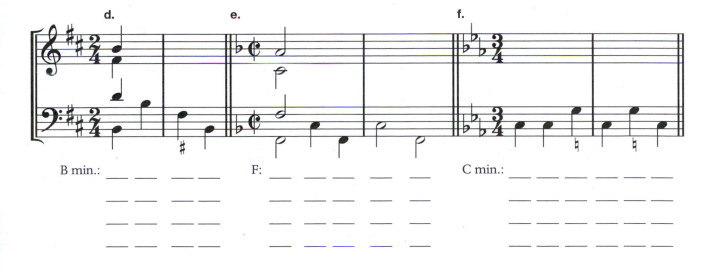

E. HARMONIZING MELODIES

For each of the following short melodies:

- In the blanks beneath the staff, list the note names of the I and V triads.
- Write the scale degrees of each melody note above the staff.
- Using only root-position I and V triads, harmonize the melody by writing Roman numerals beneath the staff and completing the bass line. Choose one chord for each note of the melody.
- Fill in the inner voices. The melody note provided must always be the highest note of the chord.

SATB format:

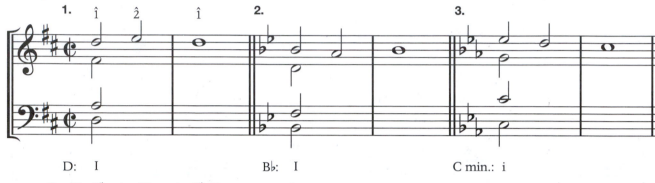

D: I
(I = D F♯ A   V = A C♯ E)

Bb: I
(I = __ __ __   V = __ __ __)

C min.: i
(i = __ __ __   V = __ __ __)

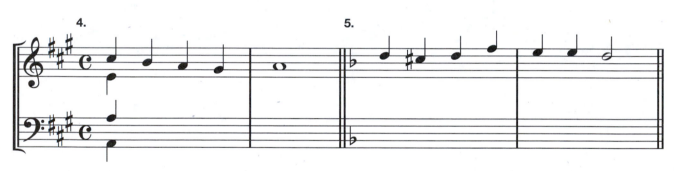

A: I
(I = __ __ __   V = __ __ __)

D min.:
(i = __ __ __   V = __ __ __)

Keyboard format:

E min.: i
(i = __ __ __   V = __ __ __)

F:
(I = __ __ __   V = __ __ __)

F. COMPOSITION

1. Provide a keyboard accompaniment for this melody by realizing the Roman numerals provided. The voice leading of the keyboard part should be good; do not worry if there are parallel octaves or unisons between the melody and the upper notes of the piano part.

a.

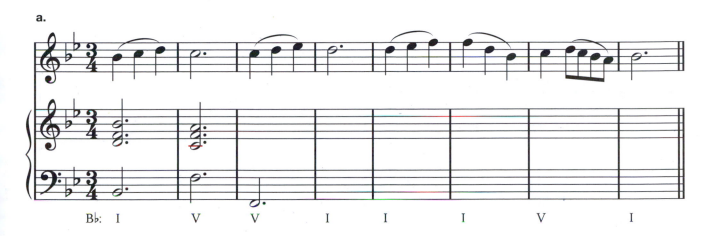

Next, elaborate on the accompaniment that you wrote above using the arpeggiated pattern begun in measures 1–2 below. Conclude the accompaniment pattern on the third beat of measure 8. The elaborated accompaniment should use the *same* pitches as in the harmonization above, although set in a different texture.

b.

2. Using one chord per measure, provide an accompaniment for this melody using only root-position i and V chords.

- The notes of the melody should either be members of the chord you choose, or embellishing tones such as passing tones or neighbor tones.
- Place triangles around any embellishing tones that are not part of the chord.
- Once you've selected the chords and completed the bass line, fill in the inner voices in keyboard format.

a.

A min.:   i

Next, elaborate on the accompaniment that you wrote above by continuing the oom-pah-pah pattern begun in measure 1; conclude the pattern with a half note in the right hand on the second beat of measure 8. The elaborated accompaniment should use the *same* pitches as in the harmonization above, although set in a different texture.

b.

G. ANALYSIS

1. Identify the key and label the chords of the following excerpts with Roman numerals. Circle every leading tone.

a. André da Silva Gomes, *Missa da Conversão de São Paulo*   **b.** Hymn from *Harmonia Unio*

key: _____ _____   key: _____ _____ _____ _____

c. Ferdinando Carulli, *Grand recueil de morceaux progressifs* for guitar, Op. 333, No. 7

Note that some embellishing tones (indicated by triangles) decorate the basic harmonies and that in the harmonies that appear in the final measure, some chord tones are merely implied.

key: _____   ___   ___   ___ ___   ___ ___ i⁶

2. Franz Schubert, "Der König in Thule"

- Identify the key and label the chords with Roman numerals.
- Place a triangle around every embellishing tone and label it as a passing tone (PT) or neighbor tone (NT).
- There is one place in this passage where a leading tone in an inner voice does not ascend directly up by step; mark this moment with a check mark.

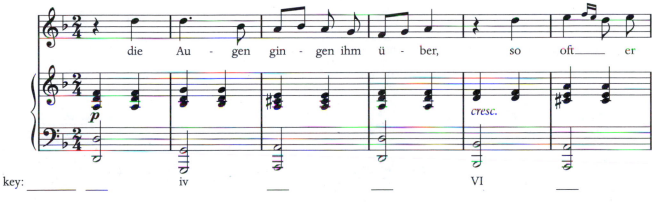

die   Au - gen gin - gen ihm ü - ber,   so oft____ er

key: _____   ___   iv   ___   ___   VI   ___

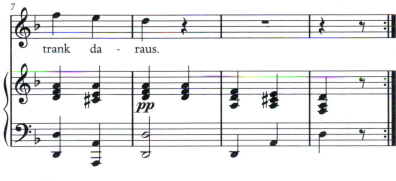

trank da - raus.

Translation: His eyes ran over with tears whenever he drank [from the goblet].

3. Frances Arkwright, "Xarifa"

- Label the key and Roman numerals, one chord per measure.

- On the blank staves below, continue the simplified harmonic model of this passage by writing its chords in four-part harmony, keyboard format, with proper voice leading. Use one chord per measure, with the top voice matching the first note found in each measure of the excerpt.

key: _____ _____ _____ _____ _____ _____ _____

4. Ludwig van Beethoven, Bagatelle No. 25 in A minor (WoO 59), "Für Elise"

Label the key and Roman numerals (one chord per measure).

key: _____ _____ _____ _____ _____ _____

- Is the first measure best understood as a i chord or a V chord? Why?

- How do mm. 1–4 and 5–8 compare? What do they have in common, and how do they differ? Which of these two phrases sounds more complete, and why?

5. W. A. Mozart, "Der Vogelfanger bin ich ja" from *The Magic Flute* (arr. Metzdorff)

- Label the key and Roman numerals in this passage.
- Place a triangle around every embellishing tone and label it as a passing tone (PT) or neighbor tone (NT).
- On the blank staves below, continue the simplified harmonic model of this passage by writing its chords in four-part harmony, keyboard format, omitting the embellishing tones.

key: _____

Translation: A bird catcher I am indeed, always cheerful, *hey-yo hopsasa!*

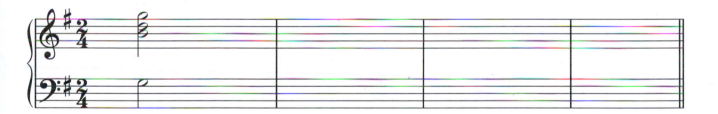

This excerpt is from an aria sung by Papageno, a character in Mozart's opera with a simple and carefree personality. What features of the music express Papageno's nature?

6. The following excerpts are notated in open-score choral format, with each voice on a separate line and the tenor sounding an octave lower than written.

- Label the Roman numerals.
- Circle the leading tone in each.
- Indicate whether the leading tone appears in an outer voice (soprano or bass) or an inner voice (alto or tenor).
- Also indicate whether the leading tone resolves up to the tonic, or if it instead moves to $\hat{5}$.

a. William Billings, "Clarimont"

C: I ____   ____ ____

Leading tone in inner or outer voice? _____

Leading tone resolves to tonic or to $\hat{5}$? _____

b. J. M. Nunes Garcia, "Cântico de Zacarias"

A: ____   ____   ____

Leading tone in inner or outer voice? _____

Leading tone resolves to tonic or to $\hat{5}$? _____

c. J. S. Bach, Chorale 250

D: IV⁶ IV⁷ ____   ____

Leading tone in inner or outer voice? _____

Leading tone resolves to tonic or to $\hat{5}$? _____

d. William Billings, "Egypt"

C: ____   ____ ____ ____ ____

Leading tone in inner or outer voice? _____

Leading tone resolves to tonic or to $\hat{5}$? _____

chapter 10

The Dominant Seventh Chord: V⁷

A. QUESTIONS FOR REVIEW

1. What are the two tendency tones within V⁷? In which direction do they each lead?

2. In a V⁷–I progression in four-part harmony, which chord tone may be omitted from V⁷? If a chord tone is omitted from V⁷, what note should be doubled?

3. In a V⁷–I progression in four-part harmony, which chord tone should be omitted from I? If a chord tone is omitted from I, what note may be tripled?

4. Which is more common, V⁷–V or V–V⁷? Why?

5. What does "V⁸⁻⁷" stand for? How is this indicated with figured bass?

6. What are the options for the dominant harmony in an authentic cadence? In a half cadence?

B. SPELLING CHORDS

Write the key signatures of the following keys. Then write the notes of the V⁷ chord twice in each key: first with all the notes, and then with the fifth omitted and the root doubled. Remember to raise $\hat{7}$ in the minor keys.

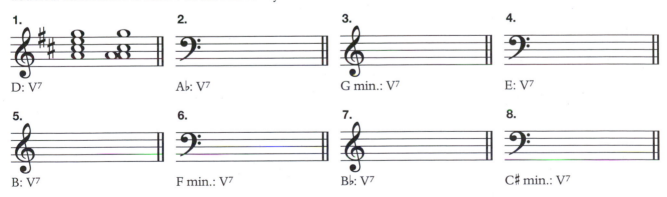

1. D: V⁷   2. A♭: V⁷   3. G min.: V⁷   4. E: V⁷

5. B: V⁷   6. F min.: V⁷   7. B♭: V⁷   8. C♯ min.: V⁷

C. REALIZING ROMAN NUMERALS

1. • On the blank lines below the staff, write the note names of the given chords; place parentheses around any note that may be omitted from the chord.

   • Then complete the Roman numeral realization.

   • Throughout, circle every leading tone and place an inverted triangle around every chordal seventh.

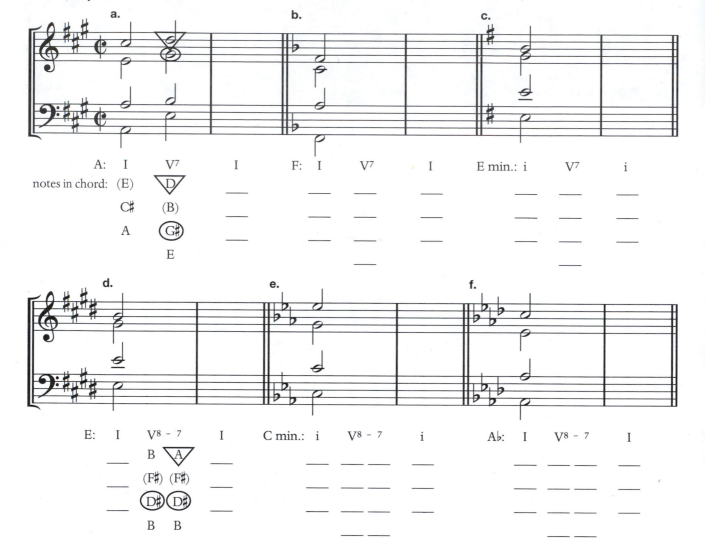

2. Realize these Roman numerals in SATB format. For both (b) and (c), you will need to provide the key signature as well.

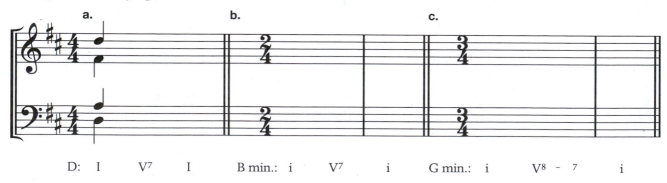

3. • On the blank lines below the staff, write the note names of the given chords; place parentheses around any note that may be omitted.

• Then complete the Roman numeral realization in keyboard format.

• Throughout, on the staff and in the spelled chords, circle every leading tone and place an inverted triangle around every chordal seventh.

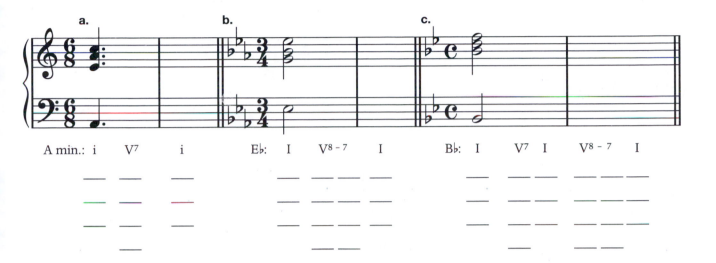

4. Realize these Roman numerals in keyboard format. For both (b) and (c), you will need to provide the key signature as well.

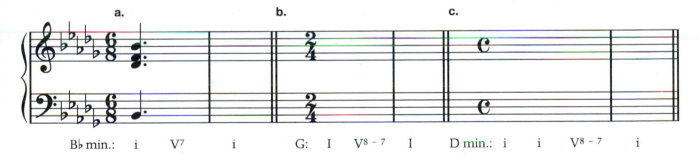

D. REALIZING FIGURED BASS

1. • On the blank lines below the staff, write the note names of the chords indicated by the figured bass.

   • Place parentheses around any note that may be omitted from the chord.

   • Then complete the figured bass realization and label the Roman numerals.

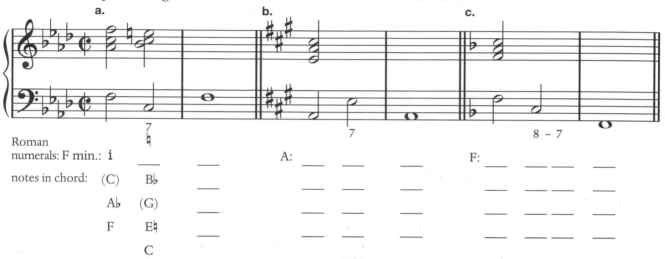

Roman
numerals: F min.: i ___ ___   A: ___ ___ ___   F: ___ ___ ___

notes in chord: (C)   B♭   ___ ___   ___ ___ ___   ___ ___ ___

                 A♭   (G)   ___ ___   ___ ___ ___   ___ ___ ___

                  F   E♮   ___ ___   ___ ___ ___   ___ ___ ___

                  C   ___ ___   ___ ___

D min.: ___ ___ ___   G: ___ ___ ___   B♭: ___ ___ ___

        ___ ___ ___   ___ ___ ___   ___ ___ ___

        ___ ___ ___   ___ ___ ___   ___ ___ ___

        ___ ___ ___   ___ ___ ___   ___ ___ ___

2. Realize these figured basses in keyboard format, and label the key and Roman numerals.

B min.: i

3. • On the blank lines below the staff, write the note names of the chords indicated by the figured bass.

   • Place parentheses around any note that may be omitted from the chord.

   • Then complete the figured bass realization and label it with Roman numerals.

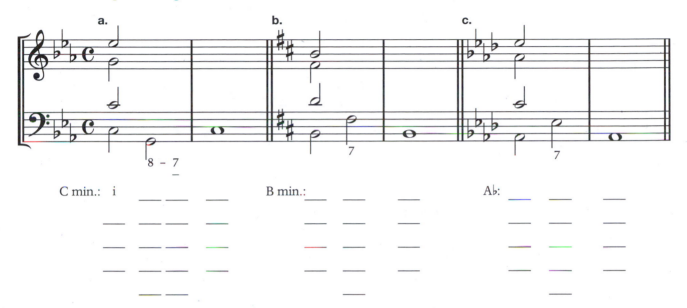

C min.: i ___ ___ ___   B min.: ___ ___ ___   A♭: ___ ___ ___

4. Realize these figured basses in SATB format, and label the key and Roman numerals.

D: I __ __   __ __ __   __ __ __

5. Complete the realization of the figured bass accompaniment for these excerpts. Do not worry about any parallel perfect intervals that may arise between your figured realization and the given melody.

a. Pierre Gaviniès, Violin Sonata Op. 1, No. 5

key: _____ _____ _____ _____ _____

b. Giovanni Battista Pergolesi (attrib.), "Medway"

key: _____ _____ _____ _____ _____ _____ _____

E. HARMONIZING MELODIES

1. *SATB format.* For each of the following melodies:

- In the blanks beneath the staff, write the note names of the I and V⁷ chords. Place parentheses around any notes that may be omitted.
- Write the scale degrees of the melody above the staff.
- Using only root-position I and V⁷ chords, harmonize the melody by writing Roman numerals beneath the staff and completing the bass line.
- Fill in the inner voices, avoiding voice-leading errors.

Bb: I __ __
I = Bb D (F)
V7 = F A (C) Eb

D: I __ __
I = __ __ __
V7 = __ __ __ __

G min.: i __ __
I = __ __ __
V7 = __ __ __ __

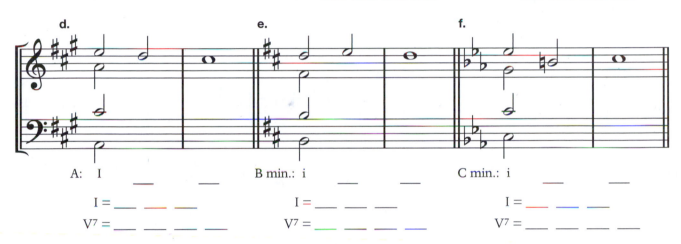

A: I __ __
I = __ __ __
V7 = __ __ __ __

B min.: i __ __
I = __ __ __
V7 = __ __ __ __

C min.: i __ __
I = __ __ __
V7 = __ __ __ __

2. *Keyboard format.* For each of the following melodies:

- In the blanks beneath the staff, write the note names of the I and V7 chords. Place parentheses around any notes that may be omitted.
- Write the scale degrees of the melody above the staff.
- Using only root-position I and V7 chords, harmonize the melody by writing Roman numerals beneath the staff and completing the bass line.
- Fill in the inner voices, avoiding voice-leading errors. As always, the given note should be the highest note of the chord.

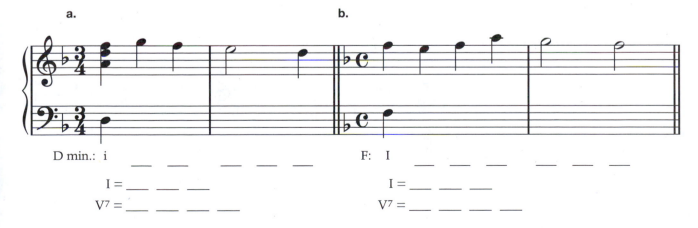

D min.: i __ __ __
I = __ __ __
V7 = __ __ __ __

F: I __ __ __ __
I = __ __ __
V7 = __ __ __ __

3. Using only root-position I , V, and V⁷ chords, harmonize the following melodies in
   SATB format, labeling the Roman numerals.

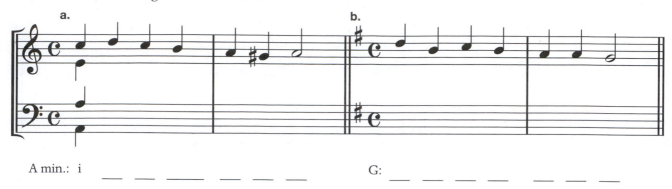

A min.: i — — — — — —   G: — — — — — —

F. ERROR DETECTION

1. Each of the following V^{8-7}–I progressions are incorrectly notated. Notate these
   progressions properly in the blank measure that follows each.

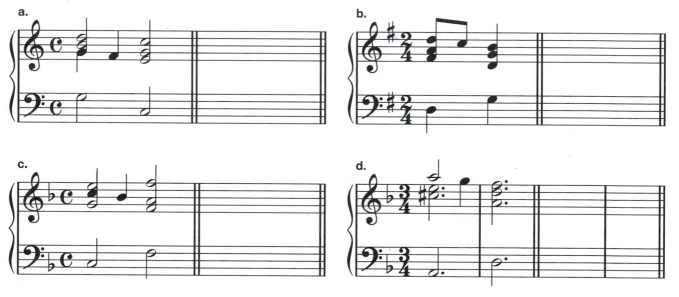

2. Mark the errors for each of the following progressions as follows:

   • *Circle* any $\hat{7}$ not raised in a minor key.

   • Place a *triangle* around any unresolved chordal seventh.

   • *Indicate with parallel lines* any parallel octaves or fifths.

   • *Write and circle Roman numerals* for faulty chord progressions.

E: G min.:   A:

G. COMPOSITION

1. Realize the following chord progression in keyboard format, using correct voice leading. Measures 5–6 should repeat measures 1–2.

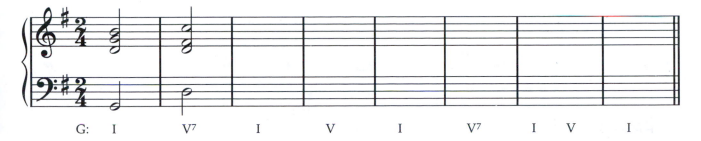

G: I   V⁷   I   V   I   V⁷   I   V   I

2. Keyboard accompaniment.

- On the lower two staves below, turn your realization of the preceding chord progression (using the same pitches) into a keyboard accompaniment, continuing the pattern given in measure 1 and concluding on the first beat of measure 8.

- Then on the top staff, finish a melody to go with the accompaniment.

- Use mostly chord tones, and decorate them with passing tones, neighbor tones, and other embellishments.

- There should not be parallel octaves or fifths between your melody and the bass line of the keyboard accompaniment. (However, there may be parallel octaves or unisons between the melody and upper voices of the accompaniment.)

- Measures 5–6 should repeat measures 1–2.

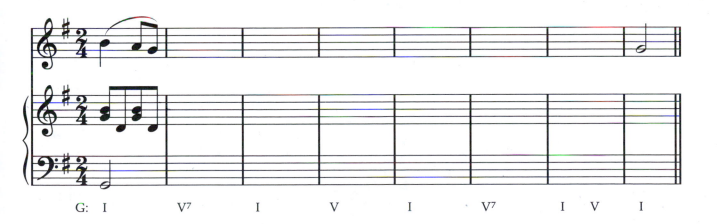

G: I   V⁷   I   V   I   V⁷   I   V   I

3. Compose an ending to this passage (which is based on a piece by Joseph Haydn) by adding four measures.

- Measure 5 should be the same as measure 1, and the style of measures 5–8 should be consistent with measures 1–4.

- Use only I, V, and V⁷ chords; you may also use passing tones, neighbor tones, and chord skips.

- End with a PAC.

- Which chord tone is absent—but implied—in the last chord of measure 2?

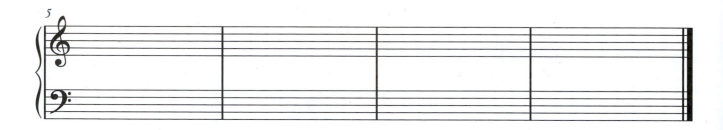

H. ANALYSIS

1. For each of the following excerpts, identify the key and label the Roman numerals. Also label each embellishing tone (indicated by a triangle) as either a passing tone (PT), neighbor tone (NT), or incomplete neighbor tone (INT). Where requested, label the cadences.

a. Jacques Offenbach, "Galop infernal" from *Orphée aux enfers*

b. Hector Berlioz, *Le carnival romain*

key: _____ ____   ____   ____   ____

2. Each of the following excerpts consists of two phrases of four measures each.

- Determine the key of each excerpt and label the Roman numerals. Also, label each cadence as either a PAC, IAC, or HC.

- Compare the two phrases within each excerpt: how are they similar, and how are they different? Is the first or second phrase more complete?

a. Ferdinando Carulli, Waltz for Guitar

cadences:

key: _____ ____   ____   ____

b. W. A. Mozart, "Sehnsucht nach dem Frühlinge"

In each measure, the lowest note of the arpeggio in the bass-clef staff serves as the bass note of the chord for the entire measure.

cadences:

key: _____ ____   ____   ____   ____

c. Carl Maria von Weber, Variations sur un Air Russe, Op. 40

Locate and label the embellishing tones in the melody in measures 2 and 6. Note that both staves use two treble clefs.

cadences:

key: _____ ____   ____   ____   ____

d. Ludwig van Beethoven, Ländler WoO 11, No. 2

cadences:

key: ___ ___ ___ ___ ___ ___ ___ ___

e. Louise Reichardt, "Für die Laute"

- There are one or two chords per measure here. Label the chords with Roman numerals. Locate and label the embellishing tones (as PT, or NT, or INT) in mm. 1, 2, 5, 6, and 7.

- On the staff following the passage, complete a four-part harmonic model of this passage based on the harmonies of your Roman numeral analysis.

cadences:

Ich wollt' ein Sträus-lein bin - den, da kam die dunk-le Nacht,   kein

key: ___ ___ ___ ___ ___ ___

cadences:

Blüm - lein war_ zu fin - den, sonst hätt' ich dir's___ ge - bracht.

___ ___ ___ ___ ___

Translation: I would bind a bouquet of flowers, had not the dark night come, no flowers were to be found, else I'd have brought you some.

- On the lower two staves below, turn your realization of the chord progression above (using the same pitches) into a keyboard accompaniment, continuing the pattern given in measure 1.

- Then on the top staff, compose a new melody to go with the accompaniment.

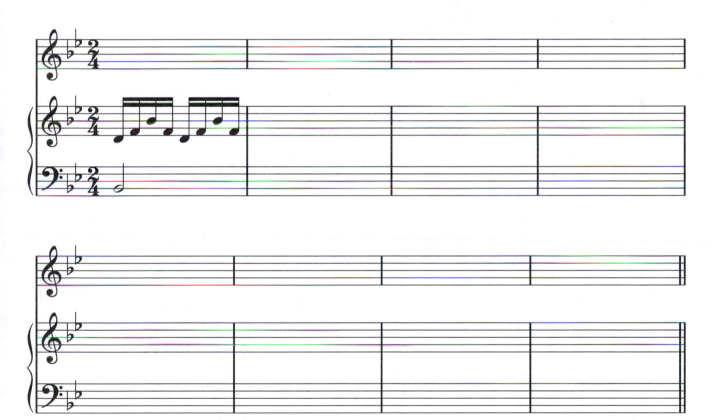

3. Giovanni Battista Ferrandini, Overture to *Catone in Utica*

- Identify the key and label the Roman numerals (one chord per measure) of the passage below. Place a triangle around every chordal seventh of a V⁷.

- On the staff below the passage, complete a four-part harmonic model of this passage based on the harmonies of your Roman numeral analysis.

key: _____ ___   ___   ___   ___

___   ___

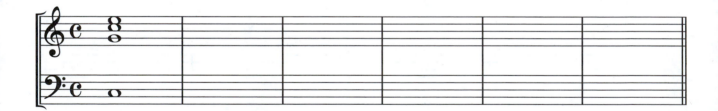

- Note that this passage is six measures long. How may it be understood to be an expansion of a simpler four-measure prototype?

- What musical features provide a sense of momentum leading to the cadence? How is a sense of closure delayed until measure 6?

- What may have motivated the skip in the viola from D to F and back in the second half of measure 3 and measure 5?

chapter 11

I⁶ and V⁶

A. QUESTIONS FOR REVIEW

1. Which chords may follow I⁶? Of the chords discussed so far (I, V, V⁷, and V⁶), which ones typically precede I⁶? Which chords do not?

2. Of the chords discussed so far, which chords may follow V⁶? Which chords may not?

3. Which notes may be doubled in I⁶? Which notes may be doubled in V⁶?

4. In what ways is I⁶ used similarly to root-position I? In what ways are I⁶ and I used differently from one another?

5. In what ways is V⁶ used similarly to root-position V? In what ways are V and V⁶ used differently from one another?

B. I⁶

1. Complete each Roman numeral realization in SATB format.

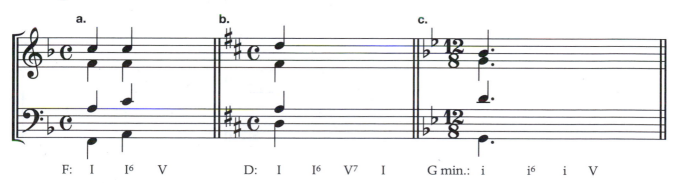

F: I   I⁶   V   D: I   I⁶   V⁷   I   G min.:   i   i⁶   i   V

2. Harmonize the progression in (a)–(c) using three different melodies, following the given guidelines.

a. On the first two beats, melody and bass move in opposite directions (creating voice exchange).

b. On the first two beats, melody and bass move in the same direction.

c. On the first two beats, melody stays on the same note.

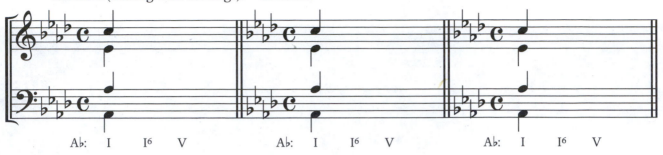

Ab: I I⁶ V   Ab: I I⁶ V   Ab: I I⁶ V

3. Complete each Roman numeral realization in keyboard format.

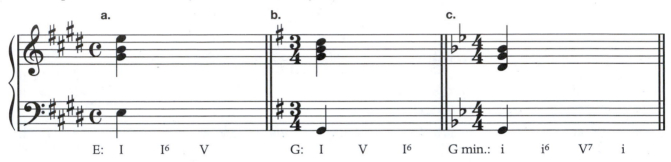

 a.   **b.**   **c.**

E: I I⁶ V G: I V I⁶ G min.: i i⁶ V⁷ i

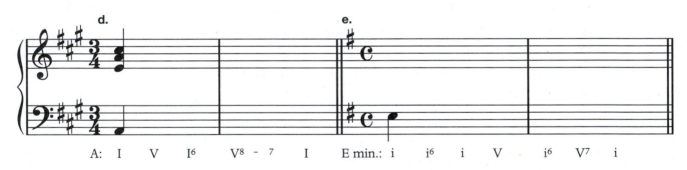

 d.   **e.**

A: I V I⁶ V⁸⁻⁷ I E min.: i i⁶ i V i⁶ V⁷ i

4. Complete each figured bass realization in keyboard format. Label the Roman numeral of each chord; in (d) and (e) also label the key.

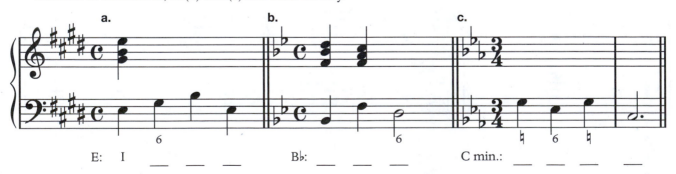

 a.   **b.**   **c.**

E: I ___ ___ ___ Bb: ___ ___ ___ C min.: ___ ___ ___ ___

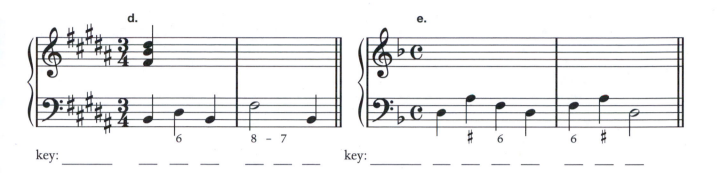

key: _____ __ __ __   key: _____ __ __ __ __ __

5. *Realizing figured bass.* Complete each figured bass realization in SATB format. Label
the key of each and the Roman numeral of each chord.

key: _____ i ___ __   key: _____ __ __   key: _____ __ __

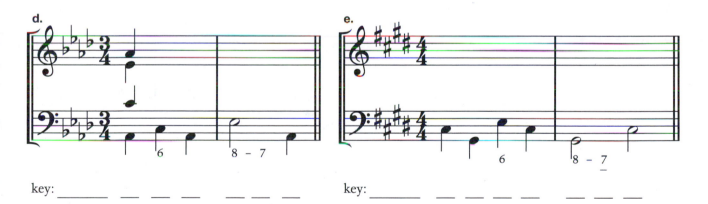

key: _____ __ __ __   key: _____ __ __ __ __

C. V⁶

1. Complete each Roman numeral realization in SATB format; circle the leading tones.

A: I   V⁶   I   B min.: i   V⁶   i   E♭: I   V⁶   I

2. Harmonize the progression in (a)–(c) in SATB format using three different melodies, following the given guidelines.

    a. On the first two beats, melody and bass move in the same direction.

    b. Melody and bass move in opposite directions.

    c. Melody and bass move in opposite directions.

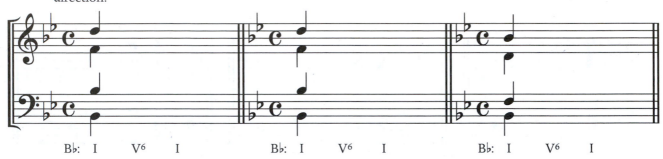

Bb: I   V⁶   I   Bb: I   V⁶   I   Bb: I   V⁶   I

3. Complete each Roman numeral realization in keyboard format; circle the leading tones.

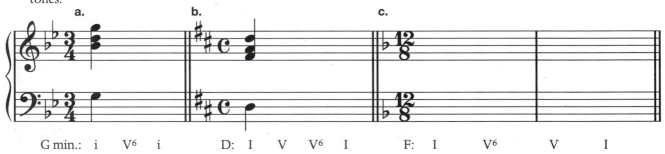

G min.: i   V⁶   i   D: I   V   V⁶   I   F: I   V⁶   V   I

4. Complete each figured bass realization. Then identify the key and label the Roman numeral of each chord.

Keyboard format:

key: _____ __ ___ __   key: _____ __ ___ __   key: _____ __ ___ __

SATB format:

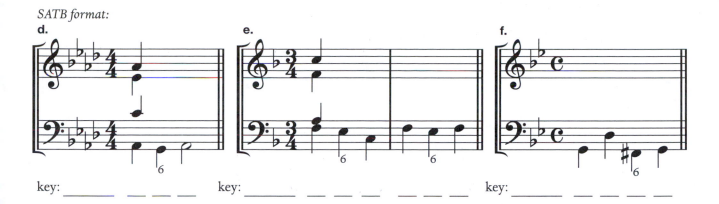

key: _____   key: _____   key: _____

D. REALIZING ROMAN NUMERALS

Complete each Roman numeral realization.

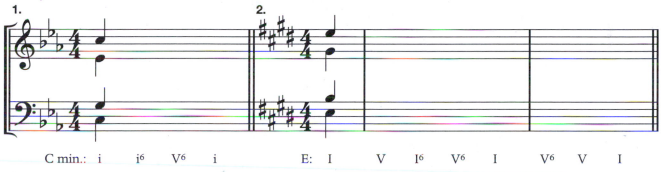

C min.: i   i⁶   V⁶   i   E: I   V   I⁶   V⁶   I   V⁶   V   I

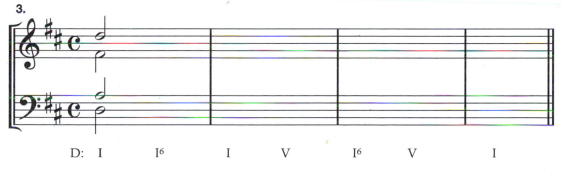

D: I   I⁶   I   V   I⁶   V   I

Keyboard format:

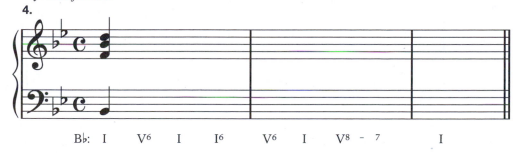

B♭: I   V⁶   I   I⁶   V⁶   I   V⁸ – 7   I

E. REALIZING FIGURED BASS

Realize each figured bass. Then label the key and the Roman numerals; in (3)–(5), also label the cadence at the end.

Keyboard format:

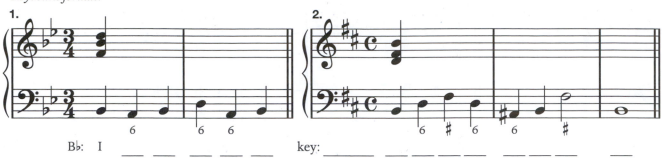

1.   **2.**

Bb: I ___ ___ ___ ___ ___ ___

key: ___ ___ ___ ___ ___ ___ ___

cadence: _____

3.

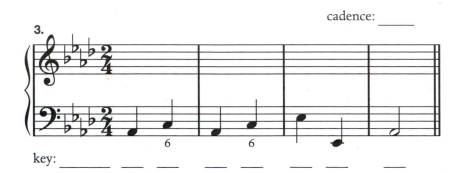

key: ___ ___ ___ ___ ___ ___ ___

cadence: _____

SATB format:

4.

key: ___ ___ ___ ___ ___

cadence: _____

5.

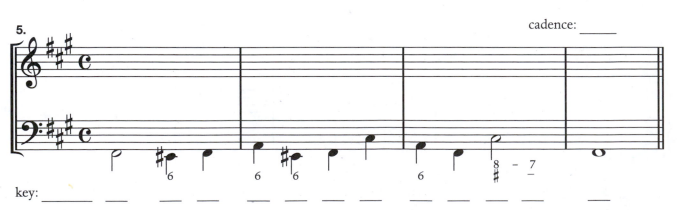

key: ___ ___ ___ ___ ___ ___ ___

F. IDENTIFYING VOICE-LEADING ERRORS

Each of the progressions have one or two of the following errors: parallel octaves, incorrect treatment of the leading tone, or incorrect treatment of the chordal seventh. Circle the problematic tone(s) and identify the error.

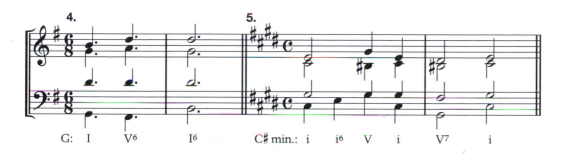

G. HARMONIZING MELODIES

1. Harmonize each melodic fragment in SATB format, using only I, I⁶, V, V⁶, and V⁷.

   - Complete the labeling of the keys and scale degrees of the melodies for each of the following fragments.

   - Harmonize the melodic fragments, using at least one I⁶ or V⁶ in each.

   - Label the chords with Roman numerals.

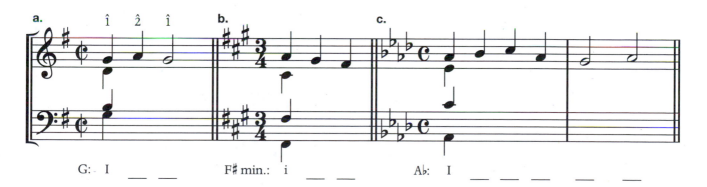

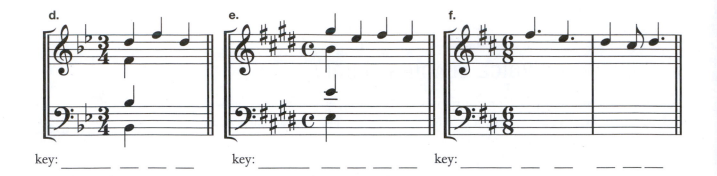

d.

e.

f.

key: _____ _ _ _   key: _____ _ _ _   key: _____ _ _ _

2. Harmonize each of the following melodies in SATB format, using only I, I⁶, V, V⁶, and V⁷ chords.

- Indicate the key of the passage and the scale degrees of the notes in the melody.

- Suggest Roman numerals and a bass line for the cadence at the end (remember, the cadence should involve root-position chords).

- Then suggest Roman numerals and a bass line for the rest of the melody; at least some of the chords should be inversions of I or V. Check that the bass does not create voice-leading errors with the melody.

- Finally, fill in the inner voices.

a.

D: I   ___   ___   ___   ___

b.

key: _____ _ _   ___   ___   ___   ___   ___

NAME: ....

c.

key: _____ __ __ __ ___ __

d.

key: _____ __ __ __ ___ __

H. FIGURED BASS ACCOMPANIMENTS

Complete a realization of the figured bass accompaniment for these excerpts. Do not worry about any parallel perfect intervals that may arise between your figured realization and the given melody.

1. Frederick the Great, Flute Sonata in B minor

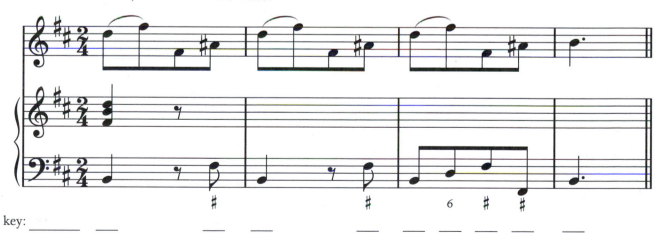

key: _____ __ __ __ ___

2. G. P. Telemann, Oboe Sonata in C minor

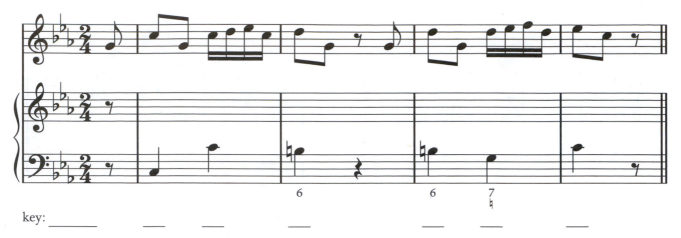

key: _____   __   __   __   __

I. COMPOSITION

1. In the following melody:

- Select one chord—I, V, I^6, V^6, or V^7—to harmonize each measure. With the exception of the notes labeled as passing tones (PT) or neighbor tones (NT), the notes in the given melody should be notes of the chord you choose for the measure.

- Write the bass line.

- In keyboard format, fill in the inner voices, being careful to avoid voice-leading errors.

- Do not worry about parallel perfect intervals that may arise between the right hand of the keyboard accompaniment and the given melody.

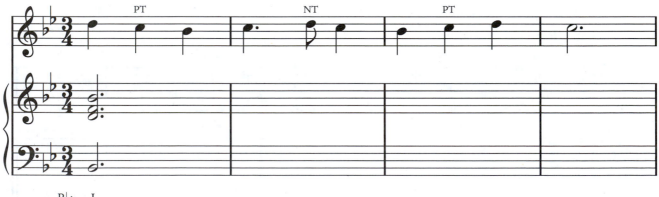

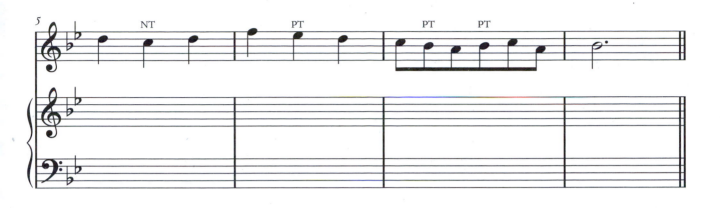

2. With the same melody as (1), rewrite the accompaniment continuing the pattern given in the first measure; use the same pitches used in your harmonization in (1).

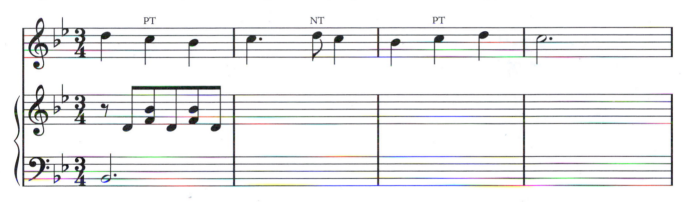

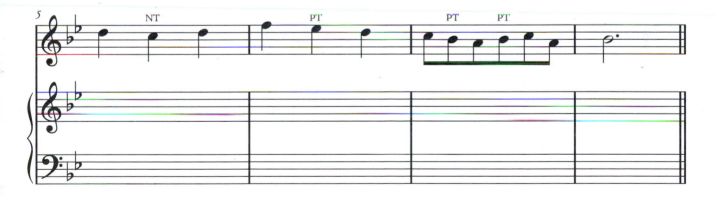

J. ANALYSIS

Label the keys and Roman numerals of the following passages. Where indicated, label the cadence.

1. *The Chorale Book for England,* No. 18

Label the scale degrees of the melody as well.

2. *The Chorale Book for England,* No. 12

Label the scale degrees of the melody as well.

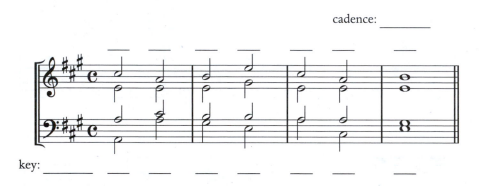

3. W. A. Mozart, Variations on "Salve tu Domine"

Note: The chordal third is implied in the second chord of measure 4.

4. Jean Baptiste Lully, Overture to *Alceste*

Label the embellishing tones in the melody.

key: _____ _____ _____ _____ _____ _____ _____ _____

5. Ferdinando Carulli, *Grand Recueil de morceaux progressifs* for guitar, Op. 333, No. 12

Two chords have been labeled for you.

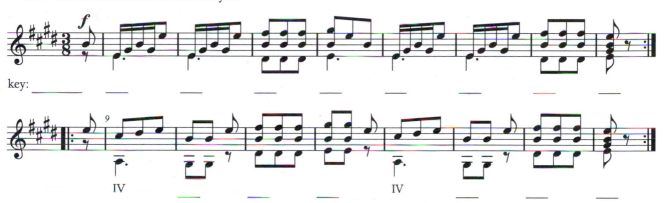

key: _____ _____ _____ _____ _____ _____ _____

IV _____ _____ _____ _____ IV _____ _____

6. Joseph Haydn, Symphony No. 45 ("Farewell"), iv

cadence: _____

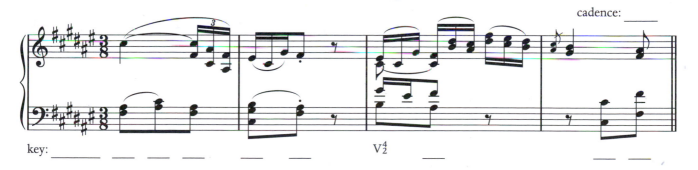

key: _____ _____ _____ V_2^4 _____ _____

Which chord tone is missing—but implied—in the second-to-last chord? _____

7. Baldassare Galuppi, "Madre natura," from *Il mondo alla roversa*

C min.: ___ ___ ___ ___ ___ iv ___ ___ ___ iv ___

cadence: ___

___ ii°6 ___ ___

- Which notes of the chord are implied in the second half of measure 7? Which chord note is implied in measure 8?

- At two points in this phrase the expected arrival of a PAC is averted. Where do these evaded cadences occur, and how are they brought about?

- What makes the final cadence in measure 7–8 sound particularly striking?

8. Ignatius Sancho, "Who'd a Thought It"

The chords are suggested with just two voices. Thus, in every chord, one or two tones are implied.

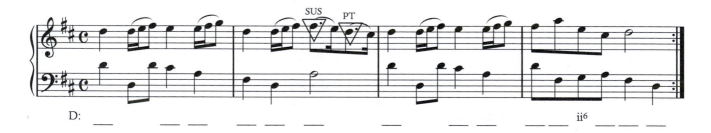

D: ___ ___ ___ ___ ___ ___ ___ ___ ___ ___ ___ ii6 ___ ___ ___

12

V^6_5 and V^4_2

A. QUESTIONS FOR REVIEW

1. What chord member (root, third, fifth, or seventh) of V^7 is in the bass of V^6_5? What scale degree is in the bass of V^6_5?

2. What chord member of V^7 is in the bass of V^4_2? What scale degree is in the bass of V^4_2?

3. What chords may follow V^6_5? What chords may precede V^6_5?

4. What chords may follow V^4_2? What chords may precede V^4_2?

5. Where within a phrase would you not find V^6_5 and V^4_2? What chords are used there instead?

6. In four-part harmony, what chord members (if any) are typically doubled in V^6_5 and V^4_2?

7. In which direction does the chordal seventh within V^6_5 and V^4_2 resolve? In which direction does $\hat{7}$ within V^6_5 and V^4_2 resolve?

B. SPELLING CHORDS

Write the key signatures of the following keys. Then write the notes of V^7, V^6_5, and V^4_2 in each key. Notice the clef changes. Remember to raise $\hat{7}$ in the minor keys, indicating it in all three positions of V^7.

1.　G:　V^7　V^6_5　V^4_2　2.　B♭:　V^7　V^6_5　V^4_2　3.　E min.:　V^7　V^6_5　V^4_2

4. A: V^7 V$_5^6$ V$_2^4$ **5.** D min.: V^7 V$_5^6$ V$_2^4$ **6.** F min.: V^7 V$_5^6$ V$_2^4$

7. E: V^7 V$_5^6$ V$_2^4$ **8.** D♭: V^7 V$_5^6$ V$_2^4$

C. REALIZING ROMAN NUMERALS

1. Realize these Roman numerals in SATB format.

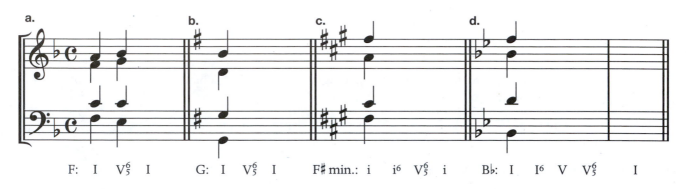

a. F: I V$_5^6$ I   b. G: I V$_5^6$ I   c. F♯ min.: i i^6 V$_5^6$ i   d. B♭: I I^6 V V$_5^6$ I

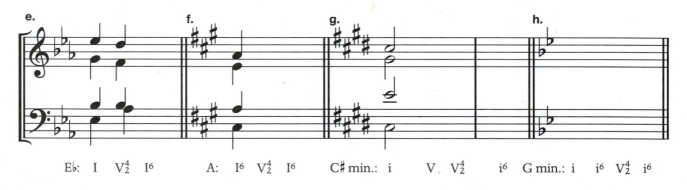

e. E♭: I V$_2^4$ I^6 f. A: I^6 V$_2^4$ I^6 g. C♯ min.: i V V$_2^4$ i^6 h. G min.: i i^6 V$_2^4$ i^6

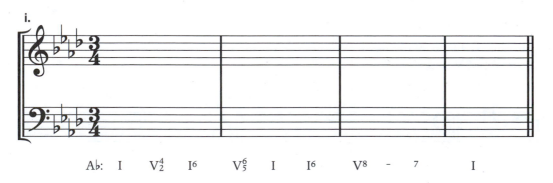

i. A♭: I V$_2^4$ I^6 V$_5^6$ I I^6 V^8 – ^{7} I

j.

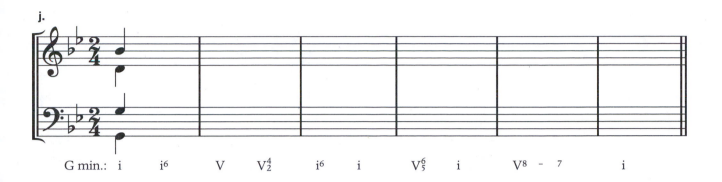

G min.:　i　　i⁶　　V　　V$_2^4$　　i⁶　　i　　V$_5^6$　　i　　V⁸ – ⁷　　i

2. Realize these Roman numerals in keyboard format.

a.　　　　　　　**b.**　　　　　　　**c.**　　　　　　　**d.**

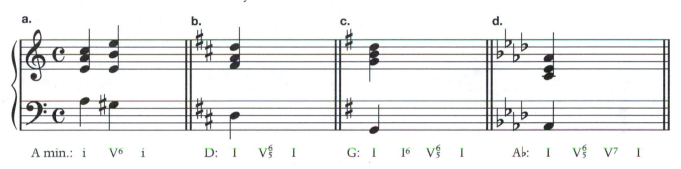

A min.:　i　V⁶　i　　　D:　I　V$_5^6$　I　　　G:　I　I⁶　V$_5^6$　I　　　A♭:　I　V$_5^6$　V⁷　I

e.　　　　　　　**f.**　　　　　　　**g.**　　　　　　　**h.**

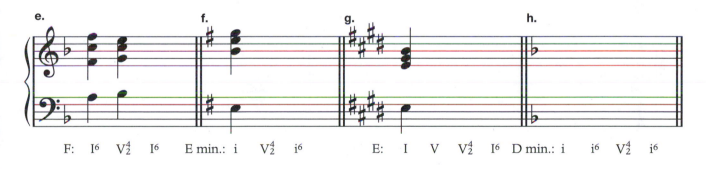

F:　I⁶　V$_2^4$　I⁶　　E min.:　i　V$_2^4$　i⁶　　　E:　I　V　V$_2^4$　I⁶　　D min.:　i　i⁶　V$_2^4$　i⁶

i.

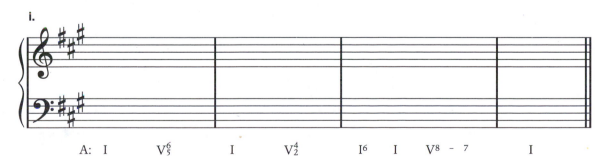

A:　I　　V$_5^6$　　I　　V$_2^4$　　I⁶　I　V⁸ – ⁷　　I

D. REALIZING FIGURED BASS

1. Realize each figured bass in keyboard format. Label the key; then label each chord using Roman numerals.

NAME: ....

2. Realize each figured bass in SATB format. Then label the key and chords using
Roman numerals.

C min.: ____ ____ ____

key: _____ ____ ____

key: _____ ____ ____ ____

key: _____ ____ ____ ____

key: _____ ____ ____ ____ ____ ____ ____

key: _____ ____ ____ ____ ____ ____ ____

E. IDENTIFYING VOICE-LEADING ERRORS

Progressions (1)–(4) each have at least one of the following errors: parallel octaves, incorrect treatment of the leading tone, or incorrect treatment of the chordal seventh. Circle the problematic tone(s) and identify the error.

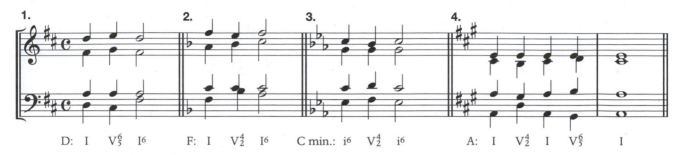

D: I   V$^6_5$ I^6 F: I   V$^4_2$ I^6 C min.: i^6 V$^4_2$ i^6 A: I   V$^4_2$ I   V$^6_5$ I

F. HARMONIZING MELODIES

1. *Short harmonizations.* Harmonize each of the following melodic fragments in SATB format.

   - First indicate the key of the passage and the scale degrees of the notes in the melody.

   - In each passage, write the bass and Roman numerals, checking that there are no voice-leading errors between your bass and the melody.

   - Use only I, I^6, V$^6_5$, and V$^4_2$ chords.

   - After deciding on the bass and Roman numerals for the entire passage, fill in the inner voices.

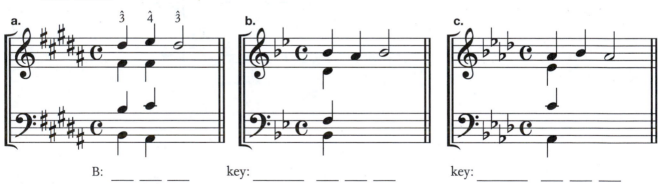

B: __ __ __   key: _____ __ __ __ __   key: _____ __ __ __ __

key: _____ __ __ __ __ __

2. *Harmonization with cadences.* Harmonize each of the following melodies in SATB format.

- First indicate the key of the passage and the scale degrees of the notes in the melody.
- In each passage, write the bass and Roman numerals, checking that there are no voice-leading errors between your bass and the melody.
- Use only I, I^6, V, V^7, V$^6_5$, and V$^4_2$ chords.
- End each melody with a cadence (remember, cadences must involve root-position chords), and indicate the type of cadence (HC, IAC, PAC).
- After deciding on the bass and Roman numerals for the entire passage, fill in the inner voices.

cadence: _____

key: _____ __ __ __ __ __ __ __

cadence: _____

key: _____ __ __ __ __ __ __

cadence: _____

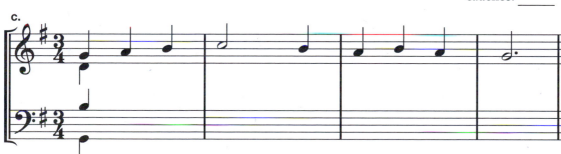

key: _____ __ __ __ __ __ __ __ __ __

d.

key: _____ __ __ __ __ __ __ __ __ __ __ __ __ __ __ __ __

G. FIGURED BASS ACCOMPANIMENT

Complete a realization of the figured bass accompaniment for these excerpts from flute sonatas. Do not worry about any parallel perfect intervals that may arise between your figured realization and the given melody.

1. J. J. Quantz, Sonata in G

2. Franz Benda, Sonata in A minor

A min.: i

H. COMPOSITION

1. Continue this passage in a style that is consistent with the first two measures.
   - End with a PAC in measures 7–8.
   - Use only i, i⁶, V, V⁶, V⁷, V⁶₅, or V⁴₂ chords. Passing and neighbor tones are allowed.

repeats mm. 1–2

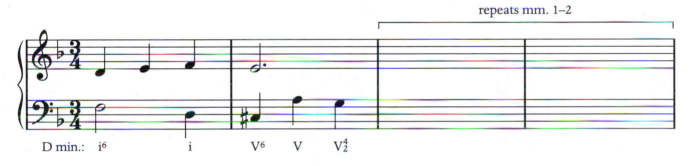

D min.: i⁶　　　i　　　V⁶　V　V⁴₂

moves toward PAC

2. Realize the chord progression below in keyboard format, using correct voice leading.

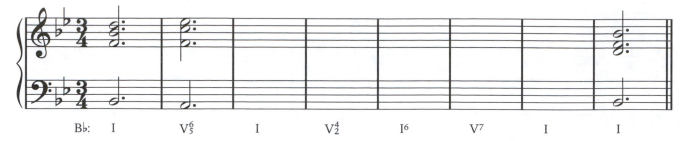

Bb: I   V$^6_5$ I   V$^4_2$ I^6 V^7 I   I

3. Melody and accompaniment

- On the following lower two staves, turn your realization of the preceding chord progression into a keyboard accompaniment, continuing the pattern given in measures 1–2.

- Then on the top staff, finish the melody to go with the accompaniment, ending the melody on the tonic on the downbeat of measure 7.

- Your melody should consist mostly of chord tones, but may include passing tones, neighbor tones, and other embellishments. Measure 5 of the melody should be the same as measure 1.

- The melody should *not* form any parallel octaves or parallel fifths with the bass of the accompaniment. Also, if there is a leading tone or chordal seventh in the bass, it should not be doubled in the melody.

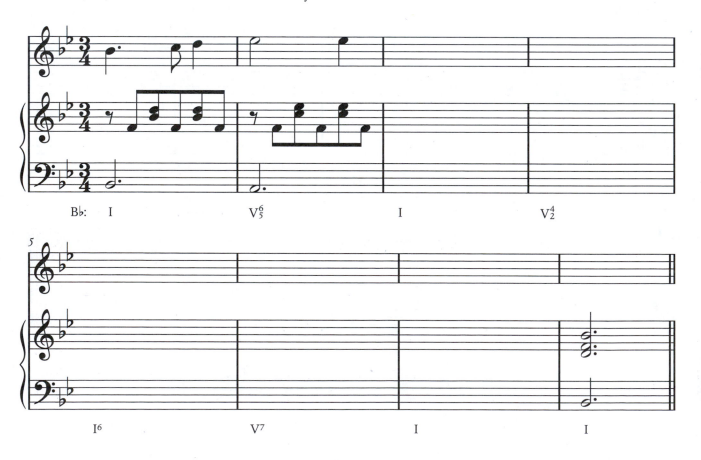

Bb: I   V$^6_5$ I   V$^4_2$

I^6 V^7 I   I

I. ANALYSIS

Label the key and the Roman numerals in each of the following excerpts. Where indicated, also label the cadence (PAC, IAC, or HC)

1. Dmytro Bortniansky, Concerto No. 35

G: _____ _____ V$^4_3$ _____ _____ _____ _____ _____

2. Ludwig van Beethoven, Sonata for Piano, Op. 13 ("Pathétique"), ii

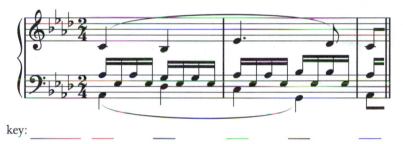

key: _____ _____ _____ _____ _____ _____

3. Franz Schubert, "Heidenroslein" ("Wild Rose")

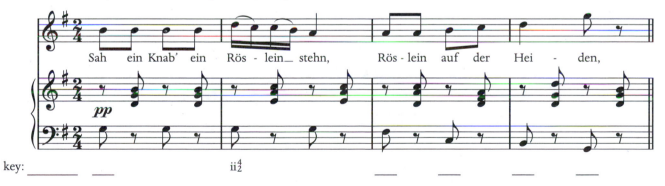

key: _____ ___ ii$^4_2$ _____ _____

Translation: A young boy saw a rose growing amid the heather.

4. Baldassare Galuppi, *Il mondo alla roversa*, Act I, scene vii

key: _____

ii⁶

key: _____

Translation: In that visage is a goddess who smites my heart.

5. Sophie Gail, "Ma Fanchette est charmante" from *Les deux jaloux*

cadence: _____

key: _____ _____

Translation: Your Fanchette is charming in her simplicity.

6. Josephine Auernhammer, Theme and Variations

cadence: _____

key: _____

cadence: _____

7. Jacques-Martin Hotteterre, First Suite for Flute and Continuo, Gavotte 2

Locate the voice exchange between the bass and the melody.

key: _____ ____   ____ ____ ____ ____ ____

8. Joseph Haydn, Sonata in C, Hob. XIV:35, iii

cadence: _____

key: _____ ____ ____ ____

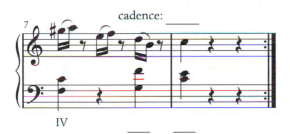

cadence: _____

IV

____ ____

9. Franz Schubert, *Valses sentimentales*, D. 779, No. 21

Each bass note here is implied to last for the entire measure. Label the cadence.

cadence: _____

key: _____ ____   ____ ____ ____ ____ ____ ____

Describe some of the specific features that promote the sense of stability in measures 1–4 and the increased energy in measures 5–8.

10. Haydn, String Quartet in A, Op. 2, No. 2

- Compare measures 1–2 with measures 3–4 and with measures 5–6. In which ways are they similar and in which ways are they different?

- What creates a sense of momentum as this phrase leads toward the cadence?

chapter 13

V^4_3 and vii$^{\circ 6}$

A. QUESTIONS FOR REVIEW

1. What note of the V^7 chord—root, third, fifth, or seventh—is in the bass of V^4_3?

2. In what ways are V^4_3 and vii$^{\circ 6}$ similar to each other?

3. What scale degree is in the bass of the following chords? Which of these chords can lead to I? Which can lead to I^6?

   a. V   **b.** V^7 **c.** V^6 **d.** V^4_3 **e.** V^6_5 **f.** V^4_2 **g.** vii$^{\circ 6}$

4. What types of V chords may appear as parts of cadences?

5. In four-part harmony, what note can be doubled, if any, in V^4_3?

6. What note cannot be doubled in vii$^{\circ 6}$?

7. What chord progressions may be used to harmonize $\hat{1}$–$\hat{2}$–$\hat{3}$ in the melody?

8. What chord progressions may be used to harmonize $\hat{3}$–$\hat{4}$–$\hat{5}$?

9. When can a perfect fifth move to a diminished fifth? When can a diminished fifth move to a perfect fifth?

10. What special exceptions to standard voice-leading practices are allowed within the progressions I–V^4_3–I^6?

B. PRELIMINARY EXERCISES

1. Write the indicated key signature and the chords; remember to raise $\hat{7}$ in minor keys.

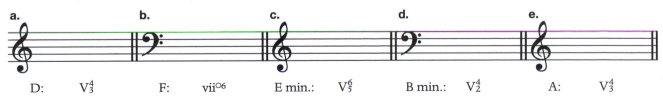

a.   D: V^4_3 b.   F: vii$^{\circ 6}$ c.   E min.: V^6_5 d.   B min.: V^4_2 e.   A: V^4_3

2. For each indicated key, write the key signature and then write V_3^4 and vii^{o6}.

a.
G: V_3^4 vii^{o6}

b.
B♭: V_3^4 vii^{o6}

c.
F min.: V_3^4 vii^{o6}

d.
D♭: V_3^4 vii^{o6}

e.
C♯ min.: V_3^4 vii^{o6}

3. Write the key signature and then the indicated chords.

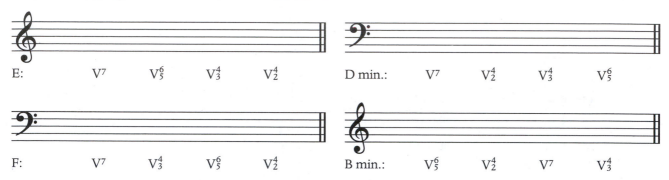

E: V^7 V_5^6 V_3^4 V_2^4

D min.: V^7 V_2^4 V_3^4 V_5^6

F: V^7 V_3^4 V_5^6 V_2^4

B min.: V_5^6 V_2^4 V^7 V_3^4

4. For each of the two-chord progressions below:

- Indicate whether the first chord could be followed by I, I^6, or either, by circling the correct answer.

- Resolve the first chord to the second in keyboard format (if either I or I^6 will work, choose one).

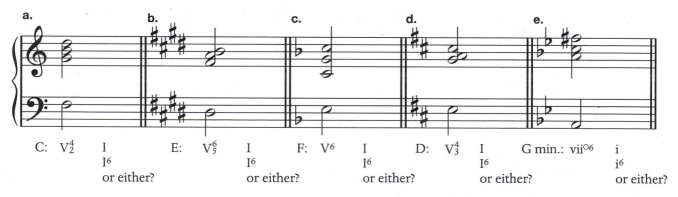

a.
C: V_2^4 I
    I^6
    or either?

b.
E: V_5^6 I
    I^6
    or either?

c.
F: V^6 I
   I^6
   or either?

d.
D: V_3^4 I
    I^6
    or either?

e.
G min.: vii^{o6} i
        i^6
        or either?

C. REALIZING ROMAN NUMERALS

1. Realize each Roman numeral in SATB format.

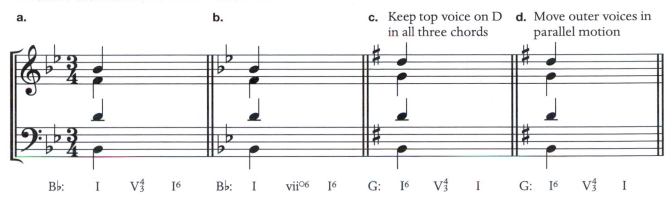

a.

b.

c. Keep top voice on D in all three chords

d. Move outer voices in parallel motion

Bb: I   V$_3^4$ I^6 Bb: I   vii^{O6} I^6 G: I^6 V$_3^4$ I   G: I^6 V$_3^4$ I

e.

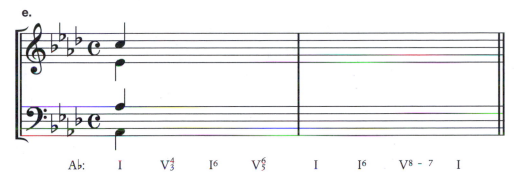

Ab: I   V$_3^4$ I^6 V$_5^6$ I   I^6 V$^{8-7}$ I

f. Use $\hat{1}$ in the soprano of the first chord.

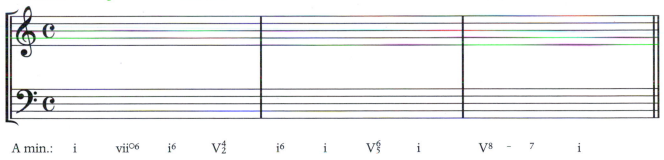

A min.:   i   vii^{O6} i^6 V$_2^4$ i^6 i   V$_5^6$ i   V$^{8-7}$ i

2. Realize each Roman numeral in keyboard format.

a. Move outer voices in contrary motion

b. Move outer voices in parallel motion

c.

d.

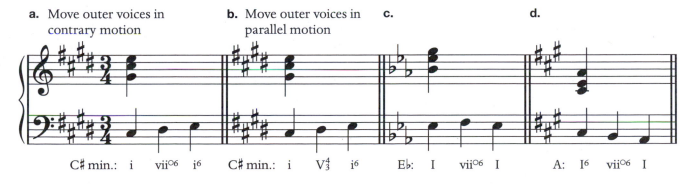

C# min.:   i   vii^{O6} i^6 C# min.:   i   V$_3^4$ i^6 Eb: I   vii^{O6} I   A: I^6 vii^{O6} I

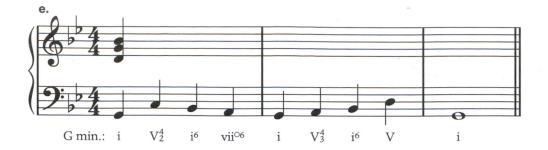

e.

G min.: i V$^4_2$ i^6 vii^{o6} i V$^4_3$ i^6 V i

D. REALIZING FIGURED BASS

1. Realize each figured bass in keyboard format. Then identify the key of each and
label the Roman numerals.

a.

4
3   6

key: _____

b.

6   #6

key: _____

c.

#6
4
3   #6

key: _____

d.

6   6   6   6   6
5

key: _____

e.

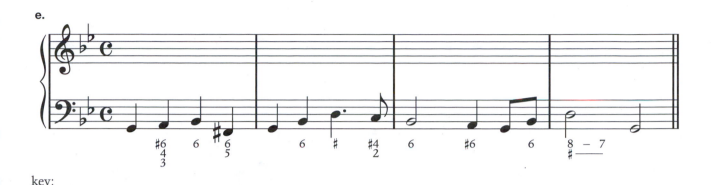

key: ___ ___ ___ ___ ___ ___ ___ ___ ___

2. Realize each figured bass in SATB format. Then identify the key of each and label the Roman numerals.

key: ___

key: ___ ___ ___

key: ___ ___ ___

key: ___ ___ ___

e.

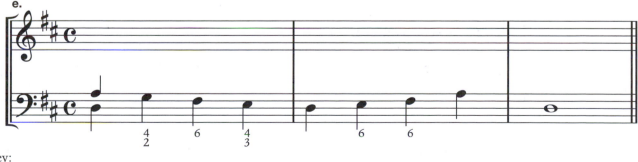

key: ___ ___ ___ ___ ___ ___ ___

3. Realize the figured bass accompaniment for the following excerpts, and label the Roman numerals. Do not worry about any parallel perfect intervals that may arise between your figured bass realization and the given melody.

a. G. P. Telemann, Sonata for Oboe in C minor

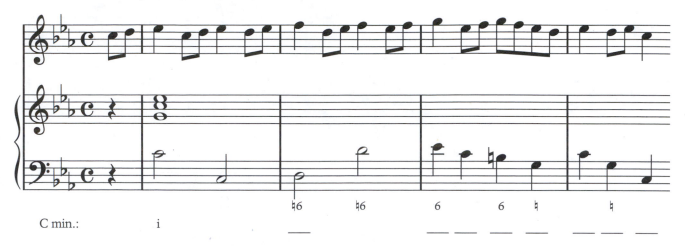

C min.:   i   ____   ____ ____ ____ ____ ____ ____ ____ ____

b. Frederick the Great, Sonata for Flute in C minor

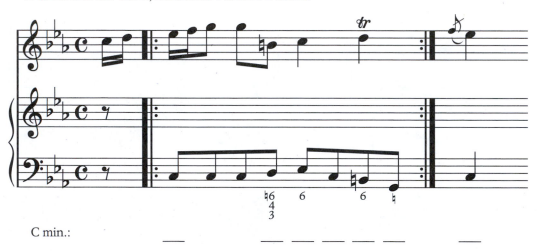

C min.:   ____   ____ ____ ____ ____ ____   ____

E. HARMONIZING MELODIES

1. Short harmonizations:

   • Label the scale degrees of the soprano.

   • Suggest a harmonization by providing a bass line and Roman numerals.

   • Use V_3^4 or vii°⁶ at least once in each exercise.

   • Fill in the inner voices.

   • Mark any voice exchanges between the bass and soprano with lines between the exchanged notes.

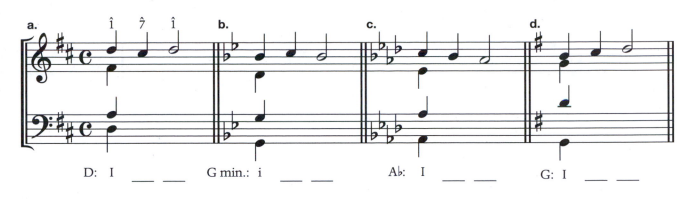

2. Harmonize the following phrases, using a different chord for every note in the melody.

- First determine the key of each passage and scale degrees of each note of the melody.

- Then determine the bass and Roman numerals of the cadence.

- Choose a Roman numeral and bass for the other notes of the melody, making sure that there are no voice-leading errors between the given melody and your bass line. Use V_3^4 or vii^{o6} at least once in each exercise; other chords can be I, I^6, V, V^6, V^7, V$_5^6$, or V$_2^4$.

- Finally, fill in the inner voices in SATB format.

key: _____ ___ ___ ___ ___ ___ ___ ___ ___ ___ ___

key: _____ __

key: _____ — — — — — —

F. COMPOSITION

1. Provide a keyboard accompaniment for the following melody:

- Select one chord per measure, except in measure 7, which should use two chords. Use only the chords discussed thus far, and write Roman numerals and a bass line.

- There should be no parallel fifths or octaves between the given melody and the bass line of the accompaniment.

- There should be a cadence in measure 4 and measure 8.

- In keyboard format, fill in the inner voices, being careful to avoid voice-leading errors.

C min.:   i V_3^4

2. Rewrite the accompaniment below continuing the pattern given in the first measure; use the same pitches as in the harmonization in (1). The final measure has been given.

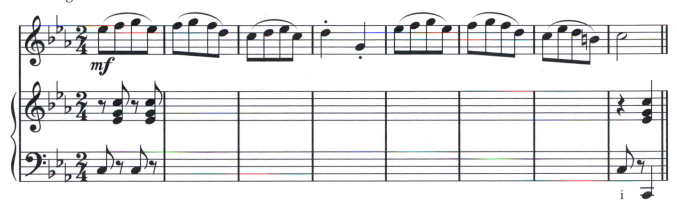

G. ANALYSIS

- Label the key and Roman numerals of the following excerpts. Identify cadences where indicated.
- Beneath each instance of a vii°⁶ or V⁴₃, indicate whether the chord involves a passing motion in the bass (P), a neighbor motion in the bass (N), or arpeggiation to or from the bass of another **D**ominant chord (ARP).

1. Alessandro Scarlatti, "Spesso vibra per suo gioco"

key: _____ ____ ____ ____ ____ ____

Translation: Often vibrates for his sport. . .

2. Jerome Kern, "Gloria's Romance"

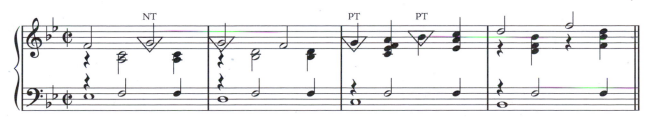

key: _____ ____ ____ ____ ____

3. Jean-Baptiste Lully, Minuet from *Cadmus et Hermione*

key: _____ _____ _____ _____

4. Dave Braham, "The Babies on Our Block"

cadence: _____

there's the Pha - lons and the Wha - lens from the Sweet Dun - och - a - dee,

key: _____ _____ _____ _____

5. Mauro Giuliani, Easy Pieces for Guitar, No. 8

key: _____ _____ _____

cadence: _____

_____ _____ _____ _____

6. W. A. Mozart, "Non ti fidar" from *Don Giovanni*

cadence: _____

Non_____ ti fi - dar, o mi - se - ra, die quel ri - bal - do cor!

p

SUS

key: _____

Translation: Don't believe, O miserable one, in the cheating heart.

7. J. M. Nunes Garcia, *Matinas e encomendação de defuntos*, Responsório I

cadence: _____

(di) - e de ter - ra su - re - ctu - rus sum:

di - e de ter - ra su - re - ctu - rus sum:

di - e de ter - ra su - re - ctu - rus sum:

di - e de ter - ra su - re - ctu - rus sum:

key: _____

Translation: I shall be resurrected from the earth.

8. Ambroise Thomas, Gavotte, from *Mignon*

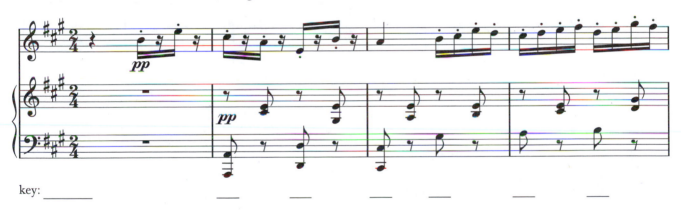

pp

pp

key: _____

cadence: _____

9. W. C. Handy, "Memphis Blues"

key: _____ __

10. Louise Reichardt, "Das Veilchen" ("The Violet")

The example includes a voice exchange between the melody and the bass. Mark it
by drawing lines between the two voices that are exchanged.

Klei - ne   Veil - chen,   süss   und blass,   Schaut ihr   durch das   jun - ge Gras

key: _____ __   ii$_5^6$ V$_5^6$/V __

Translation: Tiny violet, sweet and pale, peeking though the young grass.

11. Franz Schubert, Impromptu, D. 935, No. 2

Mark the voice exchanges between the melody and bass.

key: _____ __

12. Frédéric Chopin, Scherzo No. 2, Op. 31

Label the key and one chord per measure. There are voice exchanges between the
bass and one of the upper voices. Located and mark them in the music.

key: _____   _____   _____   _____   _____

_____   _____   _____

Complete the simplified harmonic model of measures 1-8 of this excerpt in four-part
SATB style.

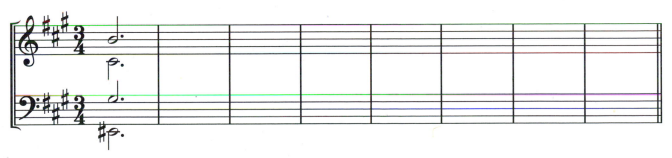

key: _____

13. Marianna Martines, Keyboard Sonata in A, ii

Provide two levels of Roman numerals for this passage:

- In the detailed level (second row), label every chord, labeling three chords per measure (with the exception of m. 7, which has only a single chord).

- On the main level above it (first row), label only one or two of the most important chords per measure, omitting the embellishing harmonies (there are two main chords in measures 4 and 6, and just one main chord in the other measures).

The first and last measures have been completed for you.

chapter 14

Approaching the Dominant: IV, ii^6, and ii$^6_5$

A. QUESTIONS FOR REVIEW

1. What do IV, ii^6, and ii$^6_5$ have in common?

2. In minor keys, what is the quality of the triad whose root is $\hat{4}$, with the natural minor form of $\hat{6}$? With raised $\hat{6}$? What are the qualities of the triad and seventh chord whose root is $\hat{2}$ with the natural minor form of $\hat{6}$? With raised $\hat{6}$?

3. What chords may follow IV, ii^6, and ii$^6_5$?

4. What chords may not precede IV, ii^6, or ii$^6_5$?

5. In four-part harmony, what tone is best to double in a IV chord? In ii^6? ii$^6_5$?

6. When voice leading between two root-position chords with bass notes a step apart, how do the upper voices typically move?

7. What scale degree is the chordal dissonance in ii$^6_5$? How should it be approached? Resolved?

8. In which direction does the minor form of $\hat{6}$ (that is, $\hat{6}$ as it appears in the natural or harmonic minor scales) tend to lead?

B. REALIZING ROMAN NUMERALS

1. Realize the Roman numerals in SATB format.

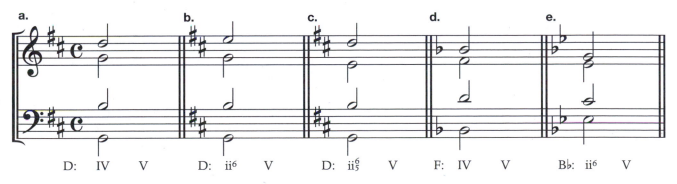

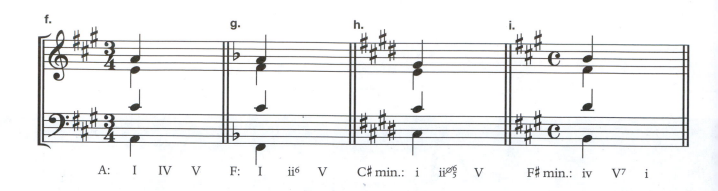

A: I   IV   V   F: I   ii⁶   V   C♯ min.:   i   ii°⁶₅   V   F♯ min.:   iv   V⁷   i

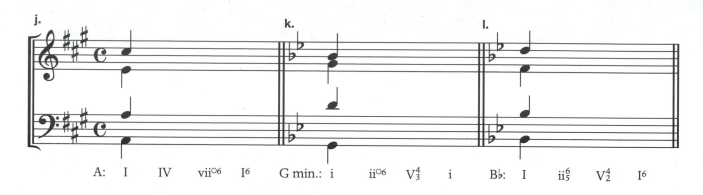

A: I   IV   vii°⁶   I⁶   G min.:   i   ii°⁶   V⁴₃   i   B♭:   I   ii⁶₅   V⁴₂   I⁶

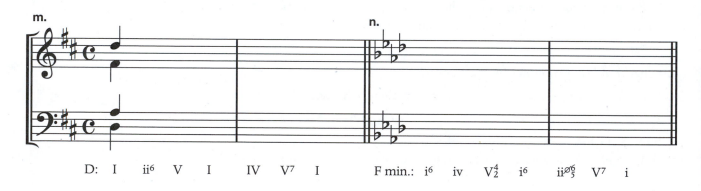

D: I   ii⁶   V   I   IV   V⁷   I   F min.:   i⁶   iv   V⁴₂   i⁶   ii°⁶₅   V⁷   i

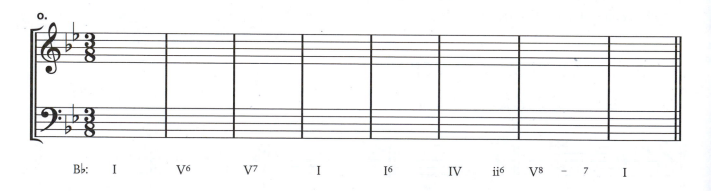

B♭:   I   V⁶   V⁷   I   I⁶   IV   ii⁶   V⁸ – ⁷   I

NAME: ....

2. Realize the Roman numerals in keyboard format.

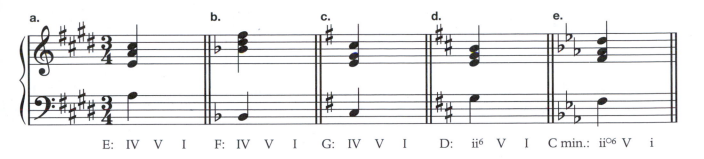

E: IV V I   F: IV V I   G: IV V I   D: ii⁶ V I   C min.: ii°⁶ V i

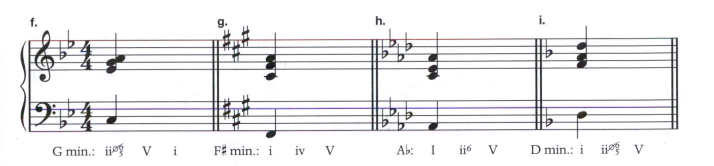

G min.: ii⌀⁶₅ V i   F♯ min.: i iv V   A♭: I ii⁶ V   D min.: i ii⌀⁶₅ V

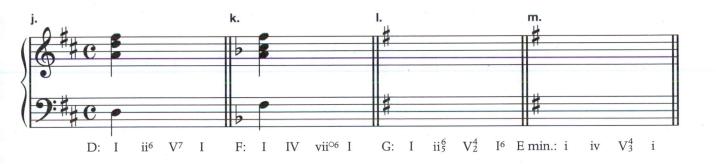

D: I ii⁶ V⁷ I   F: I IV vii°⁶ I   G: I ii⁶₅ V⁴₂ I⁶   E min.: i iv V⁴₃ i

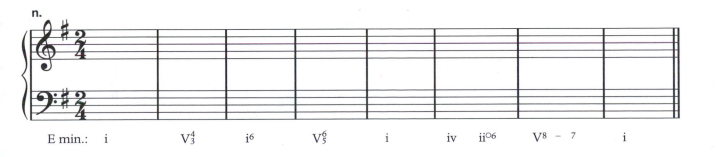

E min.: i   V⁴₃   i⁶   V⁶₅   i   iv   ii°⁶   V⁸ ⁻ ⁷   i

C. REALIZING FIGURED BASS

1. Realize each of these short figured basses in keyboard format; label the key and Roman numerals. Also label the cadences (either IAC or PAC) where indicated.

F: I   ii$^6_5$ ___

key: _____

key: _____

key: _____

key: _____

key: _____

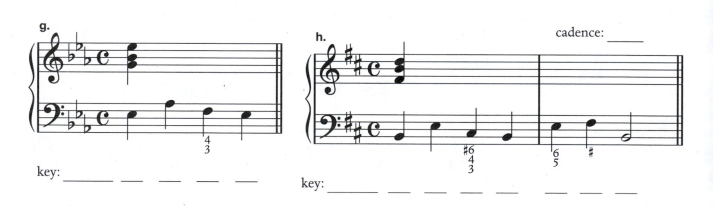

                                                          cadence: ____

key: _____

key: _____

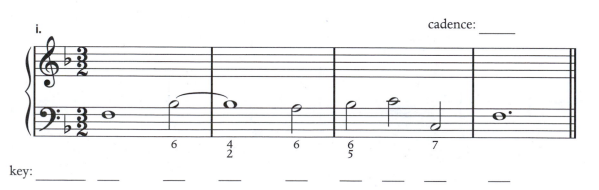

                                                           cadence: ____

key: _____

j.

cadence: _____

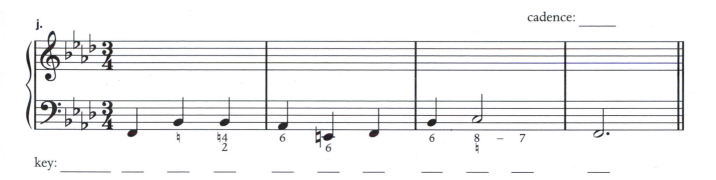

key: _____ _____ _____ _____ _____ _____ _____ _____

2. Realize each of these short figured basses in SATB format; label the key and Roman numerals. Also label the cadences (either IAC or PAC) where indicated.

a.

D: ___ ___ ___ ___

b.

key: _____ ___ ___

c.

key: _____ ___ ___

d.

key: _____ ___ ___

e.

key: _____ ___ ___

f.

key: _____ ___ ___ ___

g.

key: _____ ___ ___ ___

h.

cadence: _____

key: _____ ___ ___ ___ ___

i.

cadence: ____

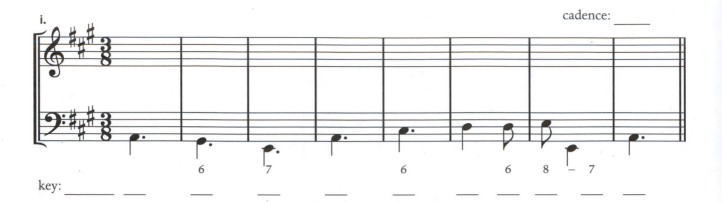

key: _____ __ __ __ __ __ __ __ __ __ __

3. Realize the following figured bass accompaniments in keyboard format, and label the key and Roman numerals. Do not worry about any parallel perfect intervals that may arise between your figured bass realization and the given melody.

a. Elizabeth Turner, "In Pity, Sophy"

key: _____ __ __ __ __ __

b. From *Calliope* collection

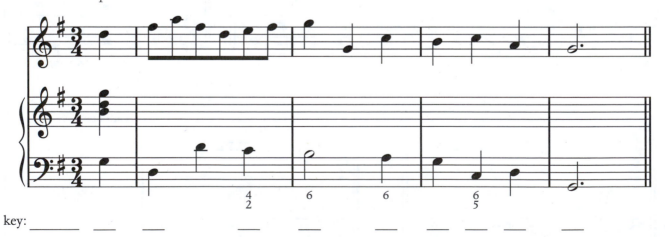

key: _____ __ __ __ __ __ __

c. Anne Danican Philidor, *Premier livre*, for flute and continuo, No. 5

key: _____ ____   ____ ____ ____ ____ ____   ____ ____ ____ ____ ____

D. IDENTIFYING VOICE-LEADING ERRORS

Most (though not all) of the following have one of these errors: parallel octaves, parallel fifths, unresolved chordal seventh, melodic augmented second. Circle the problematic tones and identify the error. If there is no error, place a check mark above the example.

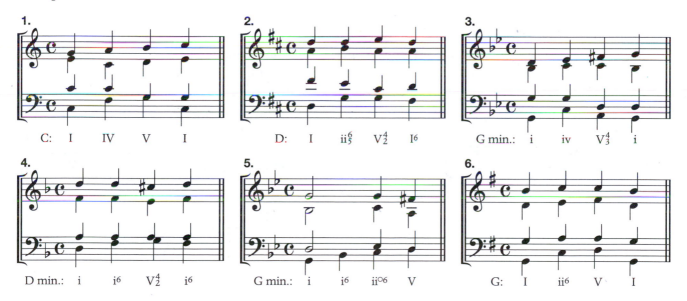

E. HARMONIZING MELODIES

1. In the following harmonic fragments, the bass line and the Roman numerals for the last two chords are given.

- Label the scale degrees in the melody, and below each excerpt list the note names in the IV, ii⁶, and ii⁶₅ chords in the given key.

- Then choose a harmony for the first chord of each (either IV, ii⁶, or ii⁶₅; note that sometimes only one of these might fit the given melody).
- Finally, fill in the inner voices in either SATB or keyboard format.

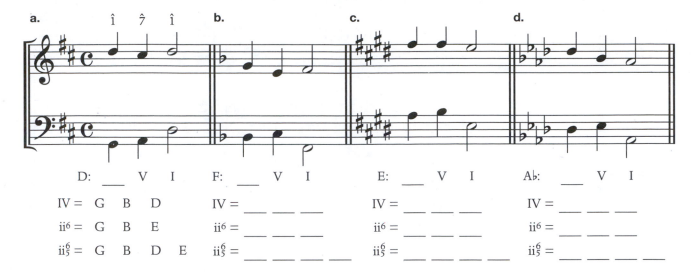

D: ___ V I	F: ___ V I	E: ___ V I	A♭: ___ V I
IV = G B D	IV = ___ ___ ___	IV = ___ ___ ___	IV = ___ ___ ___
ii⁶ = G B E	ii⁶ = ___ ___ ___	ii⁶ = ___ ___ ___	ii⁶ = ___ ___ ___
ii⁶₅ = G B D E	ii⁶₅ = ___ ___ ___ ___	ii⁶₅ = ___ ___ ___ ___	ii⁶₅ = ___ ___ ___ ___

2. Harmonize the following melodies in SATB format.
   - Prepare for the harmonization by first identifying the scale degrees of the notes in the melody and writing the note names of the chords that you may use.
   - Then provide a bass and Roman numerals for each note.
   - Finally, fill in the inner voices.
   - Use either IV, ii⁶, or ii⁶₅ for the notes marked by an asterisk—but don't use these chords anywhere else in the harmonization.
   - Elsewhere in the passage, you may use I (or I⁶), V (or V⁶), or V⁷ (in root position or inversion); somewhere in each, use at least one inverted V⁷ chord.

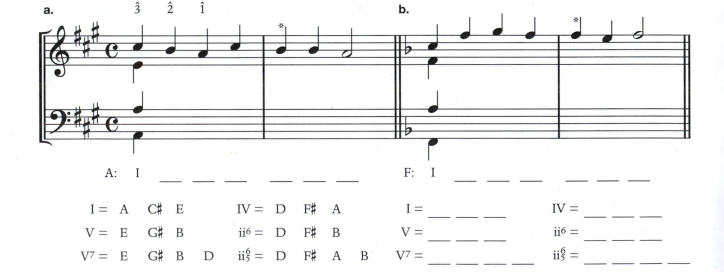

A: I ___ ___ ___ ___ ___ ___		F: I ___ ___ ___ ___ ___ ___	
I = A C♯ E	IV = D F♯ A	I = ___ ___ ___	IV = ___ ___ ___
V = E G♯ B	ii⁶ = D F♯ B	V = ___ ___ ___	ii⁶ = ___ ___ ___
V⁷ = E G♯ B D	ii⁶₅ = D F♯ A B	V⁷ = ___ ___ ___ ___	ii⁶₅ = ___ ___ ___

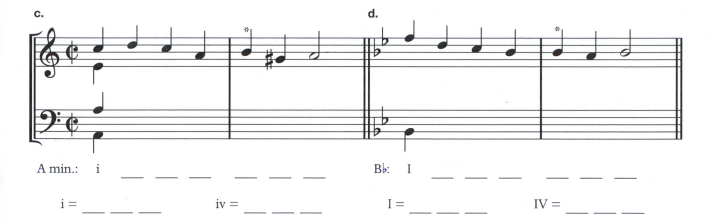

c.

d.

A min.:   i __ __ __ __ __ __ __

Bb: I __ __ __ __ __ __ __

i = __ __ __   iv = __ __ __

V = __ __ __   ii°⁶ = __ __ __

V⁷ = __ __ __ __   ii⌀⁶₅ = __ __ __ __

I = __ __ __   IV = __ __ __

V = __ __ __   ii⁶ = __ __ __

V⁷ = __ __ __ __   ii⁶₅ = __ __ __ __

3. Harmonize the following melodies in SATB format.

- Prepare for the harmonization by identifying the scale degrees of the notes in the melody and writing the note names of the chords that you may use.

- Then provide the bass and Roman numeral for each note.

- Finally, fill in the inner voices.

- Use I (or I⁶), V (or V⁶), or V⁷ (in root position or inversion), and—at least once per exercise—either IV, ii⁶, or ii⁶₅.

- Each passage should end with a cadence, using root-position V (or V⁷) to root-position I.

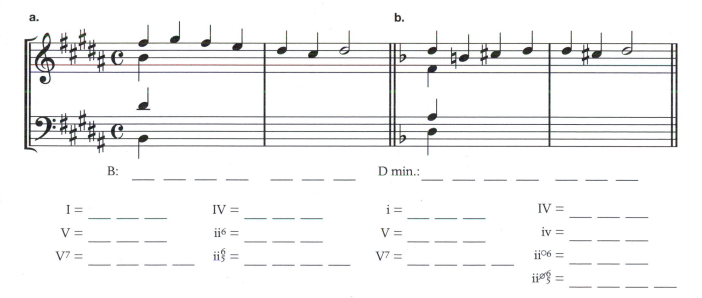

a.

b.

B: __ __ __ __   __ __ __

D min.: __ __ __ __   __ __ __

I = __ __ __   IV = __ __ __

V = __ __ __   ii⁶ = __ __ __

V⁷ = __ __ __ __   ii⁶₅ = __ __ __ __

i = __ __ __   IV = __ __ __

V = __ __ __   iv = __ __ __

V⁷ = __ __ __ __   ii°⁶ = __ __ __

ii⌀⁶₅ = __ __ __ __

c.

Ab: __ __ __ __ __ __ __ __ __ __ __ __ __ __ __ __

I = __ __ __   IV = __ __ __

V = __ __ __   ii⁶ = __ __ __

V⁷ = __ __ __ __   ii₅⁶ = __ __ __ __

d.

C min.: __ __ __ __ __ __ __ __ __ __ __

i = __ __ __   iv = __ __ __

V = __ __ __   ii°⁶ = __ __ __

V⁷ = __ __ __ __   ii°⁶₅ = __ __ __ __

4. Harmonize the following melodies in the manner outlined in the previous exercise, but now use keyboard format. In each chord, the given melody note should be the highest note.

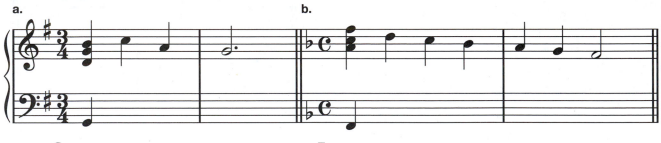

a.

G: __ __ __ __ __

I = __ __ __   IV = __ __ __

V = __ __ __   ii⁶ = __ __ __

V⁷ = __ __ __ __   ii₅⁶ = __ __ __ __

b.

F: __ __ __ __ __ __

I = __ __ __   IV = __ __ __

V = __ __ __   ii⁶ = __ __ __

V⁷ = __ __ __ __   ii₅⁶ = __ __ __ __

c.

G min.: ___ ___ ___ ___ ___ ___ ___ ___ ___

i = ___ ___ ___   iv = ___ ___ ___

V = ___ ___ ___   ii°⁶ = ___ ___ ___

V⁷ = ___ ___ ___ ___   ii⌀⁶₅ = ___ ___ ___ ___

F. COMPOSITION

1. Realize these Roman numerals in keyboard format, using good voice leading. Do
not use any unisons between the three upper voices.

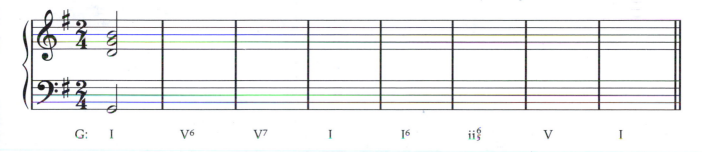

G: I   V⁶   V⁷   I   I⁶   ii⁶₅   V   I

2. Construct a piano accompaniment by continuing the accompaniment pattern
shown in measure 1, using the *same* pitches as in (1); end with a half note I chord on
the downbeat of measure 8. Then write a melody that fits with these harmonies,
taking care not to have parallel octaves between the melody and the bass line
of the piano accompaniment. The melody should conclude on the downbeat of
measure 8.

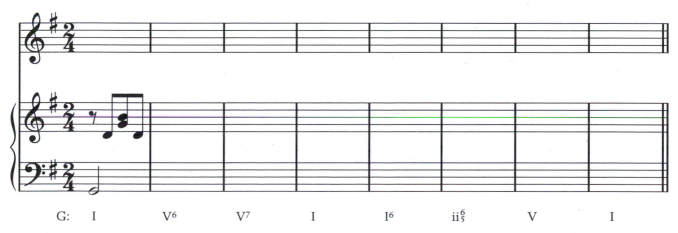

G: I   V⁶   V⁷   I   I⁶   ii⁶₅   V   I

3. Compose a passage for keyboard, guitar, or an ensemble of your choice, following these guidelines:

- The passage should be in D major, in $\frac{4}{4}$.
- The first four measures should embellish the tonic with these harmonies:

  Tonic | **Dominant** | **Dominant** | Tonic
  (For example, the first four measures might be: I | V⁶ | V⁷ | I |)
- In the last four measures, use these harmonies:

  I⁶ | IV (or ii⁶, or ii⁶₅) | V⁷ | I ||
- Conclude with a PAC.

G. ANALYSIS

Label the keys and Roman numerals. If the excerpt ends with a cadence, label the cadence as well (PAC, IAC, or HC).

1. Arthur Sullivan, "Ever Faithful"

2. J. S. Bach, Chorale 63

3. Ludwig van Beethoven, Piano Sonata, Op. 111, ii

4. Ludwig van Beethoven, Piano Sonata, Op. 26, iii

NAME: ....

5. Fernando Sor, Theme No. 1 from Op. 11, for guitar

key: _____   _____   _____

6. Franz Schubert, "Morgengruss" ("Morning Greeting")

key: _____   _____   _____

7. Anna Bon, Harpsichord Sonata Op. 2, No. 3, Minuetto

key: _____   _____   _____

8. Sophie Gail, "Les Langueurs" ("Languors")

key: _____   _____   _____   _____

Translation: The languors into which love has thrown me, although I have sought to save myself from them . . .

9. The next three excerpts each include one or two phrases.
   - Label the key and Roman numerals.
   - Locate and label the cadences in each.

   a. Justin Holland, "Chant Bohemian"

   Label one chord per measure.

key: _____

   b. Frédéric Chopin, Mazurka, Op. 33, No. 2

   Label one chord per measure, except in m. 4, where you could label two chords.

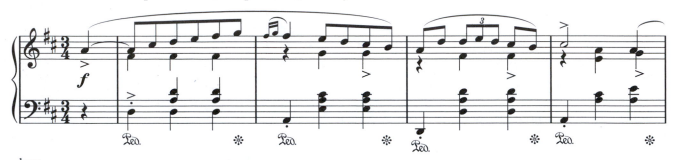

key: _____

c. Francis Johnson, "Augustus"

Label one or two chords per measure.

key: _____

10. Joseph Haydn, Symphony No. 72, iv

- Label the key, cadence, and Roman numerals (one chord per bass note).
- On the staff below, complete a simplified harmonic version of the passage in four-part harmony, keyboard format, using smooth voice leading.
- What is surprising about the last two notes of Haydn's melody?

key: _____

11. Joseph Haydn, Symphony No. 69, iii

- Complete a Roman numeral analysis beneath the example.

- On the staff below, complete a simplified harmonic model (one or two chords per measure) of this passage in keyboard format.

- Note that this passage is six measures long. How may it be understood to be an expansion of a simpler four-measure phrase?

key: _____

Compose a short piece for a solo instrument accompanied by keyboard, in either duple or triple meter, based on the harmonies of this passage.

chapter 15

Embellishing V: Cadential $^6_4$

A. QUESTIONS FOR REVIEW

1. What scale degree is in the bass of a cadential $^6_4$? What intervals appear above the bass?

2. What chord(s) should directly follow a cadential $^6_4$?

3. When a cadential $^6_4$ moves to V, what happens in the bass?

4. What chord(s) may precede a cadential $^6_4$? What chord(s) may not precede a cadential $^6_4$?

5. What note should be doubled in a cadential $^6_4$?

6. Rhythmically, where should a cadential $^6_4$ appear?

7. How is a cadential $^6_4$-V progression labeled with Roman numerals?

8. The notes in a cadential $^6_4$ are the same as in what other chord?

9. In what part of a phrase may a cadential $^6_4$ appear?

B. REALIZING ROMAN NUMERALS

1. For each V–I progression given below, spell the cadential $^6_4$ in the appropriate key.
   Then embellish the progression with that chord.

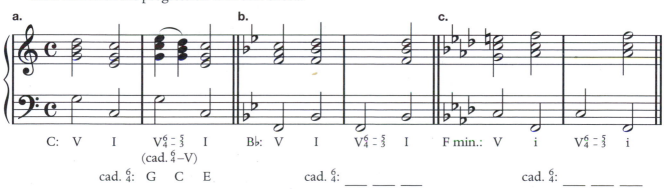

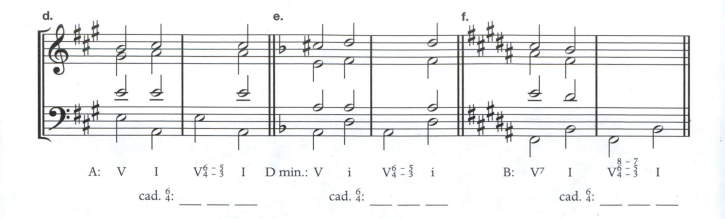

A: V I V$^6_4$ = $^5_3$ I D min.: V i V$^6_4$ = $^5_3$ i B: V^7 I V$^{6\ 8-7}_{4}$ = $^{5}_{3}$ I

cad. $^6_4$: ___ ___ ___ cad. $^6_4$: ___ ___ ___ cad. $^6_4$: ___ ___ ___

2. Realize the Roman numerals in SATB format.

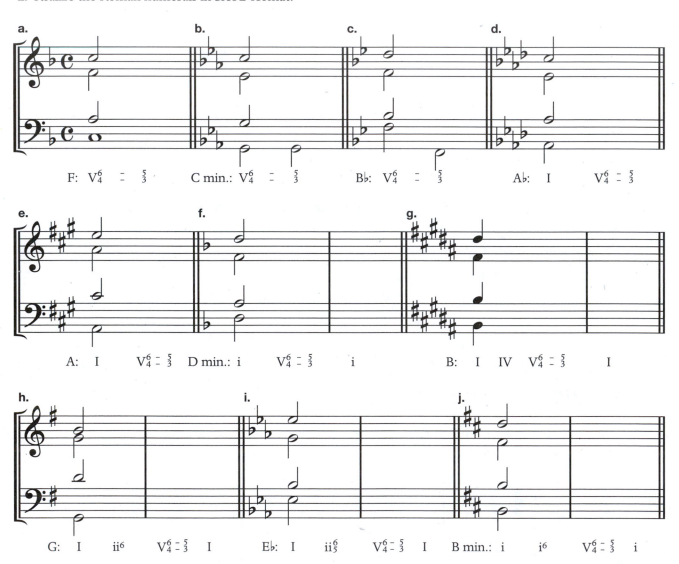

F: V$^6_4$ = $^5_3$ C min.: V$^6_4$ = $^5_3$ B♭: V$^6_4$ = $^5_3$ A♭: I V$^6_4$ = $^5_3$

A: I V$^6_4$ = $^5_3$ D min.: i V$^6_4$ = $^5_3$ i B: I IV V$^6_4$ = $^5_3$ I

G: I ii^6 V$^6_4$ = $^5_3$ I E♭: I ii$^6_5$ V$^6_4$ = $^5_3$ I B min.: i i^6 V$^6_4$ = $^5_3$ i

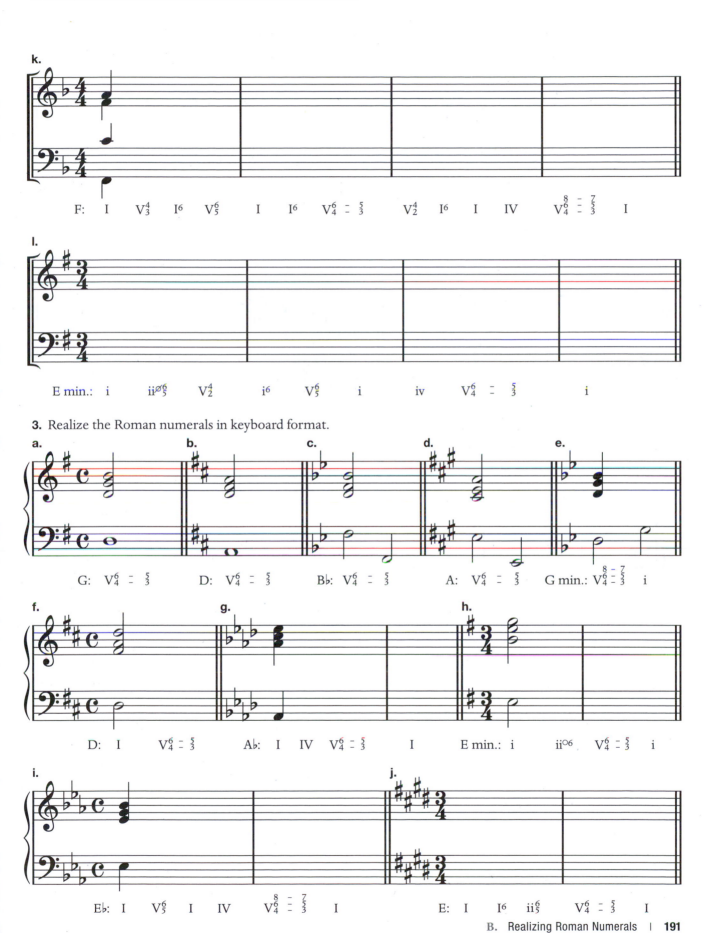

k.

F: I V$_3^4$ I^6 V$_5^6$ I I^6 V$_4^6$ – $_3^5$ V$_2^4$ I^6 I IV V$_4^6$ $_8^8$ – $_3^7$ I

l.

E min.: i ii$^{ø6}_5$ V$_2^4$ i^6 V$_5^6$ i iv V$_4^6$ – $_3^5$ i

3. Realize the Roman numerals in keyboard format.

a.   **b.**   **c.**   **d.**   **e.**

G: V$_4^6$ – $_3^5$ D: V$_4^6$ – $_3^5$ B♭: V$_4^6$ – $_3^5$ A: V$_4^6$ – $_3^5$ G min.: V$_4^6$ $_8^8$ – $_3^7$ i

f.   **g.**   **h.**

D: I V$_4^6$ – $_3^5$ A♭: I IV V$_4^6$ – $_3^5$ I   E min.: i ii^{o6} V$_4^6$ – $_3^5$ i

i.   **j.**

E♭: I V$_5^6$ I IV V$_4^6$ $_8^8$ – $_3^7$ I   E: I I^6 ii$_5^6$ V$_4^6$ – $_3^5$ I

C. REALIZING FIGURED BASS

1. Realize each figured bass in keyboard format. Then label the keys and Roman numerals. Also give the type of cadence (PAC, IAC, HC) where indicated.

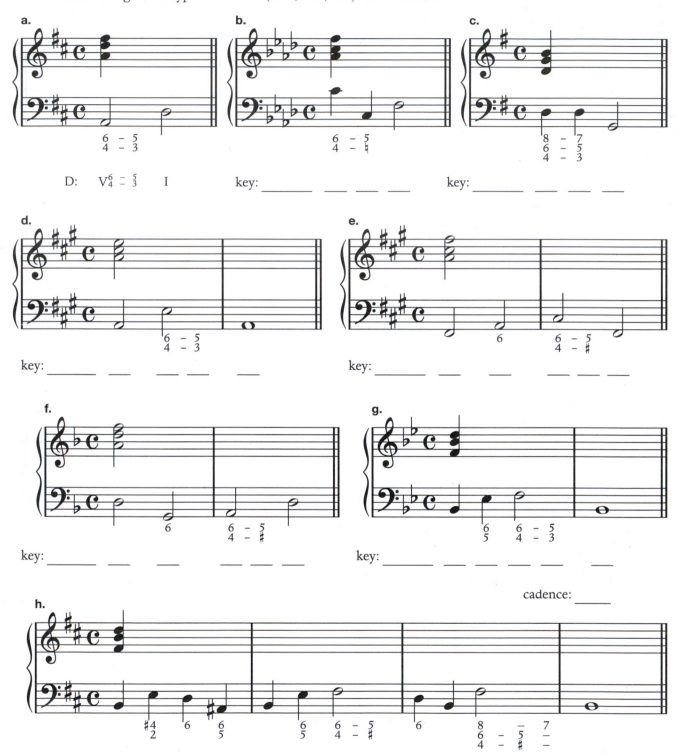

i. *Start with the tonic in the top voice.*

cadence: _____

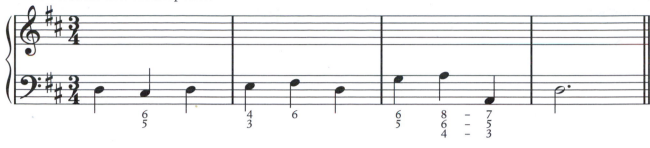

key: _____ ___ ___ ___ ___ ___ ___ ___ ___

2. Realize each figured bass in SATB format. Then label the keys and Roman numerals. Also give the type of cadence (PAC, IAC, HC) where indicated.

key: _____ ___ ___ ___   key: _____ ___ ___ ___   key: _____ ___ ___ ___

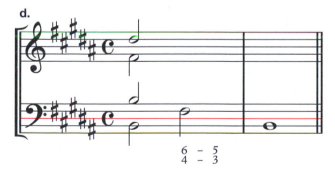

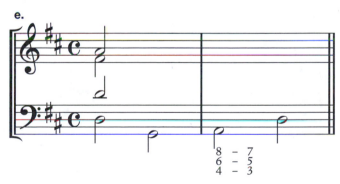

key: _____ ___ ___ ___   key: _____ ___ ___ ___ ___ ___

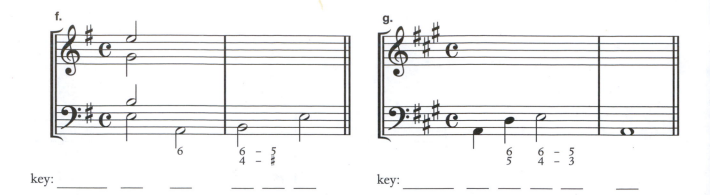

f.

key: _____ __ __ __

g.

key: _____ __ __ __ __

cadence: _____

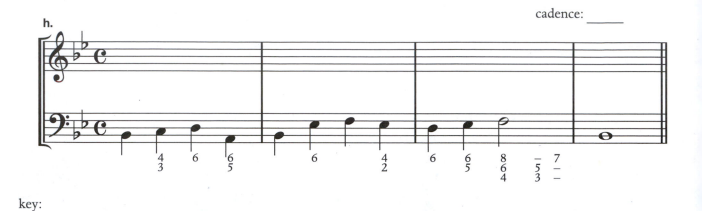

h.

key: _____ __ __ __ __ __ __ __ __

3. Realize the figured bass accompaniments (in keyboard format) for these excerpts; label the key and Roman numerals. Don't worry about parallel perfect intervals between the solo voice and accompaniment.

a. Martin Cannabich, Flute Sonata, Op. 1

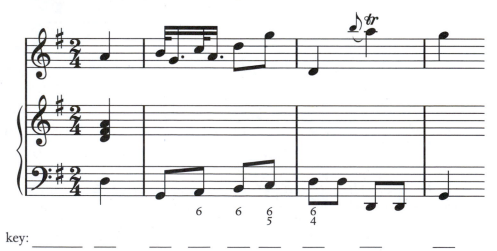

key: _____ __ __ __ __ __

b. Václav Vodiĉha, Flute Sonata, Op. 2

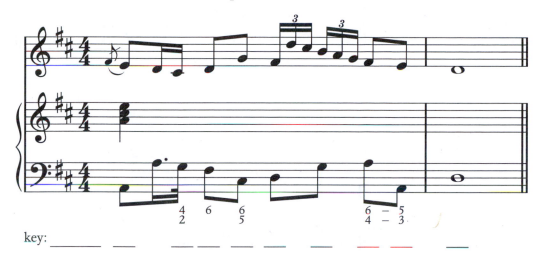

key: _____ ___ ___ ___ ___ ___ ___ ___

c. Elizabeth Turner, "Not Chloris"

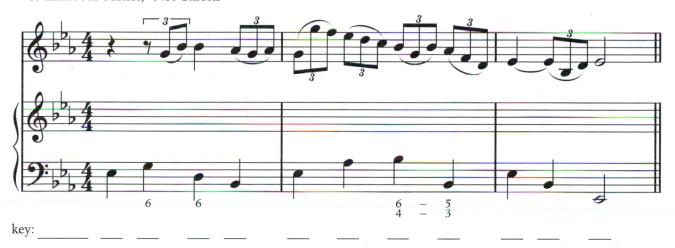

key: _____ ___ ___ ___ ___ ___ ___ ___ ___ ___ ___

D. HARMONIZING MELODIES

1. Harmonize the following short melodies in SATB format:

- Label the scale degrees of the melody; then complete the bass line and add Roman numerals, using one chord for each note in the melody.

- Whenever possible, write a cadential $^6_4$ (not every progression will include a $^6_4$). Cadential $^6_4$-V will be particularly helpful in harmonizing the melodic pattern $\hat{3}$–$\hat{2}$ or $\hat{8}$–$\hat{7}$. However, remember that a cadential $^6_4$ must appear in a stronger metrical position than the V that follows it.

- Complete the inner voices, avoiding voice-leading errors.

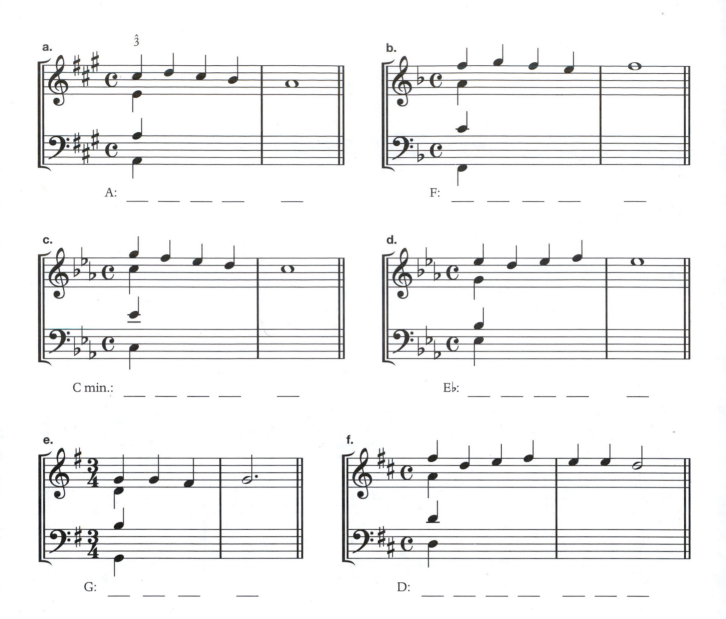

a. A: ___ ___ ___ ___ ___ ___

b. F: ___ ___ ___ ___ ___

c. C min.: ___ ___ ___ ___ ___ ___

d. E♭: ___ ___ ___ ___ ___ ___

e. G: ___ ___ ___ ___ ___

f. D: ___ ___ ___ ___ ___

2. Harmonize the following longer melodies in SATB format, and use a cadential ⁶₄ within each. Each note of the melody (except those labeled as passing tones) should be harmonized with a chord, and each passage should end with a cadence.

a.

B♭:   I   ___ ___ ___ ___ ___ ___ ___ ___ ___

b.

A: I   _ _ _ _ _ _ _ _ _

c.

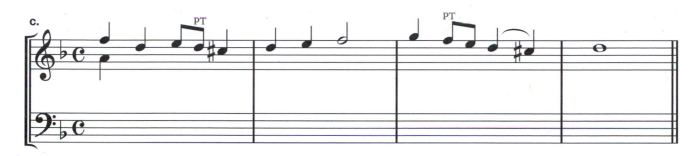

D min.:   i   _ _ _ _ _ _ _ _ _ _ _ _ _ _

3. Harmonize the following melodies in keyboard format. Harmonize each note of the melody with a chord, and end with a cadence that includes a cadential $^6_4$. In every chord, the given melodic note should be the highest note.

a.   **b.**

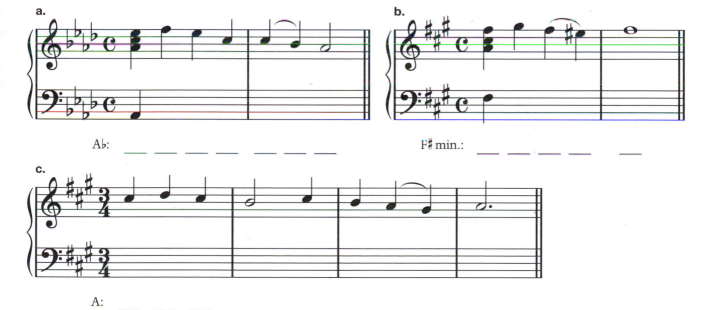

A♭:   _ _ _ _ _ _ _ _   F♯ min.:   _ _ _ _ _ _ _ _

c.

A: _ _ _ _ _ _ _ _

E. COMPOSITION

1. Realize these Roman numerals. Where there are two chords in a single measure, the rhythm should be a half note followed by a quarter note.

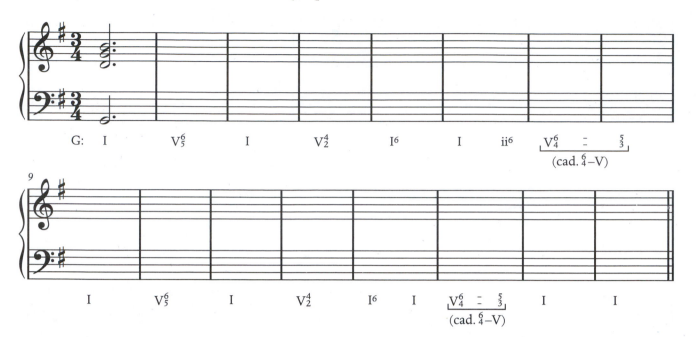

2. Compose a piece for keyboard and another instrument, based on your realization of (1).

- Choose an accompaniment pattern for the keyboard part such as an oom-pah-pah pattern or arpeggiation (you can find examples in earlier composition assignments). Rewrite the notes of the chord progression using that pattern.

- Then compose a melody to go with the keyboard part; measures 9-12 should be the same (or almost the same) as measures 1-4.

- Be sure to check for parallel octaves or fifths between the bass of the accompaniment and your melody. Also, if there is a leading tone or chordal seventh in the bass, do not double this note in the melody.

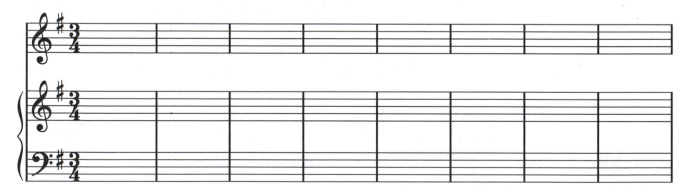

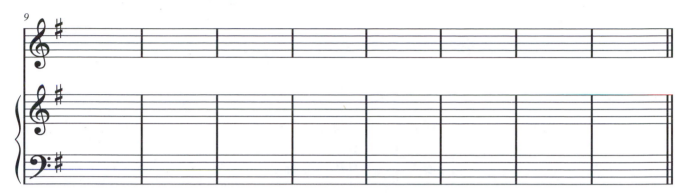

3. Continue this passage (from a composition by Gaetano Brunetti) in a style that is
consistent with the first four measures.

- Measure 5-6 should repeat measures 1-2.

- Conclude with a PAC in measure 8.

4. Compose a passage for keyboard, guitar, or an ensemble of your choice, following
these guidelines:

- The passage should be in C minor, in $\frac{4}{4}$.

- The first four measures should embellish the tonic with either

  Tonic | Dominant | Dominant | Tonic

or

  Tonic | Subdominant | Dominant | Tonic

(For example, the first four measures might be: I | iv | V$_3^4$ | I |)

- In the last four measures, lead to a cadence, using V$_{4-3}^{6-5}$ in the second-to-last
  measure.

- Conclude with a PAC.

F. ANALYSIS

In each of the following excerpts, indicate the key, and label the harmonies with Roman numerals. Then indicate the type of cadence. Blank lines are provided below the staff to fill in the label for each chord, with two lines for each V^{6-5}_{4-3} (i.e., cad. $^6_4$—V).

1. Pyotr Tchaikovsky, "L'Église" ("The Church")   **2.** J. S. Bach, Chorale 53

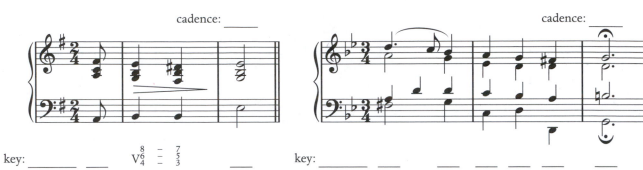

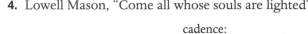

key: _____ ___ $V^{8-7}_{6-5}_{4-3}$ ___   key: _____ ___ ___ ___ ___

3. Elizabeth Cuthbert, "Howard"   **4.** Lowell Mason, "Come all whose souls are lighted"

key: _____ ___ ___ ___ ___   key: _____ ___ ___ ___

5. Maria Theresia von Paradis, "Sophie an Siegwart"

Label the embellishing tone on the downbeat of m. 2.

key: _____ ___   ___ ___ ___ ___

6. Domenico Cimarosa, Keyboard Sonata No. 29

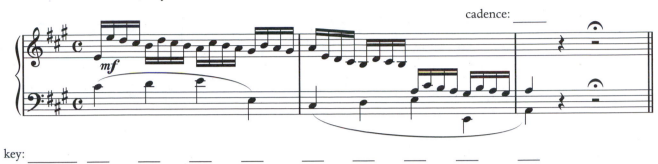

cadence: _____

key: ___ ___ ___ ___

7. Christoph Willibald Gluck, "J'ai perdu mon Eurydice" from *Orphée et Eurydice*

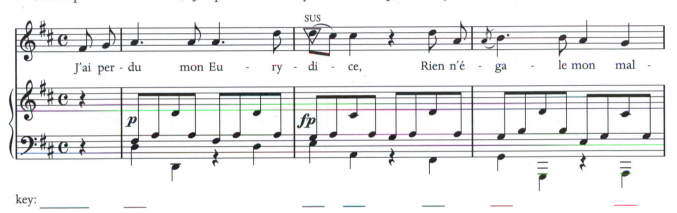

J'ai per - du   mon Eu - ry - di - ce,   Rien n'é - ga - le mon mal -

key: ___ ___ ___ ___

- heur,   Sort_ cru - el_   quel - le ri - gueur!_   Rien_ n'é - ga - le_ mon mal -

cadence: _____

- heur,   Je_ suc - com - be à_ ma_ dou - leur!

Translation: I have lost my Eurydice, nothing equals my sadness.

8. W. A. Mozart, "An Chloë" ("To Chloë")

key: _____ _____ _____ _____ _____

cadence: _____

off - nen Au-gen sieht,___ und vor Lust hin - ein zu schau - en

_____ _____

cadence: _____

mir's_____ im___ Her - zen klopft___ und___ glüht;

_____

Translation: When love shines out from your blue, clear, open eyes, and from the joy of looking into them my heart beats and glows;

How many measures are in each of the two phrases? What features of the music cause them to extend past four measures?

9. Christoph Willibald Gluck, "Vive aimé des jours" from *Alceste*

key: _____   _____   _____ _____ _____

In what way are the harmonies on the first two beats of m. 2 similar to the harmonies on the first two beats of m. 3?

10. Anna Bon, Harpsichord Sonata, Op. 2, No. 2, iii

key: _____   _____   _____   _____

11. Antonio Sacchini, *Oedipe à Colone*, Act I, scene v

The first few chords have been filled in for you.

B♭: I   V$^8_4$ $^{—7}_{—5}$ $^{—}_{—3}$ I⁶   I   _____

_____   _____   _____

12. Joseph Haydn, String Quartet, Op. 33, No. 4, iv

- Label the key and Roman numerals.
- On the staff below, complete a simplified harmonic model of this passage in four-part harmony, keyboard format. Use proper, smooth voice leading, and omit any embellishing tones.

key: _____

Identify at least three ways in which measures 1–4 and 5–8 are similar to each other and three ways in which they are different.

16 Leading to the Tonic: IV

A. QUESTIONS FOR REVIEW

1. What are some common progressions that involve IV moving directly to a tonic chord?

2. What are some melodic patterns that are harmonized with I–IV–I?

3. Which is more common: a root-position IV moving to I⁶, or IV⁶ moving to root-position I?

4. What is a plagal cadence? After what other type of cadence does it often appear?

B. REALIZING ROMAN NUMERALS

1. Realize each of these short progressions, then label the scale degrees of the melody.

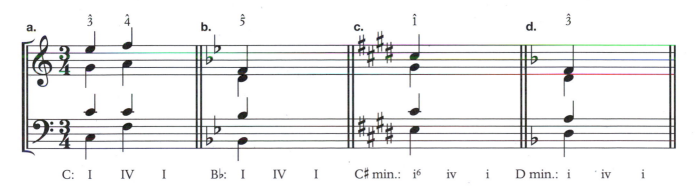

a. $\hat{3}$ $\hat{4}$ b. $\hat{5}$ c. $\hat{1}$ d. $\hat{3}$

C: I IV I   Bb: I IV I   C# min.: i⁶ iv i   D min.: i iv i

2. Realize the Roman numerals for each progression. For each I–IV–I progression, label the scale degrees in the melody.

SATB format:

a.

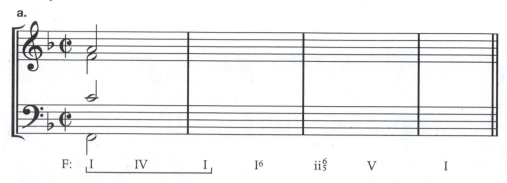

F: I   IV   I   I⁶   ii⁶₅   V   I

b.

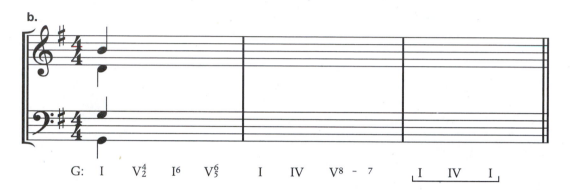

G: I   V⁴₂   I⁶   V⁶₅   I   IV   V⁸ – ⁷   I   IV   I

Keyboard format:

c.   **d.**

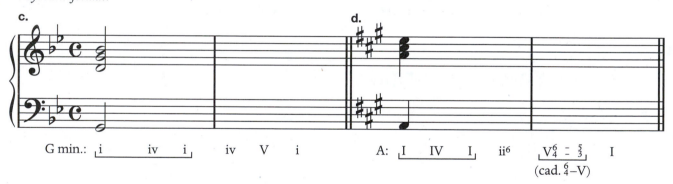

G min.: i   iv   i   iv   V   i   A: I   IV   I   ii⁶   V⁶₄ – ⁵₃   I
                                                              (cad. ⁶₄–V)

e.

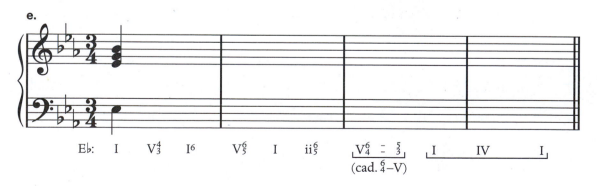

E♭: I   V⁴₃   I⁶   V⁶₅   I   ii⁶₅   V⁶₄ – ⁵₃   I   IV   I
                                            (cad. ⁶₄–V)

C. REALIZING FIGURED BASS

1. Realize each short figured bass in keyboard format. Then label the chords with Roman numerals in the key indicated.

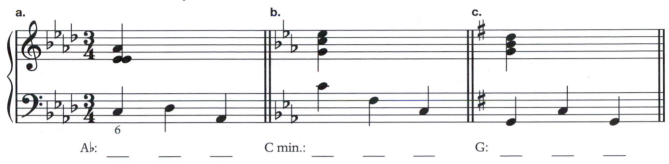

A♭: ___ ___ ___ C min.: ___ ___ ___ G: ___ ___ ___

2. Realize each figured bass. Then determine the key and label the chords with Roman numerals.

Keyboard format:

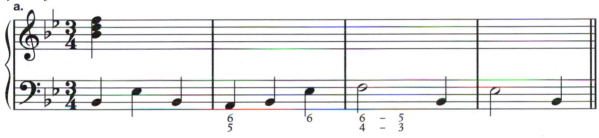

key: ___ ___ ___ ___ ___ ___

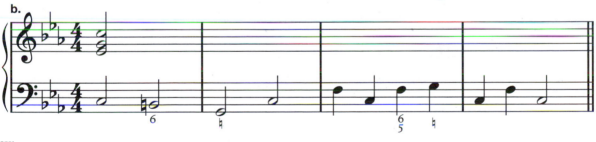

key: ___ ___ ___ ___ ___

SATB format:

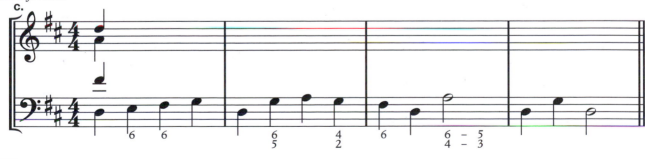

key: ___ ___ ___ ___ ___ ___ ___ ___

3. Realize the following figured bass accompaniments in keyboard format:

- Complete the upper voices on the middle staff, being careful to avoid voice-leading errors with the bass.

- Don't worry about parallel perfect intervals between the melody and the upper voices of the keyboard part.

a. Ignatius Sancho, "The Sweetest Bard"
(In some chords you may need to double a note at the unison.)

key: _____ ___ ___ ___ ___ ___ ___ ___

b. "Ladies Lamentation," from *Calliope* Collection

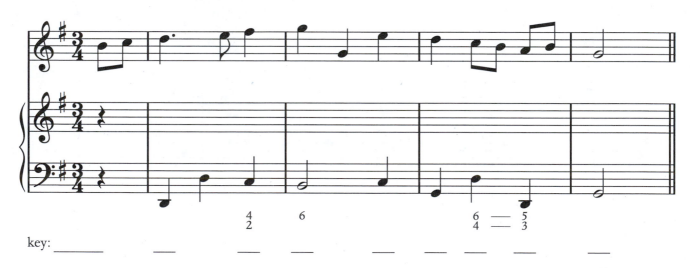

key: ___ ___ ___ ___ ___ ___ ___ ___

D. HARMONIZING MELODIES

1. Harmonize each short melody below:

- Label the scale degrees.
- Select one chord for each note; supply Roman numerals and a bass line.
- Fill in the inner voices.

SATB format:

Keyboard format:

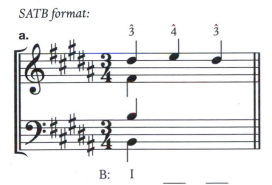

2. Harmonize these melodies.
- Label the scale degrees of these melodies.
- Then harmonize each melody by providing a bass line and Roman numerals.
  - For each melody, use at least one I–IV–I progression.
  - Avoid using root-position V or V7 in the first two measures.
- Finally, fill in the inner voices, using good voice leading.

a.

b. *Use a plagal cadence in measure 4.*

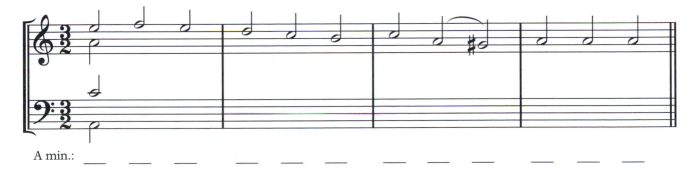

E. IDENTIFYING VOICE-LEADING ERRORS

Circle and identify the voice-leading errors in the following example.

F. COMPOSITION

1. Harmonize the melody below, with a half cadence in measure 4 and an authentic cadence in measure 8:

- Determine the key, then write a bass line. Be sure to check for parallel octaves and fifths between the bass and the melody. If there is a leading tone or chordal seventh in the melody, do not double it in the bass.
- Indicate harmonies with Roman numerals, using only one or two chords per measure. Make sure the chords create the indicated cadences.
- Label the embellishing tones in the melody.
- Complete the inner voices in keyboard format, avoiding voice-leading errors.

key: _____ _____ _____ _____

2. Rewrite the accompaniment that you completed in (1), using an accompaniment pattern of your choice (such as an oom-pah-pah pattern or arpeggiation; see previous assignments for examples).

3. Write a harmonic outline that will be the basis of a composition in (4). The key, the time signature, and Roman numerals for the first eight bars are given.

- Following the indicated structure, complete the Roman numerals and bass line.
- Complete the harmonies in keyboard format, checking for voice-leading errors.

the first phrase should end in measure 8 with an IAC

F: I   I   IV   I   IV   I⁶   I   vii°⁶ V⁷   I

measures 9–12 should be the same as measures 1–4   compose a progression that leads to a PAC

4. Using the harmonic outline you created in (3), compose a melody and accompaniment for keyboard, guitar, or an ensemble of your choice.

- Keep the key, time signature, chords, and cadences of (3).
- Measures 9–12 should be the same as measures 1–4.

G. ANALYSIS

Analyze the following excerpts. For each excerpt:

- Label the key and the Roman numerals.
- For each Roman numeral, label its function (**T**, **S**, or **D**).
- Locate and circle the I$^{(6)}$–IV–I$^{(6)}$ progressions.

1. Ludwig van Beethoven, Symphony No. 6, i

```
F:       I   ___ ___ ___
function: T   ___ ___ ___ ___
```

2. César Franck, Symphony in D Minor, ii (arr. Franck)

```
B♭ min.: ___ ___ ___ ___
function: ___ ___ ___ ___ ___
```

3. Robert Schumann, "Aus meinen Thränen spriessen"

Aus mei - nen Thrä - nen spries - sen viel blü - hen-de Blu - men her - vor,

```
key: ___ ___ ___          ___      ___      ___
function: ___              ___      ___      ___
```

Translation: From my tears sprouted many blossoming flowers.

4. Johannes Brahms, "Die Wollust in den Mayen"

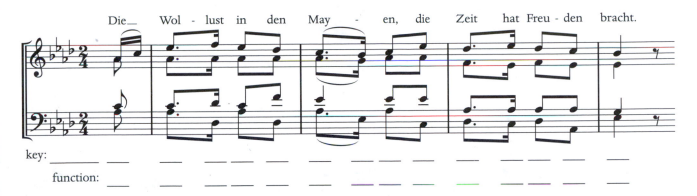

Die— Wol - lust in den May - en, die Zeit hat Freu - den bracht.

key: _____ ___   ___   ___   ___   ___   ___   ___

function: _____   ___   ___   ___   ___   ___   ___   ___

Translation: The splendor of spring time, which this time of year brings.

5. Marianna Martines, Keyboard Sonata in A, i

key: _____ ___   ___   ___

function: _____   ___   ___

6. Woolson Morse, "Ask the Man in the Moon"

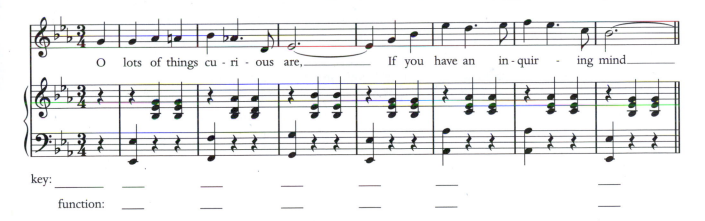

O   lots of things cu - ri - ous are,_____ If you have an   in - quir - ing mind___

key: _____ ___   ___   ___   ___   ___   ___   ___

function: _____   ___   ___   ___   ___   ___   ___

7. Franz Schubert, Sonata in A Minor for Arpeggione and Piano, D. 821

key: _____

function: ___ ___ ___

8. Frédéric Chopin, Mazurka Op. 17, No. 1

key: _____

function: ___ ___ ___

There are two phrases here. Are they each best understood as ending with a perfect authentic cadence, or with an imperfect authentic cadence? Explain the rationale for your answer, and consider how the interpretation of how these cadences should be labeled might affect the performance of this passage.

17 The Leading-Tone Seventh Chord: vii°7 and viiø7

A. QUESTIONS FOR REVIEW

1. What is the function of vii°7?

2. What chord tone (root, third, fifth, or seventh) of vii°7 needs an accidental in major keys? In minor keys?

3. How many notes need to change when moving between vii°7 and V7? Which note(s)? In what way?

4. What are the tendency tones in vii°7? How do they resolve?

5. What is a potential voice-leading problem when progressing from vii°7 to I? How can you avoid it?

6. What is similar about vii°7 and viiø7? What is different?

B. SPELLING CHORDS

1. Write each of the indicated key signatures; then supply the requested chords. Note that in each case, the V7 and vii°7 chords share three notes.

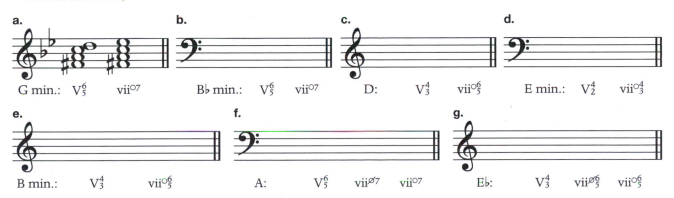

a. G min.: V_5^6 vii°7
b. B♭ min.: V_5^6 vii°7
c. D: V_3^4 vii°$_5^6$
d. E min.: V_2^4 vii°$_3^4$
e. B min.: V_3^4 vii°$_5^6$
f. A: V_5^6 viiø7   vii°7
g. E♭: V_3^4 viiø$_5^6$ vii°$_5^6$

2. Write each of the indicated key signatures; then supply the requested chords.

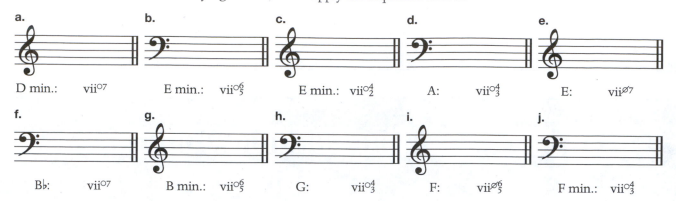

a. D min.: vii°7   b. E min.: vii°65   c. E min.: vii°42   d. A: vii°43   e. E: viiø7

f. B♭: vii°7   g. B min.: vii°65   h. G: vii°43   i. F: viiø65   j. F min.: vii°43

C. REALIZING ROMAN NUMERALS

1. Realize the Roman numerals in SATB format.

a. F min.: vii°7 i   b. B♭ min.: i vii°7 i   c. B♭: I vii°7 I   d. G: I vii°65 I6

e. B min.: i6 vii°43 i6   f. A: I IV vii°65 I6   g. G min.: i i6 vii°7 V65 i ii°6 vii°43 i6

h. E min.: i V vii°43 i6 vii°7 i iiø65 V64 – 53 i iv i
(cad. 64–V)

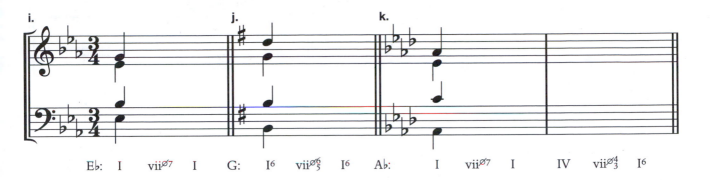

Eb: I   vii^{ø7}   I   G: I⁶   vii^{ø6}₅   I⁶   Ab: I   vii^{ø7}   I   IV   vii^{ø4}₃   I⁶

2. Realize the Roman numerals in keyboard format.

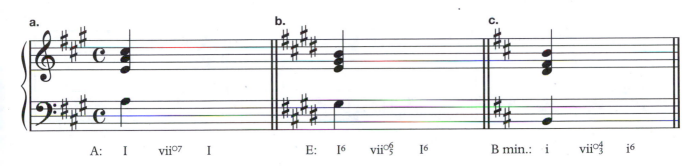

A: I   vii^{o7}   I   E: I⁶   vii^{o6}₅   I⁶   B min.:   i   vii^{o4}₃   i⁶

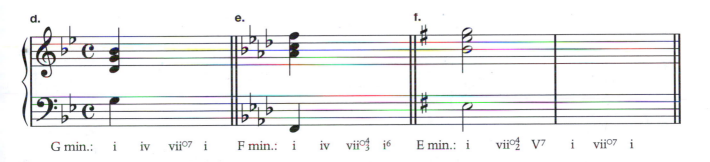

G min.:   i   iv   vii^{o7}   i   F min.:   i   iv   vii^{o4}₃   i⁶   E min.:   i   vii^{o4}₂   V⁷   i   vii^{o7}   i

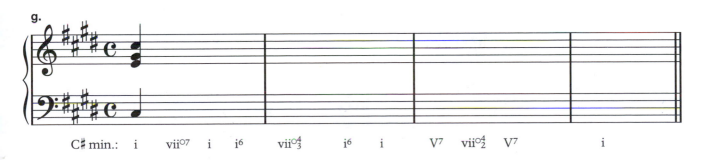

C# min.:   i   vii^{o7}   i   i⁶   vii^{o4}₃   i⁶   i   V⁷   vii^{o4}₂   V⁷   i

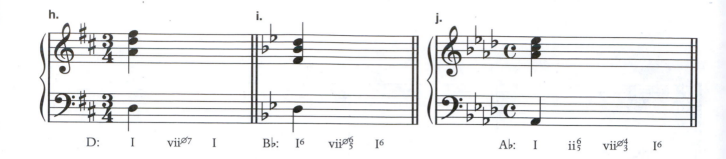

h.   i.   j.

D: I   vii°⁷   I   B♭:   I⁶   vii°⁶₅   I⁶   A♭:   I   ii⁶₅   vii°⁴₃   I⁶

D. REALIZING FIGURED BASS

1. Realize each figured bass in keyboard format. Then label the keys and Roman numerals.

a.   b.   c.

               7   4   6   ♮6   6
                         ♭3   5

key: _____ ___ ___ ___   key: _____ ___ ___ ___   key: _____ ___ ___ ___

d.

          7   ♯4   6   ♯6   6   7   ♯4   7
                    3   5   ♯   2   ♯

key: _____ ___ ___ ___ ___ ___ ___ ___ ___ ___ ___

2. Realize each figured bass in SATB format. Then label the keys and Roman numerals.

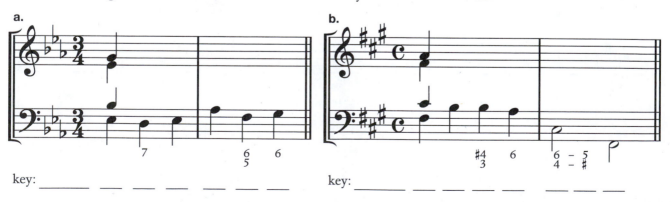

a.   b.

          7   6   6   ♯4   6   6 – 5
                       5   3   4 – ♯

key: _____ ___ ___ ___   key: _____ ___ ___ ___

c.

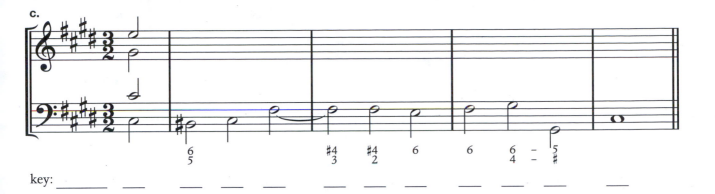

key: ____ ____ ____ ____ ____ ____ ____ ____ ____ ____ ____

E. HARMONIZING MELODIES

1. Harmonize each of the following short melodies:

- Label the scale degrees of the melody.

- Then, in SATB format, harmonize the melody in two ways: first using the indicated inversion of V⁷, then using vii°⁷ or an inversion of vii°⁷. Remember to use the appropriate accidentals.

- On the blank line provided, label the diminished seventh chord with Roman numeral and figures to indicate its position or inversion.

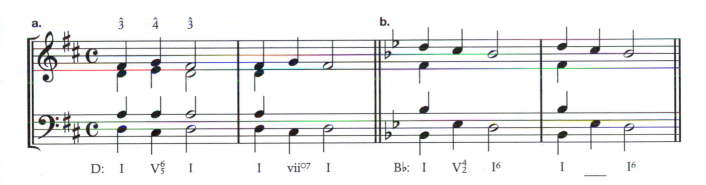

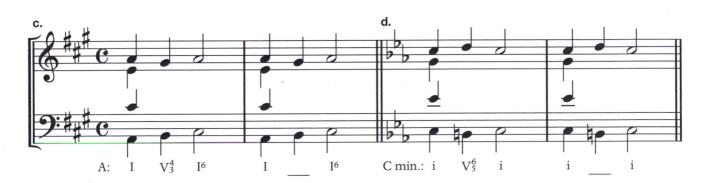

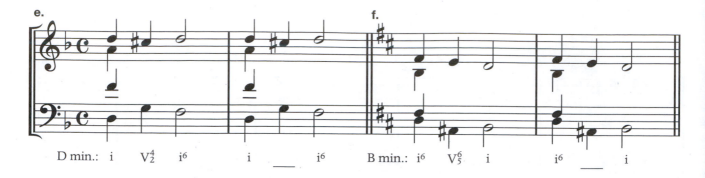

D min.: i V$_2^4$ i^6 | i ____ i^6 | B min.: i^6 V$_5^6$ i | i^6 ____ i

2. Harmonize each of the following melodies:

- Label the scale degrees of the melody.

- Then harmonize each note of the melody in SATB format.

- Use at least one vii°7 or viiø7 chord (in root position or inversion) in each.

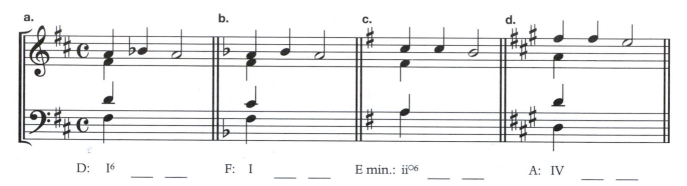

D: I^6 ____ ____ | F: I ____ ____ | E min.: ii^{o6} ____ ____ | A: IV ____ ____

F♯ min.: i ____ ____ ____

E: ____ ____ ____ ____

F. ANALYSIS

1. Analyze each of the following excerpts:

- Label the key and Roman numerals.
- Circle any instances of vii°7–I or viiø7–I progressions (in root position or inversion), and identify the scale degrees of the melody that are harmonized by these progressions.

   a. W. A. Mozart, Requiem Mass, K. 626, Agnus Dei

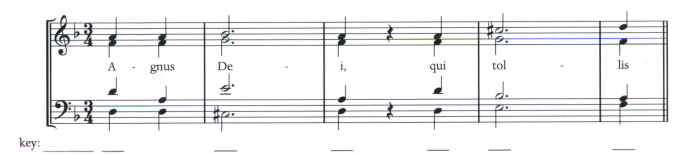

key: _____

Translation: Lamb of God, who takes away [the world's sins].

   b. W. A. Mozart, "Schon weichet dir, Sonne" ("Already you depart, sun"), from *King Thamos*

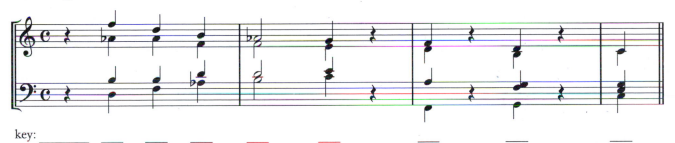

key: _____

   c. Felix Mendelssohn, *Paulus*, No. 1

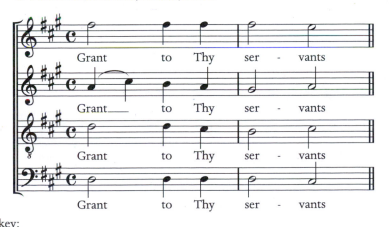

key: _____

d. C. P. E. Bach, Rondo Wq. 56, iii

key: _____ ___ _ ___ _ _ _ _ _ _

2. Analyze each of the following excerpts by labeling the key and Roman numerals. Where indicated, identify cadences.

a. Joseph Haydn, Keyboard Sonata in F, Hob. XVI:29

cadence: _____

key: _____

b. Fernando Sor, Eight Short Pieces for Guitar, Op. 24, No. 4

• In m. 4, indicate the detailed harmonies by labeling a chord for each bass note.

key: _____

V⁷/IV

• Which harmonic succession here is atypical? _____

• Which underlying harmony is embellished in m. 4? _____

c. Joseph Haydn, Symphony No. 64, Trio

Oboes and Horns:

Strings:

key: _____   ii

d. Ludwig van Beethoven, Piano Sonata, Op. 10, No. 1, i

- In what ways are the rhythm, harmony, and melody of measures 1–4 like measures 5–8? In what ways are they different?

- What is unusual about the treatment of the cadential $^6_4$ in this passage?

key: _____

cadence: _____

3. François Joseph Gossec, Overture to *Toinon et Toinette*

- Label the Roman numerals, one chord per measure in mm. 1–7 and 10, two chords in measures 8–9 (consider V_{4-3}^{6-5} as two separate chords).

- Label the embellishing tones and the cadence.

- Do measures 3–4 (and measures 5–6) embellish a i? or a V? Or first i and then V? Explain your answer.

key: _____

cadence: _____

On the staff below, complete a simplified harmonic model of this passage based on your Roman numeral analysis.

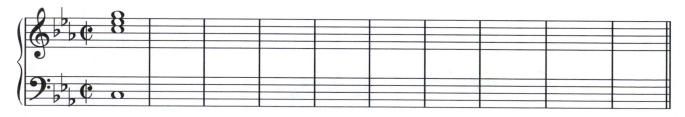

chapter 18

Approaching V: IV⁶, ii, ii⁷, and IV⁷

A. QUESTIONS FOR REVIEW

1. What is the function of IV⁶, ii, ii⁷, and IV⁷? To what type of chord do they lead?
2. In major keys, what note(s) of IV⁶ may be doubled? What note(s) of iv⁶ may be doubled in minor keys?
3. What is a Phrygian cadence?
4. What tone is usually doubled in a root-position ii?
5. What are some of the voice-leading problems that may arise with ii⁷ and IV⁷? What are some ways to avoid them?
6. What are some progressions between Subdominant chords that occur frequently? What are some progressions between Subdominant chords to avoid?

B. SPELLING CHORDS

Write the following key signatures and chords.

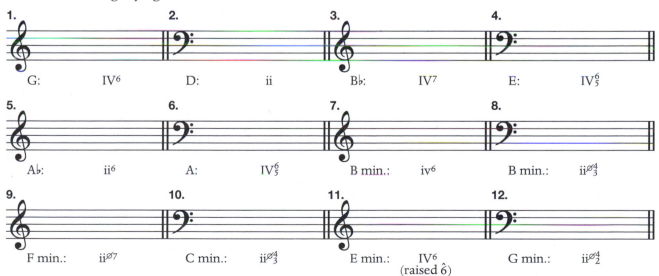

C. REALIZING ROMAN NUMERALS

1. Realize the Roman numerals in SATB format, using progressions with IV⁶.

G: IV⁶ V   F min.: iv⁶ V   E: I IV⁶ V   F♯ min.: i iv⁶ V

B♭: I IV⁶ V⁶ I   B min.: i iv⁶ ii°⁶₅ V i iv⁶ V

2. Realize the Roman numerals in SATB format, using progressions with ii⁵₃.

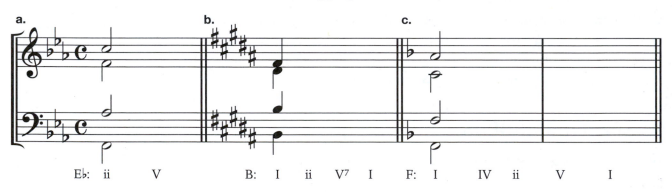

E♭: ii V   B: I ii V⁷ I   F: I IV ii V I

3. Realize the Roman numerals in SATB format, using progressions with ii⁷.

G: ii⁷ V   A: I ii⁶ ii⁷ V   F min.: i ii°⁴₂ V⁶₅ i ii°⁴₃ V

4. Realize the Roman numerals in SATB format, using progressions with IV^7.

a.　　　　　　　　　　　　　　**b.**　　　　　　　　　　**c.** This progression requires a leap in an inner voice following IV$^6_5$.

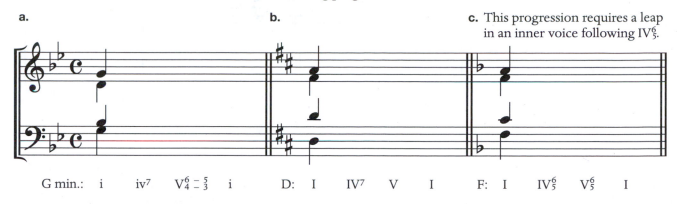

G min.:　i　　iv^7　　V$^{6-5}_{4-3}$　i　　D:　I　　IV^7　　V　　I　　F:　I　　IV$^6_5$　　V$^6_5$　　I

5. Realize the Roman numerals in SATB format, using progressions with various Subdominant chords.

a.

B min.:　i　　ii$^{ø4}_2$　　V$^6_5$　　i　　iv^7　　V$^4_2$　　i^6　　ii^{ø7}　　V　　i　　iv^6　　V

b.

G:　I　　IV^6　　V$^6_5$　　I　　ii　　V　　I^6　　ii^6　　ii^7　　V$^{6-5}_{4-3}$　　I

c.

A min.:　i　　IV^6　　V$^6_5$　　i　　iv　　ii^{ø7}　　V$^{6-5}_{4-3}$　　i　　iv^6　　V

6. Realize the Roman numerals in keyboard format.

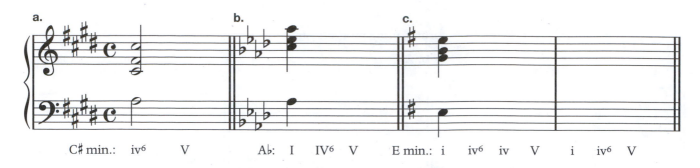

C# min.:　iv⁶　　V　　　　Ab:　I　IV⁶　V　　　E min.:　i　iv⁶　iv　V　　i　iv⁶　V

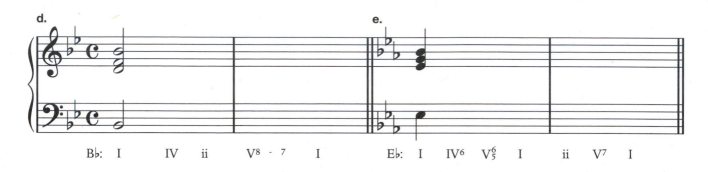

Bb:　I　　　IV　　ii　　V⁸ ⁻ ⁷　　I　　　　Eb:　I　IV⁶　V⁶₅　I　　ii　V⁷　I

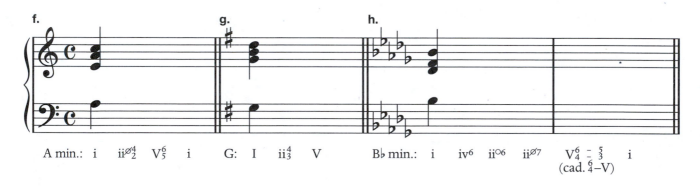

A min.:　i　ii⁰⁴₂　V⁶₅　i　　G:　I　ii⁴₃　V　　Bb min.:　i　iv⁶　ii⁰⁶　ii⁰⁷　V⁶₄ ⁻ ⁵₃　i
(cad. ⁶₄–V)

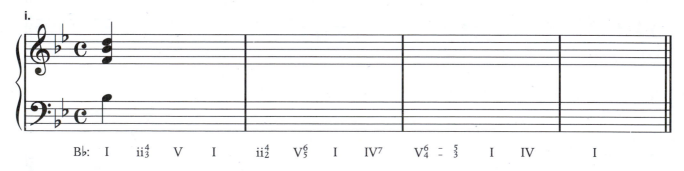

Bb:　I　ii⁴₃　V　I　ii⁴₂　V⁶₅　I　IV⁷　V⁶₄ ⁻ ⁵₃　I　IV　　　I

NAME: ....

D. REALIZING FIGURED BASS

1. Realize each figured bass in keyboard format. Then label the key and Roman numerals.

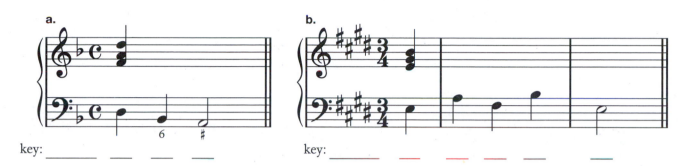

key: ____ ____ ____   key: ____ ____ ____ ____ ____ ____

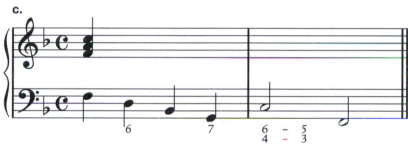

key: ____ ____ ____ ____ ____

key: ____ ____ ____ ____ ____ ____ ____ ____ ____ ____ ____

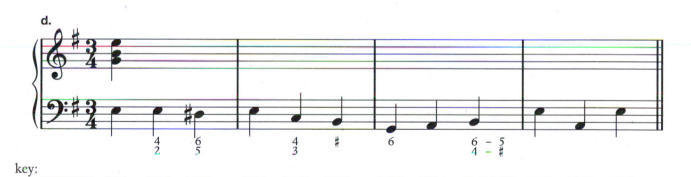

key: ____ ____ ____ ____ ____ ____ ____ ____ ____

2. Realize each figured bass in SATB format. Then label the key and Roman numerals.

a.

key: _____ ____ ____ ____ ____ ____ ____ ____

b.

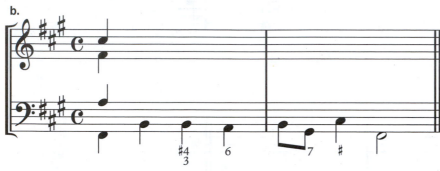

key: _____ ____ ____ ____ ____ ____ ____

c.

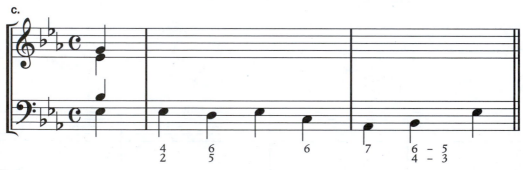

key: _____ ____ ____ ____ ____ ____ ____ ____

d.

key: _____ ____ ____ ____ ____ ____ ____ ____

3. Realize the figured bass accompaniment for each excerpt. Do not worry about parallel perfect intervals between your figured bass realization and the given melody. Then label the Roman numerals and cadences.

a. Élisabeth Jacquet de la Guerre, Violin Sonata in F, iii

F:

b. Carl Friedrich Abel, Flute Sonata, Op. 6, No. 6, iii

G:

c. Tomaso Albinoni, Sonata, Op. 4, No. 3, iv

F:

E. HARMONIZING MELODIES

1. For each of the melodic fragments below, suggest three different bass lines, along with Roman numerals, that might be used to harmonize the melody.

   - The harmonies for each should form a **Tonic–Dominant–Dominant–Tonic** progression or a **Tonic–Subdominant–Dominant–Tonic** progression.

   - Do not fill in the inner voices.

a.

A: __ __ __ __ __ __ __ __ __ __ __ __

b.

Bb: __ __ __ __ __ __ __ __ __ __ __ __

c.

F: __ __ __ __ __ __ __ __ __ __ __ __

2. Harmonize the melodies. Each note of the melody should be harmonized with a separate chord.

   - First label the scale degrees. Notice any scale-degree patterns that might suggest a standard harmonization.

   - Then write the bass and Roman numerals, starting by planning the final three to five chords that lead to the cadence.

   - Finally, fill in the inner voices.

a.

Ab: I   —   —   —   —   —   —   —   —   —   —   —

b.

G: —   —   —   —   —   —   —   —   —   —   —   —

c.

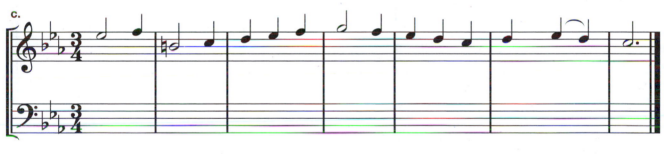

C min.:   —   —   —   —   —   —   —   —   —   —   —   —   —   —

3. Harmonize the following melodies:

- Write a bass line and Roman numerals.
- Then fill in the inner voices (SATB format).
- Harmonize each note with a different chord, and use only I, V, V^7, and their inversions, along with the most common **S**ubdominant chords—that is, IV (or iv), ii^6, or ii$^6_5$.

a.

Eb: I   —   —   —   —   —   —   —   —   —

b.

D min.: ___ ___ ___ ___ ___ ___ ___ ___ ___ ___ ___

4. Harmonize the following melodies—the same as seen in (3) above—but this time, in each use at least one of the following chords: ii$^5_3$, IV^6 (or iv^6), ii^7 (or ii$^{\varnothing 7}$), or IV^7.

a.

E♭:   I ___ ___ ___ ___ ___ ___ ___ ___

b.

D min.: ___ ___ ___ ___ ___ ___ ___ ___ ___ ___ ___

F. COMPOSITION

1. Realize the figured bass in keyboard format, then complete a Roman numeral analysis. The first phrase should end with an IAC (m. 4) and the second with a PAC (m. 8).

key: _____

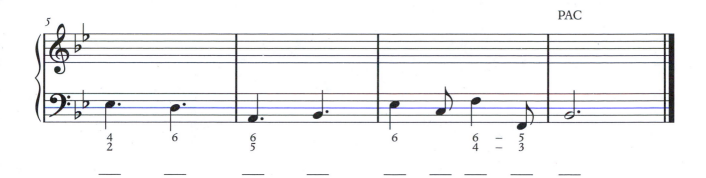

2. Compose a duet for two instruments or for piano, based on the harmonies in (1).

   • The bass line of the duet should be the same as above.

   • The melody should be based on the harmonies above, decorated by embellish-
     ing tones. End the first phrase with an IAC (m. 4) and the second with a PAC
     (m. 8).

   • Be careful to avoid parallel perfect intervals between the bass and the melody.

G. ANALYSIS

1. Label the key, Roman numerals, and cadences in the blanks provided.

a. Frederick Atkinson, "Morecambe"

cadence: ____

C: ____   ____   ____

b. J. S. Bach, Chorale 192

cadence: ____

B♭: ____ ____   ____ ____   ____ ____   ____

c. J. S. Bach, Chorale 117

cadence: ____

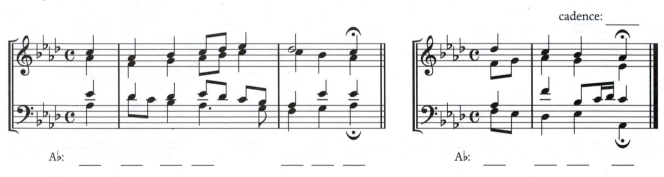

A♭: ____ ____ ____   A♭: ____ ____ ____

d. J. M. Nunes Garcia, *Matinas e encomendação de defuntos*

cadence: ____

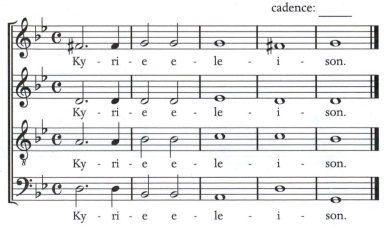

Ky - ri - e   e - le - i - son.

Ky - ri - e   e - le - i - son.

Ky - ri - e   e - le - i - son.

Ky - ri - e   e - le - i - son.

key: ____ ____   ____   ____

e. George Gershwin, "Argentina"

The chord in measure 2 has already been labeled.

cadence: _____

And her be-witch-ing art, told me at the start, ev - er in my heart, she would rule as queen.

key: _____ ___   IV

f. G. F. Handel, "Lascia ch'io pianga" ("Let Me Weep")

Also label the embellishing tones.

cadence: _____

key: _____ ___ ___ ___

cadence: _____

- What rhythmic and melodic features make the beginning of the phrase sound stable?

- What features create a sense of momentum as the music approaches the cadence?

g. Domenico Gallo, Trio Sonata No. 1, i

Two of the chords have already been labeled.

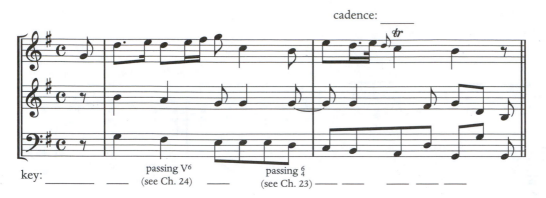

cadence: _____

key: _____ _____ passing V⁶ (see Ch. 24) _____ passing ⁶₄ (see Ch. 23) _____

h. Robert "Bobo" King, "Beautiful Ohio"

Locate and label the cadences. (Note: there is at most one chord per measure here.)

Long, long, a - go, some - one I know had a lit - tle red ca-

key: _____ _____ _____

-noe, in it on - ly room for two. Love found its start,

then in my heart, and like a flow - er grew. _____

cadence: _____

2. Label the Roman numerals and cadences in the following excerpts.

    a. Arcangelo Corelli, Concerto Op. 6, No. 8 ("Christmas Concerto")

cadence: _____

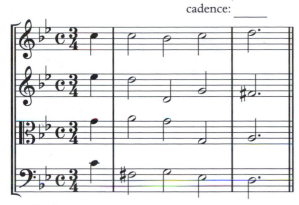

G min.:

    b. Jane Guest, "Marion"

cadence: _____

C:

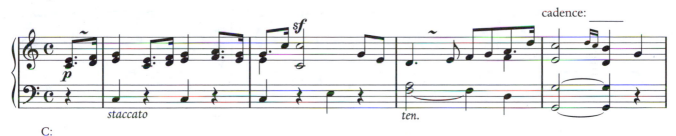

    c. Pyotr Tchaikovsky, Symphony No. 5 in E Minor, ii

cadence: _____

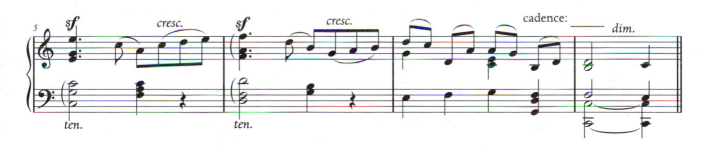

D:

d. Felix Mendelssohn, Concerto for Violin in E minor, i

The Roman numerals for two chords have already been provided.

E min.:   arp. i$_4^6$ iv$_4^6$

cadence: _____

e. Anna Bon, Harpsichord Sonata Op. 2, No. 6, i

cadence: _____

C:

chapter 19

Multiple Functions: VI

A. QUESTIONS FOR REVIEW

1. What chords typically follow vi?

2. What chords do *not* typically precede vi?

3. When voice leading between two root-position chords a third apart in four-part harmony, how do the upper voices usually move?

4. Which is more common: root motion upward by thirds (such as ii–IV–vi–I) or downward by third (I–vi–IV–ii)?

5. Describe the most common voice-leading pattern from V to vi. What note(s) are doubled? Which voices move up and which move down?

6. What standard cadence ends with a vi chord? What harmonic progression does it use? What usually follows it?

7. What is "vi⁶"? Why is it in quotation marks? When is it used?

B. REALIZING ROMAN NUMERALS

1. Realize the Roman numerals in SATB format.

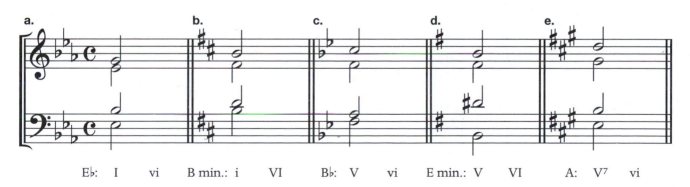

a.   Eb: I   vi   b. B min.: i   VI   c. Bb: V   vi   d. E min.: V   VI   e. A: V⁷   vi

G: vi ii$^6_5$ V   C♯ min.: i VI iv V   Ab: I vi ii V^7 I

B: I V vi ii^6 V I   F: I V^7 vi I^6 IV V I

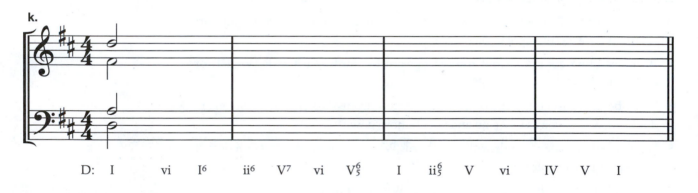

D: I vi I^6 ii^6 V^7 vi V$^6_5$ I ii$^6_5$ V vi IV V I

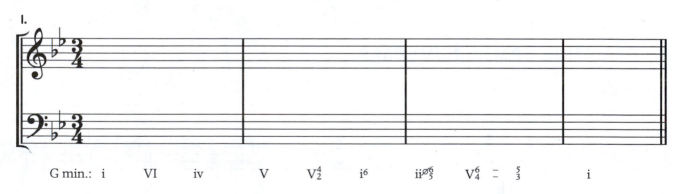

G min.: i VI iv V V$^4_2$ i^6 ii$^{⌀6}_5$ V$^6_4$ — $^5_3$ i

2. Realize the Roman numerals in keyboard format. Note that at times two voices might double a note in unison, so that only three notes sound.

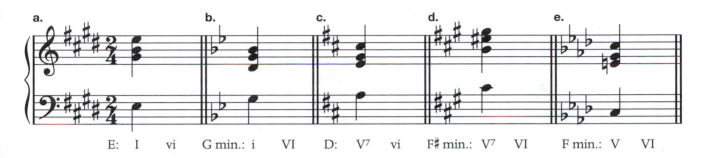

E: I vi G min.: i VI D: V⁷ vi F♯ min.: V⁷ VI F min.: V VI

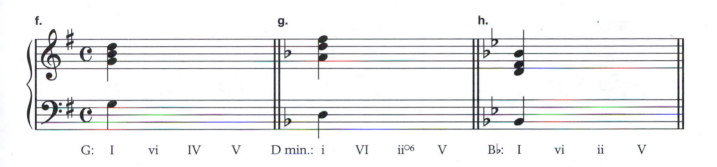

G: I vi IV V D min.: i VI ii°⁶ V B♭: I vi ii V

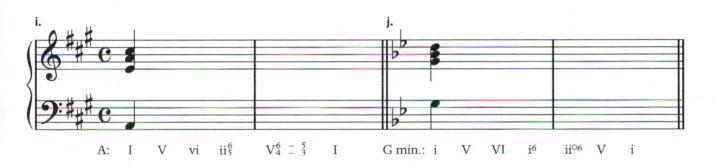

A: I V vi ii⁶₅ V⁶₄ − ⁵₃ I G min.: i V VI i⁶ ii°⁶ V i

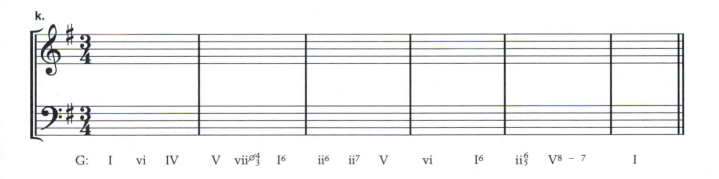

G: I vi IV V vii°⁴₃ I⁶ ii⁶ ii⁷ V vi I⁶ ii⁶₅ V⁸ − ⁷ I

C. REALIZING FIGURED BASS

1. Realize the following figured basses in keyboard format. Then label the key and Roman numerals for each.

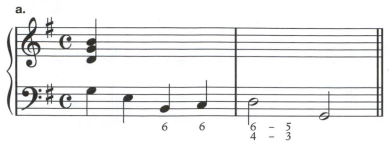

key: _____ ___ ___ ___ ___

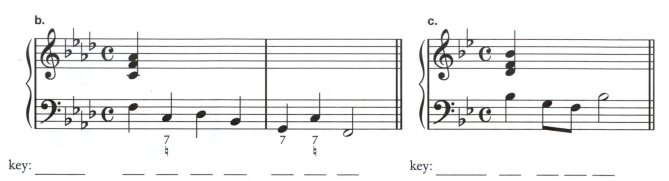

key: _____ ___ ___ ___

key: _____

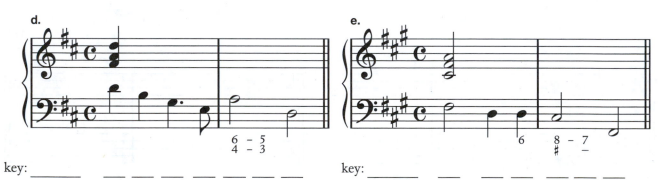

key: _____ ___ ___ ___

key: _____ ___ ___ ___

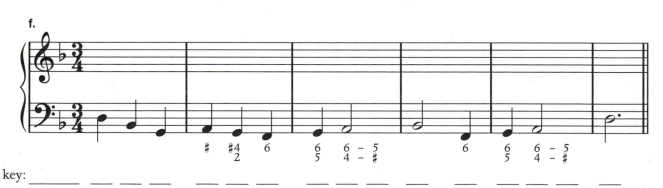

key: _____ ___ ___ ___ ___ ___ ___ ___

2. Realize the following figured basses in SATB format. Then label the key and Roman numerals for each.

a.

key: _____ __ __ __

b.

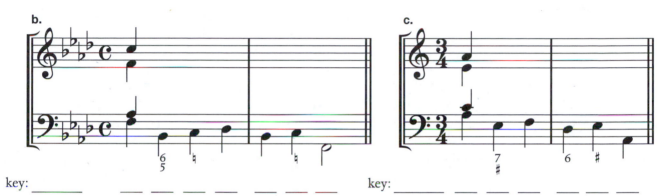

key: ____ __ __ __

c.

key: _____ __ __ __

d.

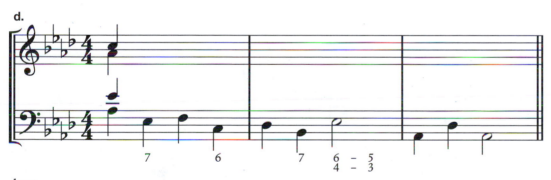

key: _____ __ __ __ __

e.

key: _____ __ __ __ __ __ __

3. Complete the realization of the figured bass accompaniments for each excerpt. Do not worry about parallel perfect intervals between your figured bass realization and the given melody. Label the Roman numerals and, where indicated, the cadences.

a. J. E. Galliard, Sonata No. 6 for Bassoon (or Cello) and Thorough Bass, iv

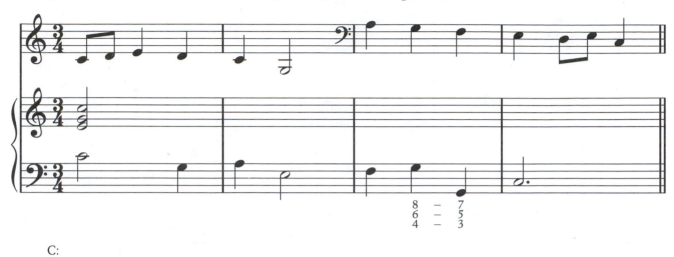

C: ___ ___ ___ ___ ___

b. Arcangelo Corelli, Chamber Sonata, Op. 2, No. 9, Sarabanda

cadence: ___

F♯ min.: ___ ___ ___ ___ ___

c. G. F. Handel, *Water Music*, Air (melody and bass only)

cadence: ___

D: ___ ___ ___ ___ ___ ___ ___

D. HARMONIZING MELODIES

Harmonize the following melodies:

- Provide a bass line and Roman numerals, using one chord for each note of the melody.
- End each with a perfect authentic cadence.
- Use one vi or VI chord in the middle of each harmonization.
- Finally, fill in the inner voices in SATB format.

E. COMPOSITION

1. Compose short chord progressions (each at most two measures) in four-part harmony, in a meter of your choice, following the given instructions.

- Each progression should begin with a tonic chord and end with an authentic cadence.
- Make sure to write the key signature and time signature. Add a barline if necessary.

   SATB format:

a. Progression in D major that begins with I moving though vi to ii⁶

b. Progression in E♭ major that begins with I moving though vi to ii⁶₅

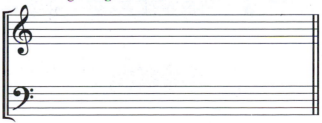

c. Progression in F♯ sharp minor that begins with i moving though VI to iv

d. Progression in A major that includes V moving to vi

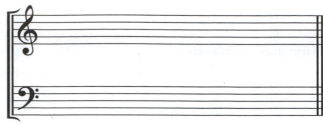

Keyboard format:

e. Progression in B major that begins with I moving though vi to ii

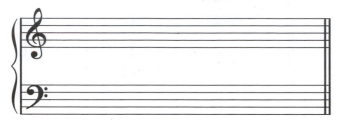

f. Progression in D minor that includes V⁷ moving to VI

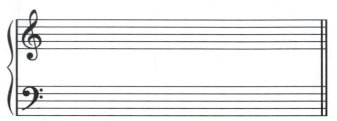

2. Suggest chords that may accompany the following melody.

- Use one chord per measure, except for measures 15, 16, and 17, which may have two chords. For variety's sake, do not use the same harmony in the same inversion for two measures in a row.
- Label the embellishing tones in the melody. Indicate the chords with Roman numerals.
- Use a half cadence at measure 8 and a deceptive cadence at measure 16 as indicated; conclude with a perfect authentic cadence.
- The chords you write should use good voice leading, and there should be no parallel octaves or fifths between the bass and the melody.

3. Construct a piano accompaniment using the same pitches as in (2), but now set with an accompaniment pattern (such as an arpeggiated texture or an oom-pah texture).

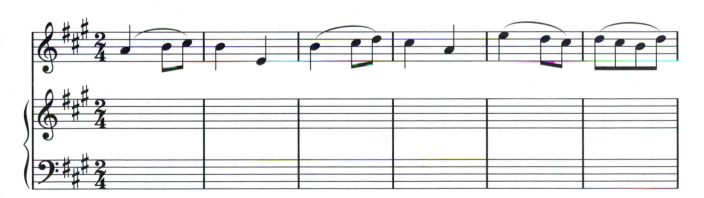

F. ANALYSIS

1. Label the key, Roman numerals, and cadences on the blanks provided.

   a. Jeremiah Clarke, "Hark the glad sound" (hymn)

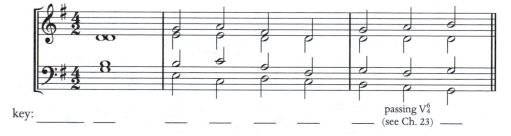

key: _____ _____   _____ _____ _____ _____ _____ _____
                                                              passing V_4^6
                                                              (see Ch. 23) _____

   b. William Henry Monk, "Abide with me" (hymn)

cadence: _____

key: _____ _____ _____ _____ _____ _____ _____ _____

c. "Medway" (hymn)

cadence: _____

key: _____ _____ _____

d. Fanny Robinson, "St. Monica" (hymn)

cadence: _____

key: _____ _____ _____

e. Joseph Haydn, Symphony No. 5, i

cadence: _____

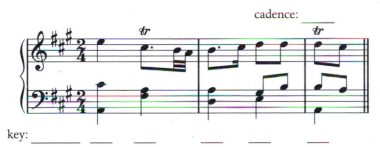

key: _____ _____ _____

f. Elisabetta de Gambarini, Canzonetta

cadence: _____

key: _____ _____ _____

g. G. F. Handel, "V'adoro, pupille," from *Giulio Cesare*

key: _____

Translation: I adore you, eyes, arrows of love, my heart welcomes your sparks.

h. Franz Schubert, "Pax vobiscum" ("Peace Be with You")

key: _____

Translation: "Peace be with you!" That was your farewell blessing.

i. Marie Antoinette / Jean-Baptiste Weckerlin, "C'est mon ami" ("He's My Friend")

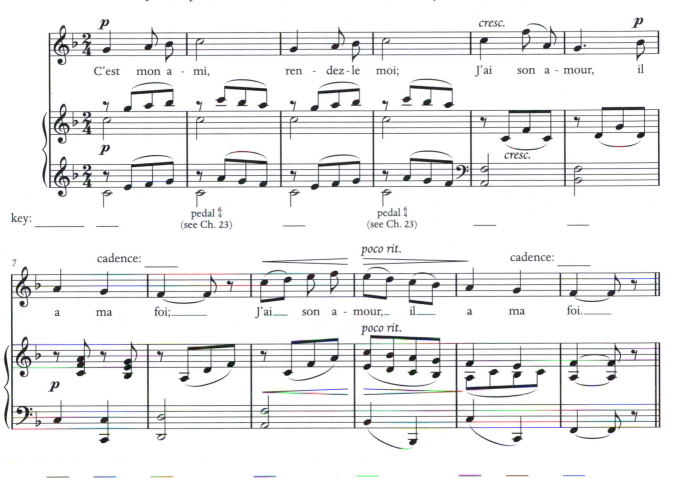

C'est mon a - mi, ren - dez - le moi; J'ai son a - mour, il
a ma foi; J'ai son a - mour, il a ma foi.

key: _____ ____

cadence: _____

Translation: He's my friend, return him to me, I have his love, he has my devotion.

j. Bert Williams, "Dora Dean"

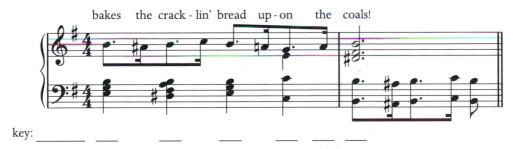

bakes the crack - lin' bread up - on the coals!

key: _____ ____

2. Analyze the harmonies in the following excerpts, and label them with Roman numerals. Then locate and label the cadences.

a. W. A. Mozart, Piano Sonata, K. 545, ii

G:

b. Robert Schumann, "Hör ich das Liedchen klingen"

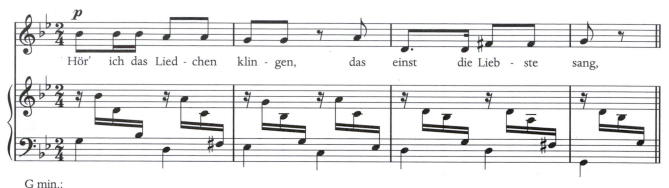

G min.:

Translation: I hear the song resounding that my beloved once sang.

c. Élisabeth Jacquet de la Guerre, Sarabande, from *Pièces de clavecin* (with optional violin accompaniment)

G:

What note is implied in the chord on the first beat of measure 3?

d. Jean-Baptiste Lully, "Suivons l'amour" ("Let Us Follow Love"), from *Cadmus et Hermonie*

C:

Translation: Let us follow love, let it enflame us.

e. Anna Amalia, "Das Veilchen" ("The Violet")

G:

f. Ludwig van Beethoven, Sonata for Violin and Piano, Op. 24, i

F:

- How does the harmonic rhythm (that is, the pace of the changes of harmonies) evolve throughout the course of the phrase? Does it speed up or slow down? Where?

- This ten-bar phrase seems expanded by two measures from a more normal eight-bar phrase. Which measures seem added? What makes them seem as though they are added? What effect is created by this expansion?

3. Label the Roman numerals and cadences. On the staves below, complete a simplified harmonic model of each passage in SATB format, using proper voice leading and smooth motion in the upper voices.

a. Fernando Sor, *Exercises facile for guitar*, Book II, No. 18

E min.:

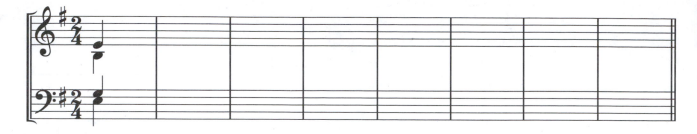

b. W. A. Mozart, Violin Sonata K. 379, ii

G:

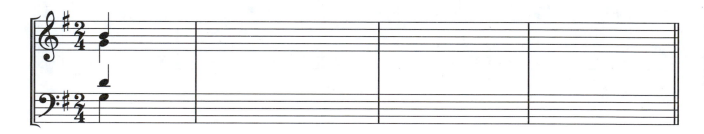

What voice-leading features in Mozart's score would be unusual in a four-part harmony exercise? What might explain the freer treatment of voice leading in Mozart's composition?

20 Voice Leading with Embellishing Tones

A. QUESTIONS FOR REVIEW

1. In what ways might embellishing tones create parallel fifths and octaves?

2. In what situations can adding an embellishing tone eliminate parallel fifths or octaves? In what situations does adding an embellishing tone not eliminate parallel octaves?

3. What is a pedal point? In what voice does it usually appear?

4. What does the figured bass symbol "4–3" indicate? What does the figured bass symbol "4–♯" indicate?

5. What does a dash under a note in figured bass indicate?

6. What does the number 2 indicate when it appears in a figured bass?

7. What does the figure "9–8" mean? Why do you suppose this figure is not written as "2–1"?

B. ADDING EMBELLISHMENTS

1. Rewrite each of the following chord pairs, adding one embellishing tone—either a passing tone or neighbor tone—between the chords. The first example has been completed for you.

a.

b.

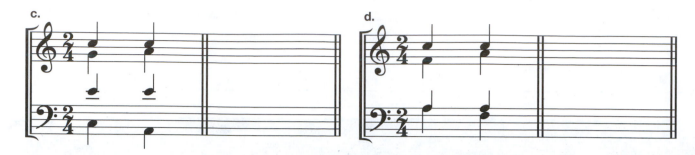

2. Rewrite each of the following chord pairs, adding two simultaneously sounding embellishing tones between the chords. The first example has been completed for you.

3. Realize the following Roman numerals in SATB format, adding at least one passing tone, one neighbor tone, and one suspension to each progression. Label the embellishing tones.

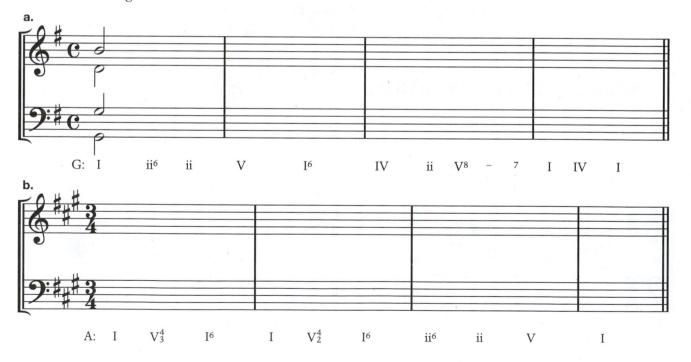

a.

G: I   ii⁶   ii   V   I⁶   IV   ii   V⁸ – ⁷   I   IV   I

b.

A: I   V₃⁴   I⁶   I   V₂⁴   I⁶   ii⁶   ii   V   I

C. READING FIGURED BASS

1. For each of the following sonorities:

- Above the staff, name the notes in the upper voices as indicated by the figured bass.

- Note that none of these involves an inversion of a standard chord: in each case, the notes in the chord must be determined by counting the intervals above the bass.

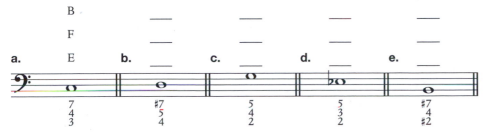

2. For each of the following sonorities:

- Above the staff, name the notes in the three upper voices as indicated by the figured bass.

- Note that some of the figures are standard abbreviations for chords that use four different notes, while others are sonorities using only three different notes.

- If only three notes are indicated, decide which note you want doubled, write that as the fourth note, and circle it.

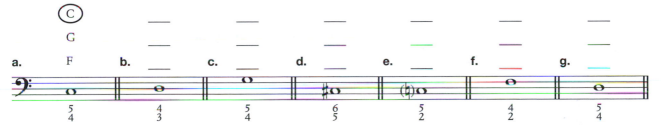

3. For each of the following progressions or pairs of sonorities:

- Above the staff, name the notes in the upper voices, as indicated by the figured bass.

- Use parentheses to indicate notes in the second chord that are held over from the first.

- When the figured bass indicates a three-note sonority or chord, decide which note you want doubled, write that as the fourth note, and circle it.

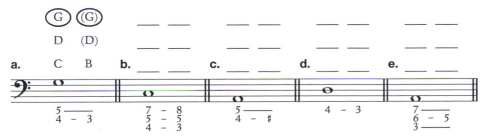

D. REALIZING FIGURED BASS

1. For each of the following:
   - Realize the figured bass.
   - Remember that "4–3" = "$\frac{5}{4-3}$" = "$\frac{5-5}{4-3}$," and "4–♯" = "$\frac{5-5}{4-♯3}$."
   - Then label the keys, Roman numerals, and embellishing tones.

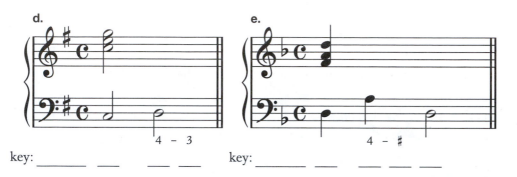

2. For each of the following:
   - Below each bass note, write the names of the notes as implied by the figured bass.
   - Then realize the figured bass in keyboard format.
   - With complicated or less familiar figures (such as $\frac{5}{4}$), determine the notes by counting intervals above the bass.
   - Remember that when there is a "2" in the figured bass, the bass note should not be doubled.

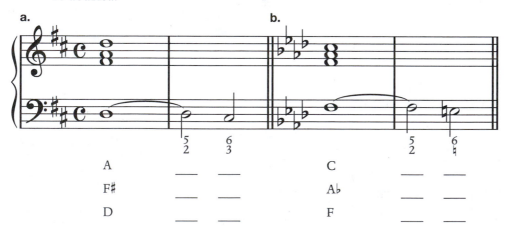

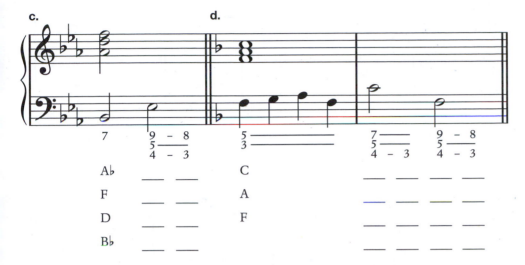

3. Realize each figured bass in keyboard format. Remember that the use of a dash within the figures indicates that the notes in the upper voices should repeat or be sustained.

c. G. F. Handel, *Exercise for Princess Anne*

Remember, the figure $9 = \frac{9}{5}$.

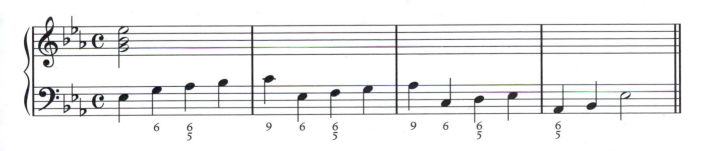

4. Realize each figured bass in SATB format.

5. Complete the realizations of these chorale excerpts by J. S. Bach in SATB format. Then label the Roman numerals, embellishing tones, and (where indicated) the cadences.

a. "Eins ist Noth!" ("One thing's needful")

b. "Ich lasse dich nicht" ("I won't let you go")

Hint: With the figure 7–6 in the second measure, omit the fifth above the bass.

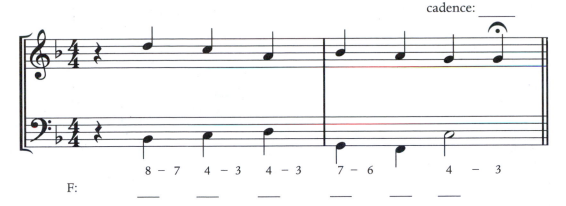

cadence: _____

8 – 7   4 – 3   4 – 3   7 – 6   4 – 3

F: ___   ___   ___   ___   ___

c. "Ich freue mich in dir" ("I rejoice in you")

—   6 — ♮ — 6 — $\frac{5}{2}$ $\frac{6}{3}$

C min.: ___   ___   ___   ___   ___

d. "Kein Stündlein geht dahin" ("No hour goes by")

Remember, 9–8 = $\frac{9-8}{5-5}$.
$ = \frac{3-3}{}$

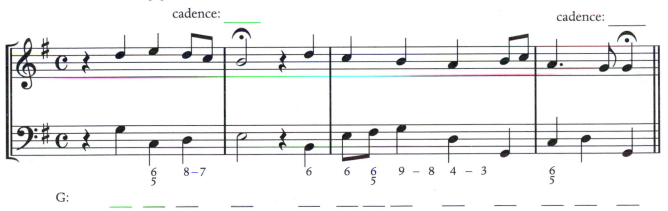

cadence: _____   cadence: _____

$\frac{6}{5}$ 8–7   6   6 $\frac{6}{5}$ 9 – 8   4 – 3 $\frac{6}{5}$

G: ___   ___   ___   ___   ___   ___   ___   ___

D. Realizing Figured Bass | **263**

E. HARMONIZING MELODIES

For each of the following melodies:

- Provide a bass line and Roman numerals.

- Then fill in the inner voices in SATB format.

- Label the embellishing tones in the melody. (If you wish, you may add some embellishing tones to the bass and inner voices as well.)

1.

B♭: I

2. Use one chord for the last half of the final measure.

B min.: i

F. ERROR DETECTION

Below is a faulty realization of a figured bass, with numbers placed above each mistake. On the blank lines following the score, describe each of these errors.

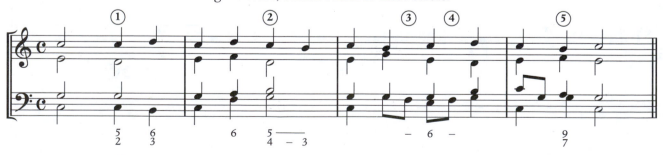

1. _____

2. _____
_____

3. _____
_____

4. _____

5. _____
_____

G. COMPOSITION

1. Realize the following figured bass in keyboard style.

2. Compose a melody above the following bass line.

- Use half notes, quarter notes, and eighth notes, with a dotted half note in measure 16.
- The notes should either be chord tones—that is, notes of the chord as seen in (1) above—or embellishing tones. Label each embellishing tone.
- Octaves or fifths on the downbeat of a measure should be approached in contrary motion.
- No two measures in a row should begin with a perfect octave or perfect fifth.
- The melody in measures 9–16 should be different than in measures 1–8.

H. ANALYSIS

Label the key, Roman numerals, cadences (where indicated), and embellishing tones.

1. J. S. Bach, Chorale 269

cadence: _____

key: _____ _____ _____ _____ _____ _____ _____

2. J. S. Bach, Chorale 22

cadence: _____

key: _____ _____ _____ _____ _____ _____ _____ _____

3. J. S. Bach, Chorale 154

Note: This is in open-score format; the tenor voice sounds an octave lower than notated.

key: _____ _____ _____ _____ _____ _____

4. J. S. Bach, Chorale 36

cadence: _____

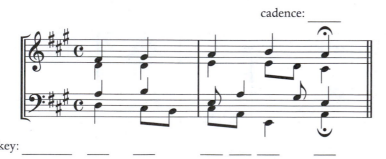

key: _____ _____ _____ _____ _____ _____

NAME: ....

5. Harriet Abrams, "A Smile and a Tear"

cadence: _____

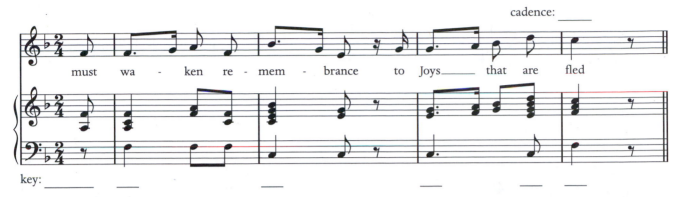

must wa - ken re - mem - brance to Joys_____ that are fled

key: _____

6. George Gershwin, "Cinderelatives"

cadence: _____

Lit - tle Cin - der - rel - a - tives._____

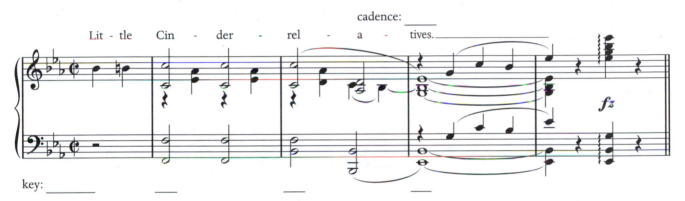

key: _____   _____   _____

7. Léopoldine Goubau d'Hovorst, Piano Sonata, Op. 13, i

The following passage is built over a pedal tone in the bass. As always, when labeling
Roman numerals above a bass pedal tone, do not worry about indicating the chord
inversions. What scale degree is the pedal tone?

key: _____   _____   _____   _____   _____

8. Jerome Kern, "You Found Me and I Found You"

key: _____   _____   _____   _____   _____

9. Franz Schubert, Dances, D. 365, No. 17

cadence: _____

key: _____

10. J. S. Bach, English Suite No. 2, Sarabande

key: ____ ____ ____ ____ ____

11. Ludwig van Beethoven, Piano Sonata, Op. 2, No. 2, ii

cadence: _____

key: _____

cadence: _____

_____   _____   _____

How do the two halves of this passage compare? In what ways are they similar, and in what ways do they differ?

chapter 21

III and VII

A. QUESTIONS FOR REVIEW

1. What chord is similar to iii? "iii⁶"? What are the standard uses of iii and "iii⁶"?

2. How is $\hat{7}$ treated differently within a iii chord than within a V chord? In minor keys, how is $\hat{7}$ within III treated differently than within V?

3. How often should iii or "iii⁶" be used within basic diatonic melody-harmonization exercises?

4. In what situations may root-position vii° triads be used within four-part harmony exercises?

B. REALIZING ROMAN NUMERALS

1. Realize the Roman numerals in SATB format; then label the scale degrees of the top voice.

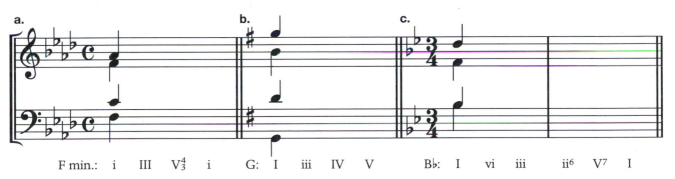

a.

F min.: i   III V$^4_3$ i

b.

G: I iii IV V

c.

B♭: I vi iii ii⁶ V⁷ I

2. Realize the Roman numerals in keyboard format, then label the scale degrees of the top voice.

D: I   I⁶   iii   ii⁶   V   I   F♯ min.:   i   VI   III   iv   V⁸ ⁻ ⁷   i

C. REALIZING FIGURED BASS

1. Realize each figured bass in SATB format, then identify the key and label the Roman numerals.

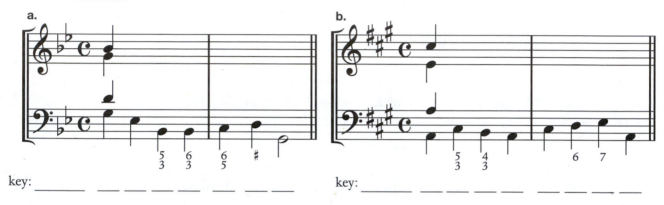

key: _____   key: _____

2. Realize each figured bass in keyboard format and label the Roman numerals.

a.

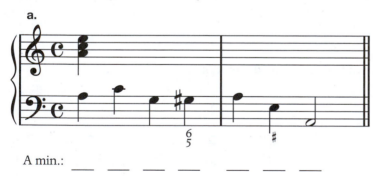

A min.: _____

b.

The melody should be a descending scale,
starting and ending on the Tonic.

F min.: _____

c.

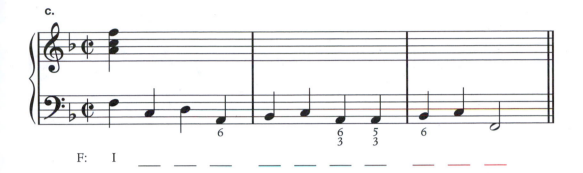

F: I   _ _ _ _ _ _ _ _ _ _ _ _ _ _

D. COMPOSITION

1. Realize the figured bass in keyboard format; the top voice is given for measures 1–6.

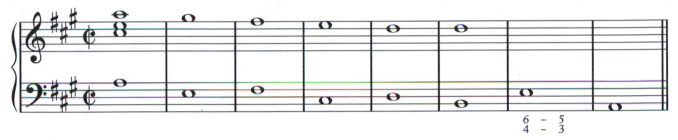

2. Compose a melody above this bass line.

- The melody should be based on the harmonies suggested by the figured bass in (1) above.
- Do not use an octave or a fifth on the downbeat of any two consecutive measures.
- The melody should end on the downbeat of measure 8.

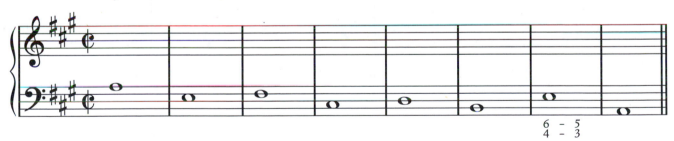

3. Compose a variation of the melody in (2).

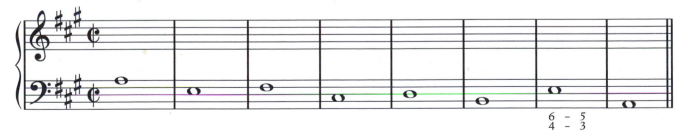

E. ANALYSIS

Label the keys and Roman numerals of the following excerpts.

1. "Old Hundredth" (hymn)

key: _____

2. Clara Schumann, *Soirées Musicales*, Mazurka, Op. 6, No. 3

key: _____

3. Robert Schumann, "Armes Waisenkind" ("Poor Orphan Child"), from *Album for the Young,* Op. 68, No. 6

Label the harmonies and cadences (two chords have already been labeled). What features of this passage seem to evoke the imagery suggested by this work's title, and why?

key: _____   V/III   cadence: _____

V/III   cadence: _____

chapter

22

Sequences

A. QUESTIONS FOR REVIEW

1. What is a sequence?

2. What are some chords and chord successions that are allowed within sequences but not common within functional progressions? Why are they allowed within sequences?

3. What are some common types of descending sequences? What are some common types of ascending sequences?

4. What voice-leading guidelines apply to parallel $\frac{6}{3}$ sequences?

5. What do the figured bass symbols "5–6" indicate?

6. What voice-leading rules apply to both functional progressions and sequential progressions?

7. How may $\hat{7}$ be treated differently in a sequence than within a functional progression?

B. MELODIC SEQUENCES

Form melodic sequences by transposing each of the following melodic fragments diatonically (that is, within the given key, using no accidentals) as indicated.

1. down by step 3 times   **2.** down by step 1 time

3. up by step 1 time

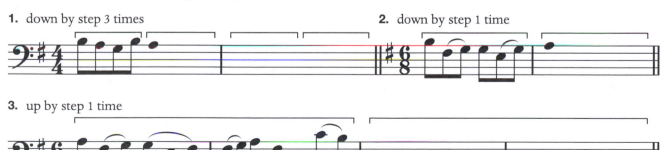

C. REALIZING ROMAN NUMERALS

1. Each of the following excerpts begins with a harmonic sequence in which a bracketed pair of chords is repeated sequentially three times. Realize the Roman numerals, continuing the sequence by transposing the bracketed progression diatonically (using only notes within the key and no accidentals).

SATB format:

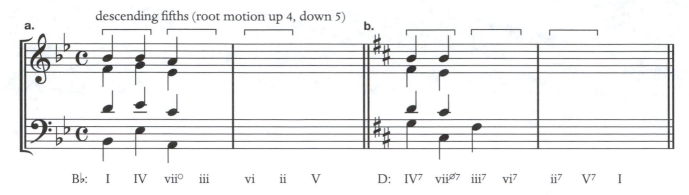

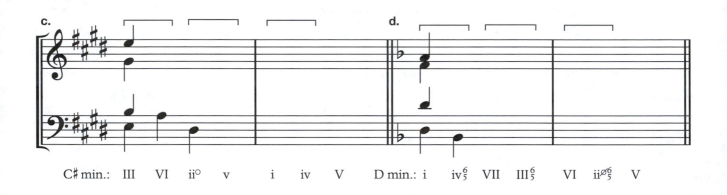

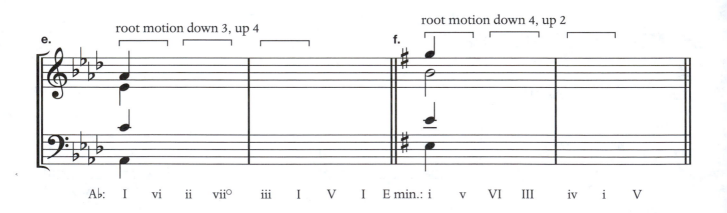

Keyboard format:

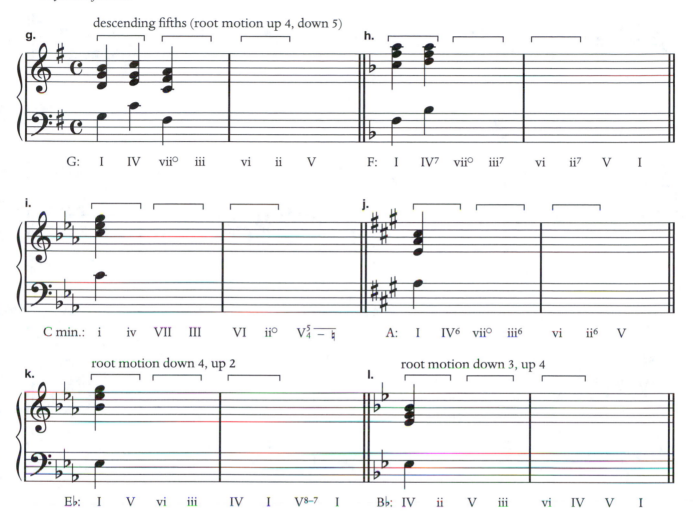

descending fifths (root motion up 4, down 5)

g. G: I IV vii° iii vi ii V

h. F: I IV⁷ vii° iii⁷ vi ii⁷ V I

i. C min.: i iv VII III VI ii° V⁵₄ — ♮

j. A: I IV⁶ vii° iii⁶ vi ii⁶ V

k. root motion down 4, up 2
E♭: I V vi iii IV I V⁸⁻⁷ I

l. root motion down 3, up 4
B♭: IV ii V iii vi IV V I

D. REALIZING FIGURED BASS

1. Realize each figured bass in four-part harmony, keyboard format, forming sequences by transposing the bracketed pair of chords diatonically (using only the notes of the key).

descending fifths (root motion alternating up 4, down 5)

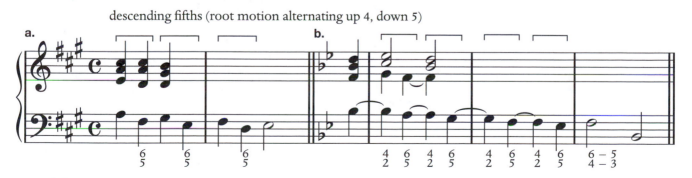

a. $\begin{matrix}6\\5\end{matrix}$ $\begin{matrix}6\\5\end{matrix}$ $\begin{matrix}6\\5\end{matrix}$

b. $\begin{matrix}4\\2\end{matrix}$ $\begin{matrix}6\\5\end{matrix}$ $\begin{matrix}4\\2\end{matrix}$ $\begin{matrix}6\\5\end{matrix}$ $\begin{matrix}4\\2\end{matrix}$ $\begin{matrix}6\\5\end{matrix}$ $\begin{matrix}4\\2\end{matrix}$ $\begin{matrix}6\\5\end{matrix}$ $\begin{matrix}6-5\\4-3\end{matrix}$

2. Realize the following in four-part harmony, keyboard format. Label the key and Roman numerals.

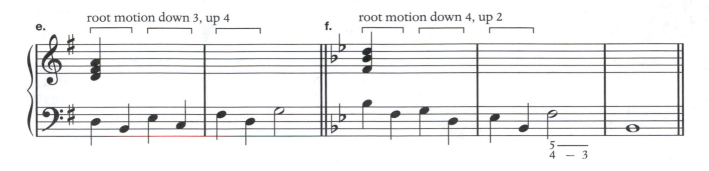

key: _____ _ _ _ _ _ _ _ _ _ _

key: _____ _ _ _ _ _ _ _ _

3. The following exercises include sequences that typically use only three voices. Realize each figured bass using only three voices (one voice in the bass, two in the treble), forming sequences by transposing the bracketed pair of chords diatonically (using only the notes of the key).

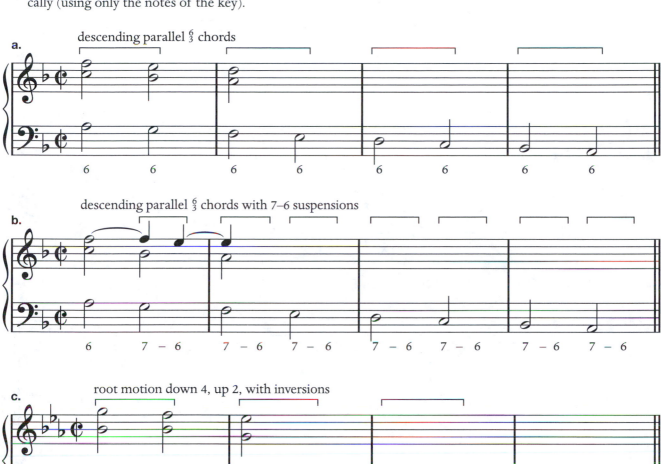

descending parallel ⁶₃ chords

descending parallel ⁶₃ chords with 7–6 suspensions

root motion down 4, up 2, with inversions

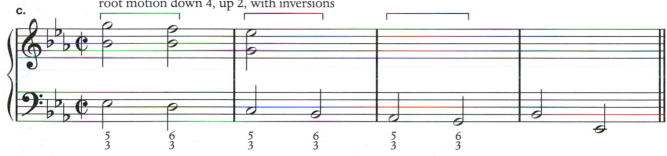

descending parallel ⁶₃ chords with 7–6 suspensions

5–6 variant of down 3, up 4

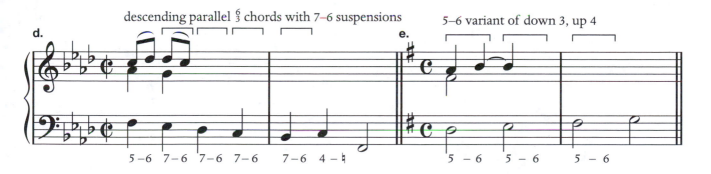

4. Realize the figured basses in SATB format. Label the key and Roman numerals.

a.

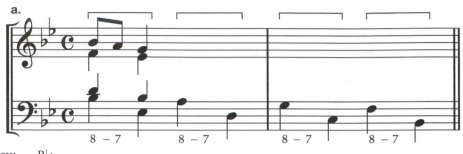

key: ___Bb:___ ___ ___ ___ ___ ___ ___ ___

b.

key: ___ ___ ___ ___ ___ ___ ___ ___ ___

c.

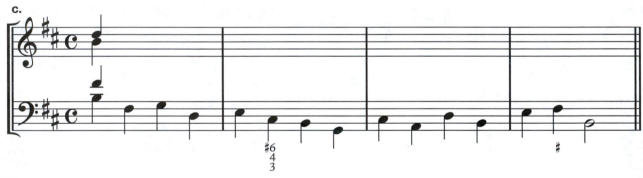

key: ___ ___ ___ ___ ___ ___ ___ ___

d.

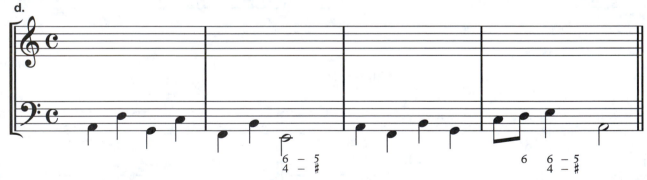

key: ___ ___ ___ ___ ___ ___ ___ ___ ___ ___ ___

E. SEQUENTIAL PATTERNS

1. Complete the figured bass accompaniments in keyboard format for the following excerpts from flute sonatas.

- Do not worry about parallel perfect intervals between your accompaniment and the given melody.

- Label the Roman numerals, chord roots, the type of sequence, and (where indicated) the cadence.

a. Giuseppe Sarti, Flute Sonata No. 3, ii

Use only three voices in the keyboard part—with only two voices in the treble staff.

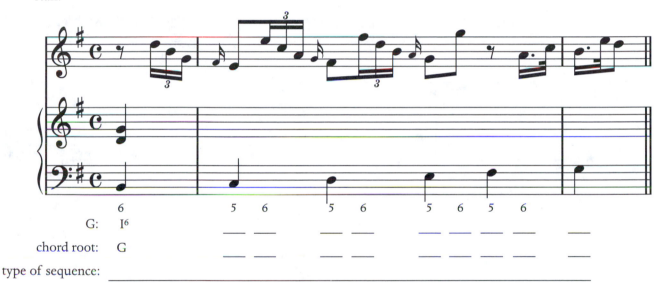

type of sequence: _____

b. Jean Baptiste Loeillet, Recorder Sonata Op. 1, No. 8, i

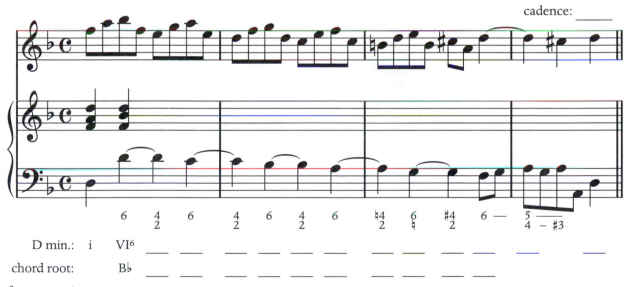

type of sequence in mm. 1–3: _____

c. G. P. Telemann, *Partita No. 3 for Oboe, Violin, or Flute,* v

C min.: ____ ____ ____ ____

cadence: ____

chord root: ____ ____ ____ ____ ____ ____ ____ ____

type of sequence in mm. 4–7: _____

2. Complete the sequences by continuing to transpose the bracketed segment, according to the instructions above the staff.

- The sequences should be diatonic, using notes within the key.
- Label the Roman numerals, chord roots, and the type of sequence.

a. Jean Baptiste Loeillet, *Lessons for Harpsichord or Spinet*, Minuet

sequence down by step 3 times

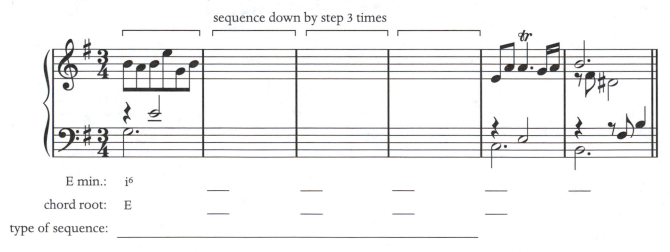

E min.: i⁶ ____ ____ ____ ____ ____

chord root: E ____ ____ ____ ____

type of sequence: _____

b. Anna Bon, Flute Sonata, Op. 1, No. 3, iii

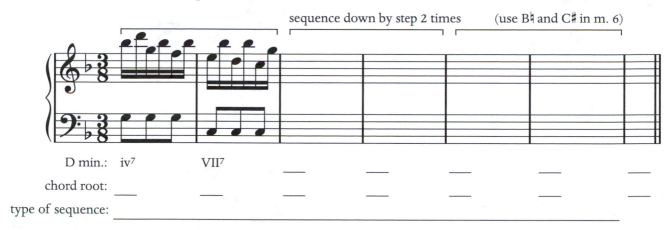

sequence down by step 2 times   (use B♮ and C♯ in m. 6)

D min.:   iv⁷   VII⁷   ___   ___   ___   ___   ___

chord root: ___   ___   ___   ___   ___   ___

type of sequence: _____

c. Giovanni Bononcini, *Cantatae e Duetti*, Prelude

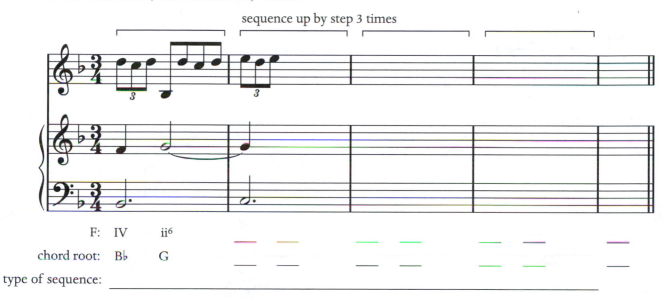

sequence up by step 3 times

F: IV   ii⁶   ___ ___   ___ ___   ___ ___   ___

chord root: B♭   G   ___ ___   ___ ___   ___ ___   ___

type of sequence: _____

3. Continue the following harmonic sequences by transposing the bracketed harmonic progression diatonically (using no accidentals). Label the Roman numerals of the chords that appear in the middle of the sequence.

Keyboard format:

a. Descending fifths

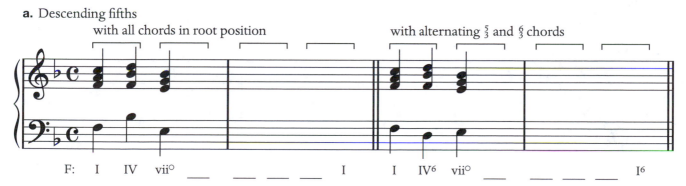

with all chords in root position   with alternating ⁵₃ and ⁶₃ chords

F: I   IV   vii°   ___   ___   ___   I   I   IV⁶ vii°   ___   ___   ___   I⁶

b. Descending fifths

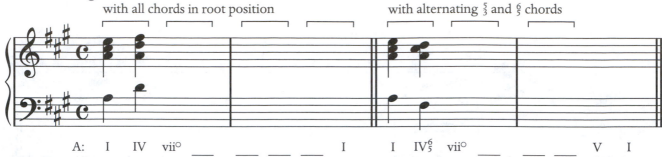

with all chords in root position   **with alternating $\frac{5}{3}$ and $\frac{6}{3}$ chords**

A: I   IV   vii°   ___   ___   ___   ___   I   I   IV$^6_5$ vii°   ___   ___   ___   V   I

SATB format:

c. Down 4, up 2

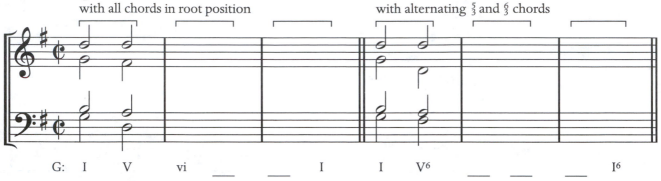

with all chords in root position   **with alternating $\frac{5}{3}$ and $\frac{6}{3}$ chords**

G: I   V   vi   ___   ___   I   I   V^6 ___   ___   ___   I^6

d. Down 3, up 4

with all chords in root position   **with alternating $\frac{5}{3}$ and $\frac{6}{3}$ chords (ascending 5–6)**

E♭:   V   iii   vi   ___   ___   ___   I   V   iii^6 vi   ___   ___   I

F. COMPOSITION

1. Realize this figured bass in keyboard format, creating a sequence by transposing
the bracketed segment down by step on each line.

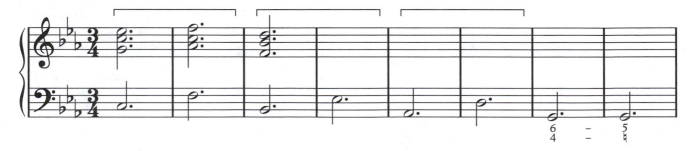

2. Compose a piece for keyboard and another instrument, based on your realization of (1).

- Choose a figuration pattern for the keyboard part such as an oom-pah-pah pattern or arpeggiation (you can find examples in earlier composition assignments). Rewrite the notes of the chord progression using that figuration.

- Then compose a melody to go with the keyboard part. The notes of the melody should either be chord tones or embellishing tones, such as passing tones or neighbor tones.

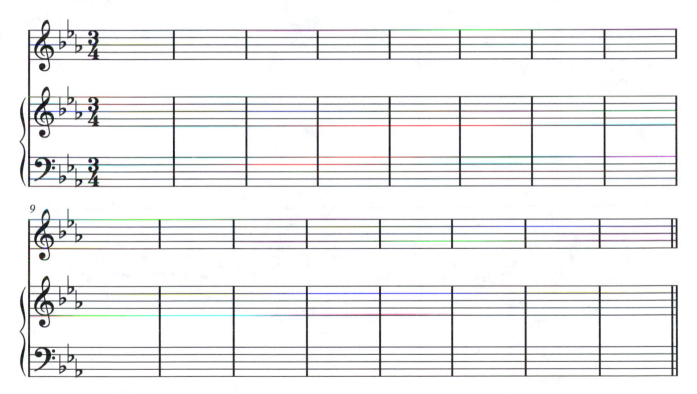

3. Compose a short piece for keyboard, guitar, or an ensemble of your choice, following these guidelines:

- Your piece can be in a major key and meter of your choice.
- It should be eight measures long, based on these harmonies:

HC   PAC

I   V | vi   iii | IV   I | V | I   V | vi   iii | IV   V | I ||

G. ANALYSIS

1. On the lines below the staves, label the Roman numerals and roots of the chords, then identify the type of sequence. Also label the cadence where indicated. Finally, indicate where the sequence leads to and from by identifying the Roman numerals of the first and last chords.

a. Anna Bon, Flute Sonata, Op. 1, No. 1, ii

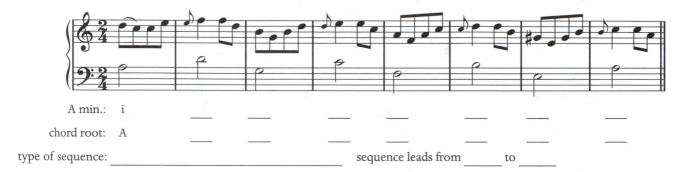

A min.:   i   ___ ___ ___ ___ ___ ___

chord root: A   ___ ___ ___ ___ ___ ___

type of sequence: _____   sequence leads from ___ to ___

b. J. S. Bach, Little Prelude in C, BWV 924a

C: ___   ___   ___   ___

chord root: ___   ___   ___   ___

type of sequence: _____   sequence leads from ___ to ___

c. J. S. Bach, Little Prelude in C, BWV 924

C: ___   ___   ___   ___

chord root: ___   ___   ___   ___

type of sequence: _____   sequence leads from ___ to ___

NAME: ....

d. G. F. Handel, Passacaglia in G Minor, HWV 432

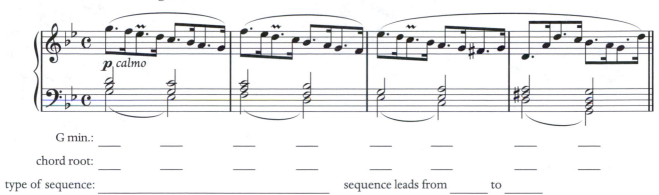

G min.: ___ ___ ___ ___ ___ ___ ___

chord root: ___ ___ ___ ___ ___ ___ ___

type of sequence: _____ sequence leads from ___ to ___

e. Henry Purcell, *Fairy Queen*

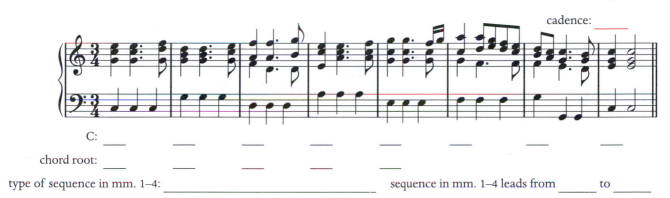

C: ___ ___ ___ ___ ___ ___

chord root: ___ ___ ___ ___ ___

type of sequence in mm. 1–4: _____ sequence in mm. 1–4 leads from ___ to ___

f. Arcangelo Corelli, Trio Sonata (for two violins and continuo), Op. 2, Preludio

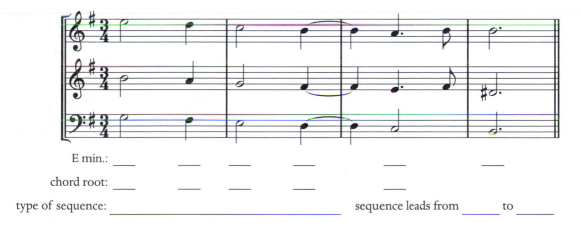

E min.: ___ ___ ___ ___ ___

chord root: ___ ___ ___ ___

type of sequence: _____ sequence leads from ___ to ___

g. Frédéric Chopin, Etude in G♭, Op. 25, No. 9

G♭: ___ ___ ___ ___ ___ ___ V$^6_5$/V ___

chord root: ___ ___ ___ ___

type of sequence in mm. 1–3: _____   sequence in mm. 1–3 leads from ___ to ___

2. Each of the following excerpts includes two sequences; identify them on the brackets provided above each passage. Also, on the score, label the cadences.

a. Joseph Haydn, Symphony No. 104, i

cadence: ___   cadence: ___

sequence in mn. 5–6: _____

sequence in mn. 13–14: _____

b. Henry Williams, Parisian Waltz No. 3

sequence in mm. 1–6: _____

sequence in mm. 9–13: _____

What produces the special rhythmic effect in mm. 1–6 and 9–13?

chapter 23

Other $^6_4$ Chords

A. QUESTIONS FOR REVIEW

1. What is a pedal $^6_4$ chord?

2. What is a passing $^6_4$ chord?

3. What is an arpeggiated $^6_4$ chord?

4. A tonic chord in second inversion (I^6_4) can serve what type of function? Can it function as a pedal $^6_4$, passing $^6_4$, arpeggiated $^6_4$, cadential $^6_4$, or all of these?

5. What harmonies are most commonly embellished with a pedal $^6_4$?

6. What is the Roman numeral of the most common type of passing $^6_4$?

B. REALIZING ROMAN NUMERALS

1. In each of the following, the $^6_4$ chords are identified by their specific function rather than by their Roman numeral: pass. (passing), ped. (pedal), arp. (arpeggiated), or cad. (cadential) $^6_4$. In the blank lines provided, label the Roman numeral of each $^6_4$ chord. Then realize the Roman numerals.

SATB format:

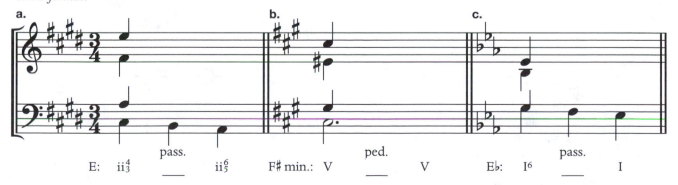

a.

pass.

E: ii^4_3 _____ ii^6_5

b.

ped.

F♯ min.: V _____ V

c.

pass.

E♭: I^6 _____ I

d.

G: I⁶   pass. I

e.

E♭: I   pass. I⁶

f.

F: V   ped. V⁷

Keyboard format:

g.

A♭: I pass. I⁶ V ped. V I arp. I⁶ I ped. I

h.

D min.: i ped. i V V⁶ arp. V i⁶ pass. i V ped. V

2. Realize the Roman numerals. Then in the blanks provided label the $^6_4$ chords according to their specific function: pass. (passing), ped. (pedal), arp. (arpeggiated), or cad. (cadential) $^6_4$.

SATB format:

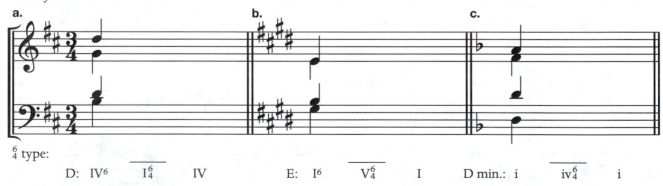

a.

$^6_4$ type: D: IV⁶ I$^6_4$ IV

b.

E: I⁶ V$^6_4$ I

c.

D min.: i iv$^6_4$ i

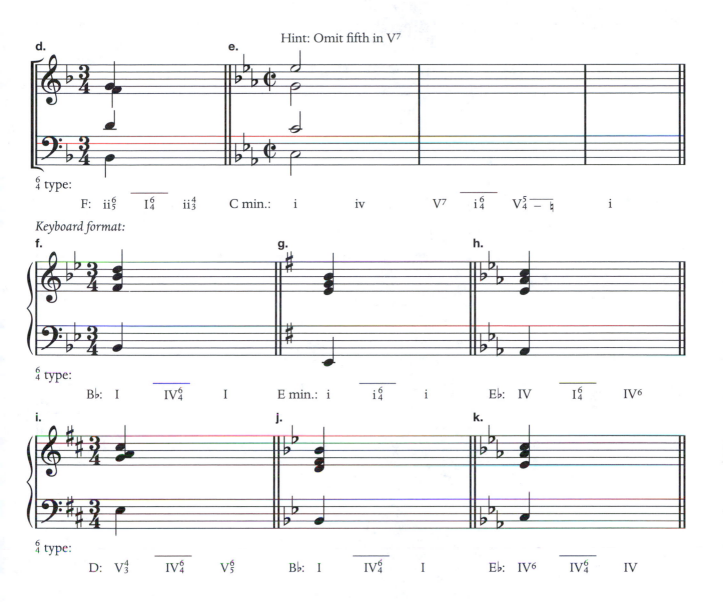

d.

e. Hint: Omit fifth in V⁷

$^6_4$ type: _____ _____

F: ii$^6_5$ I$^6_4$ ii$^4_3$ C min.: i   iv   V⁷ i$^6_4$ V$^5_4$ — ♮   i

Keyboard format:

f. **g.** **h.**

$^6_4$ type: _____ _____ _____

B♭: I IV$^6_4$ I   E min.: i i$^6_4$ i   E♭: IV I$^6_4$ IV⁶

i. **j.** **k.**

$^6_4$ type: _____ _____ _____

D: V$^4_3$ IV$^6_4$ V$^6_5$ B♭: I IV$^6_4$ I   E♭: IV⁶ IV$^6_4$ IV

C. REALIZING FIGURED BASS

1. Realize each figured bass in keyboard format. Label the key and Roman numerals, and indicate whether each $^6_4$ chord is a pass. (passing), ped. (pedal), arp. (arpeggiated), or cad. (cadential) $^6_4$.

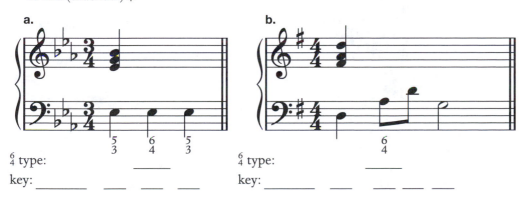

a. **b.**

$^6_4$ type: _____ $^6_4$ type: _____

key: _____ _____ _____   key: _____ _____ _____ _____

c.

$\begin{smallmatrix}6\\4\end{smallmatrix}$ type: _____

key: _____ _____ _____

d.

$\begin{smallmatrix}6\\4\end{smallmatrix}$ type: _____

key: _____ _____ _____

e.

$\begin{smallmatrix}6\\4\end{smallmatrix}$ type: _____ _____ _____

key: _____

f.

$\begin{smallmatrix}6\\4\end{smallmatrix}$ type: _____ _____ _____

key: _____

2. Realize each figured bass in SATB format. Label the key and Roman numerals, and indicate whether each $\begin{smallmatrix}6\\4\end{smallmatrix}$ chord is a pass. (passing), ped. (pedal), arp. (arpeggiated), or cad. (cadential) $\begin{smallmatrix}6\\4\end{smallmatrix}$.

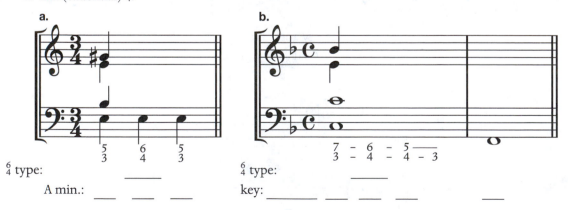

a.

$\begin{smallmatrix}6\\4\end{smallmatrix}$ type: _____

A min.: _____ _____ _____

b.

$\begin{smallmatrix}6\\4\end{smallmatrix}$ type: _____

key: _____ _____ _____

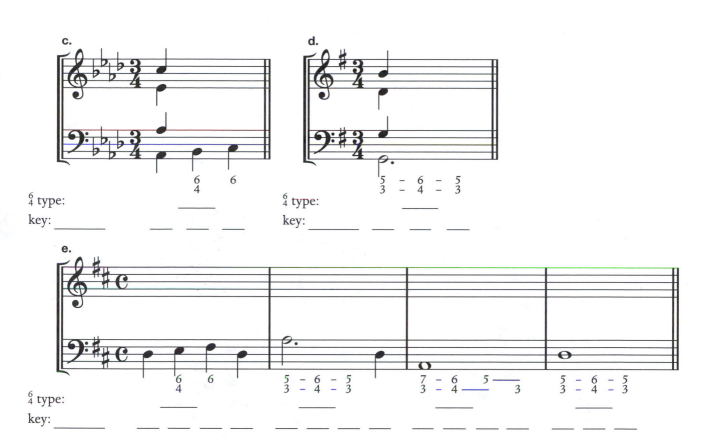

c.

$^6_4$ type: _____

key: _____ _____ _____

d.

$^6_4$ type: _____

key: _____ _____ _____ _____

e.

$^6_4$ type: _____ _____ _____

key: _____ _____ _____ _____ _____ _____ _____ _____ _____

D. ANALYSIS

Label the key, Roman numerals, and cadences (where indicated) in the following. Identify whether each of the $^6_4$ chords is a pass. (passing), ped. (pedal), arp. (arpeggiated), or cad. (cadential) $^6_4$.

1. Giovanni Battista Viotti, *Autumn* (hymn)

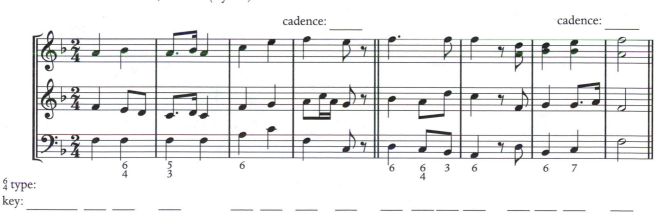

$^6_4$ type: _____

key: _____ _____

2. J. S. Bach, Chorale 59

$^6_4$ type: _____

key: _____

3. Claudia Rusca, Sacred Concerto

cadence: _____

$^6_4$ type: _____

key: _____ _____ _____

4. Georges Bizet, Overture to *Carmen*

$^6_4$ type: _____

key: _____

5. Elizabeth Anna Curteis, "Morning Hymn"

cadence: _____

$^6_4$ type: _____

key: _____ _____ _____

6. Ludwig van Beethoven, Bagatelle, Op. 33, No. 1

cadence: _____

$\frac{6}{4}$ type: _____

key: _____

7. Robert Schumann, "Wilder Reiter" ("Wild Horseman") from *Album for the Young,*
Op. 68

cadence: _____

$\frac{6}{4}$ type: _____

key: _____

cadence: _____

8. George Gershwin, "By and By"

By   and   by,   Clouds will   be   gone,_____

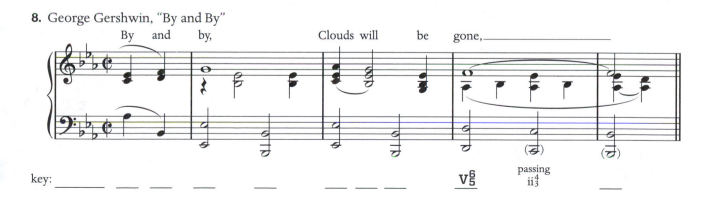

key: _____

V^6_5 passing ii$^4_3$

9. Anna Bon, Keyboard Sonata, Op. 2, No. 5, ii

$^6_4$ type: _____
key: _____ _____ _____ V^6_5/V

cadence: _____

_____ _____ _____ _____

10. W. A. Mozart, Piano Sonata, K. 311, ii

Andante con espressione

cadence: _____

$^6_4$ type: _____
key: _____

cadence: _____

_____ _____ _____

24 Other Embellishing Chords

chapter

A. QUESTIONS FOR REVIEW

1. What is an embellishing chord?

2. What are some examples of standard functional harmonic progressions that involve embellishing chords?

3. When can IV⁶ follow V?

4. When can IV⁶ follow V⁶?

5. When can IV⁶ lead directly to a tonic chord?

6. What chords may be used to harmonize an ascending scale in the bass? What chords may be used to harmonize a descending scale in the bass?

7. What is a lament bass?

B. REALIZING ROMAN NUMERALS

1. Realize the Roman numerals in SATB format.

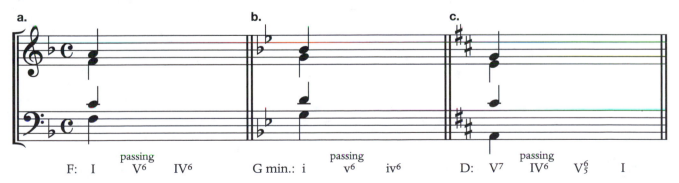

a.

b.

c.

F: I   passing
         V⁶   IV⁶

G min.: i   passing
              v⁶   iv⁶

D: V⁷   passing
          IV⁶   V⁶₅   I

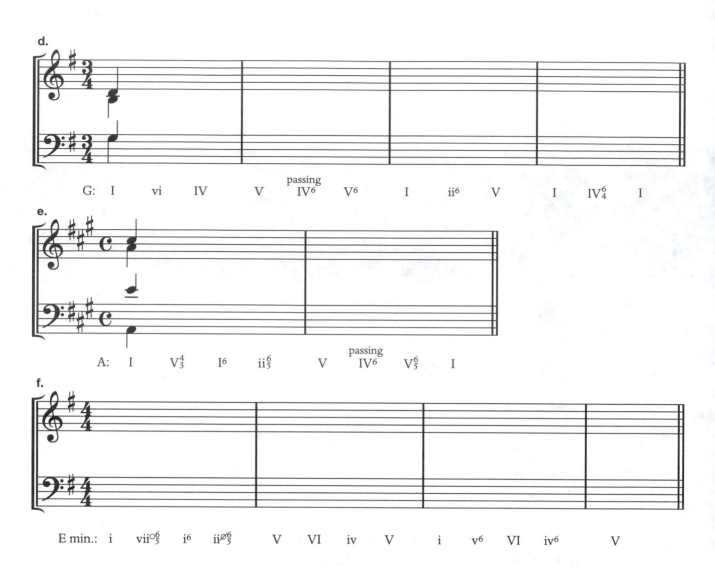

d.

G: I   vi   IV   V IV^6 _passing_ V^6 I ii^6 V   I IV^6_4 I

e.

A: I V^4_3 I^6 ii^6_5 V IV^6 _passing_ V^6_5 I

f.

E min.: i vii^{o6}_5 i^6 $ii^{ø6}_5$ V   VI   iv   V   i v^6 VI iv^6 V

2. Realize the Roman numerals in keyboard format.

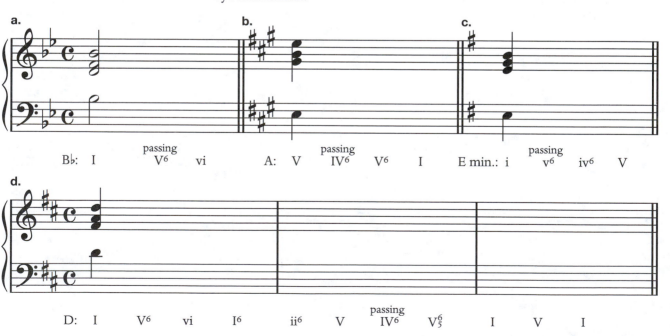

a.

B♭: I V^6 _passing_   vi

b.

A: V IV^6 _passing_ V^6 I

c.

E min.: i v^6 _passing_ iv^6 V

d.

D: I V^6 vi I^6 ii^6 V IV^6 _passing_ V^6_5 I   V   I

e.

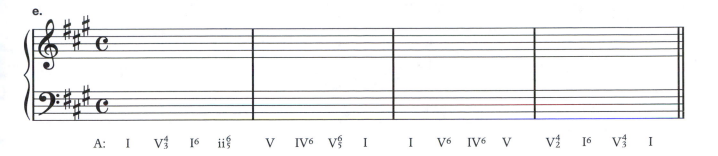

A: I V_3^4 I^6 ii_5^6 V IV^6 V_5^6 I   I V^6 IV^6 V V_2^4 I^6 V_3^4 I

C. REALIZING FIGURED BASS

1. Realize each figured bass in keyboard format. Then label the keys and Roman numerals, and indicate which chords have a primarily passing function (pass.).

- Note that two passing chords may appear in a row.

a. • Do not mark as "passing" chords that are part of a standard harmonic progress.

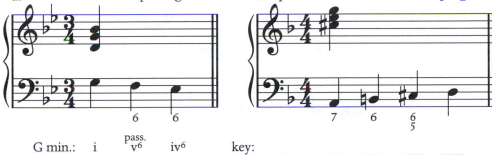

G min.:   i $\overset{\text{pass.}}{V^6}$ iv^6 key: ___ ___ ___ ___ ___

c.

key: ___ ___ ___ ___ ___

d.

key: ___ ___ ___ ___ ___ ___

e.

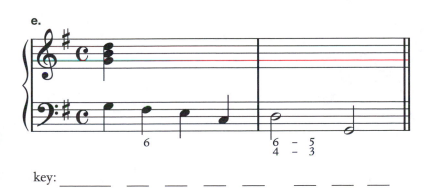

key: ___   ___ ___ ___ ___ ___

f.

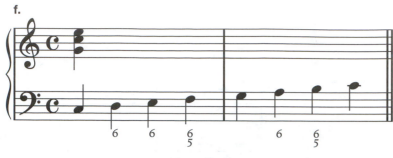

key: _____ __ __ __ __ __ __

g.

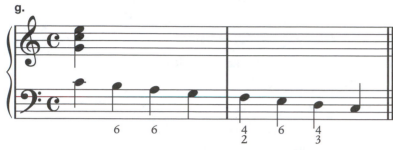

key: _____ __ __ __ __ __ __

h.

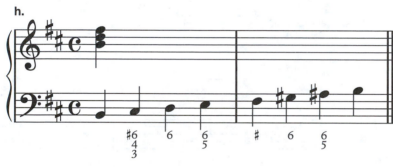

key: _____ __ __ __ __ __ __

i.

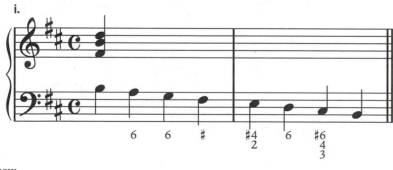

key: _____ __ __ __ __ __ __

2. Realize each figured bass in SATB format. Then label the keys and Roman numerals, and indicate which chords have a primarily passing function (pass.).

- Note that two passing chords may appear in a row.
- Do not mark as "passing" chords that are part of a standard harmonic progress.

a.

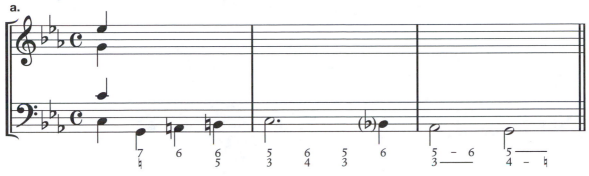

key: _____ __ __ __ __ __ __ __ __ __

b.

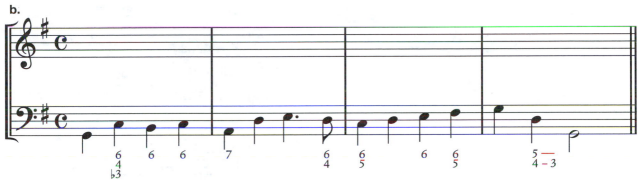

key: _____ __ __ __ __ __ __ __ __

c.

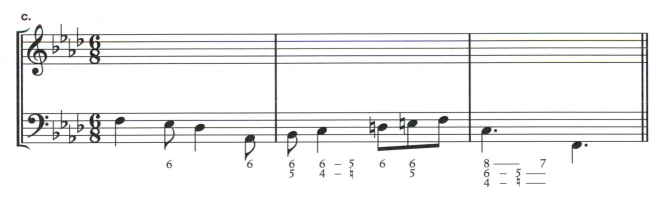

key: _____ __ __ __ __ __ __ __ __

3. Complete a realization in keyboard format of the figured bass accompaniment for these excerpts and label the Roman numerals. Do not worry about any parallel perfect intervals that may arise between your figured bass realization and the given melody.

a. Johann Ernst Galliard, Bassoon (or Cello) Sonata No. 5, ii

key: _____ _____ _____ _____ _____ _____ _____

b. William Babell, Oboe Sonata, iii

key: _____ _____ _____ _____ _____ _____ _____

c. Jean Baptiste Loeillet, Flute Sonata, Op. 1, No. 5, ii

key: _____ _____ _____ _____ _____ _____ _____ _____

D. I–IV⁶–I⁶

1. Label the scale degrees of these melodic fragments. Then harmonize them in SATB format using the indicated chords.

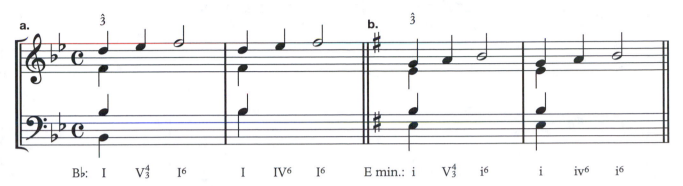

Bb: I   V⁴₃   I⁶   I   IV⁶   I⁶   E min.: i   V⁴₃   i⁶   i   iv⁶   i⁶

2. Label the scale degrees of these melodies. Then harmonize them in SATB format, using a I–IV⁶–I⁶ progression in each. Label the chords with Roman numerals.

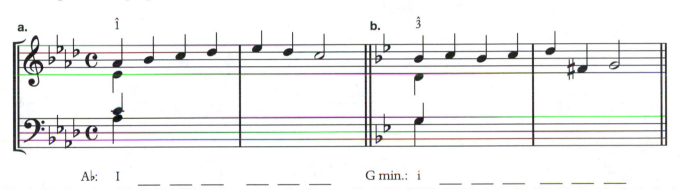

Ab: I   __ __ __ __ __   G min.: i   __ __ __ __ __ __

3. Realize the Roman numerals in SATB format. Then label the scale degrees of each melody.

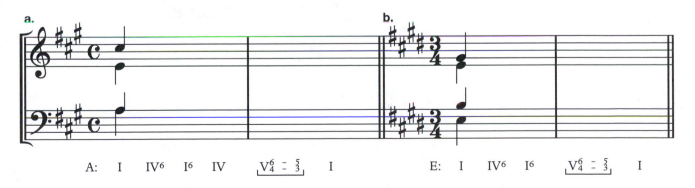

A: I   IV⁶   I⁶   IV   V⁶₄ – ⁵₃   I   E: I   IV⁶   I⁶   V⁶₄ – ⁵₃   I

4. Realize each figured bass in keyboard format. Then label the key, the scale degrees of the melody, and the Roman numerals.

a.

key: _____ ___ ___ ___ ___ ___ ___

b.

key: _____ ___ ___ ___ ___ ___ ___ ___ ___

E. COMPOSITION

1. Realize the Roman numerals in four-part harmony, keyboard format.

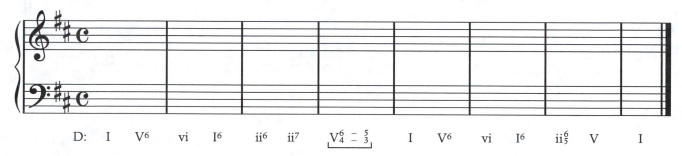

D: I   V⁶   vi   I⁶   ii⁶   ii⁷   V⁶₄ − ⁵₃   I   V⁶   vi   I⁶   ii⁶₅   V   I

2. Using the same harmonies and bass as above, write a duet (for instruments of your choice) by adding a melody.

F. ANALYSIS

1. Label the key, Roman numerals, and (where indicated) cadences in the following excerpts; then indicate which chords have a primarily passing (pass.) function.

a. J. S. Bach, Chorale 58

key: _____ ____   _____

b. J. S. Bach, *Applicatio*

key: _____

c. Jean-Philippe Rameau, Gavotte

cadence: _____

key: _____

d. Jean-Marie Leclair, Violin Sonata, Op. 2, No. 4, i

cadence: _____

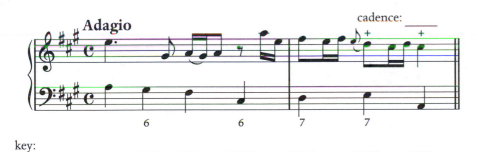

key: _____

e. Elisabetta de Gambarini, Minuet

cadence: _____

key: _____

f. Christoph Willibald Gluck, Pantomime from *Alceste*

key: _____

cadence: _____

g. Arcangelo Corelli, Chamber Sonata, Op. 2, No. 5, Sarabanda

cadence: _____

key: _____

h. Mauro Giuliani, Etude for Guitar, Op. 110, No. 15

$^6_4$ type: _____
key: _____ _____ _____ V^6_5/V _____ _____

cadence: _____

i. W. A. Mozart, String Quartet, K. 159, i

key: _____ _____ _____ _____

cadence: _____

2. Label the Roman numerals and cadences of the following excerpts.

a. Joseph Haydn, String Quartet, Op. 50, No. 4, ii

cadence: _____

key: _____ _____

b. W. A. Mozart, Piano Sonata, K. 570, ii

cadence: _____

key: _____

cadence: _____

Compare mm. 1–2 with mm. 3–4, In what ways are they similar, and in what ways are they different?

four

Chromatic Harmony

(handwritten top margin)
Ī ↗ I̅V̅
C E♭ G → G B♭ D → D F♯ A E

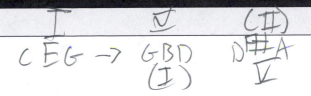

chapter

25

Applied Dominants of V

(handwritten)
Ī   V̅   (II)
C E G → G B D   D♯ A
        (I)   V

A. QUESTIONS FOR REVIEW

1. What scale degree is the root of V/V? *2nd*

2. What quality of triad (major, minor, or diminished) is V/V? What quality of seventh chord (diminished, half-diminished, minor, dominant, major) is V⁷/V? *D.*

3. V/V relates to V as V relates to what chord? *I*

4. In major keys, what chord tone in V/V and V⁷/V (root, third, or fifth) is raised with an accidental? What scale degree is this raised tone in the original key? In the key of the V chord? *Third, Fourth, Third*

5. In minor keys, what chord tones in V/V and V⁷/V (root, third, fifth, or seventh) are raised with an accidental? *Third and fifth*

6. What note may not be doubled in V/V? *Third*

7. What chords may follow V/V? *V*

8. What chord follows V$^4_2$/V? What chord follows V$^6_5$/V?

B. NOTATING V/V

1. In the following major keys, first notate the ii chord, then notate V/V. In each case, ii and V/V have the same notes *except that* the third of V/V must be raised by using an accidental.

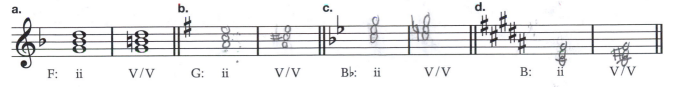

a.   b.   c.   d.

F: ii   V/V   G: ii   V/V   B♭: ii   V/V   B: ii   V/V

2. In the following minor keys, first notate the ii° chord, then notate V/V. In each case, ii° and V/V have the same notes *except that* whereas ii° does not use any accidentals in a minor key, the third and fifth of V/V must be raised by using accidentals.

F min.: ii°   V/V   G min.: ii°   V/V   B♭ min.: ii°   V/V   B min.: ii°   V/V

3. In each of the following:

- Above the staff, name the root of V and the root of V/V in the indicated major key.
- Then notate the indicated form of V/V, using the appropriate accidentals.
- Finally, name the leading tone in the key of V, and circle the note on the staff.

    a. root of V: C   **b.** root of V: E   **c.** root of V: A♭   **d.** root of V: D   **e.** root of V: B

    root of V/V: G   root of V/V: B   root of V/V: E♭   root of V/V: A   root of V/V: F♯

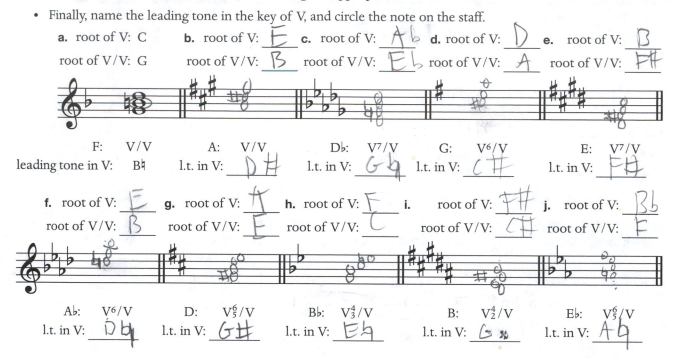

    F: V/V   A: V/V   D♭: V⁷/V   G: V⁶/V   E: V⁷/V

leading tone in V: B♮   l.t. in V: D♯   l.t. in V: G♮   l.t. in V: C♯   l.t. in V: F♯

    f. root of V: E   **g.** root of V: A♯   **h.** root of V: F   **i.** root of V: F♯   **j.** root of V: B♭

    root of V/V: B   root of V/V: E   root of V/V: C   root of V/V: C♯   root of V/V: F

    A♭: V⁶/V   D: V⁶₅/V   B♭: V⁴₃/V   B: V⁴₂/V   E♭: V⁶₅/V

l.t. in V: D♮   l.t. in V: G♯   l.t. in V: E♮   l.t. in V: G𝄪   l.t. in V: A♮

4. In each of the following:

- Above the staff, name the root of V and the root of V/V in the indicated minor key.
- Then notate the indicated form of V/V, using the appropriate accidentals.
- Finally, name the leading tone in the key of V, and circle the note on the staff.

    a. root of V: G   **b.** root of V: D   **c.** root of V: B   **d.** root of V: G♯   **e.** root of V: C

    root of V/V: D   root of V/V: A   root of V/V: F♯   root of V/V: D♯   root of V/V: G

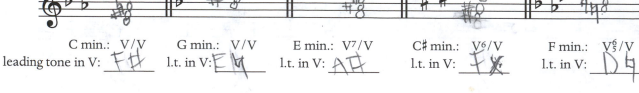

    C min.: V/V   G min.: V/V   E min.: V⁷/V   C♯ min.: V⁶/V   F min.: V⁶₅/V

leading tone in V: F♯   l.t. in V: E♮   l.t. in V: A♯   l.t. in V: F𝄪   l.t. in V: D♮

f. root of V: _____   **g.** root of V: _____   **h.** root of V: _____   **i.** root of V: _____   **j.** root of V: _____

root of V/V: _____   root of V/V: _____   root of V/V: _____   root of V/V: _____   root of V/V: _____

A min.: V/V   D min.: V$^6_5$/V   B min.: V$^4_2$/V   B♭ min.: V^6/V   F♯ min.: V$^4_3$/V

l.t. in V: _____   l.t. in V: _____   l.t. in V: _____   l.t. in V: _____   l.t. in V: _____

C. REALIZING ROMAN NUMERALS

1. Realize the Roman numerals for the following harmonic progressions in SATB format (remember to use an accidental in the V/V chords).

a.

B♭: I   V/V   V

b.

D: IV   V^7/V   V

c.

A: I   V   V^6/V   V

d.

F: V   V$^6_5$/V   V

e.

A♭: ii^6 V$^6_5$/V   V

f.

B♭: I   IV   V/V   V

g.

E♭: I   V/V   V$^6_4$ − $^5_3$
(cad. $^6_4$−V)

h.

F: I   V/V   V^7 I

i.

D: I   vi   I$^6_4$ (passing)   V^6/V   V$^6_4$ − $^5_3$ I
(cad. $^6_4$−V)

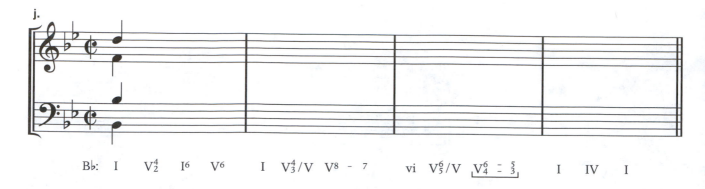

j.

Bb: I V_2^4 I^6 V^6 I V_3^4/V V^{8-7} vi V_5^6/V $\underline{V_4^6 - {}_3^5}$ I   IV   I

2. Realize the Roman numerals of the following minor-key passages in SATB format. Remember that minor keys require two accidentals in a V/V chord.

G min.:   i   V/V   V   C# min.:   i   V V^7/V V   D min.:   i iv^7 V_5^6/V V

d.

B min.:   i V_3^4 i^6 $ii^{ø6}_5$ V_2^4 i^6 $ii^{ø6}_5$ V^6/V $\underline{V_4^6 - {}_3^5}$ i $\overset{\text{pedal}}{iv_4^6}$ i
                                                              (cad. ${}_4^6$–V)

3. Realize the Roman numerals in keyboard format.

A min.:   i   V/V   V   D: I I^6 V^7/V V   Db: I V_3^4/V V

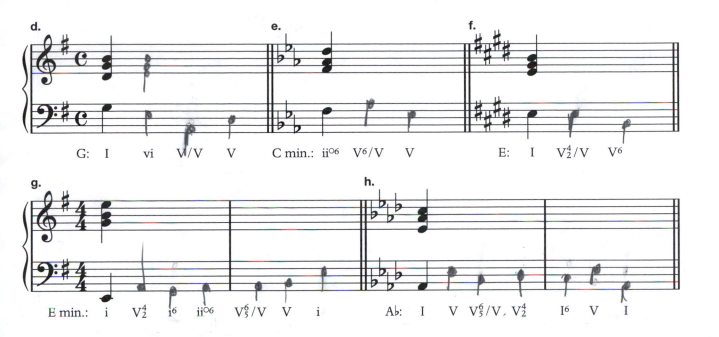

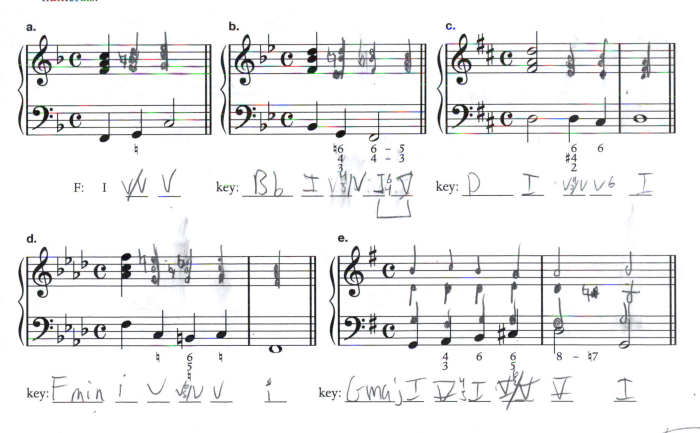

D. REALIZING FIGURED BASS

1. Realize each figured bass in keyboard format. Then identify the key and Roman numerals.

f.

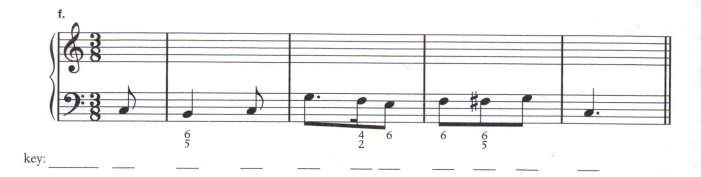

key: _____ __

2. Realize each figured bass in SATB format. Then identify the key and Roman numerals.

a.

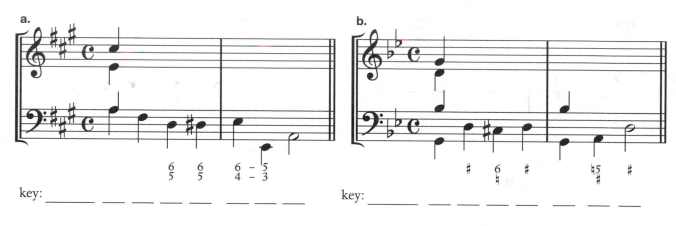

key: _____

b.

key: _____

c.

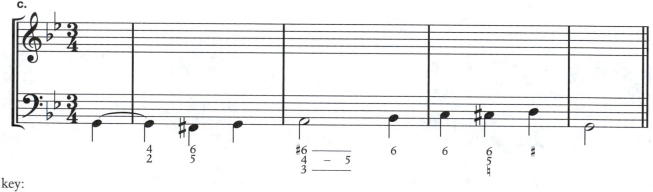

key: _____

d.

key: _____

3. J. J. Quantz, Sonata I in D, Gavotte, from *Sonatas for Flute*, Book III

- Provide a figured bass accompaniment.

- Do not worry about parallel perfect intervals between your figured bass realization and flute melody.

- Label the Roman numerals.

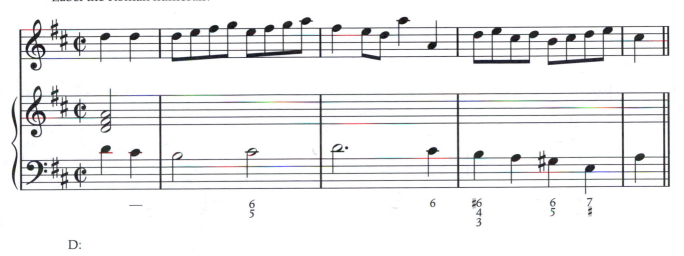

D:

E. HARMONIZING MELODIES

Harmonize each of the following melodies in SATB format.

- First label the scale degrees of the melody.

- Then provide a bass line and Roman numerals for each note of the melody.

- Use an applied dominant to harmonize the raised $\hat{4}$.

- Finally, fill in the inner voices.

Hint: V/V may move to V^7.

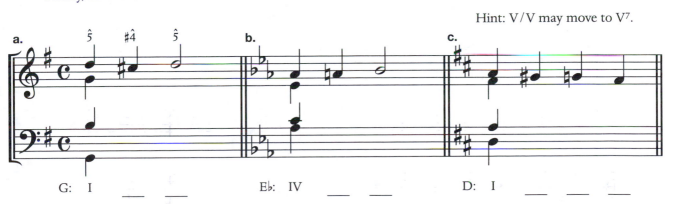

Hint: you may use two V/V chords in a row.

d.

F: I ___ ___ ___ ___ ___   F♯ min.: i ___ ___ ___ ___

f.

key: ___ ___ ___ ___

g.

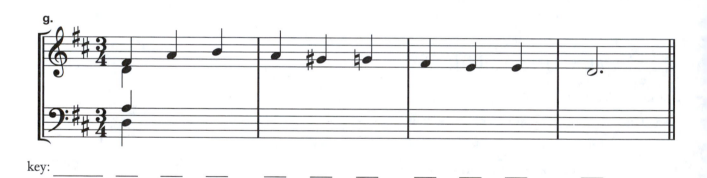

key: ___ ___ ___ ___

F. COMPOSITION

1. Realize the following Roman numerals in keyboard format. Measures 9–12 may repeat measures 1–4.

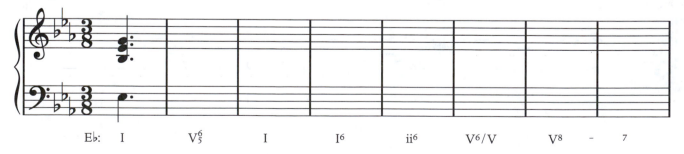

E♭:   I   V$^6_5$ I   I^6 ii^6 V^6/V   V^8 – 7

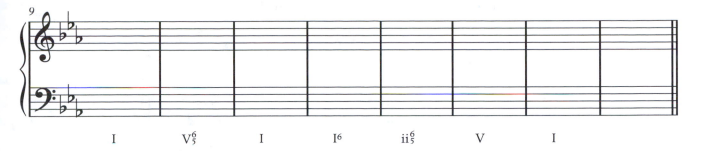

I   V$^6_5$ I   I^6 ii$^6_5$ V   I

2. Compose a melody and keyboard part based on (1):

   • Using the same notes of the harmonization in (1), choose an accompaniment
     pattern for the keyboard part such as an oom-pah-pah pattern or arpeggiation
     (you can find examples in earlier composition assignments).

   • Then compose a melody to go with the keyboard part.

   • Make sure to put in the key and time signatures for the melody part; if the
     melody is to be played by a transposing instrument, make sure to use the cor-
     rect key signature and to transpose the notes accordingly.

   • Measures 9–12 should be the same, or almost the same, as measures 1–4.

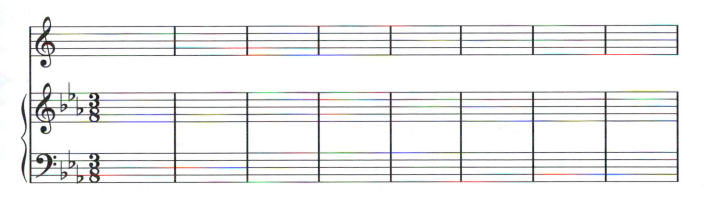

G. ANALYSIS

1. Label the keys and Roman numerals in the following excerpts, and circle the applied chords.

a. J. S. Bach, Chorale 293

b. Fanny Robinson, "St. Monica" (hymn)

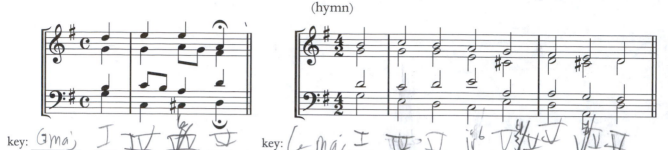

key: Gmaj I IV V̄ V̄

key: Gmaj I IV V i⁶ V̄/V̄ V̄/V̄

c. Robert Schumann, "Ein Choral" ("A Chorale")

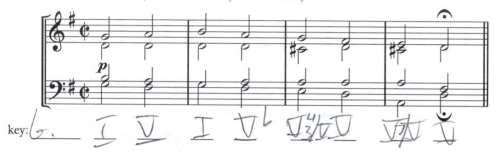

key: G. I V I V̄⁶ V̄³/V̄ V̄/V̄ V̄

d. Henry Purcell, "The Sailor's Dance," from *Dido and Aeneas*

Note that there is a somewhat unusual embellishing tone on the last quarter note of measure 3.

Violins

Viola
Cello and Bass

key: B♭ I V I⁶ IV⁶ V I V̄/V V

e. Ludwig van Beethoven, Piano Sonata, Op. 10, No. 1, iii

key: E♭ I V̄⁴₂ I V̄⁴₃ I ii⁶ V♭₅/V̄ V̄

f. W. A. Mozart, Concerto for Horn and Orchestra, K 447, i

key: _____ _____ _____ _____ _____

g. Fernando Sor, Sonata for Guitar, Op. 22, Trio

key: _____ _____ _____ _____ _____ _____

h. Luigi Cherubini, *Lodoïska*, Act I, scene i

key: _____ _____ _____ _____ _____ _____

i. Ludwig van Beethoven, Sonata for Piano Op. 2, No. 2, iii

key: _____ _____ _____

j. Niccolò Piccinni, "Se il ciel mi divide," from *Alessandro nell'Indie*

Di - vi - sa un mo - men - to dal dol - ce te - so - ro non

key: _____

vi - vo, non mo - ro, non vi - vo, non mo - ro,

Translation: Separated for a moment from my sweet treasure, I neither live nor die . . .

k. Maria Theresia von Paradis, "Vaterlandlied" ("Song of My Homeland")

Ich weiß ein deut - sches Mäd - chen, ihr Aug ist blau und

key: _____

sanft ihrBlick, und gut ihr Herz, und blau, o Her - da, blau ihr Aug.

I⁶ (V⁶/IV)

Translation: I know a German lass, her eye is blue and glance is soft, and her heart is good, and blue,
o Herda blue her eye.

1. George M. Cohan, "Josephine"

key: _____   ___   ___   _____   ___   ___   ___   ___

2. Francis Johnson, "Cotillion"

- Label the Roman numerals with a new chord each time the bass changes.
- On the staves below, complete a simplified harmonic model of the passage in four-part harmony, keyboard format.
- Compose a piece based on these harmonies, for voice or a melody instrument accompanied by keyboard, using a meter of your choice.

3. Franz Schubert, "Lied," D. 284

Label the Roman numerals.

Text and Translation:

Es ist so angenehm, so süss,
Um einen lieben Mann zu spielen,
Entzückend, wie ein Paradies,
Des Mannes Feuerkuss zu fühlen.

It is so pleasant, so sweet
To frolic with a man whom you love,
Enchanting as paradise
To feel the man's fiery kisses.

Note how the musical setting interacts with the lines and rhyme scheme of the poem.

- Where is the musical climax of the song?
- What melodic, harmonic, and rhythmic features help bring out this climax?

NAME: ....

26 Other Applied Chords

A. QUESTIONS FOR REVIEW

1. How do you determine what note should be the root of an applied V chord? How do you figure out what note should be the root of an applied vii°7 or vii°6 chord?

2. What is the quality of the triad (major, minor, or diminished) of an applied V chord?

3. What is the quality of the seventh chord (diminished, half-diminished, minor, dominant, major) in an applied V7? In an applied vii°7? In an applied viiø7?

4. In an applied dominant, what note functions as a leading tone? What special voice-leading rules apply to this note?

5. What qualities of chords (major, minor, or diminished) can follow an applied dominant? What qualities cannot, and why?

6. What applied chord might be used to harmonize lowered $\hat{7}$?

7. In a major key, what applied chord might be used to harmonize raised $\hat{1}$? Raised $\hat{5}$? Raised $\hat{2}$?

B. SPELLING APPLIED DOMINANTS

1. Spell the applied V chords:
   - Identify the root of the goal chord for the indicated applied chord.
   - Then determine the applied chord's root.
   - Finally, notate the applied chord, making sure to use the proper accidentals.

   a. root of vi: C   **b.** root of ii: C   **c.** root of vi: B   **d.** root of IV: D   **e.** root of ii: Bb
   root of V/vi: G   root of V/ii: G   root of V/vi: F#   root of V/IV: A   root of V/ii: F#

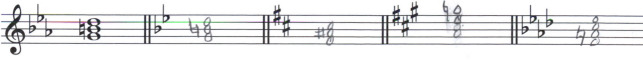

Eb: V/vi   Bb: V/ii   D: V/vi   A: V7/IV   Ab: V7/ii

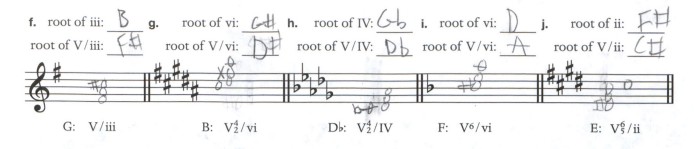

f. root of iii: __B__   g. root of vi: __G#__   h. root of IV: __Gb__   i. root of vi: __D__   j. root of ii: __F#__
root of V/iii: __F#__   root of V/vi: __D#__   root of V/IV: __Db__   root of V/vi: __A__   root of V/ii: __C#__

G: V/iii   B: V$^4_2$/vi   D♭: V$^4_2$/IV   F: V^6/vi   E: V$^6_5$/ii

2. Spell the applied vii° chords:

   • Identify the root of the goal chord for the indicated applied chord.

   • Then determine the applied chord's root.

   • Finally, notate the applied vii°^{6}, vii°^{7}, or vii°^{ø7} chord, making sure to use the proper accidentals.

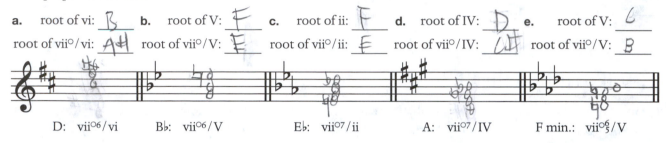

a. root of vi: __B__   b. root of V: __F__   c. root of ii: __F__   d. root of IV: __D__   e. root of V: __G__
root of vii°/vi: __A#__   root of vii°/V: __E__   root of vii°/ii: __E__   root of vii°/IV: __C#__   root of vii°/V: __B__

D: vii^{ø6}/vi   B♭: vii^{ø6}/V   E♭: vii$^{°7}$/ii   A: vii$^{°7}$/IV   F min.: vii$^{°6}_5$/V

3. Spell the applied dominant chords:

   • Identify the root of the goal chord for the indicated applied chord.

   • Then determine the applied chord's root.

   • Finally, notate the applied chord in these minor keys, making sure to use the proper accidentals.

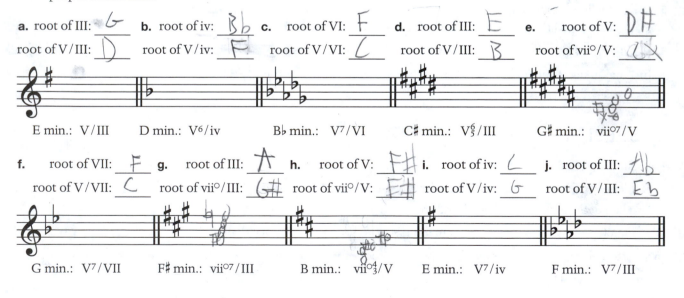

a. root of III: __G__   b. root of iv: __B♭__   c. root of VI: __F__   d. root of III: __E__   e. root of V: __D#__
root of V/III: __D__   root of V/iv: __F__   root of V/VI: __C__   root of V/III: __B__   root of vii°/V: __C#__

E min.: V/III   D min.: V^6/iv   B♭ min.: V^7/VI   C# min.: V$^6_5$/III   G# min.: vii$^{°7}$/V

f. root of VII: __F__   g. root of III: __A__   h. root of V: __F#__   i. root of iv: __C__   j. root of III: __A♭__
root of V/VII: __C__   root of vii°/III: __G#__   root of vii°/V: __E#__   root of V/iv: __G__   root of V/III: __E♭__

G min.: V^7/VII   F# min.: vii$^{°7}$/III   B min.: vii$^{°4}_3$/V   E min.: V^7/iv   F min.: V^7/III

C. REALIZING ROMAN NUMERALS

1. Realize the following Roman numerals in SATB format; make sure to use accidentals where needed.

a.

b.

c.

A: I   V/ii   ii   B♭:   V   V⁷/vi   vi   A♭:   I   V⁷/IV   IV

d.

e.

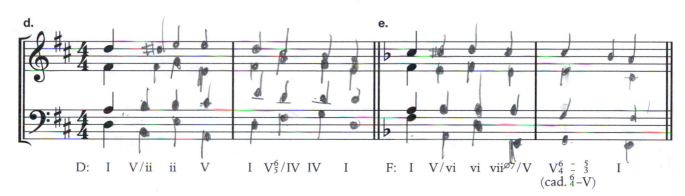

D: I   V/ii   ii   V   I   V$^6_5$/IV   IV   I   F: I   V/vi   vi   vii°⁷/V   V$^6_4$ $-$ $^5_3$ I

(cad. $^6_4$–V)

f.

g.

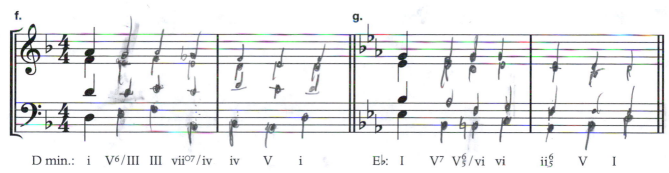

D min.:   i   V⁶/III   III   vii°⁷/iv   iv   V   i   E♭:   I   V⁷   V$^6_5$/vi   vi   ii$^6_5$ V   I

h.

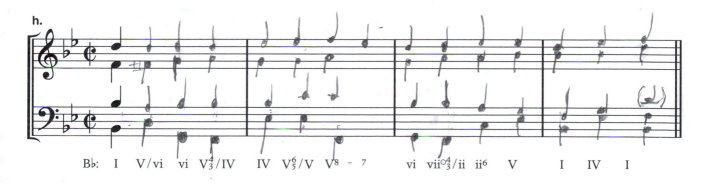

B♭:   I   V/vi   vi   V$^4_3$/IV   IV   V$^6_5$/V   V⁸ $-$ ⁷   vi   vii°$^4_3$/ii   ii⁶   V   I   IV   I

i.

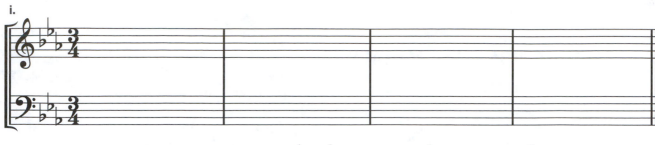

C min.:　i　V⁷/VI　VI　　vii°⁷/V　V⁶₄ — ⁵₃　　i　V⁶₅/III　III　V⁶₅/iv　iv　i
　　　　　　　　　　　　　　　　　　　　　(cad. ⁶₄–V)

j.

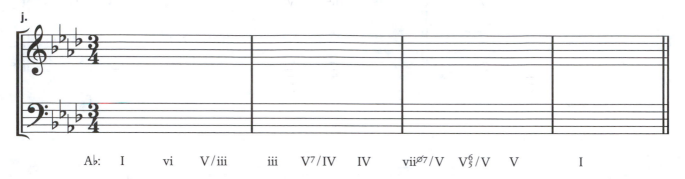

A♭:　I　vi　V/iii　iii　V⁷/IV　IV　viiø⁷/V　V⁶₅/V　V　　I

2. Realize the following Roman numerals in keyboard format; make sure to use accidentals where needed.

a.　　　　　　　　　　**b.**　　　　　　　　　　**c.**

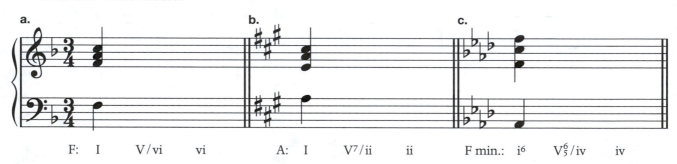

F:　I　V/vi　vi　　　A:　I　V⁷/ii　ii　　　F min.:　i⁶　V⁶₅/iv　iv

d.　　　　　　　　　　　　　　　**e.**

F♯ min.:　i　V⁶₅　i　V/III　III　ii°⁶　V　i　　Eb:　I　V⁶　vii°⁶/V　V　I　V⁷/IV　IV⁶₄　I
　　pedal

f.　　　　　　　　　　　　　　**g.**

B min.:　i　V⁶₅/III　III　V⁷/iv　iv　V　i　　G:　I　V　V⁶₅/vi　vi　vii°⁷/V　V　I

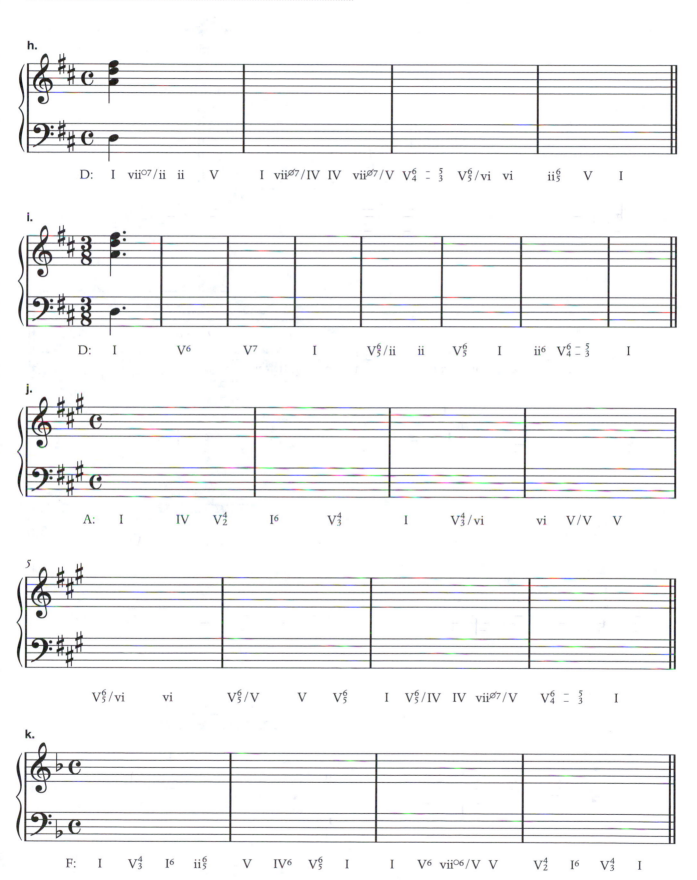

h.

D: I vii°7/ii ii   V   I vii∅7/IV IV vii∅7/V V$^6_4$ − $^5_3$ V$^6_5$/vi vi   ii$^6_5$ V   I

i.

D: I   V^6 V^7 I   V$^6_5$/ii ii V$^6_5$ I   ii^6 V$^6_4$ − $^5_3$ I

j.

A: I   IV   V$^4_2$ I^6 V$^4_3$ I   V$^4_3$/vi   vi V/V V

5

V$^6_5$/vi   vi   V$^6_5$/V   V   V$^6_5$ I   V$^6_5$/IV IV vii∅7/V   V$^6_4$ − $^5_3$ I

k.

F: I   V$^4_3$ I^6 ii$^6_5$ V   IV^6 V$^6_5$ I   I   V^6 vii°6/V V   V$^4_2$ I^6 V$^4_3$ I

D. REALIZING FIGURED BASS

1. Realize each figured bass in keyboard format. Then label the Roman numerals of the harmonies; note that there is at least one applied chord in each.

a.

b.

B♭:   I   V/ii   ii   V

G: __   __   __   __

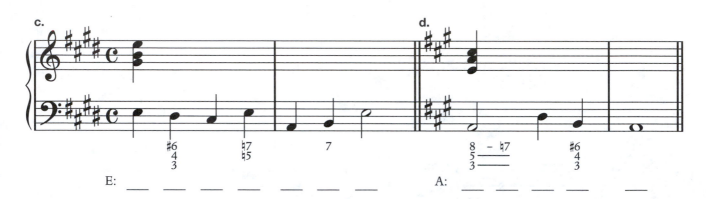

c.

d.

E: __   __   __   __

A: __   __   __   __

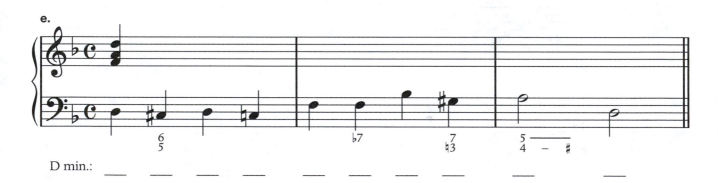

e.

D min.: __   __   __   __   __   __   __   __

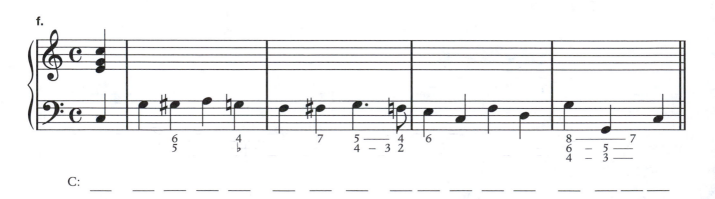

f.

C: __   __   __   __   __   __   __

g.

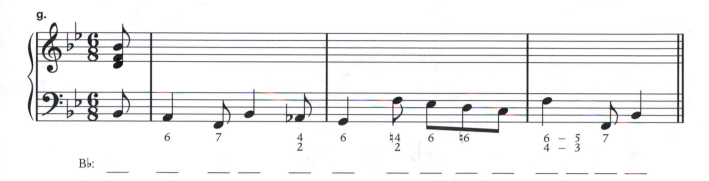

Bb: ___ ___ ___ ___ ___ ___ ___ ___ ___

h.

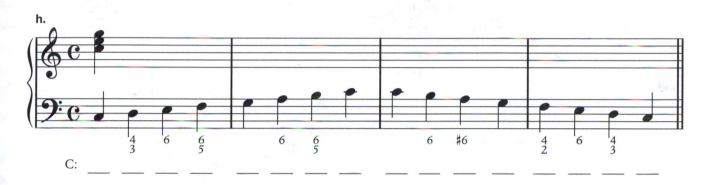

C: ___ ___ ___ ___ ___ ___ ___ ___ ___ ___

2. Realize each figured bass in SATB format and label the Roman numerals of the harmonies; note that there is at least one applied chord in each.

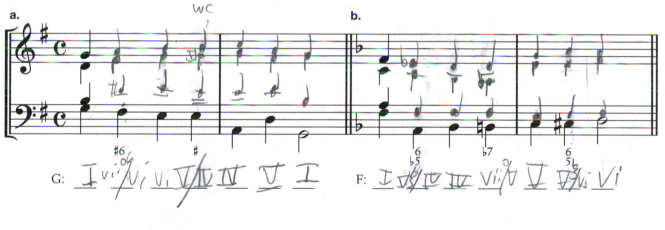

c.

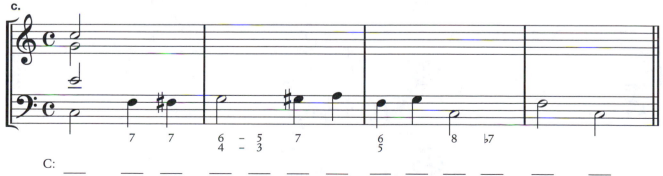

C: ___ ___ ___ ___ ___ ___ ___ ___ ___

d.

F# min.: __ __ __ __ __ __ __ __

e.

C: min.: __ __ __ __ __ __ __ __

E. HARMONIZING MELODIES

1. Determine the key and harmonize the following melodies by providing a bass line and Roman numerals, using at least one applied chord in each. Then fill in the inner voices in SATB format.

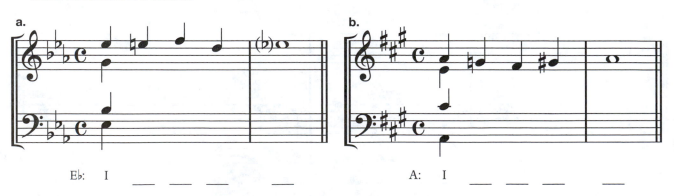

a.

E♭:   I   __ __ __ __ __ __

b.

A: I   __ __ __ __

c.

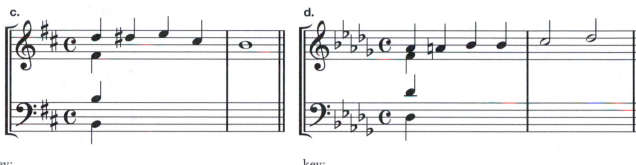

key: ____ __ __ __ __ __ __

d.

key: ____ __ __ __ __ __ __ __

e.

$$\begin{matrix} 6 & - & 5 \\ 4 & - & 3 \end{matrix}$$

key: ____ __ __ __ __ __ __ __ __

f.

key: ____ __ __ __ __ __ __ __ __ __

2. Harmonize the following melodies:

- Identify the key and provide a bass line and Roman numerals.
- Use an applied chord to harmonize each note that is marked with an asterisk. In deciding which applied chords to use, it will be helpful to first think what chord can be used to harmonize the note that follows the asterisked one (since this will be the goal chord of the applied chord).
- Then fill in the inner voices in SATB format.

a.

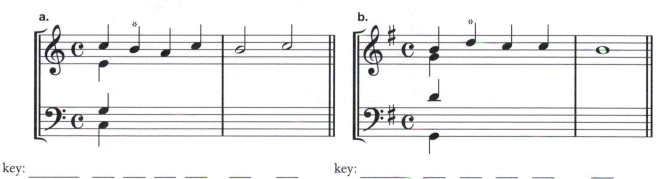

key: ____ __ __ __ __ __ __

b.

key: ____ __ __ __ __ __ __ __

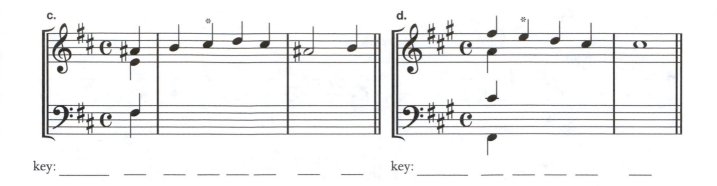

key: _____ _ _ _ _ _ _ _ _

key: _____ _ _ _ _ _ _ _

key: _____ _ _ _ _ _ _ _ _ _

F. IDENTIFYING ERRORS

In the following harmonic progressions, find and circle errors of voice leading or harmonic progression. Identify the type of error by writing above or below the staff.

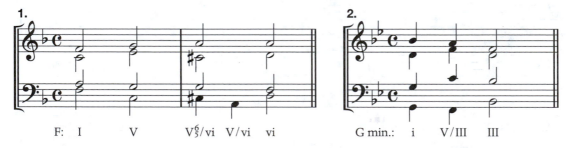

1.

F: I   V   V$^6_5$/vi V/vi vi

2.

G min.: i   V/III   III

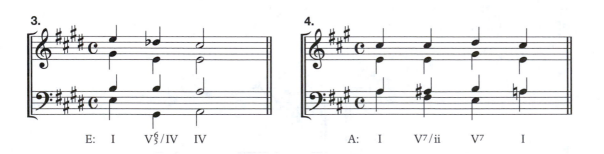

3.

E: I   V$^6_5$/IV   IV

4.

A: I   V^7/ii   V^7 I

G. COMPOSITION

1. Harmonize the following melody, using block chords, with only one chord per measure.

- Begin by providing a bass line in dotted half notes, then adding Roman numerals. The bass should not double leading tones or raised notes in the melody, and as always, there should be no parallel octaves or fifths.

- Use applied dominants where suggested by the melodic line.

- Label the embellishing tones in the melody.

- Fill in the inner voices, maintaining good voice leading.

2. Provide a keyboard accompaniment for the melody in (1), using the same harmonies and bass line, but with different time values and an accompaniment pattern, as in previous chapters.

3. Write a short composition in a key and meter of your choice, for keyboard, guitar, or an ensemble of your choice.

- Start by filling in the harmonic outline below in four-part harmony, keyboard format. In measures 1–4, choose a **T–S–D–T** or **T–D–D–T** chord progression with one chord per measure.

Embellish the tonic harmony with a
T–D–D–T or **T–S–D–T** progression

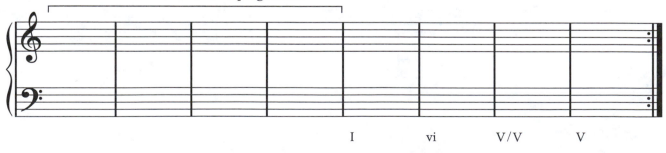

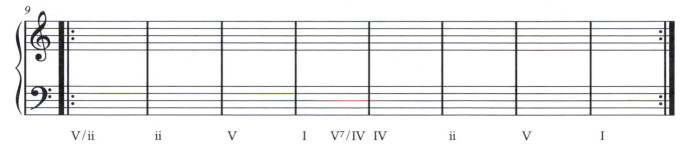

- Complete your composition, using the harmonic outline above.

H. ANALYSIS

Label the keys and Roman numerals in these excerpts; circle the secondary leading tone within each applied chord. Then, locate and label the cadences.

1. *Harmonia Sacra,* "How sad our state by nature is!"

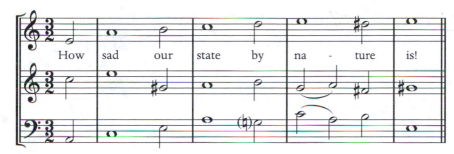

key: **A min.:**   **i** _____ _____ _____ _____ _____

2. J. S. Bach, Chorale 7

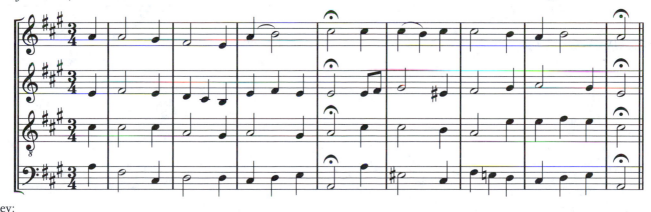

key: _____ _____ _____ _____ _____   _____ _____ _____ _____

3. J. S. Bach, Chorale 24

key: D maj   I   viib/vi vi   viib$^{4}_{3}$ V   I

4. Mauro Giuliani, Etude for Guitar, Op. 100, No. 2

5. Marie-Charlotte Campet de Saujon, "Les regrets"

de - vant té - moins   sans trou - ver de   pas - sa - ge,

pleurs   biens   a - mers_____   re - tom - bent sur__ mon cœur.

key: A min   V$^{6}_{5}$ i   V^{7}/iv   V   I   V^{7}/iv   V^{7}b   VII-06   i6   V   i

Translation: In front of witnesses, without finding a path, bitter tears fall back upon my heart.

6. Jacob J. Sawyer, "Bob-o-link Mazurka"

key: _____ _____ _____ _____ _____ _____ _____ _____

7. Corona Schröter, "Jugendlied" ("Children's Song")

Also label the embellishing tones.

Als ich noch ein Kna - be_ war, sperr - te man_ mich_

key: _____

4

ein,_____ und so sass ich man - ches Jahr

7

ü - ber_ mir al - lein,_____ wie in Mut - ter - leib.

$V_4^6 - {}_2^4$
(cad. $_4^6 - V_2^4$)

_____ _____ _____ _____ _____ _____

Translation: When I was still a boy, I was locked in. And so I remained for many years alone by myself, as if in my mother's womb.

8. Robert Schumann, "Von fremden Ländern und Menschen" ("Of Foreign Lands and People")

key: _____

9. W. A. Mozart, String Quartet, K. 458, ii

key: _____

Compare the above phrase (9) with the one in (8). Which one seems more symmetrical and balanced, and which one has more unexpected twists and turns? Describe some features in each that contribute to this sense.

10. Alessandro Scarlatti, "Son tutta duolo"

Son tut-ta duo - lo,   non ho che af-fan - ni

key: _____

e mi dà mor - te   pe - na cru - del,   pe - na cru - del

e mi_ dà mor - te   pe - na cru - del,   pe - na cru - del.

Translation: I am deeply sad, filled with worries, and dying from cruel pain.

11. Jean-Paul-Égide Martini, "Plaisir d'amour" ("The Pleasure of Love")

key: _____

Translation: The pleasures of love last but for a moment, [but] love's chagrin lasts for a lifetime.

Complete a simplified harmonic model of this passage in four-part harmony, keyboard format, one or two chords per measure.

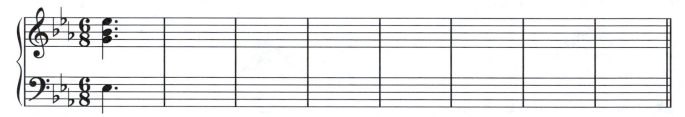

What pitch resolves in a somewhat unexpected fashion? How might this relate to the text setting?

NAME: ....

27 Modulation to the Dominant Key

A. QUESTIONS FOR REVIEW

1. What is a modulation?

2. What is a main key?

3. When modulating to the key of V, what scale degree should you raise? This raised note is equivalent to what scale degree in the new key?

4. What is a pivot chord? What are some possible pivot chords in modulating from I to V?

5. What distinguishes a modulation from a tonicization?

B. DETERMINING POSSIBLE PIVOT CHORDS

- Write the chords in the indicated major key.
- Then write the chords in the dominant key, adding accidentals where necessary.
- Circle the chords that could serve as pivots between the main key and the key of V (that is, the chords that are found in both keys) and list them beneath the staves.

1.

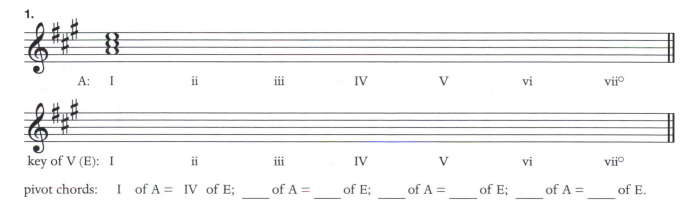

A: I   ii   iii   IV   V   vi   vii°

key of V (E):   I   ii   iii   IV   V   vi   vii°

pivot chords: I   of A =   IV   of E;   ____ of A = ____ of E;   ____ of A = ____ of E;   ____ of A = ____ of E.

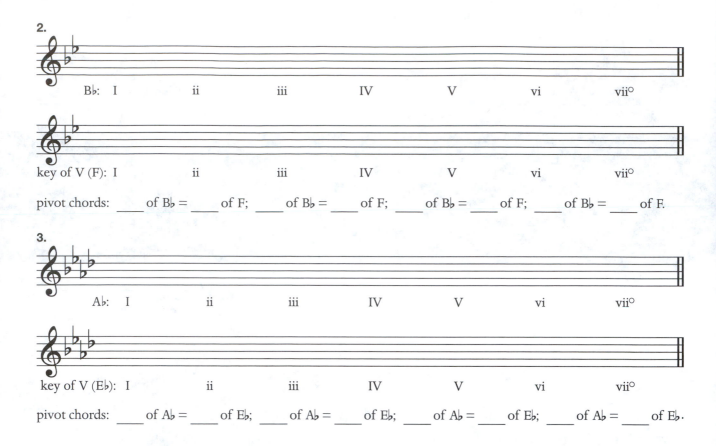

2.

Bb: I   ii   iii   IV   V   vi   vii°

key of V (F): I   ii   iii   IV   V   vi   vii°

pivot chords: ___ of Bb = ___ of F; ___ of Bb = ___ of F; ___ of Bb = ___ of F; ___ of Bb = ___ of F.

3.

Ab: I   ii   iii   IV   V   vi   vii°

key of V (Eb): I   ii   iii   IV   V   vi   vii°

pivot chords: ___ of Ab = ___ of Eb; ___ of Ab = ___ of Eb; ___ of Ab = ___ of Eb; ___ of Ab = ___ of Eb.

C. REALIZING ROMAN NUMERALS

1. Realize these Roman numerals in SATB format. Dotted boxes indicate the pivot chords. Remember to include accidentals where necessary.

2. Realize these Roman numerals in SATB format. In each case, the pivot chord is indicated in only one of the keys; on the blank line give the Roman numeral label of this pivot chord in the other key. Remember to add accidentals where necessary.

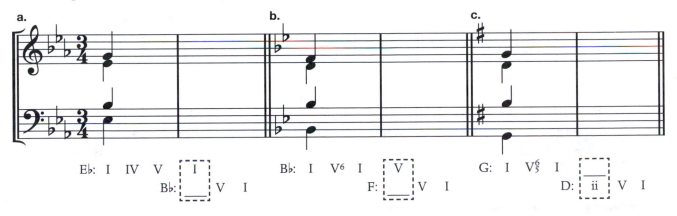

a.

Eb: I   IV   V   │ I │
Bb: │ ___ │ V   I

b.

Bb: I   V⁶   I   │ V │
F: │ ___ │ V   I

c.

G: I   V⁶₅   I   │ ii │
D: │ ii │ V   I

d.

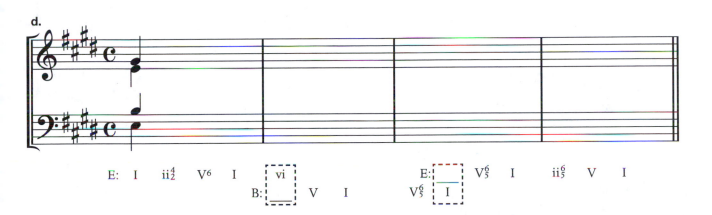

E: I   ii⁴₂   V⁶   I   │ vi │
B: │ ___ │ V   I

E: │ ___ │ V⁶₅   I   ii⁶₅   V   I
V⁶₅ │ I │

3. Realize the Roman numerals in SATB format, choosing a harmony that can serve as a pivot chord between these keys and labeling its Roman numeral (within both keys) on the blank lines provided.

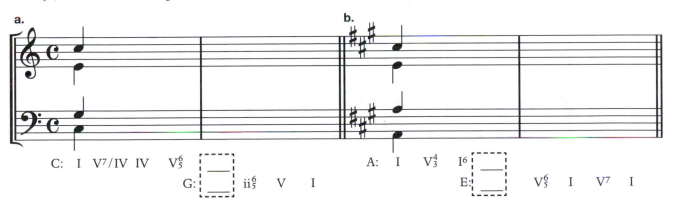

a.

C: I   V⁷/IV   IV   V⁶₅   │ ___ │
G: │ ___ │ ii⁶₅   V   I

b.

A: I   V⁴₃   I⁶   │ ___ │
E: │ ___ │ V⁶₅   I   V⁷   I

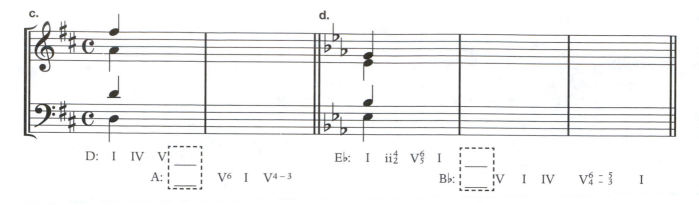

c.

D: I IV V _____
A: _____ V⁶ I V⁴⁻³

d.

E♭: I ii⁴₂ V⁶₅ I _____
B♭: _____ V I IV V⁶₄ ⁼ ⁵₃ I

4. Realize the Roman numerals in keyboard format. Where a blank line is provided, complete the labeling of the pivot chord. Where one of the pivot chords is not labeled, fill in the blank.

> Though "vi⁶" is rare in diatonic settings, it may substitute for I when used as a pivot chord.

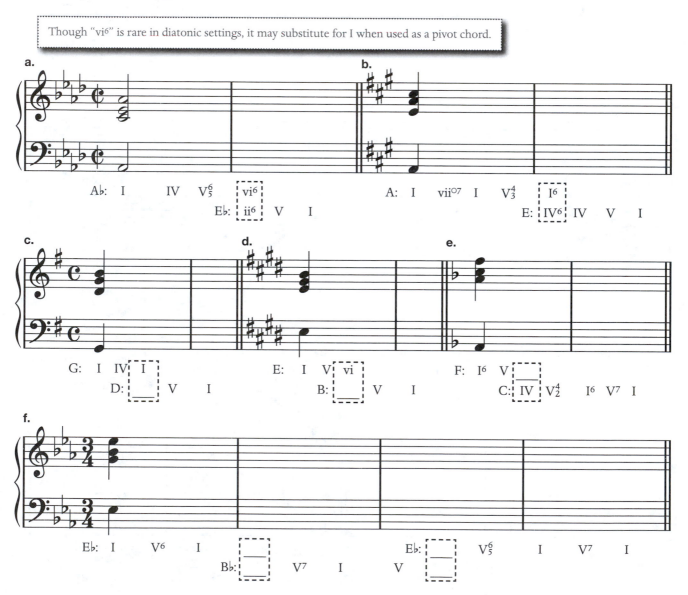

a.

A♭: I IV V⁶₅ vi⁶
E♭: ii⁶ V I

b.

A: I vii°⁷ I V⁴₃ I⁶
E: IV⁶ IV V I

c.

G: I IV I
D: _____ V I

d.

E: I V vi
B: _____ V I

e.

F: I⁶ V _____
C: IV V⁴₂ I⁶ V⁷ I

f.

E♭: I V⁶ I
B♭: _____ V⁷ I V _____
E♭: _____ V⁶₅ I V⁷ I

D. REALIZING FIGURED BASS

1. For each of the following:

- Realize the figured bass in the indicated format, then label the keys, Roman numerals, and cadences, making sure to indicate the modulations.

- Indicate pivot chords with a dotted box.

Keyboard format:

Hint: the third chord should be the pivot chord.

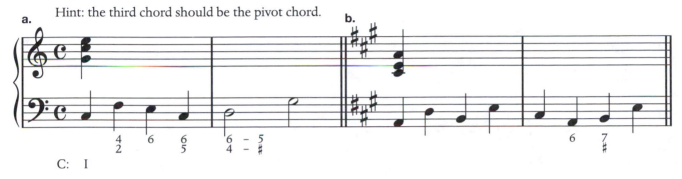

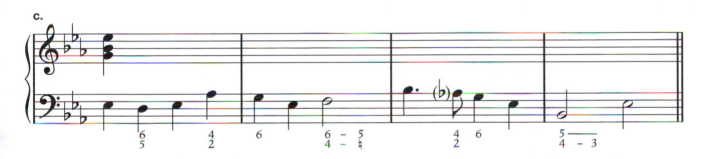

SATB format:

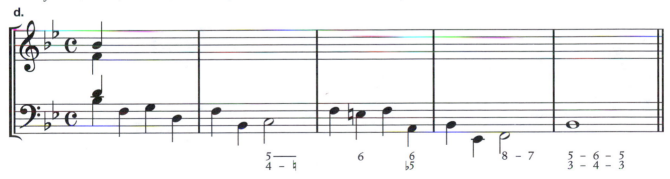

e.

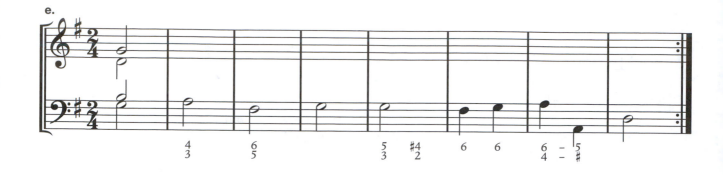

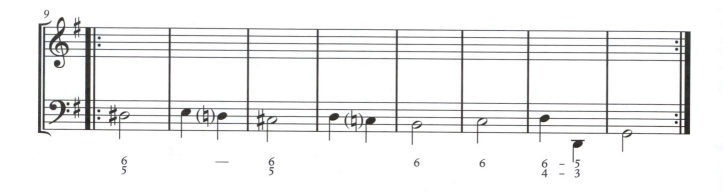

2. Realize each of the figured bass accompaniments in four-part harmony, keyboard format, indicating Roman numerals beneath the staff. Do not worry about any parallel perfect intervals that may arise between your figured realization and the given melody.

   a. Theophania Cecil, "St. Ignatius" (hymn)

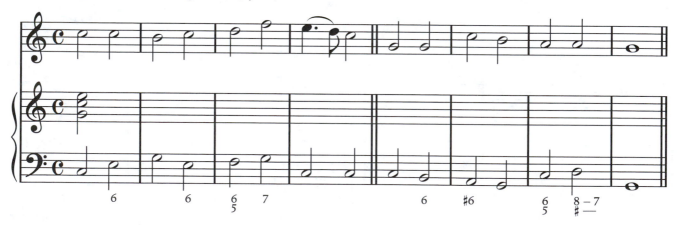

b. J. J. Quantz, Flute Sonata in D

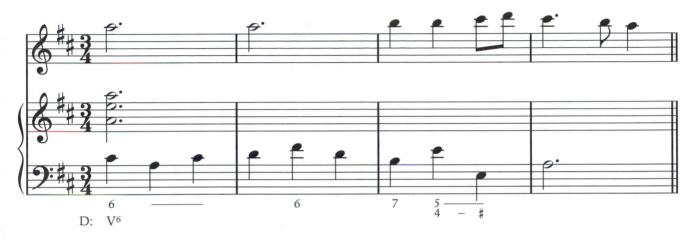

D: V⁶

c. Jacques-Martin Hotteterre, Flute Sonata, Op. 2, Rondeau, *"Le Baron"*

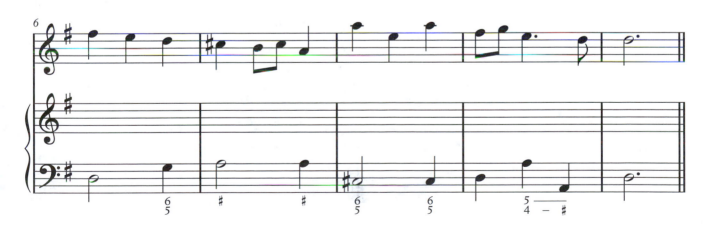

E. HARMONIZING MELODIES

1. Complete the harmonization of each melody by providing a bass line and Roman numerals and filling in the inner voices. In each case, modulate to the key of V using a pivot chord, and end with a cadence in the key of V.

2. Harmonize the following melodies in SATB format:

- Identify the key and harmonize the following melodies by providing a bass line and Roman numerals.
- Using a pivot chord, modulate to the key of V by the end of the first phrase, then back to the main key by the end of the second phrase. What in the melody hints that there will be a modulation to V in each of these?
- Finally, fill in the inner voices in SATB format.

a.

key: _____

b.

key: _____

3. Harmonize the following melodies in SATB format:

- Determine the key and add a bass line and Roman numerals, providing each note of the melody with a separate harmony.
- The fermatas indicate the location of the cadences (either an authentic cadence in the main key, a half cadence in the main key, or an authentic cadence in the key of V, as appropriate).
- Using a pivot chord, modulate to the key of V and back within each example.
- Finally, fill in the inner voices in SATB format.

a.

F: I

b.

key: _____

c.

key: _____

d.

key: _____

e.

key: _____

f.

key: _____

F. COMPOSITION

1. Realize the Roman numerals in keyboard format.

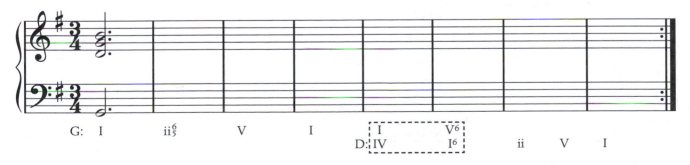

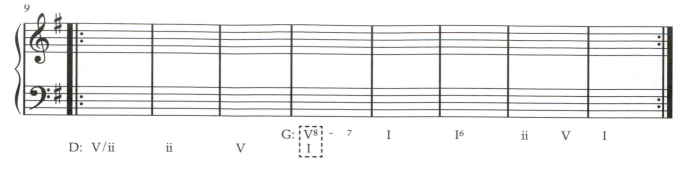

G: V⁸ – 7   I   I⁶   ii   V   I
   I

D: V/ii   ii   V

2. Realize the figured bass in keyboard format. Label the Roman numerals, indicating
pivot chords (with a dotted box) and modulations.

3. Compose a piece for keyboard and another instrument, using the same harmonies
as either (1) or (2) immediately preceding.

• Provide the key signature for all parts.

• Use the same notes in the keyboard part as previously, but use an accompaniment pattern, as in earlier chapters.

• As indicated in the score, measures 13–16 should be a transposed variant of
measures 5–8.

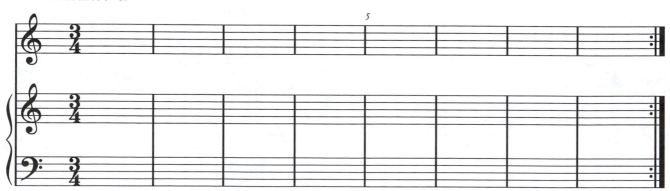

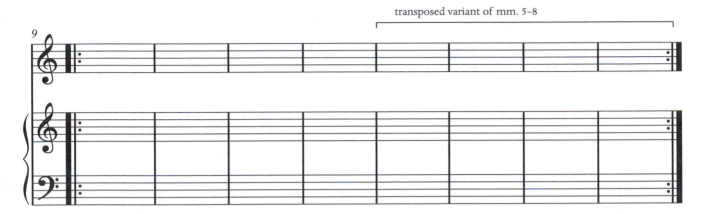

transposed variant of mm. 5–8

G. ANALYSIS

1. Analyze the following examples:

- Label the keys and Roman numerals, making sure to indicate the starting key, the change(s) of keys, and the pivot chords.
- Draw a dotted box around pivot chords showing their function in both keys.
- Label cadences, indicating key and type (PAC, IAC, HC, Phrygian, plagal).
- Notice that there are no blanks indicating where chord changes occur: you will have to determine the harmonic rhythm (the pace of the changes of harmony).

a. "Let us all with gladsome voice" (hymn)

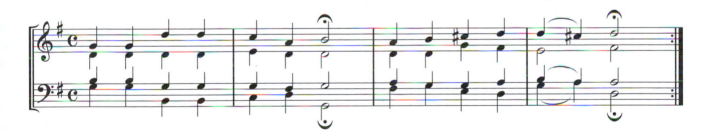

b. J. S. Bach, Chorale 192

c. Samuel Webbe, "Adeste Fidelis"

d. Jacob Sawyer, "Up in the Corner"

Most measures have one or two chords, but label three chords in measure 8.

e. Luigi Boccherini, String Quintet in E, iii

Most measures have one chord, but label two chords in measure 4 and three
chords in measure 7.

2. Decide whether each of the following examples includes modulations or tonicizations, and analyze the chords with Roman numerals accordingly. What are reasons for reading either a modulation or tonicization in each case? (There is at most one chord per bass note in each of these.)

a. "Freuet euch" (hymn)

Does this passage modulate? _____

b. W. A. Mozart, "In diesem heiligen Hallen" ("Within These Sacred Halls"), from *The Magic Flute*

In die - sen heil - gen_ Hal - len kennt man die_ Ra - che_ nicht,_ und

ist ein Mensch ge - fal - len, führt Lie - be_ ihn_ zur Pflicht

Translation: Within these sacred halls, revenge is banished. And should a person fall into sin, love will guide him back to his duty.

Does this passage modulate? _____

c. Joseph Haydn, String Quartet, Op. 50, No. 1, ii

Which measures include a voice exchange between the cello and first violin?

Does this passage modulate? ....

d. François-Joseph Gossec, Gavotte

Note: There are one or two chords at most in each bar.

Does this passage modulate? ....

e. Fernando Sor, Six Petite Pieces for Guitar, Op. 5, No. 4

Label only one or two chords per measure.

Does this passage modulate?

3. Anna Bon, Harpsichord Sonata

- Label the keys and cadences.
- Label the Roman numerals, with one or two chords per measure.
- On the staves below the score, complete a simplified harmonic model of this movement in keyboard format.
- How long are each of the four phrases in this movement? Which phrases seem expanded, and what creates this sense of expansion?
- How are the two phrases from the movement's first half altered when they return in the movement's second half?

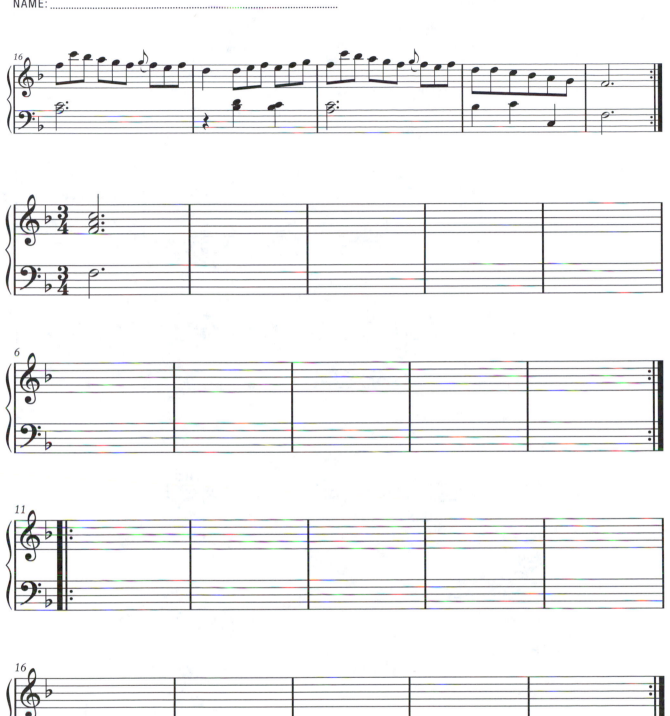

4. Carl Friedrich Abel, Flute Sonata Op. 6, No. 6, Minuet

- Label the keys, cadences, and Roman numerals.

- What helps create a sense of drive toward toward the cadence at the end of the movement's second phrase?

- What features produce an impression of instability at the start of the second half of the piece (in mm. 9–12)? How do the last four measures promote a return to stability?

28 Modulation to Closely Related Keys

chapter

A. QUESTIONS FOR REVIEW

1. What is a closely related key?

2. How can you tell that a modulation to a new key has occurred?

3. What changes when the music modulates from a minor key to its relative major? From a major key to its relative minor?

4. In a major-key piece that modulates to several keys, what key is usually the goal of the first modulation? What keys might follow this first modulation?

5. In a minor-key piece that modulates to several keys, what key is usually the goal of the first modulation? What other key might serve as the goal of the first modulation? What keys might follow the first modulation?

B. DETERMINING CLOSELY RELATED KEYS AND PIVOT CHORDS

1. List the closely related keys of the following:

    a. main key = A major; closely related keys = _____, _____, _____, _____, _____

    b. main key = E♭ major; closely related keys = _____, _____, _____, _____, _____

    c. main key = D minor; closely related keys = _____, _____, _____, _____, _____

2. For each of the following:

- Write the chords in the indicated keys. Use the key signature of the first key, and make sure to add accidentals where needed.

- Circle the chords that could serve as pivots between the two keys. List them beneath the staff, giving Roman numerals in both keys.

a.

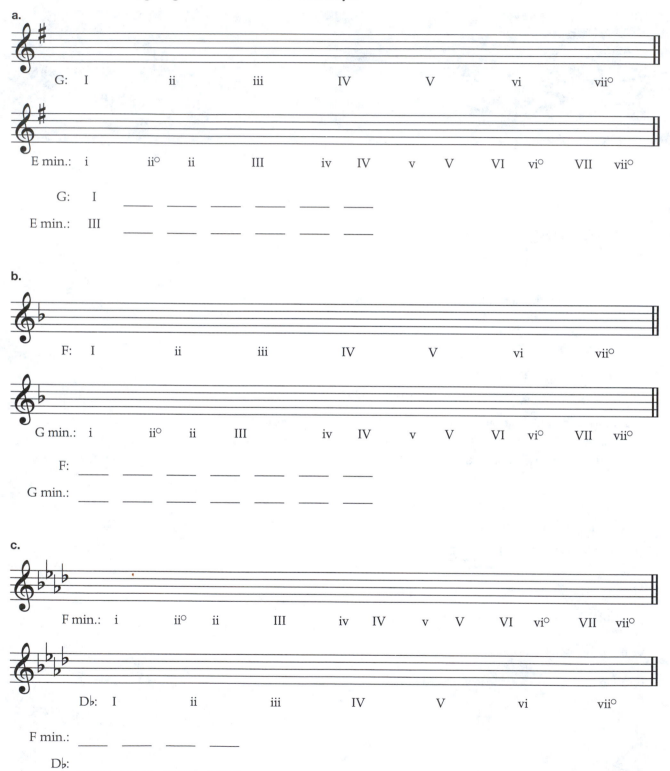

G: I   ii   iii   IV   V   vi   vii°

E min.:   i   ii°   ii   III   iv   IV   v   V   VI   vi°   VII   vii°

G: I   ___   ___   ___   ___   ___   ___

E min.:   III   ___   ___   ___   ___   ___   ___

b.

F: I   ii   iii   IV   V   vi   vii°

G min.:   i   ii°   ii   III   iv   IV   v   V   VI   vi°   VII   vii°

F: ___   ___   ___   ___   ___   ___   ___

G min.:   ___   ___   ___   ___   ___   ___   ___

c.

F min.:   i   ii°   ii   III   iv   IV   v   V   VI   vi°   VII   vii°

D♭:   I   ii   iii   IV   V   vi   vii°

F min.:   ___   ___   ___   ___

D♭:   ___   ___   ___   ___

C. REALIZING ROMAN NUMERALS

1. Realize these Roman numerals in SATB format. The chords in the dotted boxes are pivot chords.

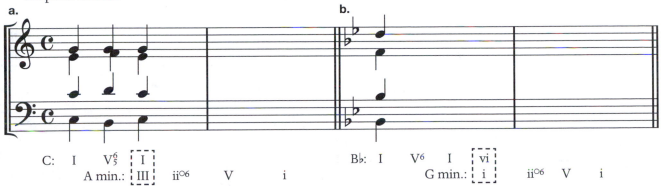

2. Complete each set of Roman numerals by supplying the pivot chord in the new key. Then realize the Roman numerals in SATB format.

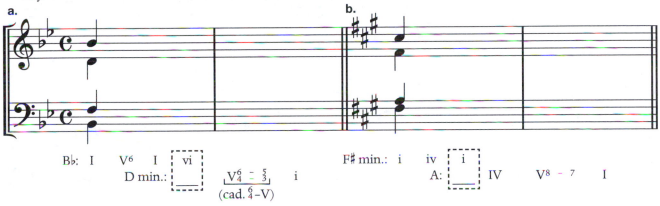

3. For each of the following:
- Choose a pivot chord that can modulate between the two keys and write its Roman numerals in the dotted box.
- To find the options for each pair of keys, you can create the same kind of list used in B2; in fact, the key relationship for the first exercise, F minor and D♭, is the same as worked out in B2(c).
- Finally, realize the Roman numerals.

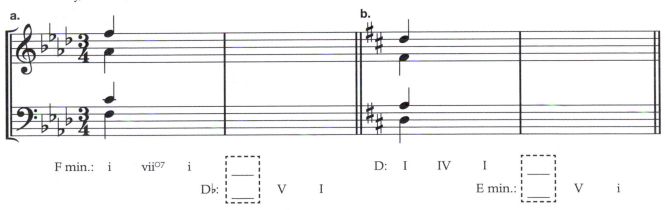

4. Realize the Roman numerals, completing the indication of pivot chords by filling in the missing Roman numerals.

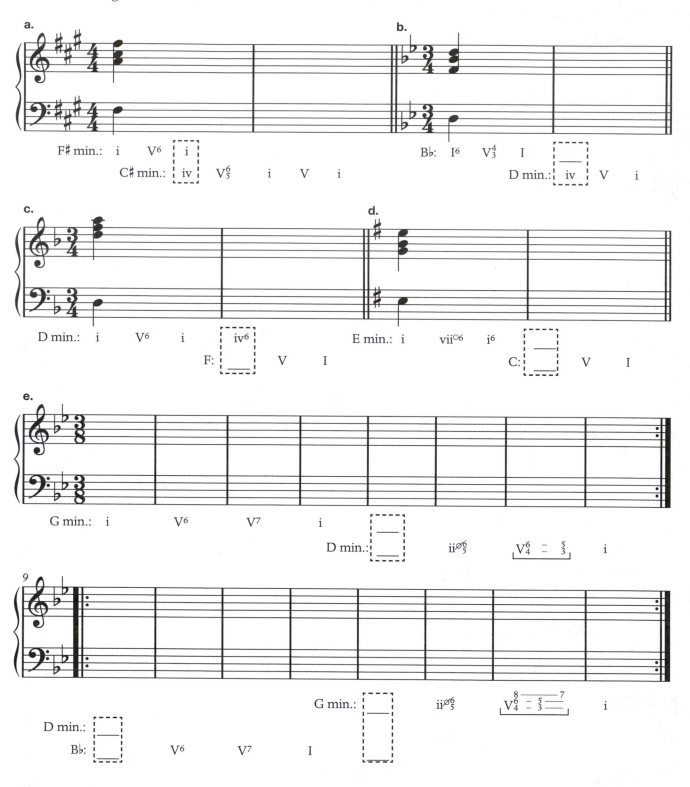

NAME: ....

5. Realize the Roman numerals in SATB format.

a.

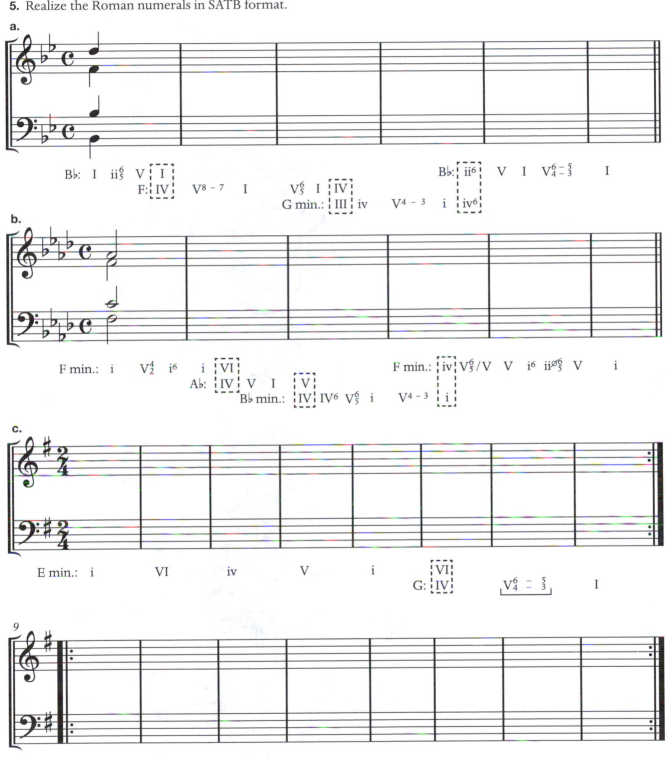

B♭: I   ii$^6_5$ V   I
F: IV   V$^{8-7}$ I   V$^6_5$ I   IV
G min.: III iv   V$^{4-3}$ i   iv^6

B♭: ii^6 V   I   V$^{6-5}_{4-3}$ I

b.

F min.: i   V$^4_2$ i^6 i   VI
A♭: IV V I   V
B♭ min.: IV IV^6 V$^6_5$ i   V$^{4-3}$ i

F min.: iv V$^6_5$/V V i^6 ii$^{ø6}_5$ V   i

c.

E min.: i   VI   iv   V   i   VI
G: IV   V$^{6\ -\ 5}_{4\ -\ 3}$ I

E min.: iv   V$^6_5$/V   V   V$^4_2$ i^6 ii^{o6} V$^{5}_{4\ -\ 3}$ i
G: V$^6_5$/ii   ii

D. REALIZING FIGURED BASS

For each of the following:

- Realize the figured bass in the indicated format.
- Then label the keys and Roman numerals, making sure to indicate the modulations.
- Mark pivot chords with dotted boxes.
- Finally, above the staff, label the key and type of cadences.

Keyboard format:

SATB format:

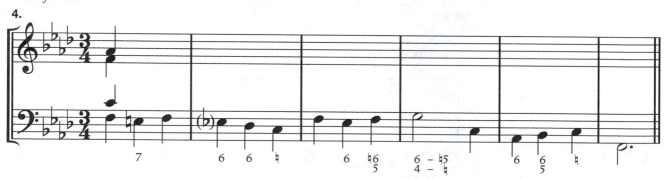

NAME: ....

5.

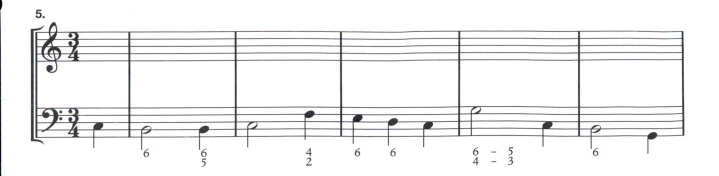

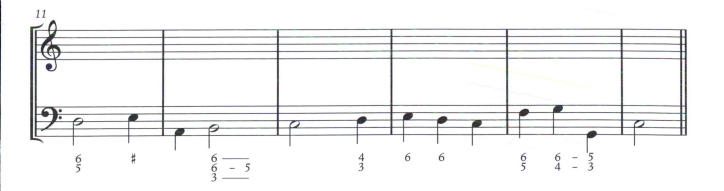

E. HARMONIZING MELODIES

Harmonize each of the following melodies:

- Write a bass line and Roman numerals, modulating to the keys indicated.
- Indicate the pivot chords.
- Then fill in the inner voices in SATB format.

1. Modulate to B♭ major   **2.** to F♯ minor

G min.: i   A: I

3. to C minor   **4.** to F♯ minor

A♭: I   B min.: i

5. main key: C   PAC in V   PAC in vi

C: I

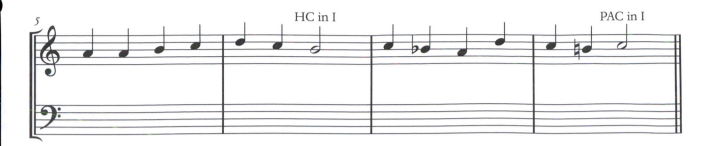

G min.:   i

F. COMPOSITION

1. Compose progressions in SATB format:

- Modulate from the main key to the second key via a pivot chord.
- Include at least one **Dominant–Tonic** progression in each key.
- Label the chords using Roman numerals.

a. E major to C♯ minor: **b.** C minor to G minor:

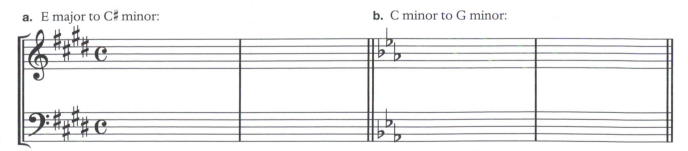

c. F♯ minor to A major: **d.** B♭ major to D minor:

. Realize these Roman numerals in keyboard format and label the key and type of cadences.

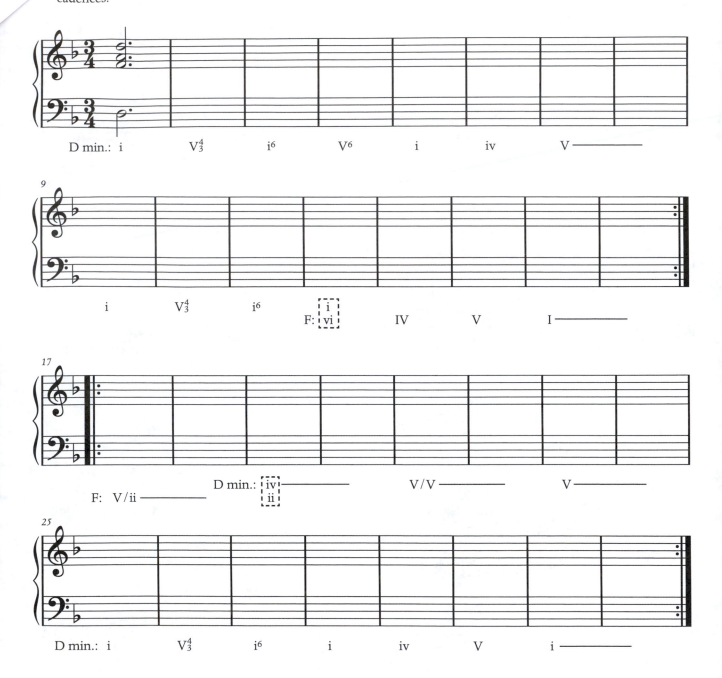

3. Compose a piece for keyboard and another instrument.

- Use the same harmonies as in (2).
- Be sure to add the clef and key signature of the melody instrument.
- As indicated in the score itself, certain measures should involve repetitions of earlier measures. The melody should conclude on the downbeat of the last measure.
- As always, there should be no parallel octaves between the melody and the bass line of the accompaniment.

NAME: ....

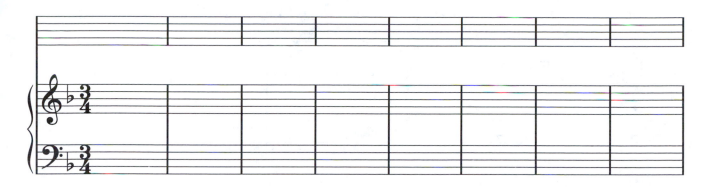

(mm. 9–10 should be the same as mm. 1–2)

9

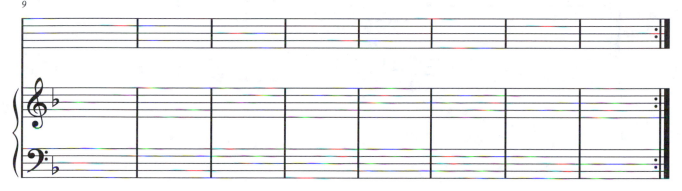

17

(mm. 25–26 should be the same as mm. 1–2)

25

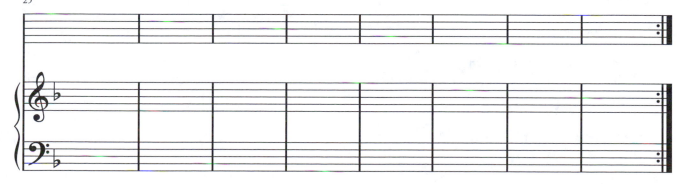

4. Write a short composition in G minor, following these guidelines:

- Write a harmonic outline for your composition in four-part harmony, keyboard format, below.

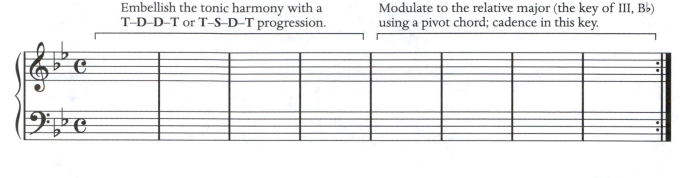

Embellish the tonic harmony with a
T–D–D–T or **T–S–D–T** progression.

Modulate to the relative major (the key of III, B♭) using a pivot chord; cadence in this key.

Conclude with a PAC in the home key (G minor).

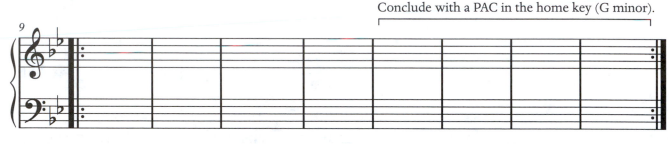

G min.:   iv   V/V   V
B♭:   I   V/ii   ii

5. Using the harmonies from the outline above (4), compose a piece for keyboard, guitar, or an ensemble of your choice, using a meter of your choice.

G. ANALYSIS

1. In the following excerpts:

- Identify the main key and the keys of modulation.
- Label the chords using Roman numerals.
- Indicate pivot chords with a dotted box.
- Above the staff, label the type of cadences within the key.

a. "Freuet euch" (hymn)

G: I

b. J. S. Bach, Chorale 51

c. J. S. Bach, Chorale 48

d. J. S. Bach, Chorale 102

e. Gioachino Rossini, *Tancredi*

f. Ludwig van Beethoven, *Equali* for Four Trombones, WoO 30, No. 3

g. Gaetano Donizetti, *Anna Bolena*, Act I (arr. Czerny)

Ger⁺⁶
(see Chapter 31)

Compare the two halves of this excerpt. What are some ways in which they are similar to one another, and what are some ways in which they are different?

h. Joseph Haydn, Symphony No. 63, ii

It^{+6}
(see Chapter 31)

What keys are tonicized rather than modulated to? In which measure does the series of tonicizations appear most rapid? In what measure does the theme from the opening four measures return?

i. Scott Joplin, "Elite Syncopations"

How do the two phrases in this passage compare? In what ways are they similar to one another? In which ways do they differ?

2. In each example, label the cadences above the staff, indicating both the key and the cadence type. Then answer the questions.

a. Johann Adolph Hasse, Flute Sonata, Op. 1, No. 6, iii

- Describe the key scheme: this piece begins in the main key of _____, then modulates first to _____, then to _____, and then to _____ before finally returning to the main key of _____.

- Where does the theme from measures 1–4 return? How is it changed when it returns?

- In a number of places, the chordal dissonance implied in the figured bass is either embellished or transferred to the bass voice before resolving. Can you locate any instance of this?

b. Arcangelo Corelli, Chamber Sonata Op. 2, No. 5, Sarabanda

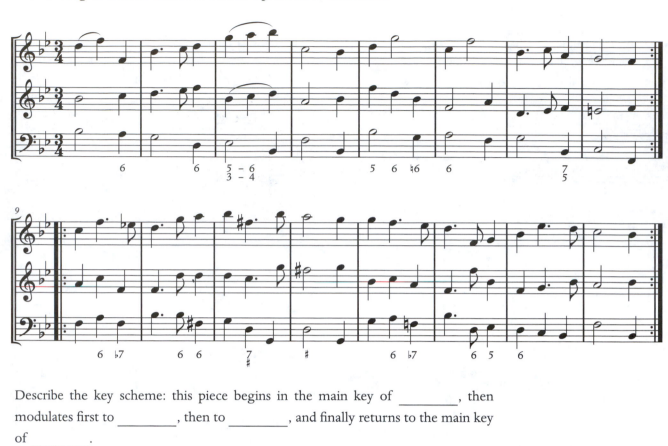

Describe the key scheme: this piece begins in the main key of _____, then modulates first to _____, then to _____, and finally returns to the main key of _____ .

c. Margarethe Danzi, Variations in F Minor

Describe the key scheme: This piece is the main key of _____, then modulates first to _____, then to _____, and finally returns to the main key of _____ .

chapter

29

Modal Mixture

A. QUESTIONS FOR REVIEW

1. What is modal mixture?

2. Why is motion between parallel major and minor keys not considered to be modulation?

3. What is a borrowed chord?

4. What scale degrees are usually altered in a borrowed chord? What are the most common borrowed chords?

5. What is a Picardy third?

B. SPELLING BORROWED CHORDS

1. Add the accidentals that are missing from the following borrowed chords.

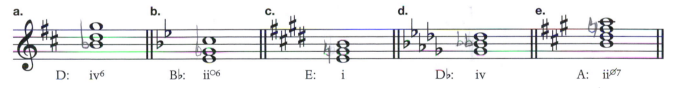

a. D: iv⁶   b. B♭: ii°⁶   c. E: i   d. D♭: iv   e. A: ii⌀7

2. Write the key signatures of the following major keys; then notate the indicated chords, adding the appropriate accidentals.

a. G: ♭III   b. B: iv   c. A♭: ii°⁶   d. F: ♭VI   e. F♯: i⁶

C. REALIZING ROMAN NUMERALS

1. Realize the following Roman numerals in SATB format.

k.

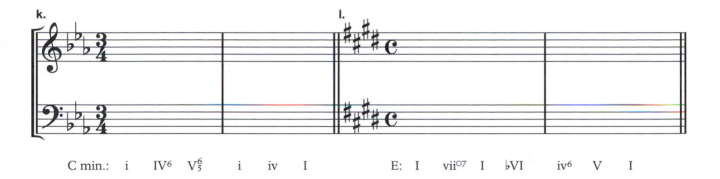

C min.:   i   IV⁶   V⁶₅   i   iv   I   E: I   vii°⁷   I   ♭VI   iv⁶   V   I

2. Realize the following Roman numerals in keyboard format.

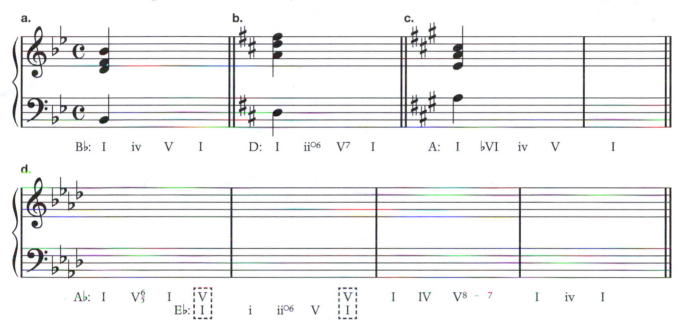

B♭: I   iv   V   I   D: I   ii°⁶   V⁷   I   A: I   ♭VI   iv   V   I

A♭: I   V⁶₅   I   ⌈V⌉   ⌈V⌉   I   IV   V⁸⁻⁷   I   iv   I

E♭: ⌊I⌋   i   ii°⁶   V   ⌊I⌋

3. In each of the following:

- Realize the progression in SATB format.
- Then rewrite the progression using almost the same chords and notes—but with modal mixture for at least one of the chords.
- Label the Roman numerals, making sure to adjust the labels for the *altered* chords.

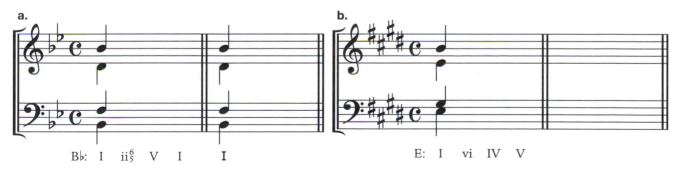

B♭: I   ii⁶₅   V   I   I   E: I   vi   IV   V

c.

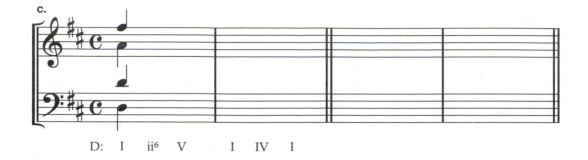

D: I   ii⁶   V   I   IV   I

D. REALIZING FIGURED BASS

For each of the following:

- Realize each figured bass.
- Then label the key and Roman numerals.
- Finally, circle the Roman numeral of any chord that involves mixture.

Keyboard format:

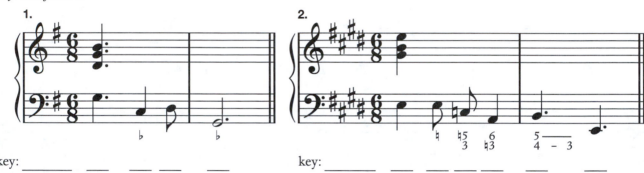

key: _____ ___ ___ ___ ___ ___ ___ ___

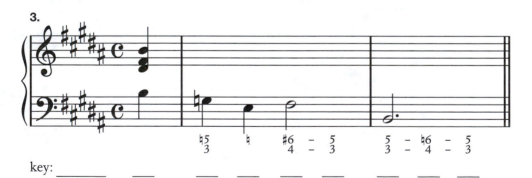

key: _____ ___ ___ ___ ___ ___ ___ ___

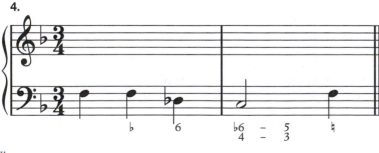

key: _____ ___ ___ ___ ___ ___ ___ ___

key: _____ ___ ___ ___ ___ ___ ___ ___

SATB format:

5.

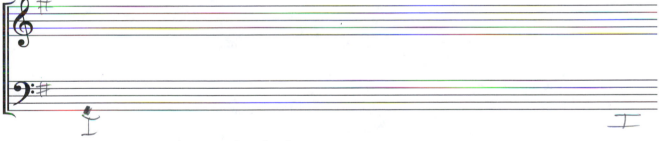

key: _____ — — — — — — — — — — —

E. COMPOSITION

1. Compose short progressions in four-part harmony, one to three measures long, using the following guidelines:

   - The progressions should be in SATB format.

   - Make sure to provide the key signature, a time signature of your choice, and bar lines where necessary.

   a. Progression in B major that uses a iv chord

[handwritten: GA Bm C D E# · Cm · 3rd↑ Steps↓ · G · Cm · G]

   b. Progression in E♭ major that uses a ♭VI chord

   c. Progression in D major that begins with a sequence that uses at least one borrowed chord.

   - The sequence should use all root-position chords in which the bass alternates moving down a fourth, then up a second, leading from I to IV (or I to iv).

   - Following the sequence, conclude the progression with a cadence in D major.

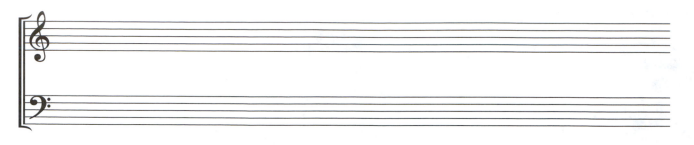

2. Realize the Roman numerals in keyboard format.

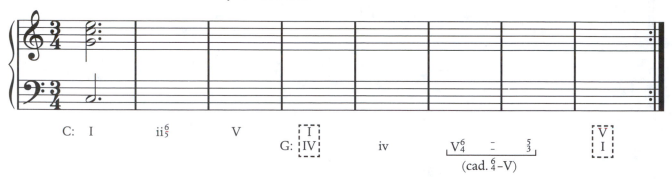

C: I   ii$^6_5$ V

G: IV   iv   V$^6_4$ — $^5_3$ V I

(cad. $^6_4$–V)

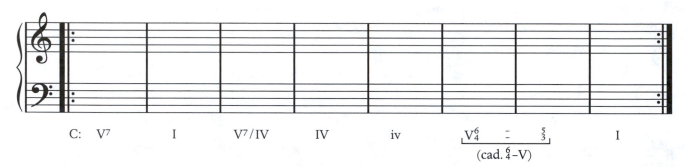

C: V^7 I   V^7/IV   IV   iv   V$^6_4$ — $^5_3$ I

(cad. $^6_4$–V)

3. Compose a work for piano, or for another instrument with piano accompaniment, based on (2).

- Compose the melody based on the harmonies given.
- Construct an accompaniment from the harmonies, using figuration, as in earlier chapters.

NAME: ....

F. ANALYSIS

1. Scott Joplin, "Maple Leaf Rag"

Label the key. Then locate the chords in this excerpt that use mixture, and label
them with Roman numerals. You need only label the mixture chords.

key: _____

2. Label the key and Roman numerals in the following excerpts; then circle the Roman numeral of each mixture chord.

a. Elizabeth Barker, "St. John Damascene" (hymn)

Also label the embellishing tone.

key: _____

b. Ludwig van Beethoven, "Freudvoll und leidvoll" ("Joyful and Sorrowful")

key: _____

Translation: In joy and in sorrow, be thoughtful, longing and fearful, in constant pain.

What chord tone is implied in measure 10 of this excerpt, A or G? Explain the reasons for your answer.

c. Franz Schubert, "Lachen und Weinen" ("Laughter and Tears")

key: _____   I

Translation: Love gives so many reasons for laughing and weeping all the time. In the morning, I laughed for joy, and why I now weep in the twilight [is something even I don't know].

How do the harmony, melody, rhythm, and other musical features reflect the text in this song excerpt?

d. Giuseppe Verdi, *La Traviata*, Act I, scene iii

Label at most one chord per measure.

key: _____

Translation: Love is the very breath of the universe, mysterious and noble, both burden and ecstasy of the heart.

NAME: ....

e. W. C. Handy, "St. Louis Blues"

G:

f. Harry T. Burleigh, "Oh, Love of a Day"

Andante con espressivo

Oh love of a day and a night_____ And an - oth - er day__ for tears_____ And a

key: _____

ten - der dream of a bur - ied love To last for a thou - sand years._____

V^7_6

g. Charles Lawlor, "Sidewalks of New York"

Mixture appears in only one (very striking) spot in this excerpt.

chapter

30

♭II⁶: The Neapolitan Sixth

A. QUESTIONS FOR REVIEW

1. What is another name for the ♭II⁶ chord?

2. Does ♭II⁶ have a **T**onic, **D**ominant, or **S**ubdominant function?

3. What scale degree is the root of a ♭II⁶? What note of the chord is in its bass? What note should be doubled? What notes are usually not doubled, and why? Is ♭II⁶ a major or minor triad?

4. Why does ♭II⁶ appear more frequently in minor keys than major keys?

5. What note of ♭II⁶ takes an accidental? In what cases is the accidental a flat? In what cases is it a natural?

6. What chords may follow ♭II⁶? What chords may precede it?

7. What are the tendency tones in ♭II⁶? How do they usually resolve?

8. What chords can appear between ♭II⁶ and V?

9. What unusual melodic interval usually arises when progressing directly from ♭II⁶ to V?

B. SPELLING ♭II⁶ CHORDS

1. For each of the following:

- Write the key signature.
- Indicate lowered $\hat{2}$.
- Then write the ii°⁶ and ♭II⁶ chords.

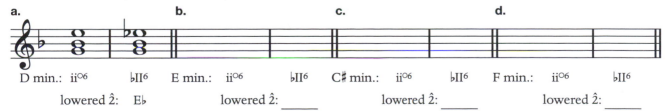

a.	b.	c.	d.
D min.: ii°⁶ ♭II⁶	E min.: ii°⁶ ♭II⁶	C♯ min.: ii°⁶ ♭II⁶	F min.: ii°⁶ ♭II⁶
lowered $\hat{2}$: E♭	lowered $\hat{2}$: _____	lowered $\hat{2}$: _____	lowered $\hat{2}$: _____

2. Below the staff spell ♭II⁶ in each of the given keys. Then write the key signature and the notes of the chord on the staff.

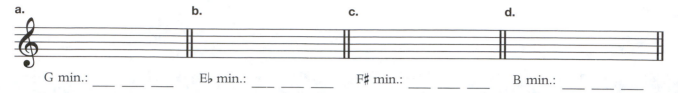

G min.: __ __ __   E♭ min.: __ __ __   F♯ min.: __ __ __   B min.: __ __ __

3. For each of the following keys, write the key signature. Then write ♭II⁶ in SATB format, with proper doubling.

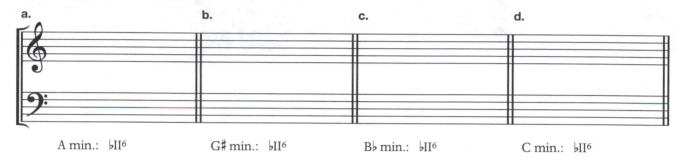

A min.: ♭II⁶   G♯ min.: ♭II⁶   B♭ min.: ♭II⁶   C min.: ♭II⁶

C. REALIZING ROMAN NUMERALS

1. Realize the Roman numerals in SATB format.

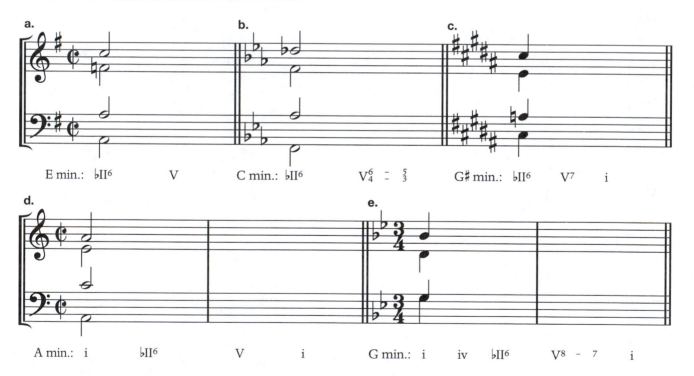

E min.: ♭II⁶   V   C min.: ♭II⁶   V⁶₄ = ⁵₃   G♯ min.: ♭II⁶   V⁷   i

A min.: i   ♭II⁶   V   i   G min.: i   iv   ♭II⁶   V⁸ – 7   i

f.

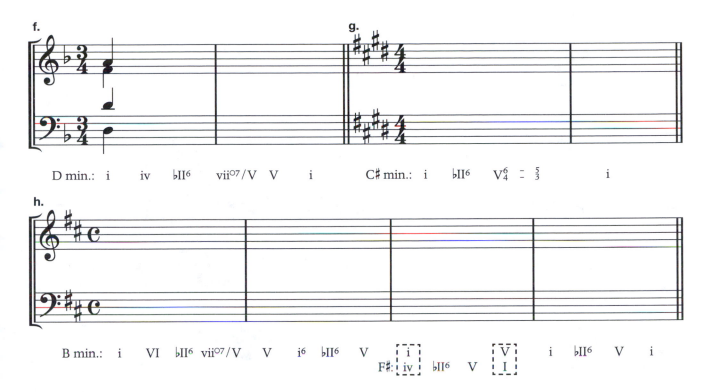

D min.: i   iv   ♭II⁶   vii°⁷/V   V   i   C♯ min.: i   ♭II⁶   V⁶₄ — ⁵₃   i

h.

B min.: i   VI   ♭II⁶   vii°⁷/V   V   i⁶   ♭II⁶   V   [i]   [V]   i   ♭II⁶   V   i

F♯: [iv]   ♭II⁶   V   [I]

2. Realize the Roman numerals in keyboard format.

a.

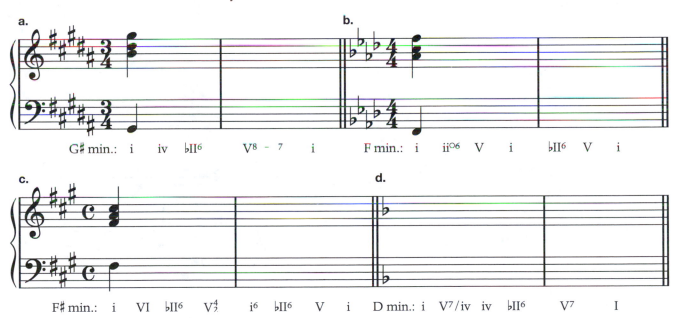

G♯ min.: i   iv   ♭II⁶   V⁸ ⁻ ⁷   i   F min.: i   ii°⁶   V   i   ♭II⁶   V   i

b.

c.

F♯ min.: i   VI   ♭II⁶   V⁴₂   i⁶   ♭II⁶   V   i   D min.: i   V⁷/iv   iv   ♭II⁶   V⁷   I

d.

D. REALIZING FIGURED BASS

1. For each of the following:

- Realize the figured bass in keyboard format.
- Then identify the minor keys and the lowered $\hat{2}$.
- Finally, label the Roman numerals.

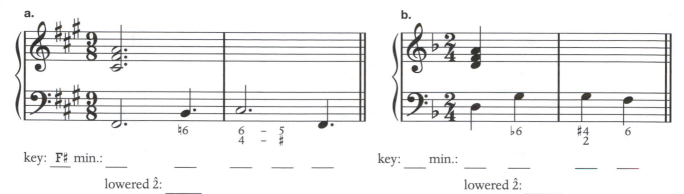

key: **F♯** min.: ___   ___   ___   ___   ___

              lowered $\hat{2}$: _____

key: ___ min.: ___   ___   ___   ___

              lowered $\hat{2}$: _____

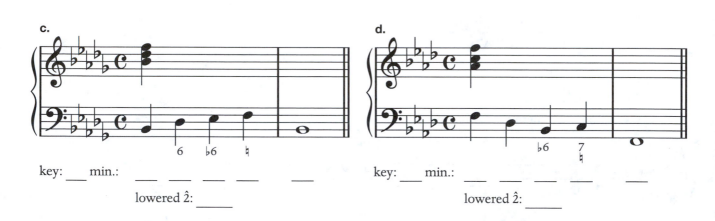

key: ___ min.: ___   ___   ___   ___   ___

              lowered $\hat{2}$: _____

key: ___ min.: ___   ___   ___   ___   ___

              lowered $\hat{2}$: _____

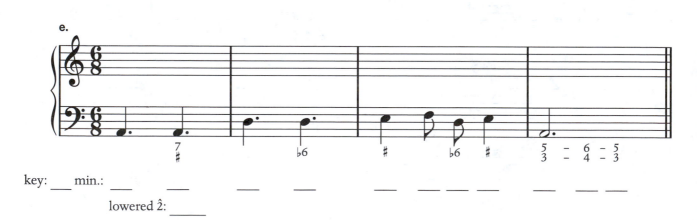

key: ___ min.: ___   ___   ___   ___

              lowered $\hat{2}$: _____

2. For each of the following:

- Realize the figured bass in SATB format.
- Then identify the minor keys and the lowered $\hat{2}$.
- Finally, label the Roman numerals.

a.

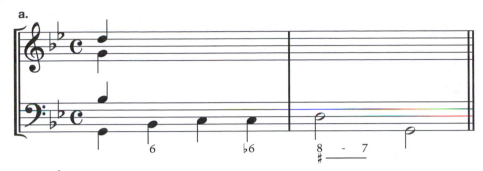

key: ___ min.: ___ ___ ___ ___ ___ ___

lowered $\hat{2}$ ___

b.

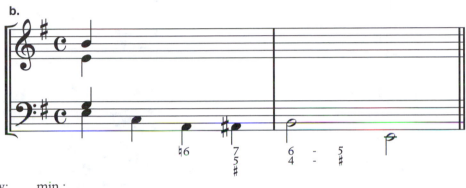

key: ___ min.: ___ ___ ___ ___ ___ ___ ___

lowered $\hat{2}$ ___

E. HARMONIZING MELODIES

For each of the following:

- Label the scale degrees for each note of the melodies.
- Then suggest a harmonization in SATB format by providing a bass line and Roman numerals.
- Fill in the inner voices.
- Use a Neapolitan sixth chord in each passage.

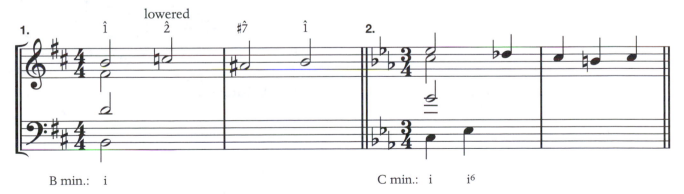

B min.: i

C min.: i   i⁶

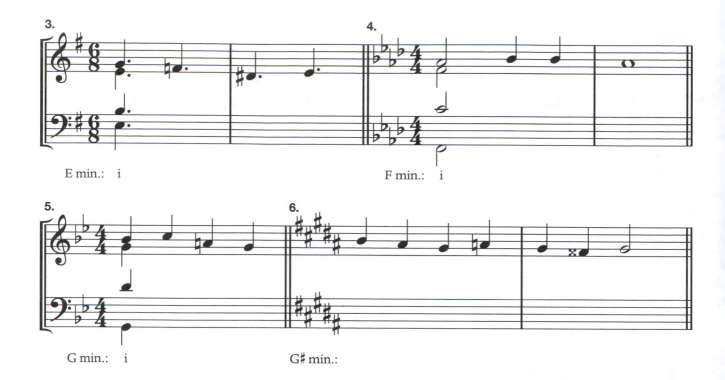

3.

E min.: i

4.

F min.: i

5.

G min.: i

6.

G♯ min.:

F. COMPOSITION

1. Realize these Roman numerals in keyboard format.

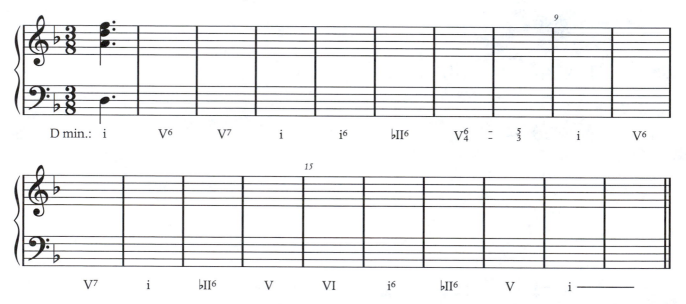

D min.: i   V⁶   V⁷   i   i⁶   ♭II⁶   V⁴₆ – ₃⁵   i   V⁶

V⁷   i   ♭II⁶   V   VI   i⁶   ♭II⁶   V   i ——

2. On the following staves, compose a piece for violin and piano, using the harmonies in (1).

- The notes in the accompaniment should be the same as in (1), but with an appropriate accompaniment texture.

- The melody in measures 9–12 should be the same as measures 1–4.

- There should be no parallel octaves between the violin part and the bass of the piano.
- Note the deceptive cadence in measure 15.
- End the violin melody on the downbeat of measure 19; end the piano accompaniment on the downbeat of measure 20.

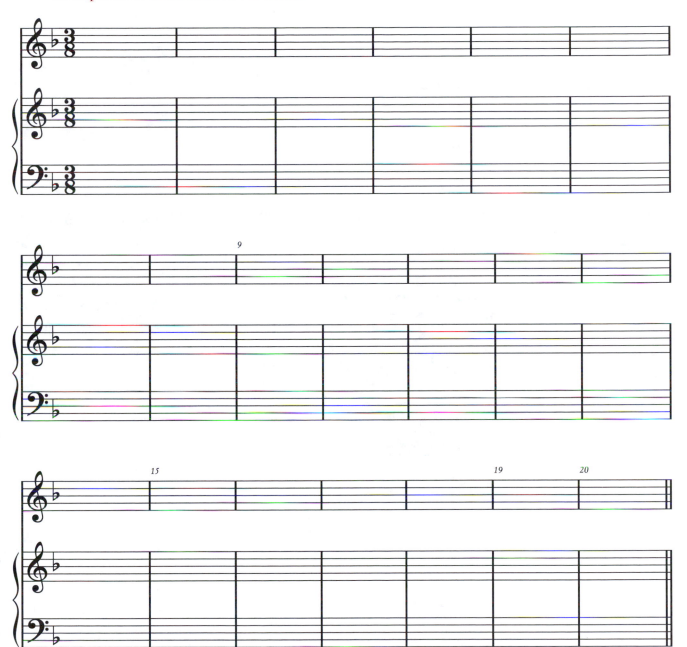

G. ANALYSIS

Analyze the following examples.

- Label the keys, cadences, and Roman numerals.
- Circle every instance of lowered $\hat{2}$ in the melody. In which of these pieces is lowered $\hat{2}$ embellished before it leads down?

1. Franz Schubert, Mass in B♭, D. 324, Gloria

key: _____

2. Louise Reichardt, "Vaters Klage" ("The Father's Lament")

Label only one chord in measure 2. Which notes in measure 2 are embellishing tones?

zu Ber - koch an der Kir - che, da ist ein neu - ge - mach - tes Grab

key: _____

Translation: In Berkoch, next to the church, there is a newly dug grave.

3. Joseph Haydn, String Quartet, Op. 17, No. 1, iii

key: _____

4. Frédéric Chopin, Waltz, Op. 34, No. 2

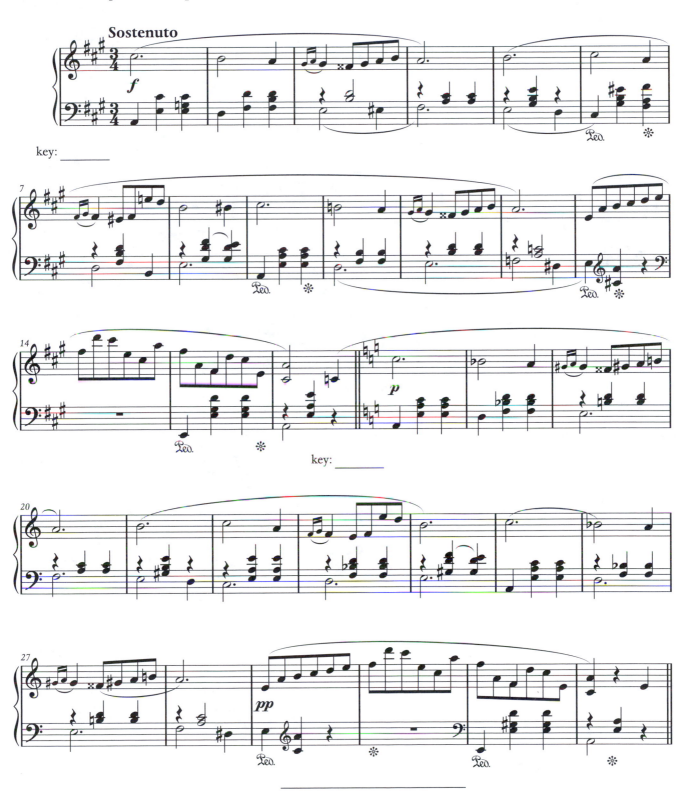

key: _____

key: _____

5. Christoph Willibald Gluck, "O malheureux Admète," from *Alceste*

key: _____

6. Ludwig van Beethoven, Sonata for Piano, Op. 27, No. 2, i

key: _____

7. Franz Schubert, "Der Müller und der Bach" ("The Miller and the Brook")

Label at most one chord per measure. Note that some harmonies are over a pedal in the bass.

key: _____

G min.:

Translation: Where a true heart dies from love, the lilies wither in every field. The moon goes behind the clouds so that no one can see its tears. The angels close their eyes and weep and sing as they bring the soul to rest.

- In one appearance of a ♭II6, lowered $\hat{2}$ in the top voice is doubled in an inner voice. In which measure does this doubling occur? Which voice (the top voice or the inner voice) moves down to the leading tone in the next chord?
- Describe ways that the musical setting reflects the text.

8. W. A. Mozart, Sonata for Violin and Piano, K. 377, ii

D min.:   i

On the staves below, complete a simplified harmonic model in four-part harmony, keyboard format, using at most one chord per measure.

9. Camille Saint-Saëns, *Introduction and Rondo Capriccioso* for Violin and Orchestra
(arr. Bizet)

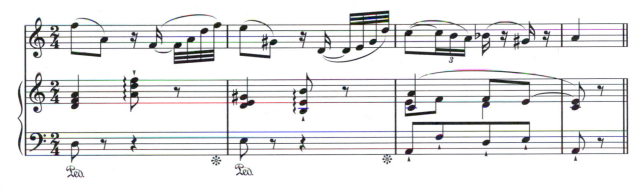

key: _____

10. Franz Schubert, "Erlkönig" ("Elf-king")

- Label at most one chord per measure, except for the second-to-last measure
  (which uses two chords).

- Note that many of the chords extend for a number of measures, and the harmonies in some measures simply consist of passing tones in the bass.

- One measure in this excerpt consists of an applied chord that appears over a
  pedal point in the bass.

key: _____

Translation: The shuddering father rode like the wind, he holds his groaning child in his arms. Struggling, he reaches his courtyard, in his arms his child lay dead.

chapter

31 Augmented Sixth Chords

A. QUESTIONS FOR REVIEW

1. What are the scale degrees of the tendency tones in an augmented sixth chord? In which voice(s) can they each appear (soprano, alto, tenor, bass)? In which direction do they each resolve?

2. What are the scale degrees in the Italian augmented sixth? The French augmented sixth? The German augmented sixth?

3. What is an alternate spelling for the German augmented sixth chord? Why is this alternate spelling used in major keys, but not minor keys?

4. In four-part harmony, what tone should be doubled in the Italian augmented sixth?

5. To what chords does each augmented sixth chord normally lead? What chords can precede an augmented sixth?

6. In a major key, what accidentals can you add to IV⁶ to turn it into an Italian augmented sixth? What accidentals can you add to ii₃⁴ to turn it into a French augmented sixth? To vii°₅⁶/V to turn it into a German augmented sixth?

7. Why do you suppose augmented sixth chords are often found at climactic cadences?

B. SPELLING AUGMENTED SIXTH CHORDS

1. For each key, provide the key signature; then write the tendency tones minor $\hat{6}$ and raised $\hat{4}$, followed by their resolutions to $\hat{5}$.

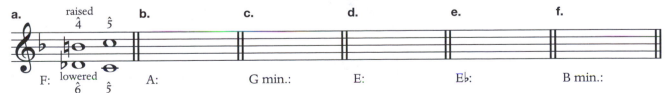

2. For each of the following:

- Write the key signature for the indicated key.

- Above the staff, name raised $\hat{4}$ and minor $\hat{6}$ in that key.

- On the staff, write the indicated augmented sixth chord, with the proper note in the lowest voice.

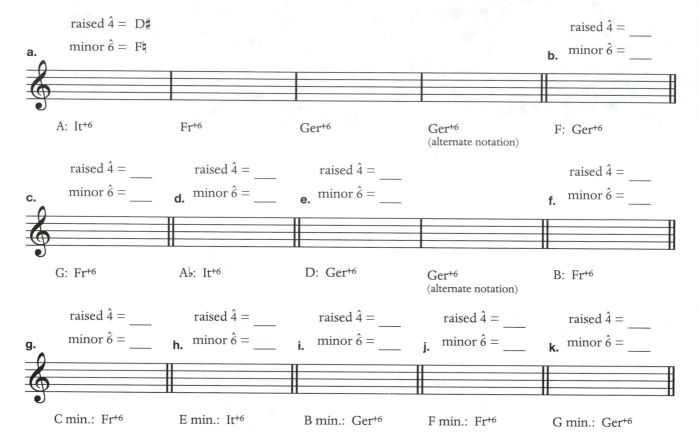

a.
raised $\hat{4}$ = D♯
minor $\hat{6}$ = F♮

b.
raised $\hat{4}$ = ___
minor $\hat{6}$ = ___

A: It^{+6} Fr^{+6} Ger^{+6} Ger^{+6} (alternate notation) F: Ger^{+6}

c.
raised $\hat{4}$ = ___
minor $\hat{6}$ = ___

d.
raised $\hat{4}$ = ___
minor $\hat{6}$ = ___

e.
raised $\hat{4}$ = ___
minor $\hat{6}$ = ___

f.
raised $\hat{4}$ = ___
minor $\hat{6}$ = ___

G: Fr^{+6} A♭: It^{+6} D: Ger^{+6} Ger^{+6} (alternate notation) B: Fr^{+6}

g.
raised $\hat{4}$ = ___
minor $\hat{6}$ = ___

h.
raised $\hat{4}$ = ___
minor $\hat{6}$ = ___

i.
raised $\hat{4}$ = ___
minor $\hat{6}$ = ___

j.
raised $\hat{4}$ = ___
minor $\hat{6}$ = ___

k.
raised $\hat{4}$ = ___
minor $\hat{6}$ = ___

C min.: Fr^{+6} E min.: It^{+6} B min.: Ger^{+6} F min.: Fr^{+6} G min.: Ger^{+6}

3. For each of the following:

- Provide the key signature.

- Write the two indicated chords.

- Place a square around raised $\hat{4}$ and minor $\hat{6}$.

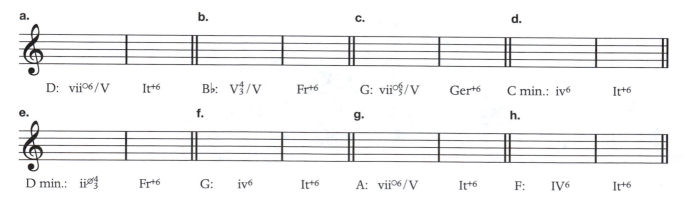

a.
D: vii^{o6}/V It^{+6}

b.
B♭: V$^4_3$/V Fr^{+6}

c.
G: vii$^{o6}_5$/V Ger^{+6}

d.
C min.: iv^6 It^{+6}

e.
D min.: ii$^{ø4}_3$ Fr^{+6}

f.
G: iv^6 It^{+6}

g.
A: vii^{o6}/V It^{+6}

h.
F: IV^6 It^{+6}

C. REALIZING ROMAN NUMERALS

1. Realize the following Roman numerals in SATB format.

A: It+6   V   D min.: Fr+6   V   C♯ min.: Ger+6   V$^6_4$ ‒ $^5_3$ G min.: iv6   It+6   V

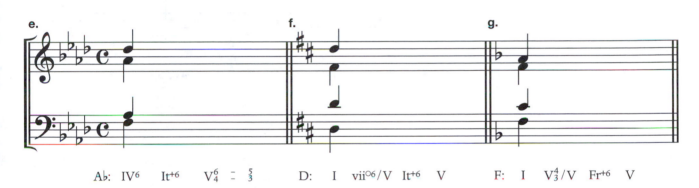

A♭: IV6   It+6   V$^6_4$ ‒ $^5_3$ D: I   vii°6/V   It+6   V   F: I   V$^4_3$/V   Fr+6   V

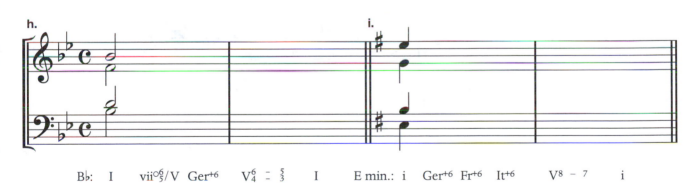

B♭: I   vii°$^6_5$/V   Ger+6   V$^6_4$ ‒ $^5_3$ I   E min.: i   Ger+6   Fr+6   It+6   V8 ‒ 7   i

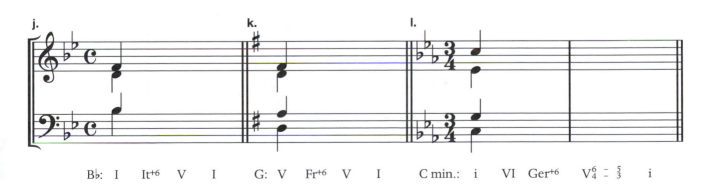

B♭: I   It+6   V   I   G: V   Fr+6   V   I   C min.: i   VI   Ger+6   V$^6_4$ ‒ $^5_3$ i

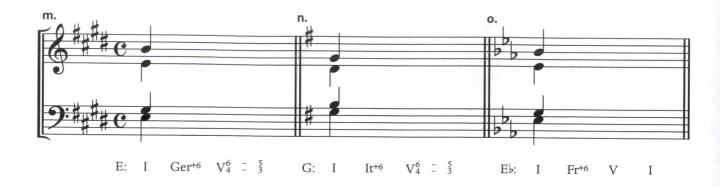

E: I Ger^{+6} V$^6_4$ — $^5_3$ G: I It^{+6} V$^6_4$ — $^5_3$ E♭: I Fr^{+6} V I

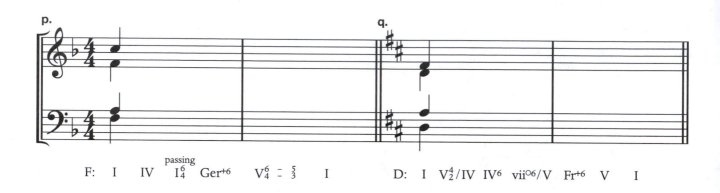

F: I IV I$^6_4$ ^{passing} Ger^{+6} V$^6_4$ — $^5_3$ I   D: I V$^4_2$/IV IV^6 vii$^{○6}$/V Fr^{+6} V I

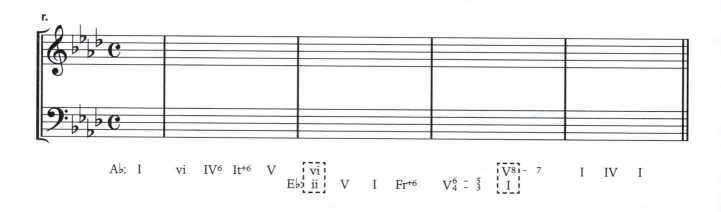

A♭: I vi IV^6 It^{+6} V ⌐vi¬   I IV I
                     E♭: ⌐ii¬ V I Fr^{+6} V$^6_4$ — $^5_3$ ⌐V^8¬ – ^{7}
                        └──┘   └I┘

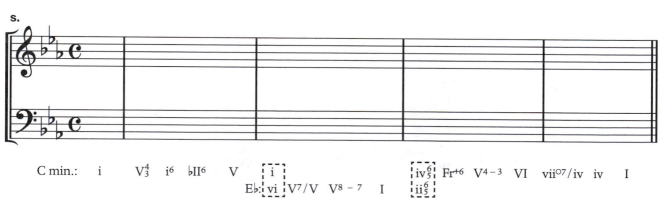

C min.: i V$^4_3$ i^6 ♭II^6 V ⌐i¬   ⌐iv$^6_5$¬ Fr^{+6} V$^{4-3}$ VI vii$^{○7}$/iv iv I
                       E♭: ⌐vi¬ V^7/V V$^{8-7}$ I   ⌐ii$^6_5$¬
                          └──┘   └──┘

2. Realize the following Roman numerals in keyboard format.

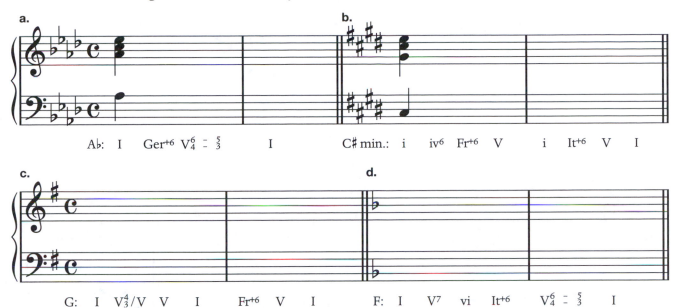

a.

Ab: I   Ger+6 V$^6_4$ − $^5_3$ I

b.

C# min.: i   iv6   Fr+6   V   i   It+6   V   I

c.

G: I   V$^4_3$/V   V   I   Fr+6   V   I

d.

F: I   V7   vi   It+6   V$^6_4$ − $^5_3$ I

D. REALIZING FIGURED BASS

1. Realize the figured basses in keyboard format. Then label the keys and Roman numerals.

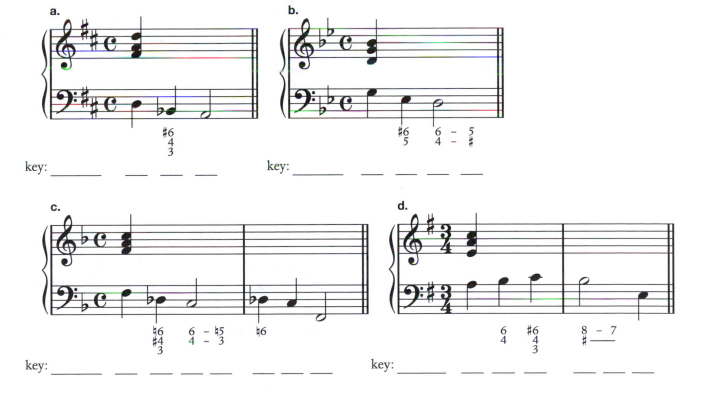

a.

#6
4
3

key: _____ ___ ___ ___

b.

#6   6 − 5
5   4 − #

key: _____ ___ ___ ___

c.

♮6   6 − ♮5   ♮6
#4   4 − 3
3

key: _____ ___ ___ ___ ___

d.

6   #6   8 − 7
4   4   #
     3

key: _____ ___ ___ ___

e.

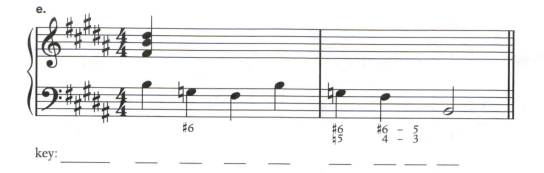

key: _____ _____ _____ _____ _____

2. Realize the figured bass in SATB format. Then label the key and Roman numerals.

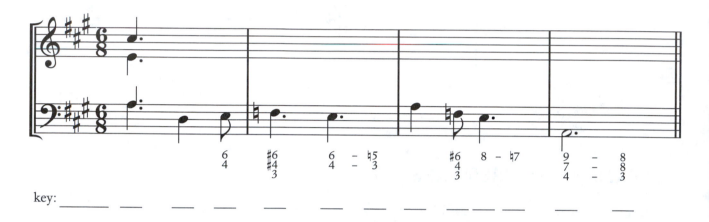

key: _____ _____ _____ _____ _____ _____ _____ _____ _____

E. HARMONIZING MELODIES

Label the key and harmonize each of the following melodic fragments in SATB format, using the indicated chromatic chord and labeling the Roman numerals.

1. use V / V

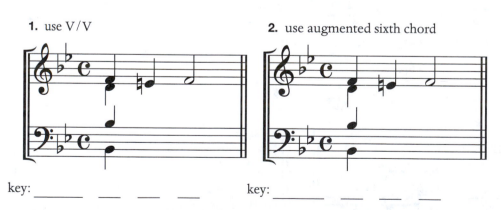

key: _____ _____ _____ _____

2. use augmented sixth chord

key: _____ _____ _____ _____

3. use augmented sixth chord

4. use augmented sixth chord

key: _____ ___ ___ ___

key: _____ ___ ___ ___ ___

F. ANALYSIS

Label the keys and the harmonies in the following passages. Identify cadences where requested.

1. Giovanni Paisiello, *Passione di Gesù Cristo (The Passion of Jesus Christ)*

il   mon - do af - flit - to.

key: _____

Translation: The afflicted world.

2. Ludwig van Beethoven, Overture to the *Creatures of Prometheus*, Op. 43

C:

3. Johannes Brahms, "Im Herbst" ("In Autumn")

se - lig - ster   Er - guß

C:

Translation: Holiest outpouring.

4. Franz Schubert, Sonata for Violin in D, D. 384, i

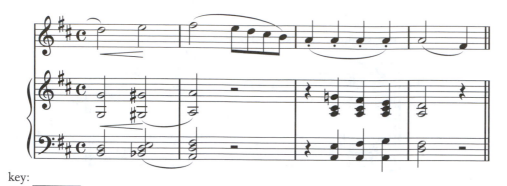

key: _____

5. Ludwig van Beethoven, Piano Sonata, Op. 13 ("Pathétique"), iii

key: _____

6. Jacob Sawyer, "Seventh Exposition Grand March"

cadence: _____

Risoluto

key: _____

7. Josephine Lang, "An den Frühling"

Hint: This excerpt includes an applied chord.

cadence: _____

mit dei - nem Blu - men - körb - chen,_____ will - kom - men auf der Flur.

C:

Translation: With your flower basket, welcome to the meadow.

8. Hortense de Beauharnais, "Eloigne toi" ("Move Away")

cadence: _____

key: _____

Translation: Move away, companion of my pain near death, said a deserter.

9. Ludwig van Beethoven, Bagatelle, Op. 119, No. 1

Label the cadence as well as the key and harmonies.

key: _____

cadence: _____

How is repetition used in measures 1–4? What features increase the momentum in measures 5–8 compared to measures 1–4?

10. George Gershwin and Will Donaldson, "Rialto Ripple Rag"

key: _____

11. Robert Schumann, Waltz, Op. 124, No. 4

Label the cadences as well as the harmonies. (Hint: In each measure, the bass note on the downbeat serves as the bass for the entire measure.)

cadence: _____

key: _____

In what ways are the two phrases in this excerpt similar to one another, and how do they differ? What creates a sense of blurring between the end of the first phrase and the start of the next one?

Complete the simplified harmonic model of Schumann's Waltz in four-part harmony, keyboard format.

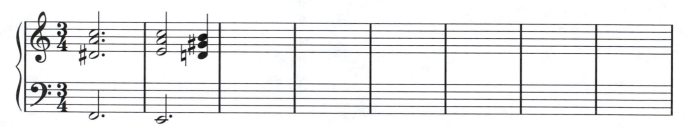

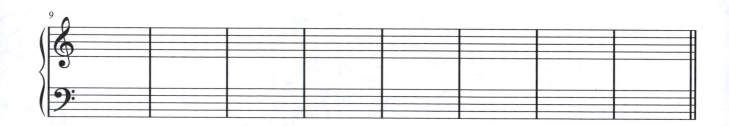

12. Giuseppe Verdi, *Il Trovatore*, Act III, scene iv

Label the key, the modulations or tonicizations, and the Roman numerals (at most one chord per measure).

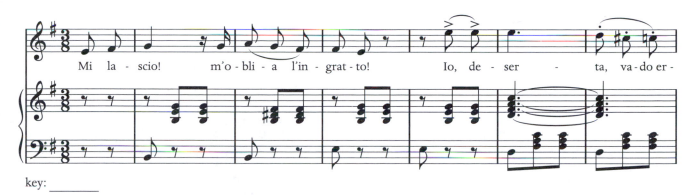

Mi la - scio!   m'o - bli - a   l'in - grat - to!   Io, de - ser - - ta, va - do er -

key: _____

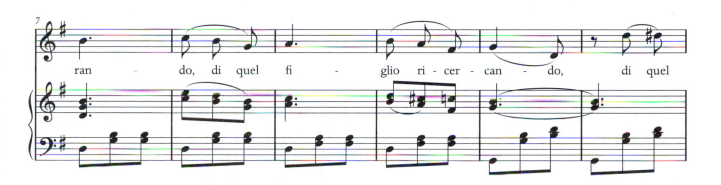

ran - do, di quel fi - glio ri - cer - can - do, di quel

cadence: _____

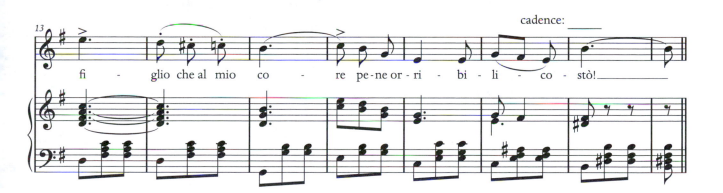

fi - glio che al mio co - re pe - ne or - ri - bi - li - co - stò!_____

Translation: I was left and forgotten by that ingrate! Deserted, I wander searching for that son who cost my heart horrible pain!

13. Fanny Mendelssohn Hensel, "Abschied von Rom" ("Farewell to Rome")

key: _____

14. Reginald De Koven, "O Promise Me"

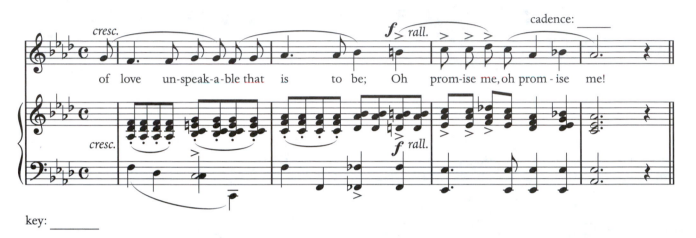

of love un-speak-a-ble that is to be; Oh prom-ise me, oh prom - ise me!

key: _____

15. Ludwig van Beethoven, Piano Sonata, Op. 57 ("Appassionata"), ii

key: _____

What is unusual about the resolution of the augmented sixth chord in this passage? Why do you suppose Beethoven opted to use the spelling with raised $\hat{2}$ rather than the minor form of $\hat{3}$ for this chord?

32

Other Chromatically Altered Chords

A. QUESTIONS FOR REVIEW

1. When does chromatic alteration of chord tones *not* involve a change of key or modal mixture?

2. Does chromatic alteration of chord tones change the quality of a chord? Does it change the basic function of the chord?

3. How does the fifth of an augmented triad resolve?

4. In what contexts is a ♭II chord typically used? In what less common contexts might a ♭II chord appear?

5. What is a diminished third chord? What is a common-tone diminished seventh chord?

B. SPELLING CHORDS

1. Add the accidentals that are missing from these chords.

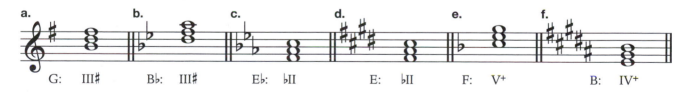

2. Write the following pairs of chords, providing the key signatures and adding accidentals where needed.

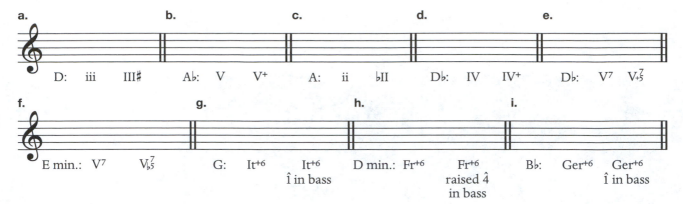

a.   D: iii   III♯   b.   A♭:   V   V⁺   c.   A: ii   ♭II   d.   D♭:   IV   IV⁺   e.   D♭:   V⁷   V₊₅⁷

f.   E min.:   V⁷   V♭₅⁷   g.   G: It⁺⁶   It⁺⁶ (Î in bass)   h.   D min.:   Fr⁺⁶   Fr⁺⁶ (raised 4̂ in bass)   i.   B♭:   Ger⁺⁶   Ger⁺⁶ (Î in bass)

C. REALIZING ROMAN NUMERALS

1. Realize the Roman numerals in SATB format.

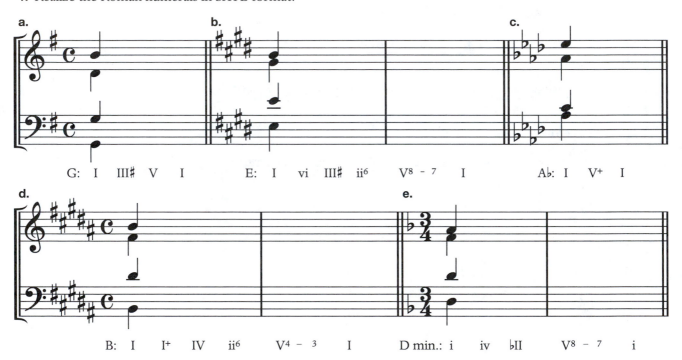

a.   G: I   III♯   V   I   b.   E: I   vi   III♯   ii⁶   V⁸ ⁻ ⁷   I   c.   A♭:   I   V⁺   I

d.   B: I   I⁺   IV   ii⁶   V⁴ ⁻ ³   I   e.   D min.:   i   iv   ♭II   V⁸ ⁻ ⁷   i

2. Realize the Roman numerals in keyboard format.

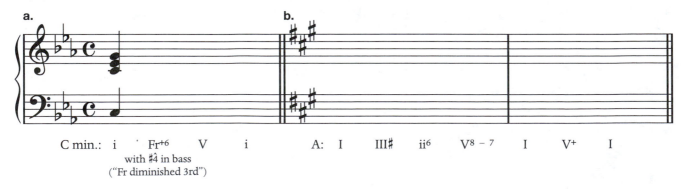

a.   C min.:   i   Fr⁺⁶ (with ♯4̂ in bass) ("Fr diminished 3rd")   V   i   b.   A: I   III♯   ii⁶   V⁸ ⁻ ⁷   I   V⁺   I

3. Realize the Roman numerals. When moving to the chord that follows it, the upper voices of the common-tone embellishing chords should either remain on the same note or move stepwise. Note that it may be necessary to double the fifth of the root-position I chord.

SATB format

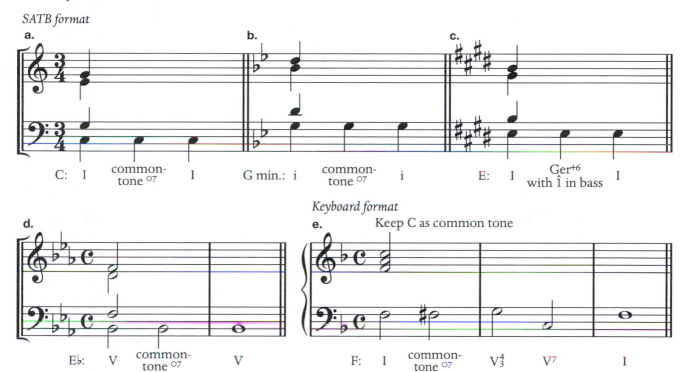

D. REALIZING FIGURED BASS

1. Realize the figured bass in keyboard format.

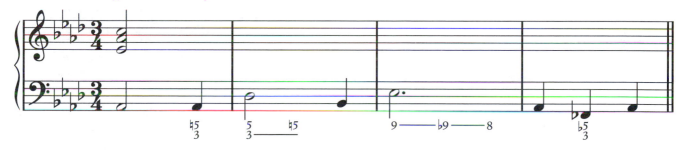

2. Realize the figured bass in SATB format.

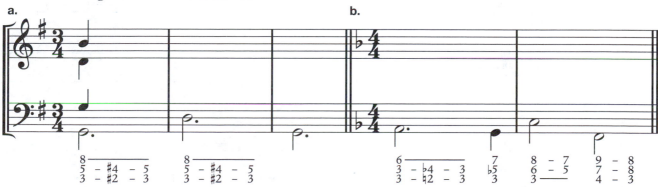

E. COMPOSITION

1. Realize the following figured bass. Then label the key and Roman numerals.

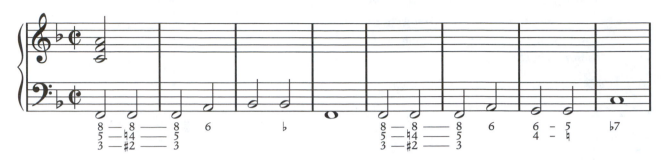

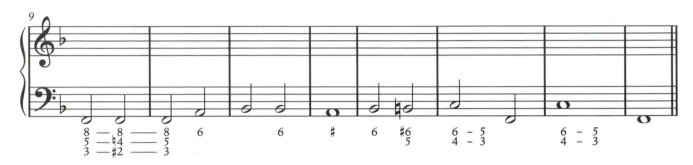

2. Compose a piece for keyboard or keyboard and another instrument using the harmonies in (1).

F. ANALYSIS

1. Label the chords in the following. Circle the appearance of chromatic chords discussed in Chapter 32.

a. Robert Schumann, Fantasy in C, Op. 17, iii

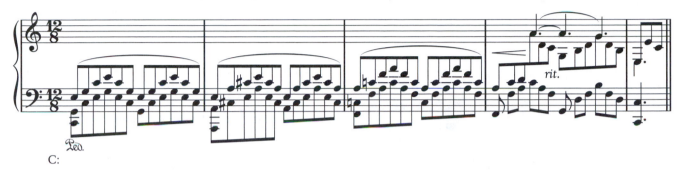

C:

b. Giovanni Paisiello, *Passione di Gesù Cristo* (*The Passion of Jesus Christ*)

key: _____

c. Hugo Wolf, "Gebet," from *Mörike Lieder*

E:

d. Robert Schumann, "Humoresque"

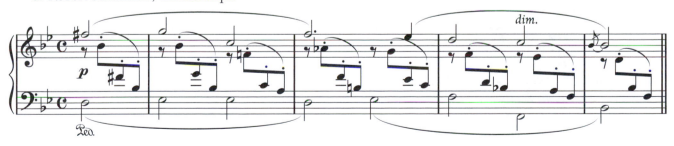

Bb:

e. Hugo Wolf, "An die Schlaf," from *Mörike Lieder*

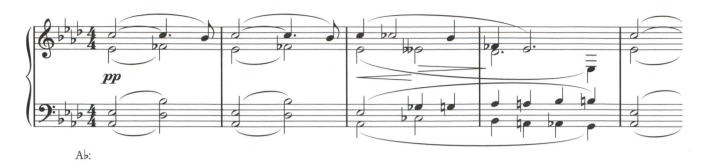

A♭:

f. Felix Mendelssohn, "Jagdlied," Op. 120, No. 1

C:

Translation: Up and onward, you men and beautiful ladies!

What is unusual about the treatment of the cadential $^6_4$ in this passage?

g. Antonín Dvořák, *The Spectre's Bride*

F:

2. Label the Roman numerals and circle the common-tone embellishing chords.

a. Franz Schubert, String Quintet in C, i

b. Franz Schubert, "Am Meer," from *Schwanengesang*

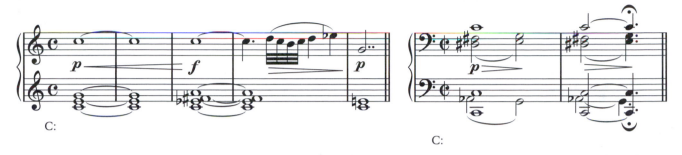

C:

C:

c. Stefan Auber, *Fra Diavolo*, Act I, scene v

beau Trem - blez_____ au sein de la___ tem - pê - te Au

G:

Translation: Tremble in the midst of the tempest

d. Franz Liszt, "Freudvoll und leidvoll" ("Joyful and Sorrowful")

A♭:

In this excerpt, what notes are spelled enharmonically? Why might Liszt have used the enharmonic spelling instead of the standard one?

e. James Reese Europe, "Castles' Half and Half"

C:

f. Franz Schubert, Waltz, Op. 9, No. 31

- Label only one chord per measure.

- Then circle and describe the common-tone embellishing chords.

C:

g. Alex Rogers, "I'm a Jonah Man," from *In Dahomey*

F:

h. Alma Mahler, "In meines Vaters Garten" ("In My Father's Garden")

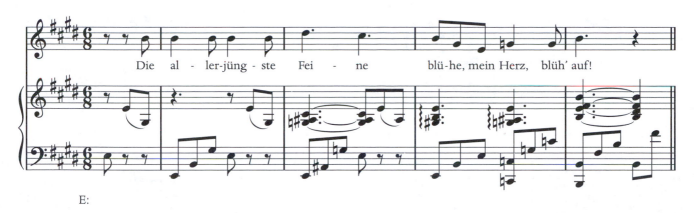

E:

Translation: The youngest of the three—bloom my heart, bloom forth!

i. Tom Turpin, "A Ragtime Nightmare"

In addition to labeling the harmonies, locate and identify the cadences. An applied chord appears between a cadential $^6_4$ and its resolution to V^7.

C:

3. Label the key and Roman numerals. On the staves below each excerpt, complete a simplified harmonic model in four-part harmony, keyboard format.

a. Ludwig van Beethoven, Piano Sonata, Op. 31, No. 2 ("Tempest"), iii

key: _____

b. John Philip Sousa, "Stars and Stripes Forever"

Label two chords per measure for the first seven measures, and one chord per measure for the remainder.

key: _____

4. W. C. Handy, "Hesitating Blues"

Label the Roman numerals.

- Describe some of the striking rhythmic features of the piece.
- At one point, a cadential $^6_4$ resolves in an unusual way. In what measure does this occur? How is it unusual?

33

Chromatic Sequences

A. QUESTIONS FOR REVIEW

1. In a sequence, why can V/V follow V/ii?

2. In a sequence consisting entirely of dominant seventh chords, how do leading tones move? Chordal sevenths?

3. How do strict chromatic sequences differ from other types of sequences?

4. Why is enharmonic reinterpretation necessary in chromatic descending fifth sequences that begin and end on the same chord?

5. How is an equal division of the octave created?

B. REALIZING ROMAN NUMERALS

Realize the Roman numerals of the following sequences in SATB format, and describe the root motion of the sequences (such as descending fifths; down 3, up 4; etc.).

root motion of sequence: _____

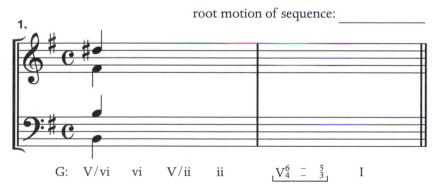

G: V/vi   vi   V/ii   ii   V$^6_4$ − $^5_3$ I

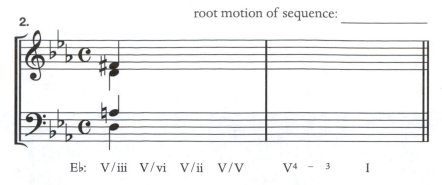

2.

root motion of sequence: _____

E♭:   V/iii   V/vi   V/ii   V/V   V⁴ – ³   I

root motion of sequence: _____

3.

D min.:   V⁶₅/iv   iv   V⁶₅/III   III   V⁶₅/♭II   ♭II   V⁶₅   i

root motion of sequence: _____

4.

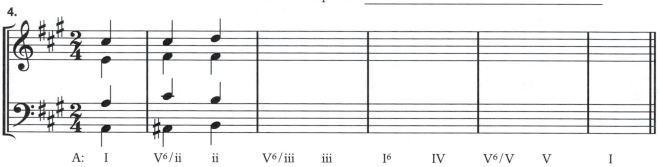

A: I   V⁶/ii   ii   V⁶/iii   iii   I⁶   IV   V⁶/V   V   I

C. COMPLETING CHROMATIC SEQUENCES

1. Complete these descending fifth sequences by continuing the pattern presented in the opening chords. Each uses applied chords.

Keyboard format

a.

b.

SATB format

c.

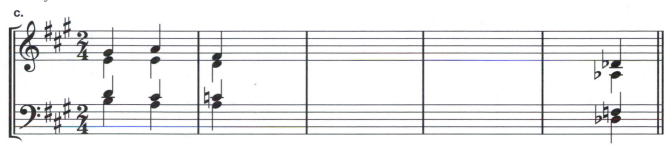

d.

2. Change the given diatonic sequences to chromatic sequences by adding accidentals where necessary to form the chords indicated by the Roman numerals below the staff.

Keyboard format

a.

Eb: I   V/vi   vi   V/V   V   I

b.

D: I   V/ii   ii   V/iii   iii   V⁷   I

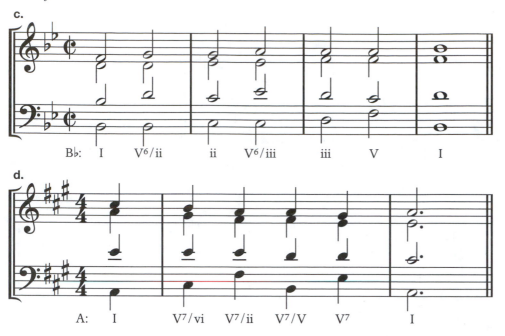

D. REALIZING FIGURED BASS

1. Realize the figured basses, and identify the root motion of each sequence (such as descending fifths; alternating down 3, up 4; and so on).

Keyboard format

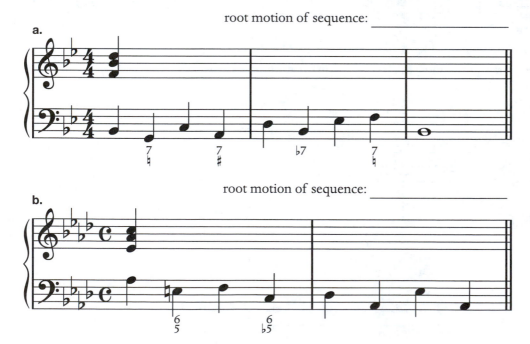

root motion of
sequence: m. 1 _____

root motion of
sequence: mm. 3–4 _____

c.

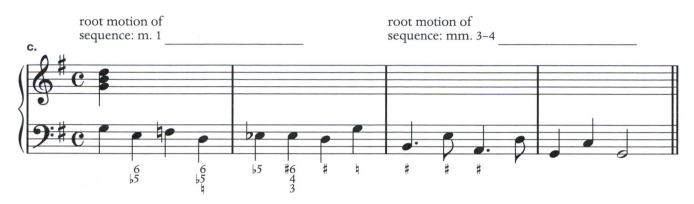

SATB format

root motion of sequence: _____

d.

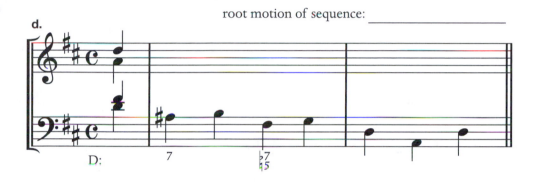

root motion of sequence: _____

e.

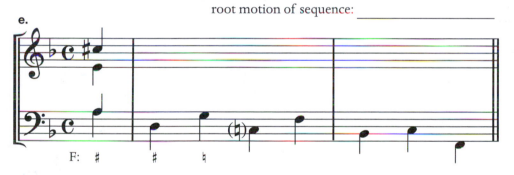

root motion of sequence (mm. 2–4): _____

f.

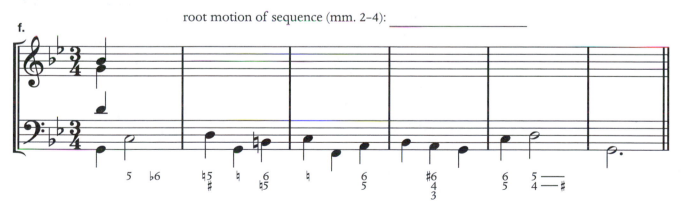

2. The following are figured bass exercises from historical sources.

- Realize the figured basses in four-part harmony.
- Write the roots for the chords indicated.
- Identify the root motion of the sequences (such as descending fifth; alternating down 3, up 4; etc.).

keyboard format

a. Exercise by Johann Gottlieb Vierling

root motion of sequence (mm. 1–2): _____

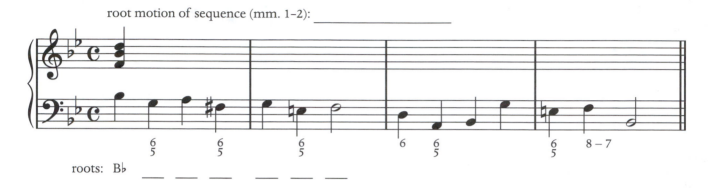

b. Exercise by G. F. Handel, for Princess Anne

root motion in sequence in mm. 1–2: _____ in mm. 4–6: _____

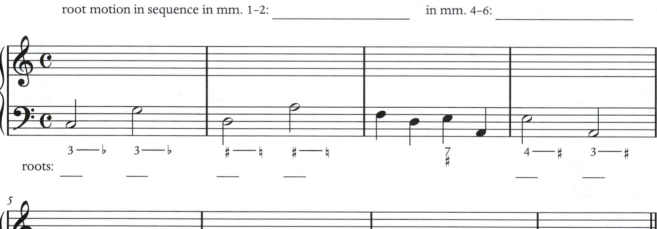

for string quartet

    c. Exercise by W. A. Mozart, for Barbara Ployer

        root motion in sequence in mm. 1–2: _____

roots: _____

3. Provide figured bass accompaniments in keyboard format for the following excerpts.

    a. G. F. Handel, *Water Music*, Adagio e staccato

        Also label the Roman numerals.

b. Tomaso Albinoni, Violin Sonata Op. 4, No. 4, iv

Label the roots of the chord in spaces provided.

roots: D

root motion sequence in mm. 1–4: _____ In mm. 4–6: _____

E. EQUAL DIVISION OF THE OCTAVE

1. Add five other notes between the given pairs of notes so as to divide the octave into six equal parts; each note should be a whole step (two semitones) higher than the previous one.

2. Add three other notes between the given pairs of notes so as to divide the octave into four equal parts.

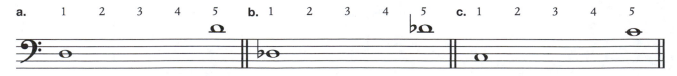

How many semitones are between the adjacent notes? ____

3. Add two other notes between the given pairs of notes so as to divide the octave
into three equal parts.

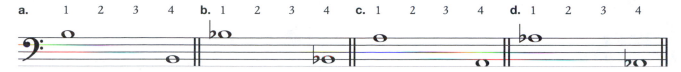

How many semitones are between the adjacent notes? ____

F. STRICT CHROMATIC SEQUENCES

Realize these figured basses; then indicate the number of semitones between each
repetition of the strict chromatic sequential pattern.

Keyboard format:

1.   semitones between each repetition of sequential pattern in mm. 1–3: ____

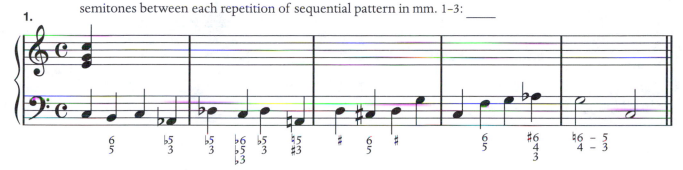

2.   semitones between each repetition of sequential pattern: ____

3. Exercise by Emanuel Aloys Förster

     semitones between each repetition of sequential pattern: ____

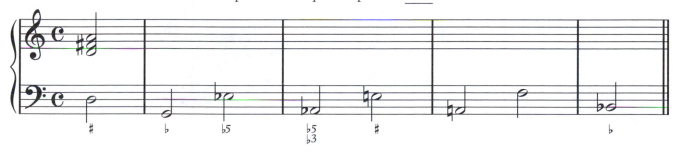

SATB format:

4. semitones in each repetition of sequential pattern from m. 1 to downbeat of m. 3: _____

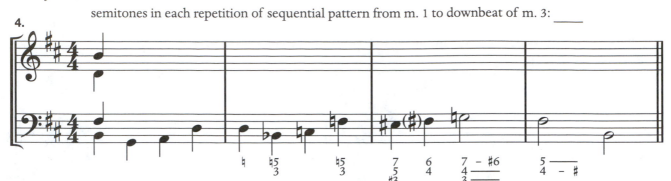

G. ANALYSIS

1. Label the Roman numerals and identify the root motion of the sequences (such as descending fifth; alternating down 3, up 4; and so on).

a. Chris Smith and Elmer Bowman, "Good Morning Carrie"

root motion in m. 1 (second beat) through m. 2: _____

Ab:

b. Clarence Williams, "Sugar Blues"

root motion (starting with second chord): _____

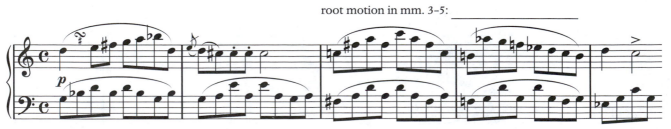

C:

c. Ludwig van Beethoven, Piano Sonata, Op. 2, No. 3, i

root motion in mm. 3–5: _____

G min.:

d. Joseph Haydn, Symphony No. 36, iii

root motion: _____

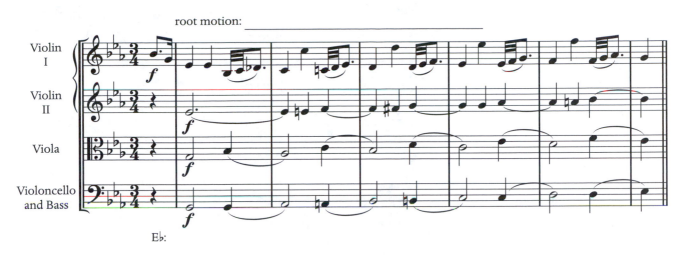

In this sequence, every measure except one includes an applied dominant. Why do you suppose an applied dominant is not used in that measure?

e. Sigismund Neukomm, *Morceaux*, Book II, No. 6

root motion in mm. 1–6: _____

f. Ludwig van Beethoven, Piano Sonata, Op. 14, No. 2, ii

root motion in mm. 1–2: _____

g. Clara Rogers, "A Match"

root motion in mm. 1–3: _____

And teach   his feet   a   meas - ure,   And find   his mouth   a   rein;

D:

2. Provide a simplified harmonic model of this passage on the staff below the score.

- The bass of each measure of the model should match the lowest note in each of the indicated group of measures.

- The upper voices in the model should match the notes of the chord (omitting embellishing tones) in each of the indicated group of measures, moving with smooth voice leading between chords.

- Where necessary, enharmonically respell the harmonic model.

Bedřich Smetana, Overture to *The Bartered Bride*

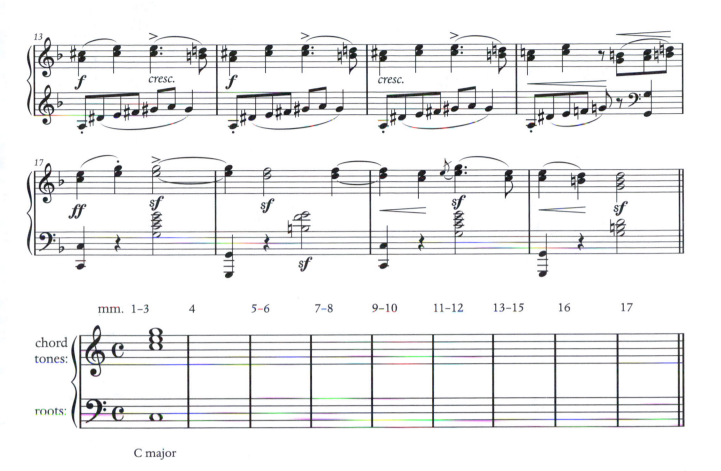

C major

- Why do mm. 137–138 include flats in the lower voice and sharps in the upper voices?

- How might this sequential pattern be described? (See also Chapter 42.)

3. Label the chord roots and qualities of the following as indicated. Then identify the root motion of the sequences.

a. Frédéric Chopin, Concerto in F Minor, Op. 21, iii

root: C   ___ ___   ___   ___   ___ ___   ___ ___

quality: maj.   ___ ___   ___   ___   ___ ___   ___ ___

type of sequence: _____

b. Clara Schumann, Prelude No. 2

root: C   ___ ___ ___   ___ ___ ___ ___   ___

quality: maj.   ___ ___ ___   ___ ___ ___ ___   ___

type of sequence in m. 1: _____ in mm. 2–3: _____

Two cadential $^6_4$ chords in this excerpt resolve atypically. Locate them and describe how they resolve.

4. James Scott, "Efficiency Rag"

Label the roman numerals and cadences.

C:

chapter 34 | Chromatic Modulation

A. QUESTIONS FOR REVIEW

1. What are distantly related keys?

2. What are some examples of chromatic pivot chords?

3. What is a common-tone modulation?

4. What chords can be reinterpreted enharmonically to create a chromatic pivot chord?

5. When did chromatic modulations begin to become commonplace?

6. How might a series of modulations or tonicizations create equal division of the octave?

B. NOTATING CHROMATIC PIVOT CHORDS

1. *Pivot chords involving mixture*: Write the indicated chord, and complete the chord identification below the staff.

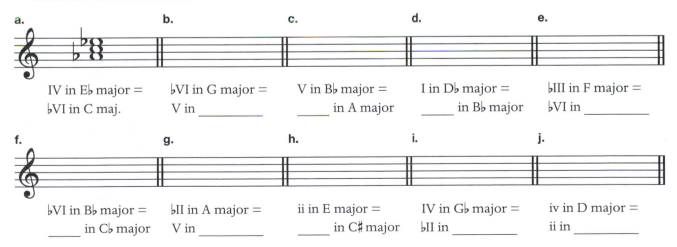

a.

IV in E♭ major =
♭VI in C maj.

b.

♭VI in G major =
V in _____

c.

V in B♭ major =
_____ in A major

d.

I in D♭ major =
_____ in B♭ major

e.

♭III in F major =
♭VI in _____

f.

♭VI in B♭ major =
_____ in C♭ major

g.

♭II in A major =
V in _____

h.

ii in E major =
_____ in C♯ major

i.

IV in G♭ major =
♭II in _____

j.

iv in D major =
ii in _____

2. *Pivot chords involving enharmonic reinterpretation:* Write the pairs of enharmonically equivalent chords, and complete the chord identification below the staff.

a.

vii°7 of F = vii°$^4_3$ of B

b.

vii°7 of G = vii°$^6_5$ of _____

c.

vii°$^6_5$ of D = vii°7 of _____

d.

V7 of C = Ger+6 of _____

e.

V7 of E♭ = Ger+6 of _____

f.

V7 of _____ = Ger+6 of F

3. Name at least three chords that can be used as pivot chords between the following pairs of keys.

- Indicate the Roman numeral of the chord in each key.

- Circle any chord that involves enharmonic reinterpretation.

a. G major and B♭ major:

G : _____♭VI_____ . _____ . _____ .
= B♭: _____IV_____ . _____ . _____ .

b. D minor and E♭ major:

D min.: _____ . _____ . _____ .
= E♭: _____ . _____ . _____ .

c. A♭ major and F major:

A♭: _____ . _____ . _____ .
= F: _____ . _____ . _____ .

4. Compose a short progression that modulates between one of the pairs of keys listed above in question (3).

- The progression should be two or three measures long, in SATB format.

- Write a time signature and the key signature of the starting key.

- Modulate between the two keys using one of the chromatic pivot chords identified above.

C. REALIZING ROMAN NUMERALS

1. Realize the Roman numerals for these progressions, each of which uses a chromatic pivot chord, in SATB format. Make sure to include the necessary accidentals.

a.

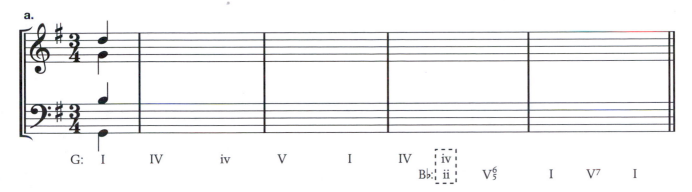

G: I   IV   iv   V   I   IV
B♭: ii   V$^6_5$ I   V^7 I

b.

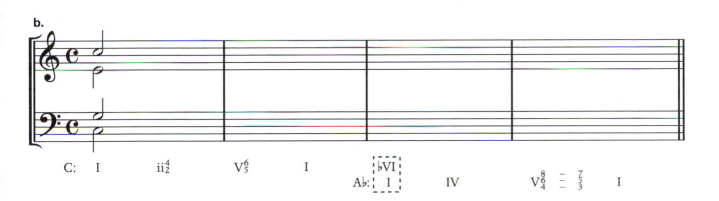

C: I   ii$^4_2$ V$^6_5$ I   ♭VI
A♭: I   IV   V$^8_4$^{6} ₌ $^7_3$^{5} I

c.

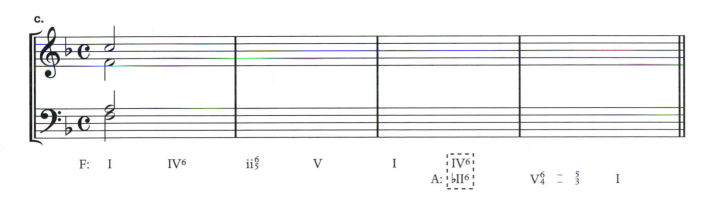

F: I   IV^6 ii$^6_5$ V   I   IV^6
A: ♭II^6 V$^6_4$ ₌ $^5_3$ I

2. Each of these passages uses an enharmonically reinterpreted pivot chord. Realize the Roman numerals, in keyboard format.

a.

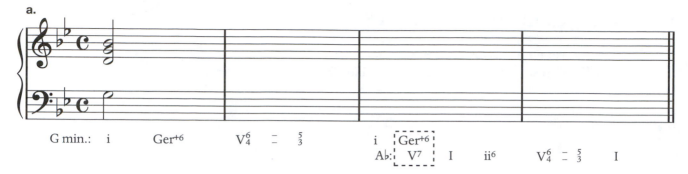

G min.: i Ger+6 V$^6_4$ — $^5_3$ i Ger+6
A♭: V^7 I ii^6 V$^6_4$ — $^5_3$ I

Also circle the Roman numerals of the enharmonically equivalent chords.

b.

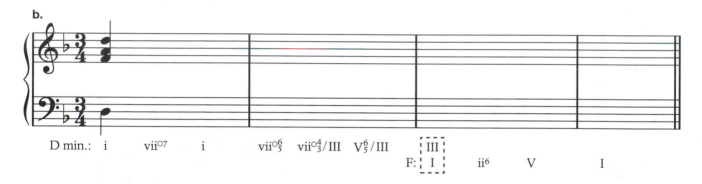

D min.: i vii°7 i vii°$^6_5$ vii°$^4_3$/III V$^6_5$/III III
F: I ii^6 V I

D. REALIZING FIGURED BASS

- Realize the following figured basses.
- Then indicate the keys of the tonicizations below the staff.

1.

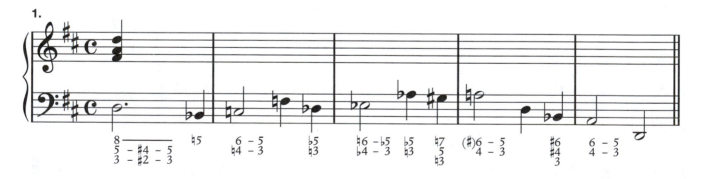

$\begin{matrix}8 \\ 5 \\ 3\end{matrix}$ — #4 — 5 — #2 — 3 ♮5 $\begin{matrix}6 \\ ♮4\end{matrix}$ — $\begin{matrix}5 \\ 3\end{matrix}$ $\begin{matrix}♭5 \\ ♭3\end{matrix}$ $\begin{matrix}♮6 \\ ♭4\end{matrix}$ — $\begin{matrix}♭5 \\ 3\end{matrix}$ $\begin{matrix}♭5 \\ ♭3\end{matrix}$ $\begin{matrix}♮7 \\ 5 \\ ♭3\end{matrix}$ (♯)$\begin{matrix}6 \\ 4\end{matrix}$ — $\begin{matrix}5 \\ 3\end{matrix}$ $\begin{matrix}♯6 \\ ♯4 \\ 3\end{matrix}$ $\begin{matrix}6 \\ 4\end{matrix}$ — $\begin{matrix}5 \\ 3\end{matrix}$

2.

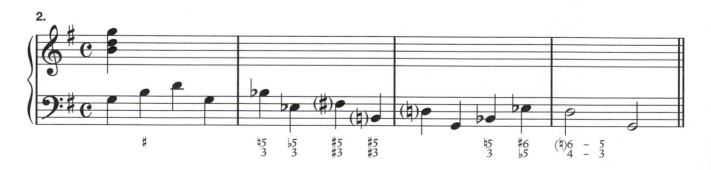

♯ $\begin{matrix}♮5 \\ 3\end{matrix}$ $\begin{matrix}♭5 \\ 3\end{matrix}$ $\begin{matrix}♯5 \\ ♯3\end{matrix}$ $\begin{matrix}♯5 \\ ♯3\end{matrix}$ $\begin{matrix}♮5 \\ 3\end{matrix}$ $\begin{matrix}♯6 \\ ♭5\end{matrix}$ (♮)$\begin{matrix}6 \\ 4\end{matrix}$ — $\begin{matrix}5 \\ 3\end{matrix}$

3.

4.

5. Using Exercise 4 as a simplified harmonic model, compose a piece. The piece could
be for keyboard or for keyboard and another instrument.

E. ANALYSIS

1. Friedrich von Flotow, *Martha*, overture

- Identify the key this passage begins in, and the key to which it modulates.
- Label the keys and Roman numerals on the score. Note that most chords last for several measures.

- What modulatory technique is used in this example? _____

_____

2. Franz Schubert, Ecossaise, D. 145

- Label the key of this piece and any keys that are tonicized.
- Label the Roman numerals.
- Name the modulatory technique used to move to each new key.
- There is an unusual chord progression in the first phrase. Circle the Roman numerals for that progression. How might this progression be explained?

3. Ludwig van Beethoven, String Quartet, Op. 18, No. 2, iv

- Label the starting key and the key to which there is a modulation, indicating its relationship to the main key, and the modulatory technique used.

- Label the return to the main key, indicating the modulatory technique used.

- Label the Roman numerals (at most one chord per measure).

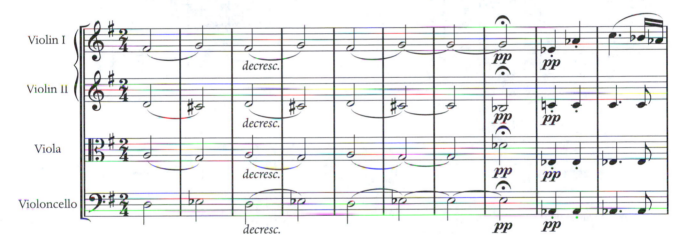

4. Franz Schubert, 20 Waltzes, D. 146, No. 10

Label the main key and any other keys that are tonicized. (Note that in some cases the V of the key might be more emphasized than its tonic.)

Complete a harmonic model of measures 13–28 in four-part harmony, using at most one chord per measure. When moving between chords all the voices should either move by step or stay on the same note (perhaps enharmonically respelled).

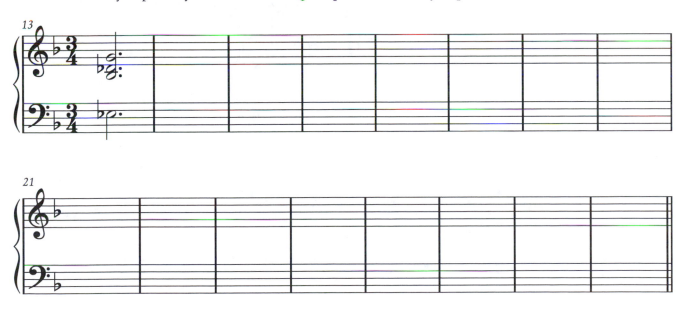

5. Franz Liszt, "Oh! Quand je dors"

Label the key and Roman numerals with one Roman numeral for each implied bass note (thus, for instance, the first Roman numeral should extend from measure 1 through measure 6, since the note E is the implied bass throughout these measures).

Translation: Oh! when I'm asleep, come to my bed, as Laura appeared to Petrarch, and as your breath touches me when you pass, suddenly my lips will open!

This piece begins in E major. What keys arrive in the following measures?

m. 1 __E__ m. 9 _____ m. 11 _____ m. 16 _____ m. 19 _____

Write a chord progression based on these keys, connecting the tonic chords in root
position, with smooth motion in the upper voices:

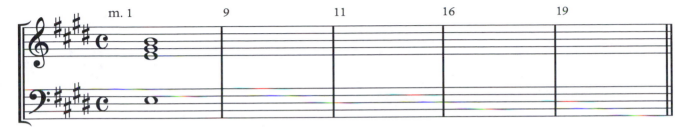

What might explain the logic of this succession of keys?

6. Franz Liszt, *Consolation* No. 1

Answer the questions that follow the excerpt.

- What are the keys of the following passages?

  mm. 1–7: _____ mm. 8–12: _____ mm. 13–16: _____ mm. 17–25: _____

- At times, the sense of key here seems merely suggested rather than strongly asserted. What features in the music create this impression?

- How does the harmonic structure of this piece compare to the harmonic structure of Liszt's song "Oh! Quand je dors" in the previous question?

7. Franz Liszt, *Consolation* No. 3

Answer the questions that follow the excerpt.

- This piece begins in D♭ major. What keys arrive in the following measures?

  measure 1 ____D♭____   measure 26 _____   measure 31 _____

  measure 35 _____   measure 39 _____   measure 43 _____

Write a chord progression based on these keys, in which the tonics of these keys are root position chords, with smooth motion in the upper voices:

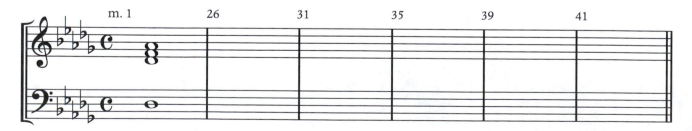

- Describe the logic behind this key structure and the modulations that lead to each new key.

part
five

Form

chapter 35

Sentences and Other Phrase Types

A. QUESTIONS FOR REVIEW

1. What is a sentence? What are its sections?

2. What does a presentation consist of? How does it differ from the segment that follows it?

3. In a typical eight-measure sentence, how long is the presentation? How long is the basic idea? How long is the repetition (or varied repetition) of the basic idea?

4. What are some ways in which the length of a standard sentence may be varied?

5. What is phrase overlap?

6. What might make it difficult to decide whether a phrase is a sentence or merely sentence-like?

B. COMPOSITION

1. Compose melodies following the instructions given.

a. *presentation*   *continuation*

		fragmentation		*cadence*
		repetition of	m. 1 trans-posed up or	PAC in C, ending on
basic idea	strict repetition of basic idea	m. 1	down a step	downbeat of m. 8

b. Same as (a), except that measures 3–4 should be a varied repetition of measures 1–2, with the same rhythm and melodic contour but transposed up or down a scale step.

c. Same as (a), except that measures 3–4 should be a contrasting idea (not a repetition or variation of measures 1–2).

2. Compose melodies following the instructions given. In each case, make sure the melody fits with the harmonies indicated by the Roman numerals.

e.

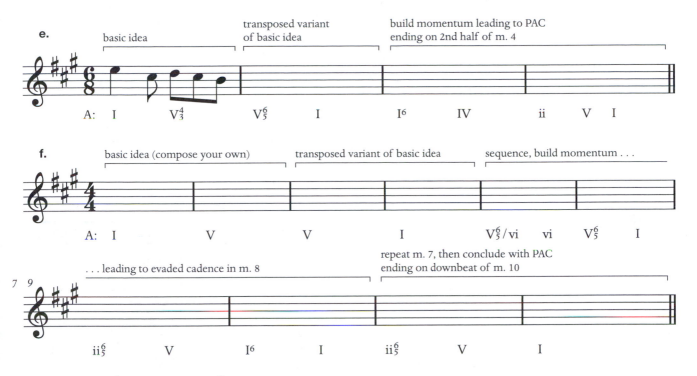

basic idea — transposed variant of basic idea — build momentum leading to PAC ending on 2nd half of m. 4

A: I V$_3^4$ V$_5^6$ I I^6 IV ii V I

f.

basic idea (compose your own) — transposed variant of basic idea — sequence, build momentum . . .

A: I V V I V$_5^6$/vi vi V$_5^6$ I

. . . leading to evaded cadence in m. 8 — repeat m. 7, then conclude with PAC ending on downbeat of m. 10

7 9

ii$_5^6$ V I^6 I ii$_5^6$ V I

3. Compose a phrase in sentence form.

   a. First, realize the Roman numerals in keyboard format:

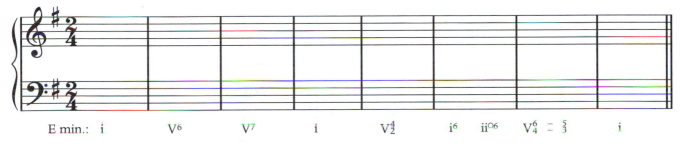

E min.: i V^6 V^7 i V$_2^4$ i^6 ii^{o6} V$_4^6$ — $_3^5$ i

   b. Using the harmonies of the progression in (a) above, compose a short piece in sentence form either for two instruments or for piano. The bass line can be exactly the same as in (a) above, or it can be a variant of the bass line in (a).

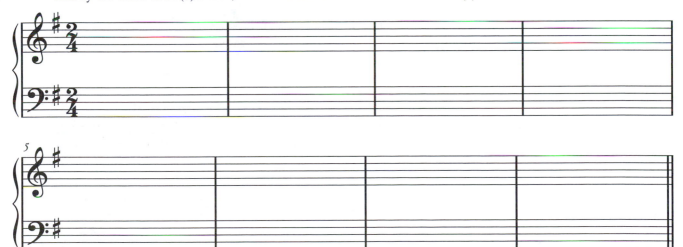

5

4. Below are the first two measures of a sentence from a string trio by Haydn. Complete this passage in sentence form. It should be playable either by a trio or by keyboard.

5. Compose a short passage in D major with a meter of your choice, for keyboard, guitar, or an ensemble of your choice.

    a. Start by composing an eight-measure harmonic model in four-part harmony, keyboard format, following the outline below.

    b. Compose a passage in sentence form based on the harmonic outline in (a), with a basic idea repeated in varied form in measures 1–4, followed by a continuation leading to a perfect authentic cadence in measures 5–8.

C. ANALYSIS

1. The following passages are sentences.

- In the score, identify the presentation, the basic idea, the repetition of the basic idea, and the continuation.

- Identify the type and key of the cadence at the end.

- On the blank lines below the staff, describe features of repetition, variation, and continuation.

a. Joseph Haydn, Quartet Op. 2, No. 1, ii

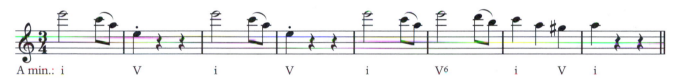

A min.: i   V   i   V   i   V⁶   i   V   i

How is the basic idea varied (if at all) when it is repeated within the presentation?

_____

Features that create momentum in the continuation:

_____

b. Louis-Claude Daquin, "La guitare"

How is the basic idea varied (if at all) when it is repeated within the presentation?

_____

Features that create momentum in the continuation:

_____

c. Fernando Sor, Grand Sonata for Guitar, Op. 22, Minuet

How is the basic idea varied (if at all) when it is repeated within the presentation?

_____

Features that create momentum in the continuation:

_____

d. W. A. Mozart, Minuet, K. 1

How is the basic idea varied (if at all) when it is repeated within the presentation?

_____

Features that create momentum in the continuation:

_____

e. François Couperin, "Les brinborions"

How is the basic idea varied (if at all) when it is repeated within the presentation?

_____

Features that create momentum in the continuation:

_____

f. Frédéric Chopin, Nocturne, Op. 32, No. 1

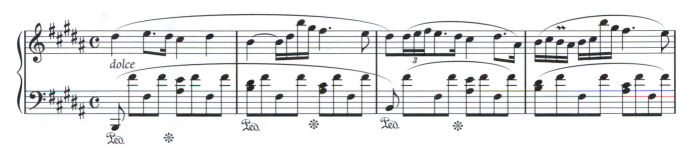

How is the basic idea varied (if at all) when it is repeated within the presentation?

_____

Features that create momentum in the continuation:

_____

g. Corona Schröter, "An eine Blume" ("To a Flower")

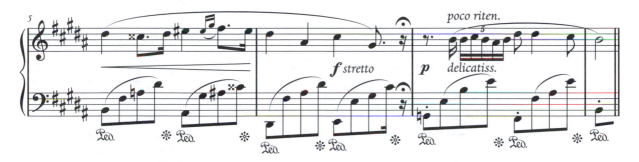

Translation: As the heavens have so beautifully adorned you, as the sun sews your garments, as you glitter with gold and silk, may my rose gladly suffer.

How is the basic idea varied (if at all) when it is repeated within the presentation?

_____

Features that create momentum in the continuation:

_____

h. Ludwig van Beethoven, Sonatina in G, Anh. 5, i

How is the basic idea varied (if at all) when it is repeated within the presentation?

_____

Features that create momentum in the continuation:

_____

i. Franz Schubert, Waltz, Op. 9, No. 17

How is the basic idea varied (if at all) when it is repeated within the presentation?

_____

Features that create momentum in the continuation:

_____

j. Giuseppe Verdi, "Pura siccome un angelo" ("As Pure as an Angel"), from *La Traviata*

Translation: [The young man], in love and beloved in turn, who was soon to marry my daughter, would now withdraw his pledge and ruin our happiness.

How is the basic idea varied (if at all) when it is repeated within the presentation?

_____

Features that create momentum in the continuation:

_____

k. Domenico Sarro, *Achille in Sciro*

Translation: If you tie a heart in knots, if you set a soul aflame, oh tyrannical love, is there something you don't demand from me?

How is the basic idea varied (if at all) when it is repeated within the presentation?

_____

Features that create momentum in the continuation:

_____

I. W. A. Mozart, "Un aura amorosa," from *Così fan tutte*

Translation: A loving aura from my beloved will sweetly refresh my heart.

How is the basic idea varied (if at all) when it is repeated within the presentation?

_____

Features that create momentum in the continuation:

_____

2. The following passages are sentences that are expanded from the eight-measure model.

- On the score, identify the presentation (including the basic idea and its repetition) and continuation.

- Label the type and key of the cadence at the end.

- On the blank lines below the staff, describe how the phrase is expanded.

a. W. A. Mozart, Symphony No. 15, K. 124, iii (violins and basses only)

How is this phrase expanded?

_____

_____

b. W. A. Mozart, Piano Sonata in G, K. 283, i

How is this phrase expanded?

_____

_____

c. W. A. Mozart, Piano Sonata in C, K. 330, i

How is this phrase expanded?

---

d. Ludwig van Beethoven, Sonata for Violin and Piano, Op. 24 ("Spring"), iv

How is this phrase expanded?

_____

_____

3. Analyze the following excerpts by labeling the parts of the phrase and cadences on the score, then answer the questions below the staff.

a. W. A. Mozart, Piano Sonata in B♭, K. 333, i

Is this a sentence? _____

If not, why not?

_____

If it is a sentence, is the basic idea repeated exactly?

_____

If not, how is it varied?

_____

b. Bob Cole, "Everybody Wants to See the Baby"

Is this a sentence? _____

If not, why not?

_____

If it is a sentence, is the basic idea repeated exactly?

_____

If not, how is it varied?

_____

c. C. P. E. Bach, Sonata for Keyboard in F, i

Is this a sentence? _____

If not, why not?

_____

If it is a sentence, is the basic idea repeated exactly?

_____

If not, how is it varied?

_____

4. The following passages—all composed during the later nineteenth century or early twentieth century—treat harmony and tonality freely. Each of these are either sentences or sentence-like (see also Chapter 47).

- On the score for each passage, label the basic idea, the repetition of the basic idea, the presentation, and the continuation.

- Label the type and key of cadence suggested at the end of each passage.

- Which features in each suggest a sense of key? Which features tend to obscure the tonality?

a. Maurice Ravel, Menuet in C♯ Minor

b. Sergey Prokofiev, Gavotte from *Classical Symphony*, Op. 25

c. Hugo Wolf, "Ein Stündlein wohl vor Tag," from *Mörike Lieder*

Translation: While I lay sleeping, a moment before daybreak, a swallow in a tree sang before my window, I barely could hear it.

36

Periods and Other Phrase Pairs

A. QUESTIONS FOR REVIEW

1. What is a parallel period? How is it different from a sequential period? From a contrasting period?

2. What is an antecedent? What types of cadences may be found at the end of the antecedent? What is a consequent, and what types of cadences may be found at the end of it?

3. Typically, how long is each phrase in a period? Under what circumstances can the lengths of phrases differ?

4. How can a sentence appear within a period?

5. In what situation might a phrase pair not form a period?

B. COMPOSITION

1. Complete each period as indicated. For parallel periods, the second phrase should begin the same way as the first (mm. 5–6 should be the same as mm. 1–2).

a. Parallel period, ending with PAC

b. Parallel period, ending with PAC

c. Parallel period, ending with PAC

d. Contrasting period (m. 5 is different from m. 1), ending with PAC

e. Parallel period, ending with PAC

f. Parallel period, ending with PAC in key of relative major

g. Sequential period, ending with PAC in tonic key

transposition up a scale step of mm. 1–2

2. Compose parallel periods by completing the following excerpts, in each case ending with a PAC.

a. Antonio Rosetti, Violin Duet in D

b. Francis Johnson, "Philadelphia Fireman's Cotillion"

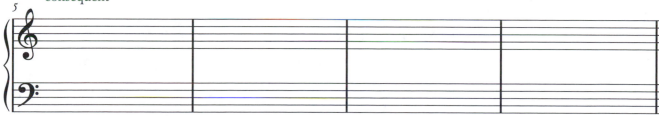

c. Ferdinando Carulli, Petites Bagatelles for Guitar, Op. 130, No. 10

antecedent

consequent
5

d. Wilhelmine von Troschke und Rosenwerth, "Eine Hand voll Erde"

antecedent   continue to half cadence

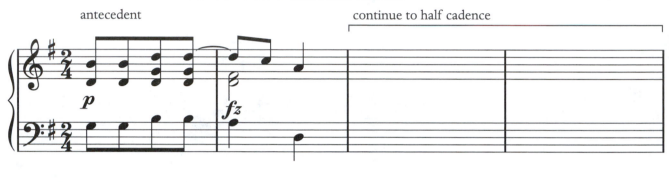

consequent

5

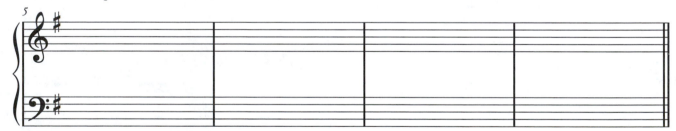

3. Compose periods based following the given instructions.

a. Compose an eight-measure parallel period in E minor, $\frac{2}{4}$ time, based on the harmonies indicated.

- The piece should be either for keyboard or for two instruments.
- Make sure to write the clefs, key signature, and time signature.

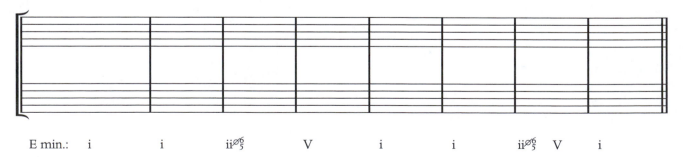

E min.:   i   i   ii⌀$^6_5$ V   i   i   ii⌀$^6_5$ V   i

b. Compose an eight-measure sequential or contrasting period in E minor, $\frac{2}{4}$ time, based on the harmonies indicated.

- The antecedent can be the same as (**a**) above.
- The piece should be either for keyboard or for two instruments.
- Make sure to write the clefs, key signature, and time signature.

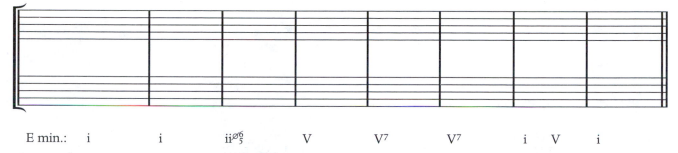

E min.:   i   i   ii°$^6_5$ V   V^7 V^7 i   V   i

c. Compose a parallel period in a key and time signature of your choice, for either keyboard, guitar, or instrument with keyboard accompaniment, following these guidelines:

- The antecedent begins on the tonic and leads to a half cadence.
- The first four measures of the consequent begin like the antecedent, but now end with a deceptive cadence.
- Following the deceptive cadence, two more measures lead to a perfect authentic cadence.

C. ANALYSIS

1. The following passages are each parallel periods.

- On the scores, bracket the antecedent and consequent.
- Label the type of each cadence; if there is a modulation, indicate the key of the cadence.

- Circle the measures at the start of the antecedent and consequent that are the same (or nearly the same, with only a slight variation).

a. "Home on the Range"

b. "Sur le pont d'Avignon"

c. "Roll the Cotton Down"

d. "My Bonnie Lies over the Ocean"

e. Wallace Willis, "Swing Low, Sweet Chariot"

2. The following passages are each periods. Label as indicated.

- On the score, bracket and label the antecedent and consequent.

- Label the cadences, indicating the type of each. If there is a modulation, indicate the key of the cadence.

- Below the score, identify the type of period (parallel, sequential, or contrasting) and whether there is a modulation within the consequent (and if there is a modulation, to what key).

- Give the number of measures in the antecedent and consequent.

a. W. A. Mozart, Divertimento, K. 213, iv

period type: _____ modulation? _____

no. of measures in antecedent = _____   no. of measures in consequent = _____

b. J. S. Bach, Minuet in G

period type: _____ modulation? _____

no. of measures in antecedent = _____   no. of measures in consequent = _____

c. Joseph Haydn, Piano Trio, Hob. XV:20, ii

period type: _____ modulation? _____

no. of measures in antecedent = _____ no. of measures in consequent = _____

d. Joseph Haydn, Symphony No. 94, ii

period type: _____ modulation? _____

no. of measures in antecedent = _____ no. of measures in consequent = _____

e. Justin Holland, Andante for Guitar

period type: _____ modulation? _____

no. of measures in antecedent = _____ no. of measures in consequent = _____

f. Richard Wagner, Bridal Chorus, from *Lohengrin*, Act III

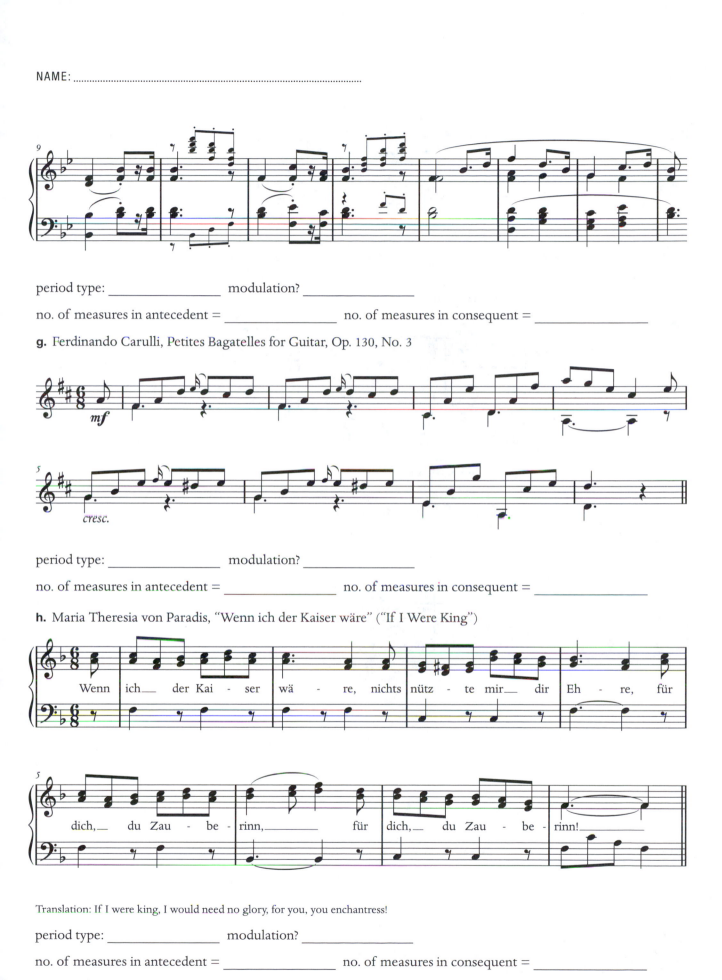

period type: _____ modulation? _____

no. of measures in antecedent = _____ no. of measures in consequent = _____

g. Ferdinando Carulli, *Petites Bagatelles* for Guitar, Op. 130, No. 3

period type: _____ modulation? _____

no. of measures in antecedent = _____ no. of measures in consequent = _____

h. Maria Theresia von Paradis, "Wenn ich der Kaiser wäre" ("If I Were King")

Wenn ich__ der Kai - ser wä - re, nichts nütz - te mir__ dir Eh - re, für

dich,__ du Zau - be - rinn,_____ für dich,__ du Zau - be - rinn!_____

Translation: If I were king, I would need no glory, for you, you enchantress!

period type: _____ modulation? _____

no. of measures in antecedent = _____ no. of measures in consequent = _____

i. Franz Schubert, Waltz, Op. 18, No. 10

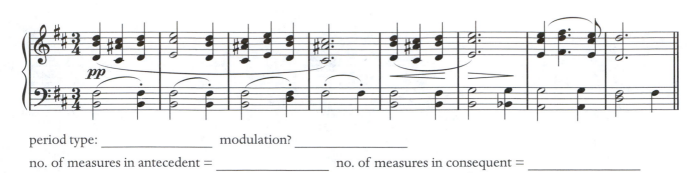

period type: _____ modulation? _____

no. of measures in antecedent = _____ no. of measures in consequent = _____

j. Ignatius Sancho, "Friendship Source of Joy"

period type: _____ modulation? _____

no. of measures in antecedent = _____ no. of measures in consequent = _____

k. Joseph Haydn, Symphony No. 64

period type: _____ modulation? _____

no. of measures in antecedent = _____ no. of measures in consequent = _____

l. G. F. Handel, Suite in D Minor, Sarabande, HWV 437

period type: _____ modulation? _____

no. of measures in antecedent = _____ no. of measures in consequent = _____

m. Étienne Méhul, Piano Sonata in D, Op. 1, i

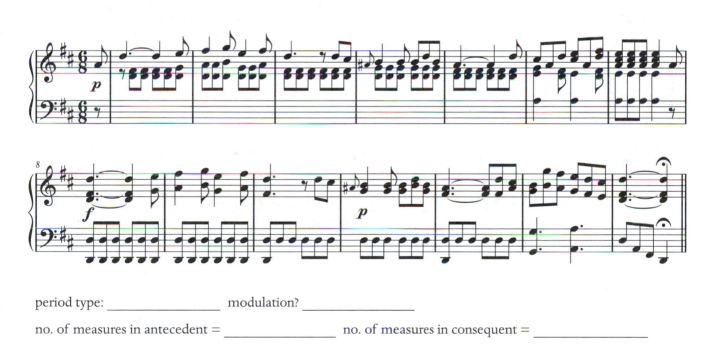

period type: _____ modulation? _____

no. of measures in antecedent = _____ no. of measures in consequent = _____

n. W. A. Mozart, "Ein Mädchen oder Weibchen" (arr. Beethoven, Op. 66, piano part only)

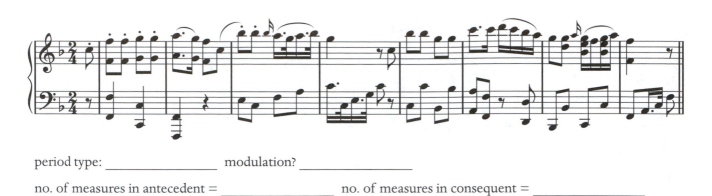

period type: _____ modulation? _____

no. of measures in antecedent = _____ no. of measures in consequent = _____

o. W. A. Mozart, "Bei Männern welche Liebe fühlen" ("In Men Who Feel Love"), from
The Magic Flute

Translation: Pamina: In men who feel love, a good heart is not lacking. Papageno: To share that sweet
emotion is a woman's highest duty.

period type: _____ modulation? _____

no. of measures in antecedent = _____ no. of measures in consequent = _____

p. W. A. Mozart, Piano Sonata in D, K. 576, i

period type: _____ modulation? _____

no. of measures in antecedent = _____ no. of measures in consequent = _____

q. Scott Joplin, "The Entertainer"

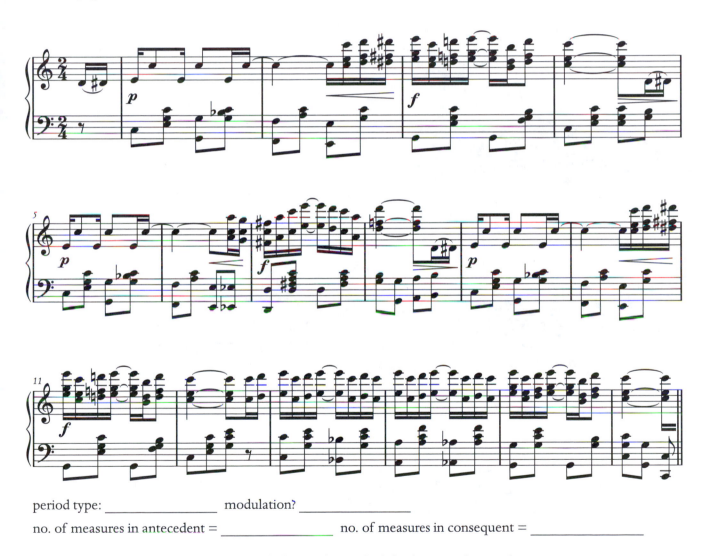

period type: _____ modulation? _____

no. of measures in antecedent = _____ no. of measures in consequent = _____

3. The following passages are each parallel periods in which both antecedent and
consequent are sentences.

- Bracket and label the antecedent and the consequent.

- Label the cadences indicating the type of each; if there is a modulation, indicate
the key of the cadence.

- Label the start of the presentation and the continuation within each sentence.
- Bracket and label the basic idea and its repetition within each presentation.

a. W. A. Mozart, Horn Concerto in E♭, K. 447, iii

b. Sophia Dussek, Harp Sonata in G, Op. 2, No. 2, ii

c. Robert Schumann, "Armes Waisenkind" ("Poor Orphan Child")

4. The following are parallel periods in which the antecedent and consequent are
different lengths.

- On the score, label the key and type of cadences, and bracket and label the
  antecedent and consequent.

- Below the score, indicate the length of the antecedent and consequent. Then
  indicate which of these phrases is longer and explain how the longer phrase was
  expanded.

a. Marianne Auenbrugger, Piano Sonata in E♭, iii

length of antecedent = _____   length of consequent = _____

Which is longer, and how was it lengthened? _____

_____

_____

b. Franz Schubert, "Wasserfluth" ("Flood Water"), from *Winterreise* (*A Winter's Journey*)

Man-che Thrän' aus mei-nen Au-gen ist ge-fal-len in den Schnee; sei-ne kal-ten

Flo-cken sau-gen dur-stig ein das hei--sse Weh,_____ dur-stig ein_ das hei--sse Weh.

Translation: Many tears from my eyes have fallen on the snow; its cold flakes thirstily absorb my burning sorrow.

length of antecedent = _____ length of consequent = _____

Which is longer, and how was it lengthened? _____

_____

c. Giacomo Meyerbeer, Coronation March, from *Le prophète*, Act IV

length of antecedent = _____   length of consequent = _____

Which is longer, and how was it lengthened? _____

_____

d. Felix Mendelssohn, *Songs without Words*, Op. 62, No. 1

length of antecedent = _____   length of consequent = _____

Which is longer, and how was it lengthened? _____

_____

e. Mozart, Piano Concerto in D Minor, K. 466, iii

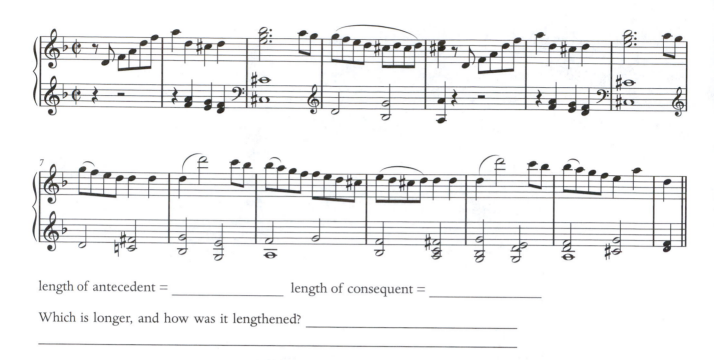

length of antecedent = _____ length of consequent = _____

Which is longer, and how was it lengthened? _____

_____

_____

5. The following passages each consist of a phrase pair that is not a period. On the score itself, label the cadence at the end of each phrase by type and, if there's a modulation, by key. On the lines below each score, indicate:

- whether the phrases begin similarly or differently;

- whether there is a modulation within the second phrase (and if so, to what key);

- the number of measures in each phrase.

a. Jean-Philippe Rameau, Rigaudon

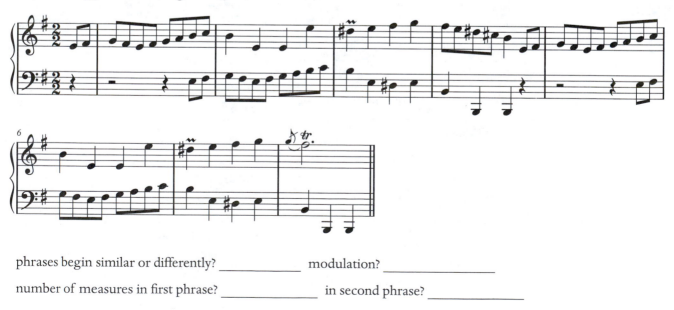

phrases begin similar or differently? _____ modulation? _____

number of measures in first phrase? _____ in second phrase? _____

b. Ludwig van Beethoven, Sonata for Violin and Piano, Op. 24 ("Spring"), iii

phrases begin similar or differently? _____ modulation? _____

number of measures in first phrase? _____ in second phrase? _____

c. W. A. Mozart, Minuet, K. 4

phrases begin similar or differently? _____ modulation? _____

number of measures in first phrase? _____ in second phrase? _____

6. Edward Elgar, "Salut d'amour"

- Label the cadences, and the antecedent and consequent phrases on the score.
- Label the Roman numerals.
- On the staves below the score, complete a simplified harmonic model.
- Compose a short parallel period based on this harmonic progression either for piano, guitar, or an instrument plus piano accompaniment.

7. The following periods—all composed during the late nineteenth or early twentieth century—treat harmony and tonality relatively freely (see also Chapter 47).

- On the score for each passage, label the antecedent and consequent phrases.
- Indicate whether the passage is best understood as a parallel, sequential, or contrasting period.
- Label the key and type of cadence found at the end of each phrase.
- What harmonies are suggested in each of these passages? Which features tend to obscure the tonality?

a. Gabriel Fauré, Sicilienne, from *Pelléas et Mélisande*

period type: _____

b. Aleksandr Scriabin, Prelude Op. 11, No. 10

Type of period _____

c. Giacomo Puccini, "Musetta's Waltz," from *La bohème*

Translation: When I stroll along the street, people stop and stare, and all admire my beauty from head to toe.

period type: _____

d. George Gershwin, "Innocent Ingenue"

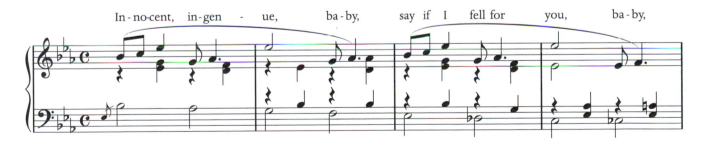

period type: _____

chapter 37 — Binary Form

A. QUESTIONS FOR REVIEW

1. What is binary form?

2. What is the difference between rounded, balanced, and simple binary forms?

3. In what ways are rounded, balanced, and simple binary forms analogous to parallel, sequential, and contrasting periods, respectively?

4. What types of cadence are usually found at the end of the first part of a binary form? What are the different effects of these various cadences?

5. What key and type of cadence is usually found at the end of the second part of a binary form?

B. COMPOSITION

Compose melodies against the given bass lines, using the harmonies suggested by the figured bass and following the instructions where given in the score.

1.

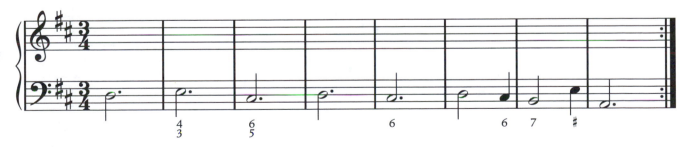

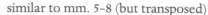

Is this in rounded or balanced binary? _____

2.

Is this in rounded or balanced binary? _____

3. Compose a rounded binary form movement by completing the following excerpt (from a cello sonata by Pleyel), following the instructions in the score.

... consequent: begins like mm. 1–4, but leads to a PAC in V   leads to V of the main key

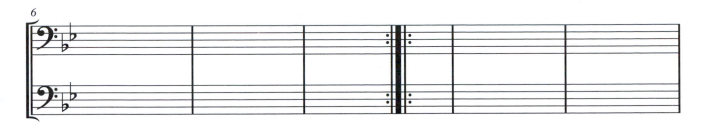

theme from mm. 1–4 returns, but now ends with PAC in main key

4. Compose a 16-measure piece in balanced binary form, following these guidelines:

- Write for keyboard, guitar, a solo instrument, or a solo instrument with piano accompaniment.

- Choose a major key and meter.

- Measures 1–4 should embellish tonic harmony with a **T–D–D–T** or **T–S–D–T** progression.

- Measures 5–8 should lead to a PAC in V with this progression:

  o **Key of V: I⁶ | ii⁶₅ | V | I |**

- Measures 9–12 should be based on one of these two progressions, in the main key:

  o **main key: V⁷/vi | vi | V⁷/V | V |**

           or

  o **main key: V⁷/ii | ii | V⁷ | I |**

- Measures 13–16 should be similar to measures 5–8, but now transposed to the main key, ending with a PAC.

C. ANALYSIS

Answer the questions about each of the following pieces.

1. Mauro Giuliani, Variations for Guitar, Op. 2

a. In what key is this movement? _____ What is the key and type of the cadence at the end of the first part? _____ What is the key and type of the cadence at the end of the second part? _____

b. Does the melody from the first few measures return in the main key in the middle of the second part? _____ (If yes, circle the return in the score.)

c. Based on the answer above, is this excerpt rounded, balanced, or simple?

_____

d. Are the two parts about the same length? _____ If the second part is longer than the first, by how much (about 1.5 times as long, twice as long)? _____

e. What is the form of measures 1-8? _____

f. What features promote a sense of instability at the start of the second part?

_____

2. W. A. Mozart, Minuet, K. 1e

Fine

a. In what key is this excerpt? _____ What is the key and type of cadence at the end of the first part? _____ What is the key and type of cadence at the end of the second part? _____

b. Does the melody from the first few measures return in the main key in the middle of the second part? _____ (If yes, circle the return in the score.)

c. Does the melody from the final measures from the first part return (perhaps slightly varied or transposed) at the end of the second part? _____ (If yes, circle it in the score.)

d. Based on the answers above, is this excerpt rounded, balanced, or simple?

_____

e. Compare the lengths of the two parts: _____

f. What features promote a sense of instability at the start of the second part (such as sequence, tonicization, or sustained V)? _____

3. Henry Purcell, Harpsichord Suite, Z. 660, Minuet

a. In what key is this excerpt? _____ What is the key and type of cadence at the end of the first part? _____ What is the key and type of cadence at the end of the second part? _____

b. Does the melody from the first few measures return in the main key in the middle of the second part? _____ (If yes, circle the return in the score.)

c. Does the melody from the final measures from the first part return (perhaps slightly varied or transposed) at the end of the second part? _____ (If yes, circle it in the score.)

d. Based on the answers above, is this excerpt rounded, balanced, or simple?

_____

e. Compare the lengths of the two parts: _____

f. What features promote a sense of instability at the start of the second part (such as sequence, tonicization, or sustained V)? _____

4. Joseph Bologne Saint-Georges, Sonata for Two Violins, Book II, No. 1, ii

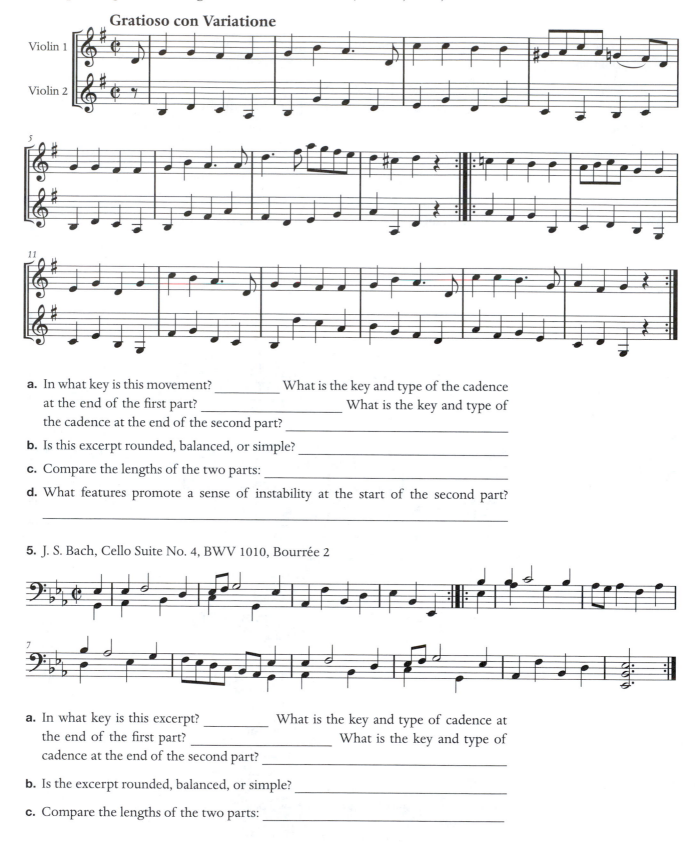

a. In what key is this movement? _____ What is the key and type of the cadence at the end of the first part? _____ What is the key and type of the cadence at the end of the second part? _____

b. Is this excerpt rounded, balanced, or simple? _____

c. Compare the lengths of the two parts: _____

d. What features promote a sense of instability at the start of the second part?

_____

5. J. S. Bach, Cello Suite No. 4, BWV 1010, Bourrée 2

a. In what key is this excerpt? _____ What is the key and type of cadence at the end of the first part? _____ What is the key and type of cadence at the end of the second part? _____

b. Is the excerpt rounded, balanced, or simple? _____

c. Compare the lengths of the two parts: _____

6. Arcangelo Corelli, Chamber Sonata Op. 2, No. 1, Gavotte

a. In what key is this movement? _____ What is the key and type of the cadence at the end of the first part? _____ What is the key and type of the cadence at the end of the second part? _____

b. Is this excerpt rounded, balanced, or simple? _____

c. Compare the lengths of the two parts: _____

d. What is the type and the key of the cadence in measure 6? _____

7. Joseph Haydn, Piano Sonata, Hob. XVI:37, iii

a. In what key is this excerpt? _____ What is the key and type of cadence at the end of the first part? _____ What is the key and type of cadence at the end of the second part? _____

b. Is the excerpt rounded, balanced, or simple? _____

c. Compare the lengths of the two parts:

_____

d. What features promote a sense of instability at the start of the second half?

_____

8. Joseph Haydn, Piano Sonata, Hob. XVI:37, iii

a. In what key is this excerpt? _____ What is the key and type of cadence at the end of the first part? _____ What is the key and type of cadence at the end of the second part? _____

b. Is the excerpt rounded, balanced, or simple? _____

c. Compare the lengths of the two parts:

_____

d. What features promote a sense of instability at the start of the second half?

_____

9. Anna Bon, Harpsichord Sonata in F, Op. 2, No. 3, Trio

a. In what key is this excerpt? _____ What is the key and type of cadence at the end of the first part? _____ What is the key and type of cadence at the end of the second part? _____ What is atypical about this final cadence? _____

b. Is the excerpt rounded, balanced, or simple? _____

c. Compare the lengths of the two parts: _____

d. What features promote a sense of instability at the start of the second part?

_____

10. Beethoven, Piano Sonata, Op. 2, No. 2, iii

(Scherzo) D. C.

a. In what key is this excerpt? _____ What is the key and type of cadence at the end of the first part? _____ What is the key and type of cadence at the end of the second part? _____

b. Is this excerpt rounded, balanced, or simple? _____

c. Compare the lengths of the two parts: _____

d. What features promote a sense of instability at the start of the second part (such as sequence, tonicization, or sustained V)? _____

11. Ludwig van Beethoven, Piano Sonata, Op. 27, No. 2 ("Moonlight"), ii

a. In what key is this excerpt? _____ What is the key and type of cadence at the end of the first part? _____ What is the key and type of cadence at the end of the second part? _____ What is the key and type of the cadence in measure 24? _____

b. Is the excerpt rounded, balanced, or simple? _____

c. Compare the lengths of the two parts:

_____

d. Is the theme in measures 1–8 a sentence, a parallel period, a sequential period, or a contrasting period? _____

e. How do measures 1–8 and 9–16 compare? In what ways are they similar, and in what ways are they different?

_____

_____

f. Why do you suppose there are no repeat signs at the end of the first part of this binary form movement?

_____

_____

12. Johannes Brahms, Waltz, Op. 39, No. 5

a. In what key is this excerpt? _____ What is the key and type of cadence at the end of the first part? _____ What is the key and type of cadence at the end of the second part? _____ What is atypical about this final cadence? _____

b. Is the excerpt rounded, balanced, or simple? _____

c. Compare the lengths of the two parts:

_____

d. What is unusual about the harmonization of the return of opening theme within the second part?

_____

chapter 38 — Ternary and Rondo Forms

A. QUESTIONS FOR REVIEW

1. Using letters, show the thematic scheme of ternary form.
2. Why is **A B C** form not an example of ternary form?
3. How does ternary form differ from rounded binary form?
4. Using letters, what are some common schemes of rondo form?
5. In which key does the **A** section of a rondo form always appear?
6. How do the contrasting sections of a five-part rondo form (that is, the **B** and **C** sections) usually differ from one another?

B. COMPOSITION

1. Realize these Roman numerals in keyboard style.

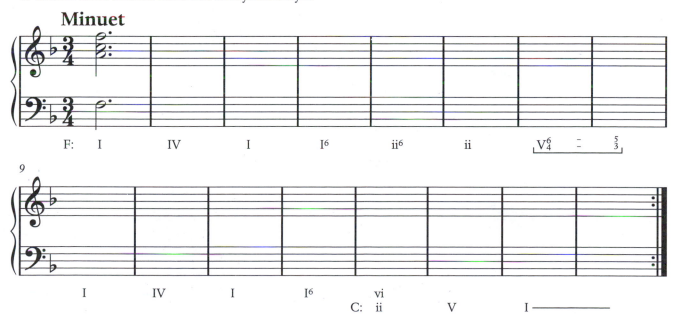

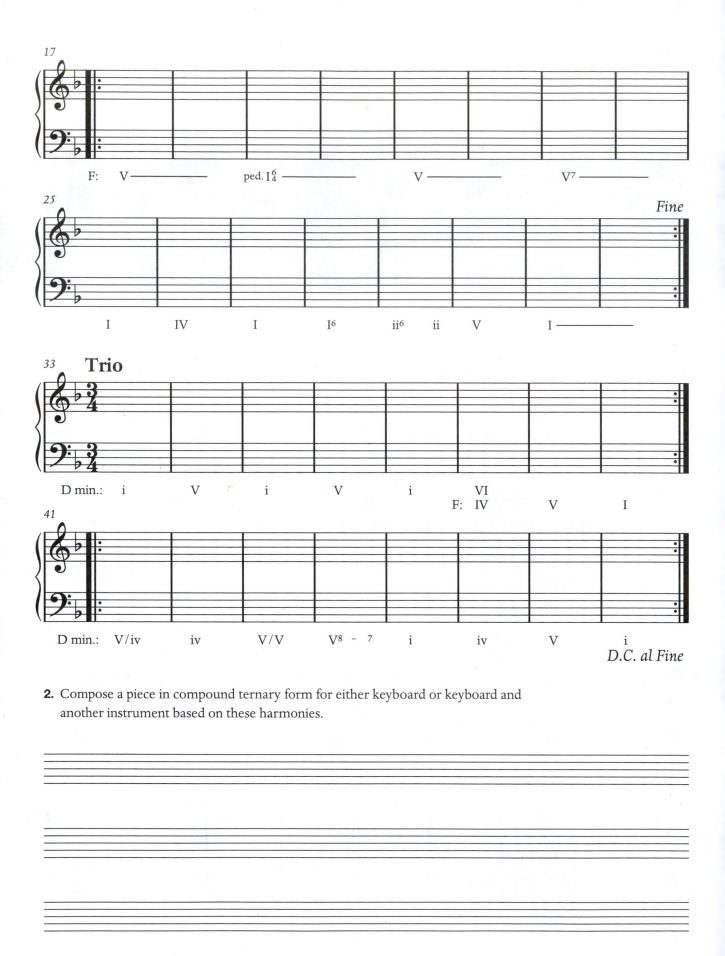

2. Compose a piece in compound ternary form for either keyboard or keyboard and another instrument based on these harmonies.

C. ANALYSIS

1. Muzio Clementi, Piano Sonatina in G, Op. 36, No. 2, ii

This piece is in ternary form, with a short bridge leading between two of the sections.

- Label the large sections with letters (**A** or **B**), and label the cadences with keys and types.
- Circle the (short) bridge that leads between the sections.
- Is the **A** section varied when it returns? _____

How does the **B** section compare to the **A** sections? In what ways is it similar, and in what ways does it differ? What features create the sense that the **B** section represents a departure or digression?

2. Robert Schumann, "Wichtige Begebenheit" ("An Important Event")

- Label the large sections of this ternary form piece with letters (**A** or **B**), and label the cadences with keys and types.

- Is the **A** section varied when it returns? _____

- Label the harmonies through the second beat of measure 4.

What features create the sense that the **B** section represents a departure or digression?

3. Joseph Haydn, Symphony No. 65, iii

This movement is in compound ternary form. On the score, label the cadences with keys and types.

Menuett

- What is the key of the Minuet? _____ To what key is there a modulation at the end of the Minuet's first half? _____
- Describe the form of the Minuet: is it binary? _____. If so, is it rounded, simple, or balanced? _____ Are the two parts of the Minuet the same length, or is the second half slightly longer, or much longer?

_____

Trio

- What is the key of the Trio? _____ To what key is there a modulation at the end of the Trio's first half? _____
- Describe the form of the Trio: is it binary? _____. If so, is it rounded, simple, or balanced? _____ Are the two parts of the Trio the same length, or is the second or half slightly longer, or much longer?

_____

Describe some striking rhythm features found in this movement. Where do they occur within the form?

NAME: ....

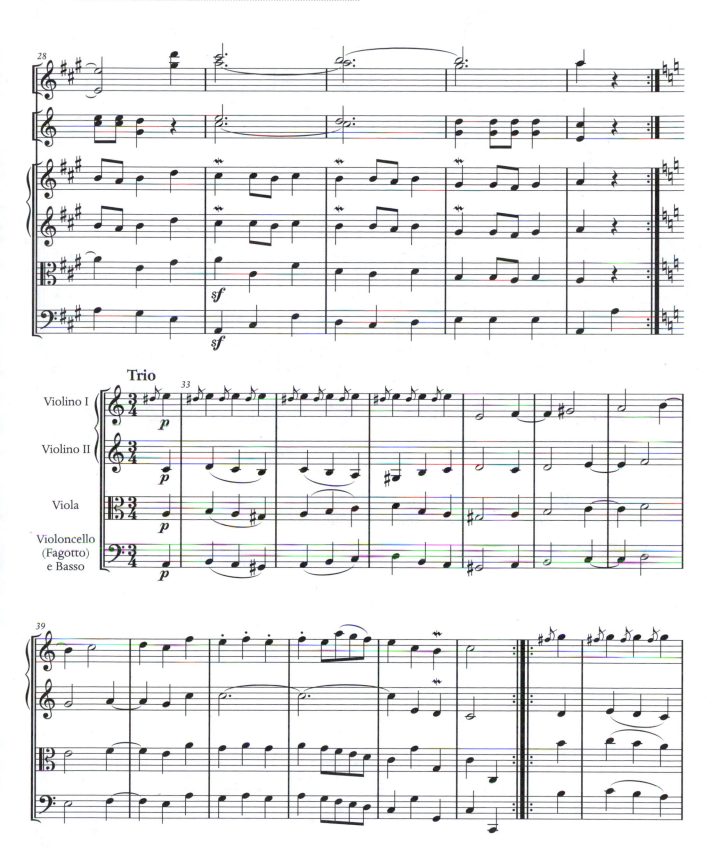

Menuetto da Capo

4. Ludwig van Beethoven, Piano Sonata, Op. 13 ("Pathétique"), ii

- Provide the keys and the beginning measure numbers of the sections.

    A section: key of _____ ; begins in measure _____

    B section: key of _____ ; begins in measure _____

    A′ section: key of _____ ; begins in measure _____

    C section: key of _____ ; begins in measure _____

    A″ section: key of _____ ; begins in measure _____

- On the score itself, label the cadences with keys and types. Note that following the final cadence toward the end of both **B** and **C** there is a bridge lasting for a few measures that leads back to **A′** and **A″**, respectively.

Adagio cantabile

NAME: ....

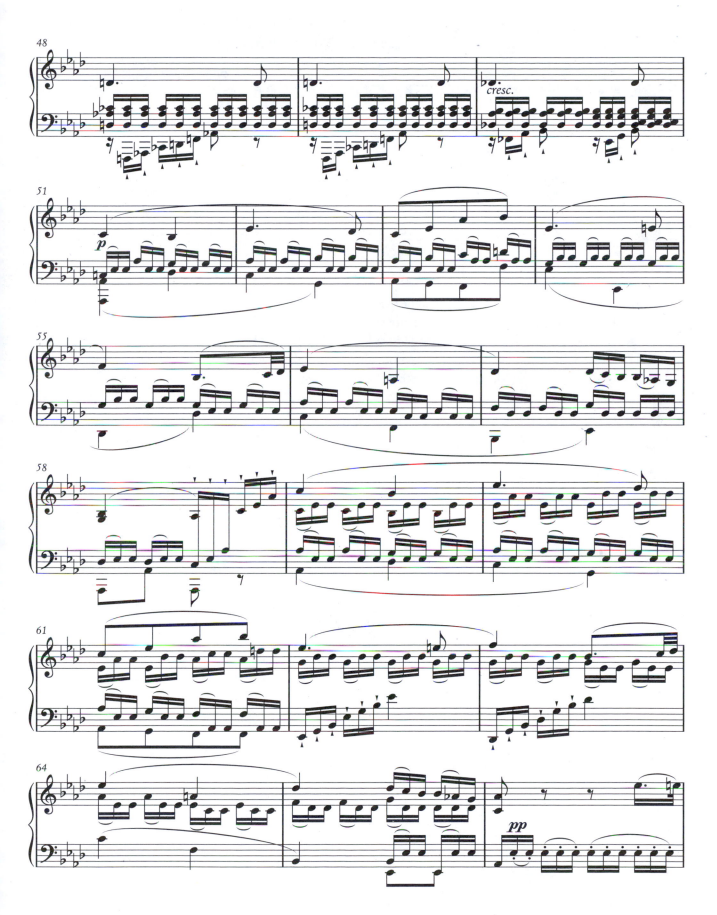

5. Describe how the **A**, **A′**, and **A″** sections differ from one another in this movement. What features create a sense of departure and instability within the **B** and **C** sections? Why is the sense of departure and instability more intense and substantial in the **C** section than in the **B** section? Describe some of the roles that the pitch E♮ and its enharmonic equivalent (F♭) play within this movement.

chapter 39

Sonata Form

A. QUESTIONS FOR REVIEW

1. What are the three large sections of sonata form?

2. How is sonata form similar to rounded binary form?

3. What are the parts of a sonata exposition? What keys are they in and what types of cadences occur at the end of each?

4. What is the medial caesura?

5. Where in the exposition does phrase overlap commonly occur? Where does it usually not occur?

6. What are the characteristic features of the development section?

7. In what ways is the recapitulation similar to the exposition and in what ways does it differ?

8. What are the characteristics of the introduction section in a sonata form movement?

9. When does the coda appear in a sonata form movement?

B. COMPOSITION

1. Realize the figured bass in keyboard format. This will be the basis of a work in sonata form, as indicated by the labels for the sections.

exposition: *main theme*

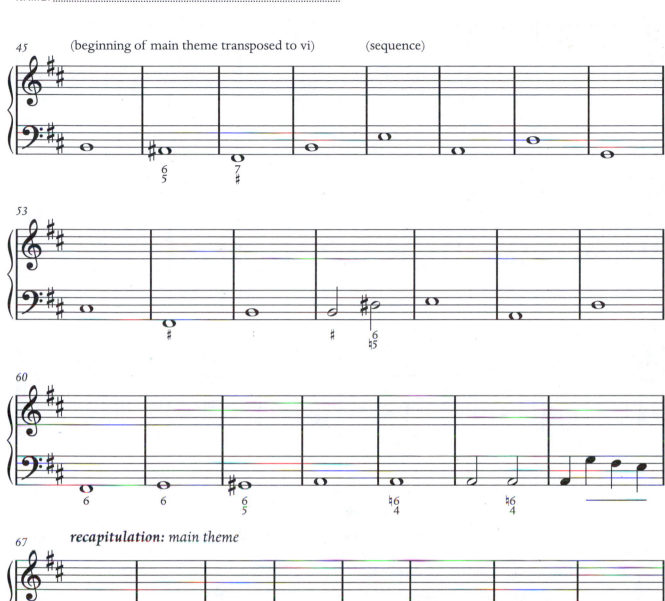

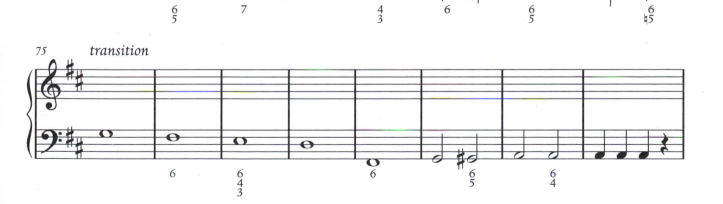

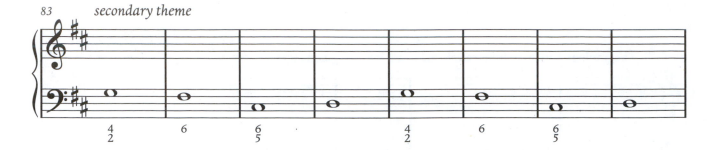

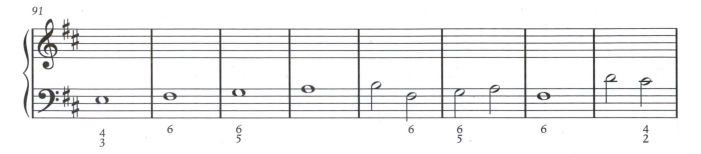

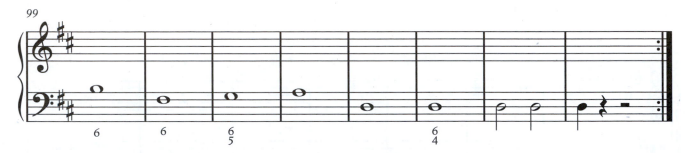

2. Based on your figured bass realization, on your own music manuscript paper compose a work in sonata form, with thematic repetitions.

- The piece can be written for (a) solo melodic instrument; (b) keyboard, with the melody in the right hand; (c) keyboard, with a varied texture; (d) solo instrument accompanied by keyboard; or (e) ensemble of three or more instruments.

- Use the same bass line and harmonies as above.

- The sections and subsections of the piece, including sequences and transitions, should match the prompts given in (1) above, with the exposition (mm.1–36), development (mm. 37–66), and recapitulation (mm. 67–106), and subsections occurring as indicated.

- Use the prompts as well as the figures to determine thematic repetitions, cadences, modulations, and other sonata form features.

- Label the sections and subsections of the completed composition.

C. ANALYSIS

Identify the measures and keys as indicated for the following pieces.

1. W. A. Mozart, Piano Sonata in C, K. 309, i

Exposition

- The **exposition** begins in measure _____ .

- **primary theme**: begins in measure _____ in the key of _____ (note: the main theme in this movement lasts for two phrases).

- **transition**: begins in measure _____ , starting in the key of _____ and ending in the key of _____ .

- **medial caesura**: appears in measure _____ .

- **secondary theme**: begins in measure _____ in the key of _____ .

- The PAC at the end of the secondary theme appears in measures _____ .

- **closing section**: begins in measure _____ in the key of _____ .

Development

- The **development** begins in measure _____ .

- Which theme returns at the start of the development section, and in what key? _____ This theme returns again in measure 67 in the key of _____ . By measure 73, there is a motion to the key of _____ , where a lengthy sequence begins.

- There are two perfect authentic cadences in this development section. In what measures do they appear, and in what key? _____

- The **retransition**, which follows the second of these perfect authentic cadences, begins in measure _____ .

Recapitulation

- The **recapitulation** begins in measure _____ .

- **primary theme**: begins in measure _____ in the key of _____ .

- **transition**: begins in measure _____ , starting in the key of _____ and ending in the key of _____ .

- **medial caesura**: appears in measure _____ .

- **secondary theme**: begins in measure _____ in the key of _____ .

- The PAC at the end of the secondary theme appears in measures _____ .

- **closing section**: begins in measure _____ in the key of _____ .

Allegro con spirito

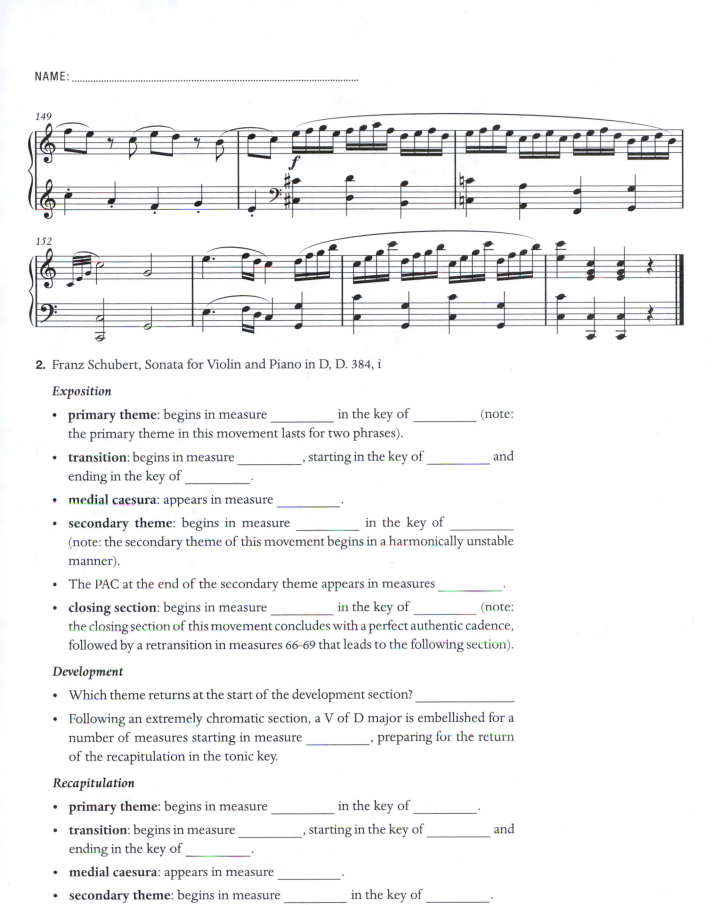

2. Franz Schubert, Sonata for Violin and Piano in D, D. 384, i

Exposition

- **primary theme**: begins in measure _____ in the key of _____ (note: the primary theme in this movement lasts for two phrases).

- **transition**: begins in measure _____, starting in the key of _____ and ending in the key of _____.

- **medial caesura**: appears in measure _____.

- **secondary theme**: begins in measure _____ in the key of _____ (note: the secondary theme of this movement begins in a harmonically unstable manner).

- The PAC at the end of the secondary theme appears in measures _____.

- **closing section**: begins in measure _____ in the key of _____ (note: the closing section of this movement concludes with a perfect authentic cadence, followed by a retransition in measures 66–69 that leads to the following section).

Development

- Which theme returns at the start of the development section? _____

- Following an extremely chromatic section, a V of D major is embellished for a number of measures starting in measure _____, preparing for the return of the recapitulation in the tonic key.

Recapitulation

- **primary theme**: begins in measure _____ in the key of _____.

- **transition**: begins in measure _____, starting in the key of _____ and ending in the key of _____.

- **medial caesura**: appears in measure _____.

- **secondary theme**: begins in measure _____ in the key of _____.

- The PAC at the end of the secondary theme appears in measures _____.

- **closing section**: begins in measure _____ in the key of _____.

3. Ludwig van Beethoven, Piano Sonata in E, Op. 14, No. 1, i

Exposition

- **primary theme**: begins in measure _____ in the key of _____ .

- **transition**: begins in measure _____ , starting in the key of _____ and ending in the key of _____ .

- **medial caesura**: appears in measure _____ .

- **secondary theme**: begins in measures _____ in the key of _____ .

- The PAC at the end of the secondary theme appears in measures _____ .

- **closing section**: begins in measure _____ in the key of _____ (note: the closing section of this movement concludes with a perfect authentic cadence, followed by a retransition in measures 57–60 that leads to the following section).

Development

- Which theme returns at the start of the development section, and in what key?

    _____

- Measure 65 marks the start of a new subsection beginning in the key of
  _____ and leading to a PAC in the key of _____, ending in measure
  _____.

- This is followed by a motion to a V of E that is sustained for a number of
  measures and that arrives in measure _____, preparing for the return of
  the recapitulation in the tonic key; this V chord is sustained for _____
  measures.

Recapitulation

- **primary theme**: begins in measure _____ in the key of _____. How
  does the primary theme differ here from its appearance in the exposition?
  _____

- **transition**: begins in measure _____, starting in the key of _____
  and ending in the key of _____. In what ways does the transition of the
  recapitulation differ from that of the exposition? _____
  _____

- **medial caesura**: appears in measure _____.

- **secondary theme**: begins in measures _____ in the key of _____.

- The PAC at the end of the secondary theme appears in measure _____.

- **closing section**: begins in measure _____ in the key of _____.

Coda

- The coda begins (with a passage not heard in the exposition) in measure
  _____, coinciding with the PAC at the end of the closing section.

4. Gioachino Rossini, Overture to *Barber of Seville* (arr. Narici)

In this work, as in many opera overtures, the exposition is not repeated. Also, there is no development section, and no transition section within the recapitulation. The medial caesura within the exposition does not involve a pause in all the instruments, but rather a marked thinning of the texture that lasts for a number of measures.

Introduction

- begins in measure _____ in the key of _____.

Exposition

- **primary theme**: begins in measure _____ in the key of _____ (note: the main theme in this movement lasts for two phrases).

- **transition**: begins in measure _____, starting in the key of _____ and ending in the key of _____.

- medial caesura: appears around measures _____ (see comments above).

- **secondary theme**: begins in measures _____ in the key of _____.

- The PAC at the end of the secondary theme appears in measures _____.

- **closing section**: begins in measure _____ in the key of _____.

Recapitulation

- **primary theme**: begins in measures _____ in the key of _____.

- **secondary theme**: begins in measures _____ in the key of _____.

- **closing section**: begins in measure _____ in the key of _____.

Coda

- begins in measure _____ in the key of _____.

NAME: ....

part.

six

Post-Tonal Theory

chapter

40 Collections and Scales I: Diatonic and Pentatonic

A. QUESTIONS FOR REVIEW

1. What is a collection? What is a scale?

2. What is a diatonic collection? How many are there? How are they labeled? How many scalar orderings are there? How are they labeled? What is a "centric tone"?

3. What is a pentatonic collection? How many are there? How are they labeled? How many scalar orderings are there? How are they labeled?

4. What is the relationship between the pentatonic and diatonic collections? What is the complement of a given pentatonic collection? A given diatonic collection? How many pentatonic collections are included in a diatonic collection?

B. WRITING SCALES

Write the indicated scales and write in the intervals (in semitones).

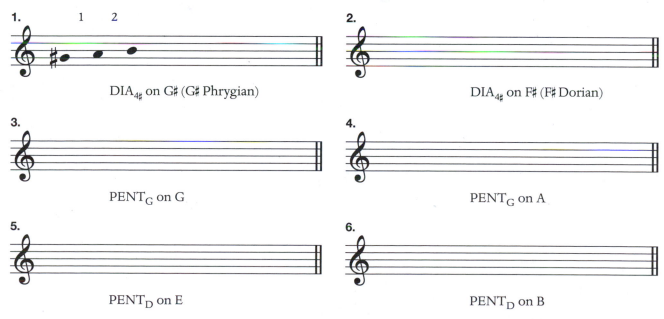

1.

$DIA_{4\sharp}$ on G♯ (G♯ Phrygian)

2.

$DIA_{4\sharp}$ on F♯ (F♯ Dorian)

3.

$PENT_G$ on G

4.

$PENT_G$ on A

5.

$PENT_D$ on E

6.

$PENT_D$ on B

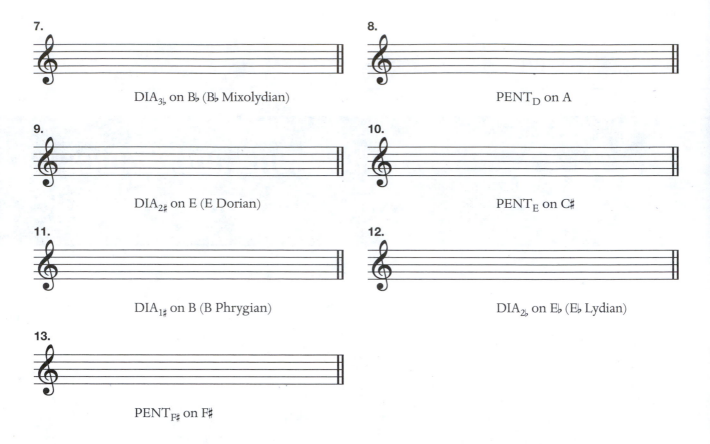

7. DIA₃♭ on B♭ (B♭ Mixolydian)

8. PENT_D on A

9. DIA₂♯ on E (E Dorian)

10. PENT_E on C♯

11. DIA₁♯ on B (B Phrygian)

12. DIA₂♭ on E♭ (E♭ Lydian)

13. PENT_F♯ on F♯

C. IDENTIFYING SCALES

- Write the intervals (in semitones) above each staff.
- Identify the collection and centric tone (for example, PENT_C on A, or DIA₁♭ on F).
- For diatonic collections, provide the scale name (for example, F♯ Mixolydian).
- For pentatonic collections, identify those that are major or minor.

1. PENT_E♭ on E (major pentatonic)

2. scale: _____

3. scale: _____

4. scale: _____

5. scale: _____

6. scale: _____

7. scale: _____

NAME: ....

D. COMPOSITION

1. Compose a short melody in F Phrygian. Begin by writing the correct key signature.

2. Using only the notes from DIA$_{3\sharp}$ on D (D Lydian), write a progression of three-note chords for piano left hand, one per measure, without using any triads. Then write a melody for piano right hand to go with it, again using only the notes of D Lydian.

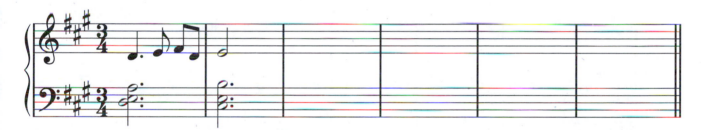

3. Using only the notes of PENT$_{B\flat}$ on G (G–B♭–C–D–F), write a simple melody with chordal accompaniment. All of the chords must either be triads, or 3rds or 6ths with one of the two notes doubled.

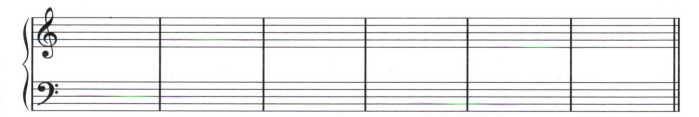

E. ANALYSIS

For each example, follow instructions that precede the example, and answer the questions that follow.

1. Béla Bartók, "Evening in Transylvania"

- Identify the collection that is formed by the melody alone, and write out its notes. _____
- Identify the collection formed by the passage as a whole and write out its notes. _____
- What scale is traversed by the bass line? _____

2. Béla Bartók, Piano Concerto No. 3, ii, strings only

- Inspect each of the five melodic lines and identify the melodic intervals. Only four different melodic intervals are used. What are they? _____
- Identify the collection and centric tone for this passage and write out its note. (The last note in the violin part is drawn from outside the prevailing collection.)
_____

3. Louise Talma, "One Need Not Be a Chamber to Be Haunted"

- What collection is used in the voice part and the piano right hand (ignore the circled notes)? Name the collection and list the notes it contains. _____

_____

- What collection is used in the piano left hand (ignore the circled notes)? Name the collection and list the notes it contains. _____

- Within the vocal line and the right hand of the piano, what are the principal melodic intervals? _____

- The two collections are related by transposition. What interval transposes the collection in the voice part and the right hand to the collection in the left hand? Is that interval heard between the parts? _____

_____

_____

- Do the two collections have any notes in common? _____

4. Xiaoyong Chen, "Wind, Water, and Shadow"

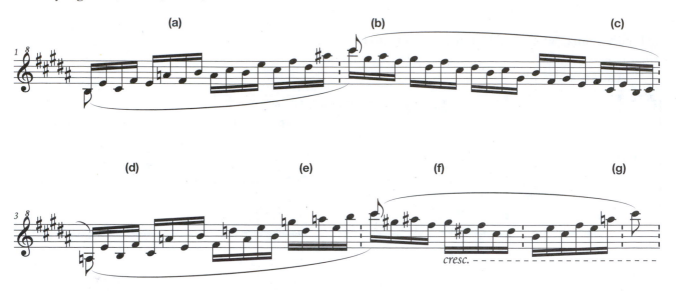

- For each boxed passage, identify the pentatonic collection and write out the notes as a scale in the "major" ordering.

- Name the common tones shared by the adjacent collections.

	COLLECTION	NOTES	COMMON TONES
(a)	PENT$_A$	A–B–C#–E–F#	
			_____
(b)	_____	_____	
			_____
(c)	_____	_____	
			_____
(d)	_____	_____	
			_____
(e)	_____	_____	
			_____
(f)	_____	_____	
			_____
(g)	_____	_____	

- Which diatonic collections are created by each of the following pairs of pentatonic collections?

PENT$_G$ + PENT$_A$ = _____

PENT$_A$ + PENT$_E$ = _____

PENT$_E$ + PENT$_{F\#}$ = _____

5. Erik Satie, *Parade*

For each melodic excerpt, identify the collection and the centric tone. Then write out the notes in the collection.

Collection: _____

Collection: _____

Collection: _____

- Which notes are held in common between the first and second collections?

  _____

- Which notes are held in common between the second and third collections?

  _____

- Which notes are held in common between the first and third collections?

  _____

- Which two collections have the same centric tone? _____

  _____

6. Béla Bartók, *Eight Improvisations on Hungarian Peasant Songs*, No. 1

- Identify the collection and write out its notes. _____
- The centric tone? (There are two strong possibilities.) _____

  _____

- What is the scale used? _____

  _____

  _____

7. Maurice Ravel, Sonata for Violin and Cello, iii

For each boxed passage identify the collection and centric tone, and label it in the lettered blank. Then list the notes in the collection.

(a) _____

(b) _____

(c) _____

(d) _____

- As the music moves from collection to collection, which notes are held in common? _____

_____

- Which notes change between collections? _____

8. Kaija Saariaho, *L'Amour de loin*, Act IV, scene i

- What is the collection and scale? Write out the notes.

  _____

- What are the most common harmonic intervals?

  _____

Collections and Scales II: Octatonic, Hexatonic, and Whole-Tone

chapter **41**

A. QUESTIONS FOR REVIEW

1. What is an octatonic collection? How many octatonic collections are there? How are they labeled? What is the interval pattern for an octatonic scale? How many scalar orderings are there?

2. Which familiar four-note chord is the complement of the octatonic collection? Which familiar chords does the octatonic collection contain?

3. What is a hexatonic collection? How many hexatonic collections are there? How are they labeled? What is the interval pattern for a hexatonic scale? How many scalar orderings are there?

4. What is the complement of a hexatonic collection? Which familiar chords does the hexatonic collection contain?

5. What is a whole-tone collection? How many whole-tone collections are there? How are they labeled? What is the interval pattern for a whole-tone scale? How many scalar orderings are there?

6. What is the complement of a whole-tone collection? What type of triad does the whole-tone collection contain?

7. What harmonies are found in both the octatonic and diatonic collections? In both the octatonic and hexatonic collections? In both the hexatonic and whole-tone collections?

B. WRITING SCALES

1. Write the indicated octatonic scales, labeling the intervals (in semitones) between adjacent notes.

a. OCT_{C♯D} on C♯ (octatonic collection that includes the notes C♯ and D written to start on C♯)

b. OCT_{C♯D} on D (same notes as in (a) but starting on D)

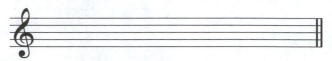

c. OCT_{C♯D} on G

d. OCT_{C♯D} on G, using different enharmonic spellings than in (c) for at least two of the notes

2. Write the indicated hexatonic scales labeling the intervals (in semitones) between adjacent notes.

a. HEX_{C♯D} on C♯ (hexatonic collection that includes the notes C♯ and D, written to start on C♯)

b. HEX_{C♯D} on D (same notes as in (a) but starting on D)

c. HEX_{C♯D} on F♯

d. HEX_{C♯D} on F♯, using different enharmonic spellings than in (c) for at least two of the notes

3. Write the indicated whole-tone scales, labeling the intervals (in semitones) between adjacent notes.

a. WT_{C♯} on F (whole-tone collection that includes the note C♯ written to start on F)

b. WT_{C♯} on G (same notes as in (a) but starting on G)

c. WT$_{C\sharp}$ on A

d. WT$_{C\sharp}$ on A, using different enharmonic spellings than in (c) for at least two of the notes

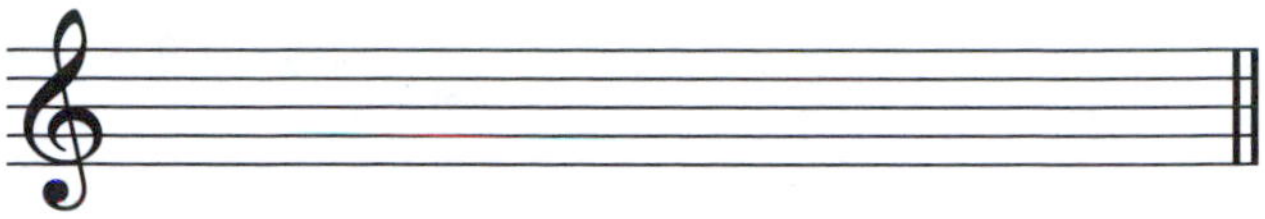

4. Write the indicated scales (octatonic, hexatonic, or whole tone), labeling the intervals (in semitones) between adjacent notes.

a. OCT$_{C\sharp D}$ on F

b. HEX$_{C\sharp D}$ on F

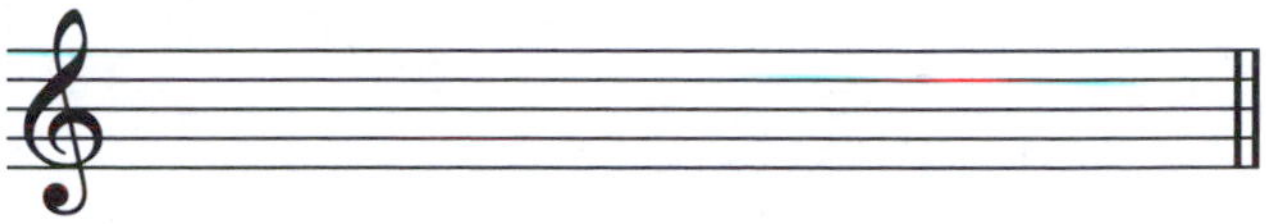

c. WT$_{C\sharp}$ on A

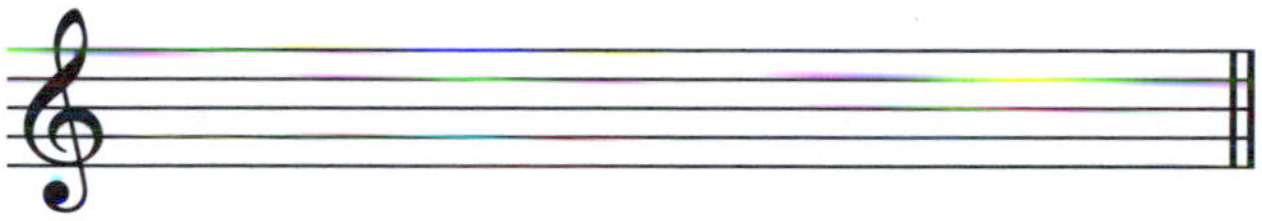

d. WT$_{C}$ on B♭

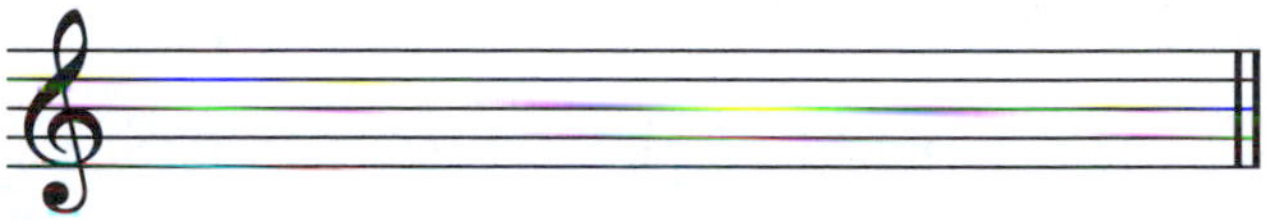

e. HEX$_{DE\flat}$ on G

f. OCT$_{C\sharp D}$ on G

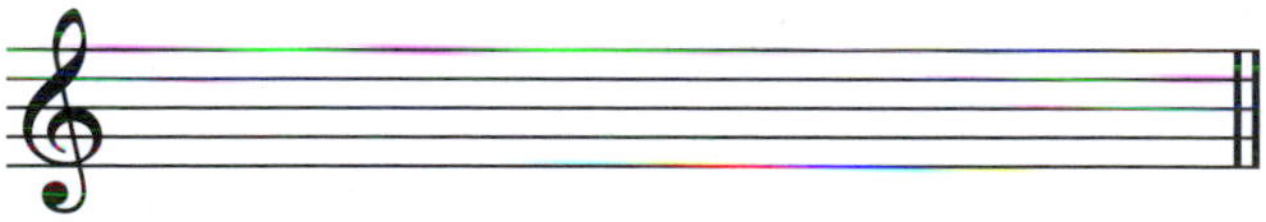

g. HEX$_{CD\flat}$ on E

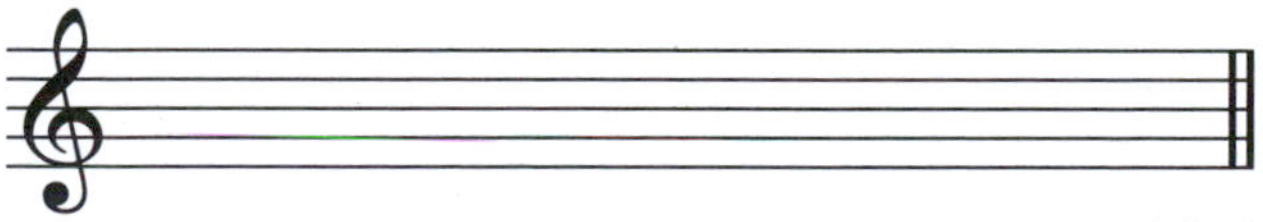

C. IDENTIFYING SCALES

For each of these scales, write the intervals between adjacent notes (in semitones) and identify the scale.

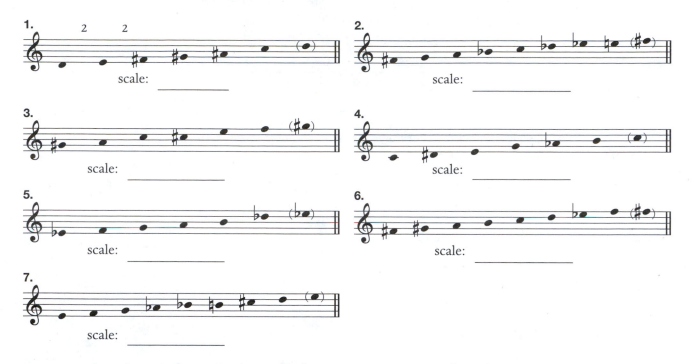

1.

2   2

scale: _____

2.

scale: _____

3.

scale: _____

4.

scale: _____

5.

scale: _____

6.

scale: _____

7.

scale: _____

D. INTERACTION BETWEEN SCALES

Name as many collections (diatonic, pentatonic, octatonic, hexatonic, or whole-tone) as you can that contain the following groups of notes (there are at least two correct answers for each question).

1. D–F♯–A–C (a dominant seventh chord)

_____

2. D–F–A♭–B (a diminished seventh chord)

_____

3. G♭–B♭–C–E (a French augmented sixth chord)

_____

4. F–A♭–A–C (a triad with both major and minor third)

_____

5. D–F♯–B♭ (an augmented triad)

_____

6. G–D–A–E (a stack of perfect fifths)

_____

7. D–E–F–G (the first four notes of a minor scale)

_____

E. COMPOSITION

Write melodies as indicated. Choose a meter and write a melody of between 8 and 16 measures, in whatever style and mood you like.

1. Use only notes from $OCT_{C\#D}$ on E: E–F–G–A♭–B♭–B–C♯–D–(E).

2. Use only notes from $HEX_{C\#D}$ on F: F–F♯–A–B♭–C♯–D–(F).

3. Use only notes from $WT_{C\#}$, starting and ending on A.

4. Start with $OCT_{CD♭}$ on E♭ (E♭–E–F♯–G–A–B♭–C–D♭) and modulate smoothly to $DIA_{2♭}$ on G (G–A–B♭–C–D–E♭–F–G), using common tones as a pivot between the collections.

5. Start with HEX$_{C\sharp D}$ on D (D–F–F♯–A–B♭–C♯) and end with D Ionian (D–E–F♯–G–A–B–C♯). A simple chordal accompaniment is provided using triads from HEX$_{C\sharp D}$, some of which are also found in D Ionian.

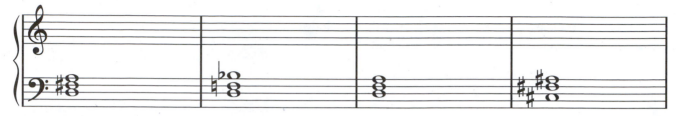

F. ANALYSIS

Identify the collections used in these examples and list their notes. Then answer any further questions.

1. Kaija Saariaho, *L'Amour de loin*

Collection: _____

2. Béla Bartók, "From the Island of Bali," *Mikrokosmos* No. 109

Collection: _____

- The four-note figure in the left hand consists of two semitones. They are related by transposition by what interval? _____

- The four-note figure in the right hand also consists of two semitones. What is the interval of transposition? _____

- The right-hand part and the left-hand part are related to each other by transposition. By what interval? _____

3. Béla Bartók, "Diminished Fifth," *Mikrokosmos* No. 101

Collection: _____

- There is one note that does not belong—circle it. How can you account for it?

_____

_____

- Compare the right-hand and left-hand parts in mm. 1–5. How are they related to each other? What happens to those parts in mm. 6–11?

_____

_____

_____

_____

4. Maurice Ravel, *Valses nobles et sentimentales*, No. 2

Assez lent – avec une expression intense ♩ = 104

en dehors

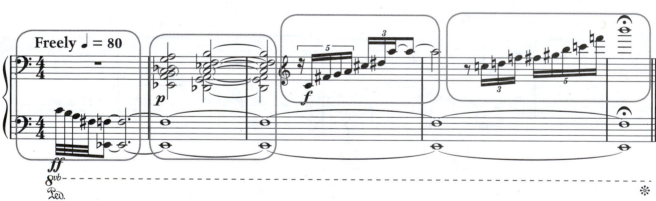

- Identify the collection in m. 1: _____
- Identify the collection in m. 2: _____
- What is the relationship between these two collections? _____

  _____

  _____

- Which familiar chords are found in each measure? How are they related to each other? _____

  _____

  _____

5. Chen Yi, *Northern Scenes*

Identify the collection for each boxed group of notes and write it in the blank below the staff. Note that collections might be missing a note. Notes that do not belong to the prevailing collection are in parentheses. Once you have identified the collections, identify any common tones between adjacent collections.

Collection: _____   _____   _____   _____

Notes: _____   _____   _____   _____

Common
tones: _____   _____   _____

6. Kaija Saariaho, *Sept papillons* (for solo cello), iii

*In this excerpt, A trills with C♯, F with F♯, and C♯ with D. S.P. indicates *sul ponticello* bowing, S.T., *sul tasto*, and N., *normal*.

- Identify the collection in use in this short piece.

  Collection: _____

- What is the centric tone? Write out the scale beginning on that tone.

  _____

- Circle any notes that do not belong to the prevailing collection. How can you account for them?

  _____
  _____
  _____

7. Béla Bartók, String Quartet No. 1, ii

Identify the whole-tone collections in each boxed segment of this passage, writing your answers next to each segment and listing the notes in each collection. (Not every collection is complete, but each includes enough notes to be identified.)

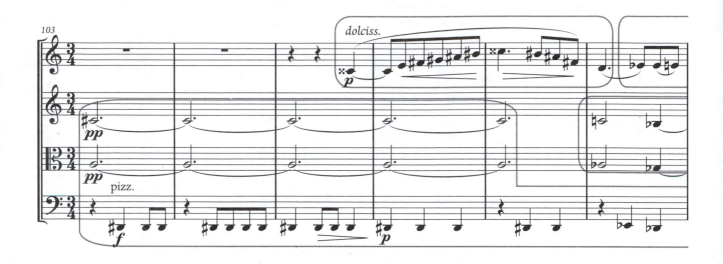

8. Béla Bartók, Forty-Four Duos for Two Violins, No. 33, "Harvest Song"

- The markings Tempo I and Tempo II divide this excerpt into three sections. Identify the collections in each section and list their notes. (Some collections are incomplete.)

Tempo I: _____

Tempo II: _____

Tempo I: _____

- What is the same and what is different in the way the three collections are presented?

_____

_____

_____

_____

_____

9. Ellen Taaffe Zwilich, String Quartet No. 2, ii

Identify the collection for each boxed segment in this passage and list the notes in each collection.

- Each instrument enters four semitones below its predecessor. What is the effect of that transposition on the key signatures of the diatonic collections?

_____

_____

- The cello starts by repeating what the first violin had at the beginning. What is it about the transpositional pattern that makes that happen?

  ....

  ....

10. Joan Tower, *In Memory* (for string quartet)

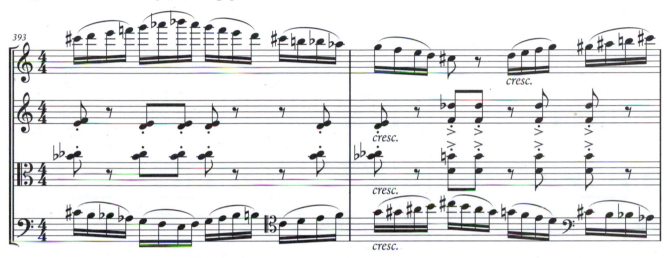

Collection: _____

- What is the centric tone? Does it change over the course of the passage?

  _____

  _____

11. Mario Davidovsky, Quartetto No. 3 (for violin, viola, cello, and piano)

- Identify the collection in the string parts and list its notes. _____

- Identify the collection in the piano parts and list its notes. _____

- What is the relationship between the two collections?

  _____

  _____

12. Aleksandr Scriabin, Prelude, Op. 74, No. 3

Allegro drammatico

Collection: _____

- Is it possible to identify a centric tone or tones?

  _____

  _____

- Circle any notes that lie outside the collection. How might you account for them?

  _____

  _____

chapter 42 — Triadic Post-Tonality

A. QUESTIONS FOR REVIEW

1. What is a triadic transformation? What is **L**? **P**? **R**? **SLIDE**? What effect does a triadic transformation have on the quality of a major triad? On a minor triad?

2. In a complete **L–P** chain, how many triads are there? How many different **L–P** chains are there? What familiar collection is created by an **L–P** chain?

3. In a complete **P–SLIDE** chain, how many triads are there? How would you describe the root motion of the triads?

4. When triads are used in parallel motion, do the traditional voice-leading rules forbidding parallel fifths and octaves apply?

5. Given a clearly audible triadic root and fifth, what tones can be added to a chord without destroying the sense of the chord as a triad?

6. What can composers do to recompose an underlying **T–S–D**-type progression?

7. What does it mean for music to be bitonal? Bi-triadic? In bi-triadic music, how might the two triads be related to each other?

B. WRITING TRIADIC TRANSFORMATIONS

Provide the missing chord(s) in these progressions.

1. Perform a **P** transformation of the following triads, and label the root and quality (maj, min) of each triad.

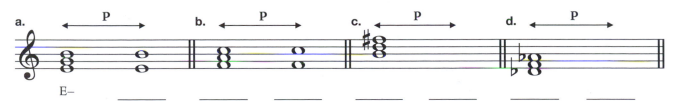

2. Perform a **SLIDE** transformation of the following triads, and label the root and quality (maj, min) of each triad.

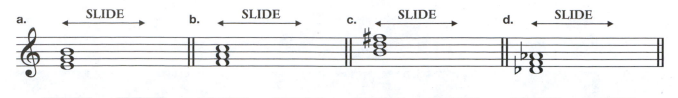

____ ____   ____ ____   ____ ____   ____ ____

3. Perform an **L** transformation of the following triads, and label the root and quality (maj, min) of each triad.

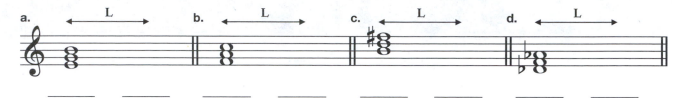

____ ____   ____ ____   ____ ____   ____ ____

4. Perform an **R** transformation of the following triads, and label the root and quality (maj, min) of each triad.

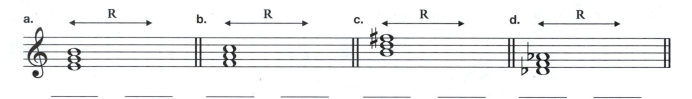

____ ____   ____ ____   ____ ____   ____ ____

5. Provide the pitches and names of the missing chords.

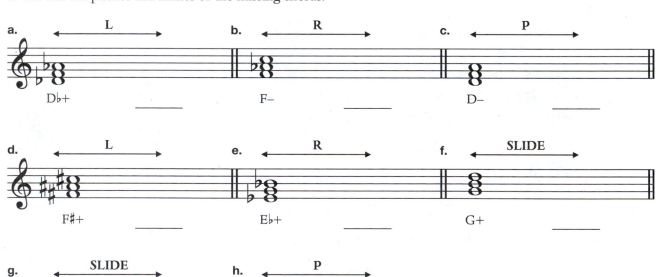

a. L   Db+   ____

b. R   F−   ____

c. P   D−   ____

d. L   F♯+   ____

e. R   E♭+   ____

f. SLIDE   G+   ____

g. SLIDE   E+   ____

h. P   A−   ____

C. IDENTIFYING TRIADIC TRANSFORMATIONS

Identify the transformation that connects these pairs of chords.

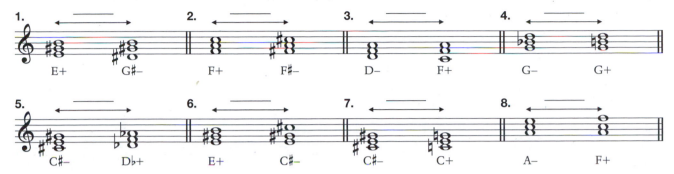

D. TRIADIC TRANSFORMATION CHAINS

Fill in and name the missing chords and, where requested, the missing transtormistions. From chord to chord, notes either are held in common or move by semitone or whole tone. Chords may be written in inversion.

1. P–SLIDE partial cycle. Fill in and name the four missing chords.

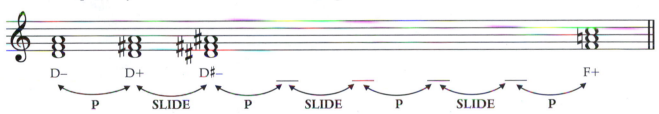

2. P–SLIDE complete cycle. There is only one **P–SLIDE** cycle, and it contains all twelve major and all twelve minor triads.

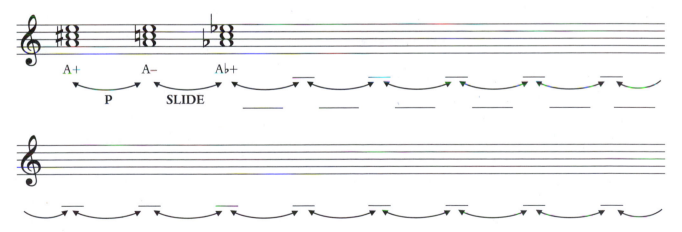

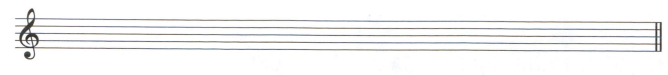

What is the root motion of the triads in this cycle? _____

_____

3. L–P cycle. Fill in and name the four missing chords.

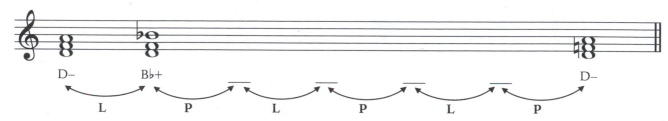

These triads all belong to which collection? List its notes. _____

4. L–P cycle. Fill out the complete **L–P** cycle that starts and ends on a B-minor triad.

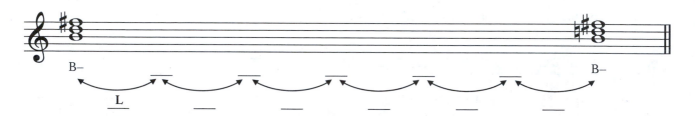

These triads all belong to which collection? List its notes. _____

What is the root motion of the triads in this cycle? _____

What chord do the roots outline? _____

5. R–P cycle. Fill in and name the five missing chords.

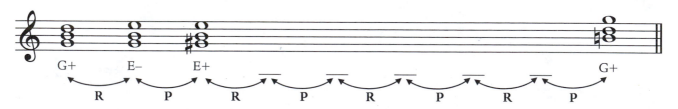

These triads all belong to which collection? List its notes.

_____

6. R–P cycle. Write out the complete **R–P** cycle that starts and ends on D major.

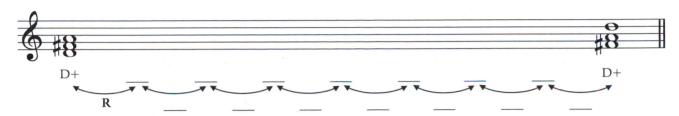

D+   R   D+

These triads all belong to which collection? List its notes.

_____

What is the root motion of the triads in this cycle? _____

What chord do the roots outline? _____

7. L–R partial cycle. Fill in and name the four missing chords.

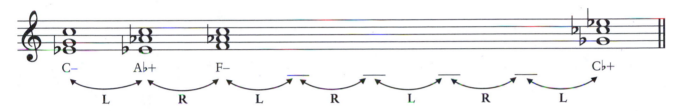

C–   A♭+   F–   C♭+

L   R   L   R   L   R   L

8. L–R cycle. Complete the **L–R** cycle, which contains all twelve major and all twelve minor triads.

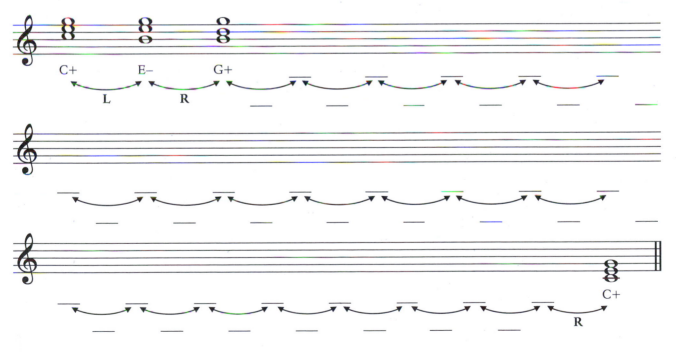

C+   E–   G+

L   R

C+

R

What is the root motion of the triads in this cycle? _____

_____

E. COMPOSITION

1. Transformation chains

  a. P–L chain

- Write out a full P–L chain in the left hand, starting and ending with a D major triad.

- Use the smoothest voice leading possible (keep two common tones and move the remaining voice by semitone).

- Then write a melody to go along with the triads. The melody may arpeggiate the triad in that measure or embellish it with passing or neighbor tones.

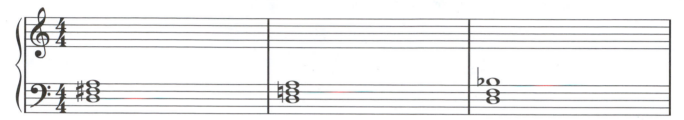

  b. R–P chain

- Write out a full R–P chain in the left hand, starting and ending with an A major triad.

- Use the smoothest voice leading possible (keep two common tones and move the remaining voice by semitone or whole tone).

- Then write a melody to go along with the triads. The melody may arpeggiate the triad in that measure or embellish it with passing or neighbor tones.

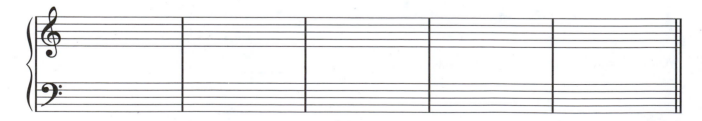

2. Parallel triads.

- Write a pentatonic melody in quarter and half notes, starting on E, roughly eight measures long

- Harmonize it with parallel triads of which the melody note is also the root. You may either keep triads within the same diatonic collection (changing their quality as necessary), or make all the triads major (which will require the addition of chromatic notes).

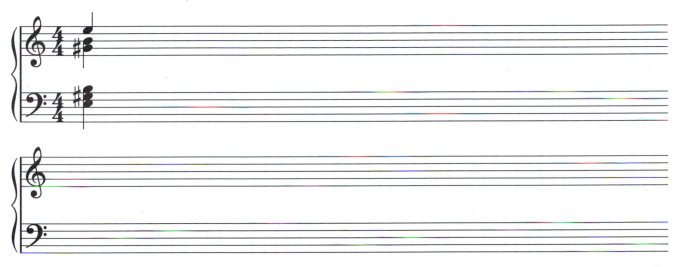

3. Triads with added notes

    a. Write out the simple progression in D major as indicated, one chord per measure. Then add tertian extensions (7ths, 9ths, and/or 11ths) to each chord. Each chord should contain six or seven notes. Do not worry about resolving dissonances or avoiding parallel fifths and octaves.

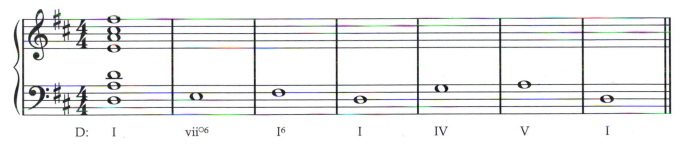

D: I   vii°⁶   I⁶   I   IV   V   I

    b. Using the same progression as in (a), this time add tones (diatonic or chromatic) that cannot be easily explained as tertian extensions. Each chord should contain six or seven notes. Do not worry about resolving dissonances or avoiding parallel fifths and octaves.

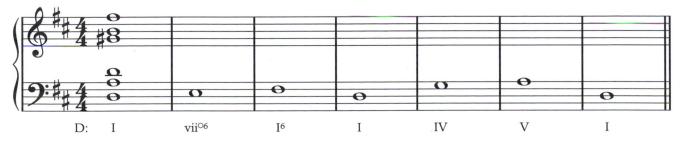

D: I   vii°⁶   I⁶   I   IV   V   I

4. Bitonal and bi-triadic music

    a. Write a duet for violin and cello, 8–16 measures long. The violin part should be in B minor; the cello part should be in B♭ major. (These two scales have three notes in common: D, G, and A.)

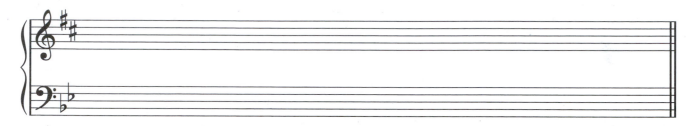

    b. Given the progression of triads in the left hand, add triads in the right hand that are related by **P**, **SLIDE**, or transposition at the tritone. Do not repeat a chord in adjacent measures.

F. ANALYSIS

1. Triadic transformations

Label the boxed chords and identify the transformation that connects them. Ignore any embellishing tones.

    a. Igor Stravinsky, *Five Fingers*, Lento

left hand   right hand

b. Igor Stravinsky, Serenade in A, i

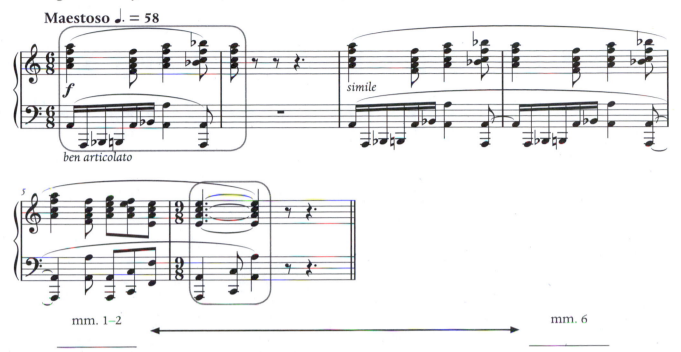

mm. 1–2   ⟷   mm. 6

c. Dmitri Shostakovich, String Quartet No. 4, ii

d. Béla Bartók, *Allegro barbaro*

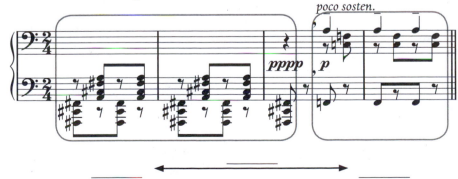

e. John Adams, *Nixon in China,* Act II

f. John Adams, *Harmonium,* Part I

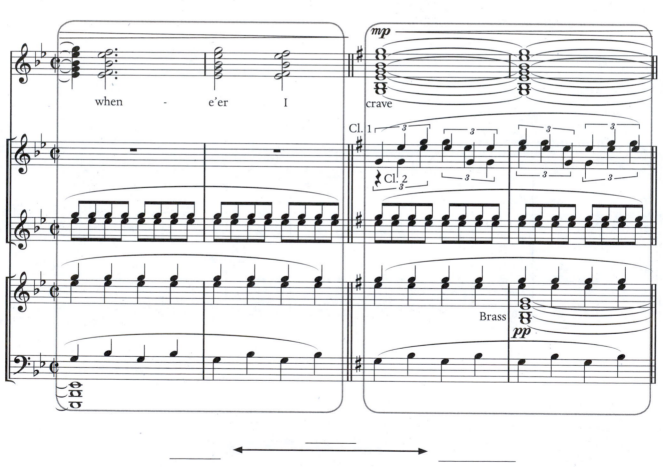

2. Transformation chains

Identify the boxed triads and the transformations that connect them.

a. Alfred Schnittke, Piano Quintet, i

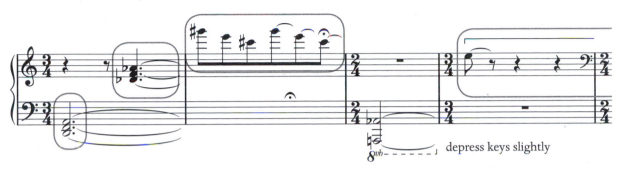

Transformation: _____ _____ _____

Triads: ← → ← → ← →

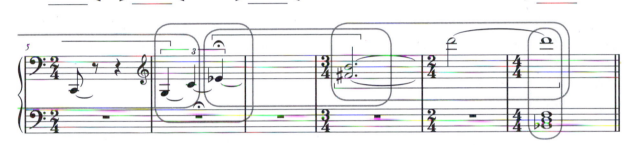

Transformation: _____ _____ _____

Triads: ← → ← → ← → ← →

b. Alfred Schnittke, Concerto Grosso No. 2, i

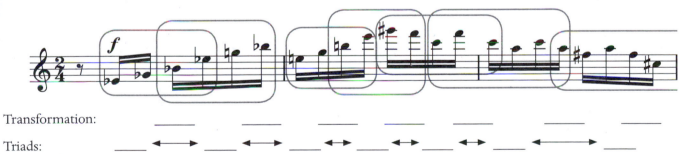

Transformation: _____ _____ _____ _____

Triads: ← → ← → ← → ← → ← → ← →

Transformation: _____ _____

Triads: ← → ← → ← → ← →

c. Ursula Mamlok, *Panta Rhei*, iii

Transformation:

Triads:

Write out the complete chain of which these triads are part and identify the transformations.

3. Parallel triads

    a. Béla Bartók, *Bluebeard's Castle*

        Label the triads at the beginning (in mm. 1–6) and end (mm. 17–22) of the excerpt in the blanks provided with root and quality. Then answer the questions below.

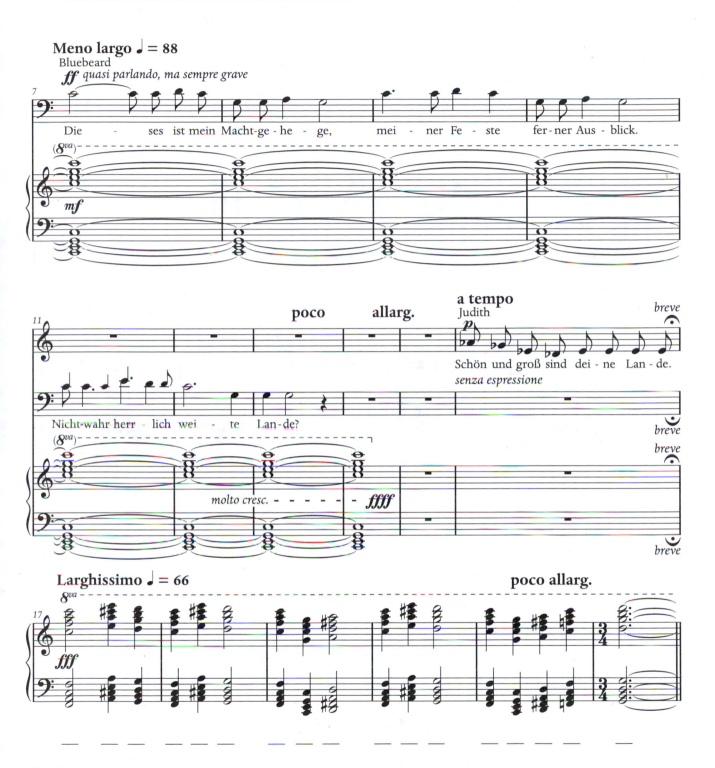

Translation:

Judith: Ah!

Bluebeard: Behold my spacious kingdom. Gaze upon its distant vistas. Is it not a noble country?

Judith: Fair and spacious is your country.

- What collection is formed by the roots of the triads in mm. 1–6? _____
- What collection or scale is formed by the vocal melody in mm. 7–10?

  _____

- What collection or scale is formed by the vocal melody in m. 16? (Note: One note is omitted.) _____

- What collection is formed by the roots of the triads in mm. 17–22? _____

b. Claude Debussy, *La cathédrale engloutie*

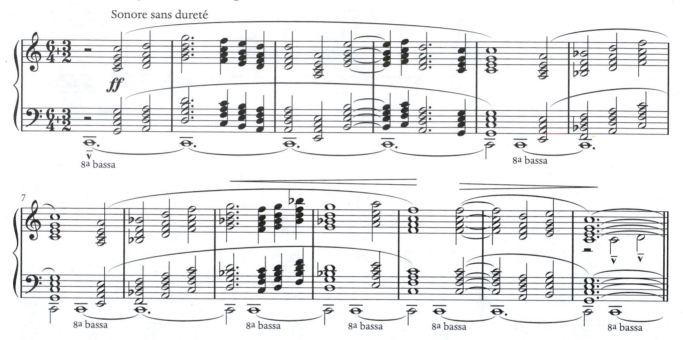

- What collection/scale is defined by the melody over the course of the passage?

  _____

- How is the melody accompanied? What is the relationship between melody notes and triad roots?

  _____

  _____

  _____

c. Sofia Gubaidulina, *So sei es*

Label the triads in the blanks provided beneath the staff.

- What collection is formed by the melody notes? _____
- Can you see any pattern of intervals in the succession of melody notes?

  _____

- What collection is formed by the triad roots? _____

d. Igor Stravinsky, *Petrushka*, "Russian Dance"

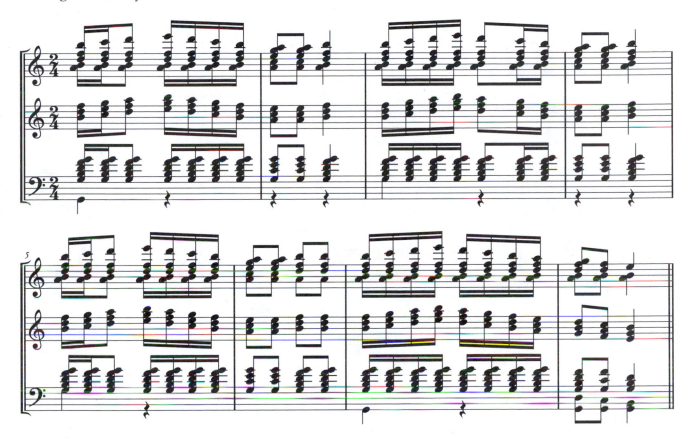

- What scale/collection is defined by the melody (highest line)?

  _____

- How is that melody accompanied?

  _____

  _____

  _____

e. George Crumb, *Makrokosmos*, "Primeval Sounds (Genesis I)"

Label the triads as indicated.

right hand:

left hand:

- What pattern do the triad roots in the right hand follow?

———————————————————————————————

- What pattern do the triad roots in the left hand follow? What is their relationship to the right-hand triads?

———————————————————————————————

———————————————————————————————

———————————————————————————————

4. Triads with added tones

a. Béla Bartók, Bagatelle, Op. 6, No. 4

- Identify the triads, and label them in the blanks below.

- Some triads include added tones; circle the added tones, and indicate their intervals above the root.

- How do the last eight triads compare to the first eight?

———————————————————————————————

- What is the collection or scale of the passage as a whole?

———————————————————————————————

b. Maurice Ravel, *Le tombeau de Couperin*, Rigaudon

- Identify the triads with root and quality, ignoring any added tones.
- Then complete a Roman numeral analysis in C major.
- Finally, circle any added tones and label them with their relationship to the bass.

triads: _____   _____   _____

Roman
numerals in C: ____   ____   ____   ____

How do the added tones avoid obscuring the identity of the triads? _____

_____

_____

c. Maurice Ravel, *Le tombeau de Couperin*, Forlane

- Identify the triads (one per measure) and label them with root and quality, ignoring the added tones. To identify the triads, focus on the bass notes.
- Then analyze the progression with Roman numerals.

triads: _____   _____   _____   _____   _____

Roman
numerals
in E min.: ____   ____   ____   ____   ____

- How would you account for the added tones: are they extensions or nonharmonic tones, and if the latter, how do they embellish the notes of the triads?

___

- How is it that the added tones do not obscure the identity of the triads?

___

d. Shulamit Ran, *Soliloquy*

- What triad is sustained throughout this passage?

___

- What tones are added to it? Give the pitch and its relationship to the chord root.

___

- Can you identify a large collection that contains the triad root, major third, and the added tones?

___

5. Transitional progressions recomposed

For each passage, try to compose a simplified, tonal prototype that might be understood to lie behind the post-tonal surface. Provide a Roman numeral analysis of your composition. Some chords and Roman numerals are provided. There will be many possible solutions!

a. Igor Stravinsky, Concerto for Piano and Winds

A min.:   i   V⁸ ————— 7   i

b. Sergey Prokofiev, *Classical Symphony*, Gavotte

The first phrase of this piece is discussed in the textbook.

D:

c. Igor Stravinsky, *The Rake's Progress*, Act I

The first phrase of this piece is discussed in the textbook.

d. Igor Stravinsky, Piano Sonata

Write your tonal prototype in $\frac{3}{4}$ throughout.

NAME: ....

e. Dmitri Shostakovich, String Quartet No. 3

6. Bitonal and bi-triadic music

Each of these examples makes use of different combinations of triads that may be related by transposition or triadic transformation (**L**, **P**, **R**, **SLIDE**), or by belonging to larger collections (hexatonic, octatonic, whole tone, diatonic). Analyze and answer the questions that follow.

a. Igor Stravinsky, *Petrushka*, Second Tableau

Identify the two triads heard in rapid alternation.

triads: ____ ____

- What is the relationship between the two triads? _____

_____

- What is the collection to which the six notes of these two triads belong?

_____

NAME: ....

b. Igor Stravinsky, *Petrushka*, Third Tableau

Identify the two triads heard in rapid alternation within each of the two boxed passages and a large collection to which each pair belongs.

triads: _____ _____

collection: _____ _____

c. Alfred Schnittke, Cello Sonata No. 1, iii

The right hand of the piano in this excerpt features a C-minor triad throughout. The left hand and cello part combine to form other chords. Complete the table below with the triads that appear in those outer voices and their relationship to C minor.

measures:	1–3	4–6
triad:	_____	_____
relationship to C minor:	_____	_____

d. Alfred Schnittke, Tuba mirum, from *Requiem* (celesta and piano parts only)

Fill in the table below with the triads in the left hand and the right hand. Then identify the transformations that relate simultaneous and successive triads.

transformation: _____ _____

right-hand triads: ____ ↔ ____ ↔ ____ ↔ ____ ↔ ____ ↔ ____ ↔ ____

transformation: ↕ ↕ ↕ ↕ ↕ ↕ ↕ ↕

left-hand triads: ____ ↔ ____ ↔ ____ ↔ ____ ↔ ____ ↔ ____ ↔ ____

transformation: _____ _____ _____

Every vertical harmony consists of two triads in what relationship? _____

e. Darius Milhaud, "Ipanema," from *Saudades do Brazil*

Identify the two triads embedded in the string parts.

triads: _____ _____

- How are the two triads related to each other? _____
_____

- How does the changing bass note affect your perception of which of the triads is principal and which secondary? _____
_____

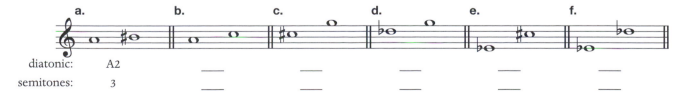

NAME: ....

chapter

43

Intervals

A. QUESTIONS FOR REVIEW

1. What is enharmonic equivalence?

2. What is a pitch? How many different pitches are represented on the piano keyboard?

3. What is an ordered pitch interval? An unordered pitch interval?

4. What is octave equivalence?

5. What is a pitch class? How many pitch classes are there?

6. What is an ordered pitch-class interval? An unordered pitch-class interval?

7. What is an interval class?

8. What is an interval inversion?

9. What is the difference between ordered and unordered intervals? What is the difference between pitch and pitch-class intervals? Which is the most concrete, specific way of describing an interval? Which is the most abstract, general way of describing an interval?

10. What is a motive?

B. IDENTIFYING INTERVALS

1. For each of these intervals, give the diatonic name (e.g., M3) and the number of semitones (i.e., the unordered pitch interval).

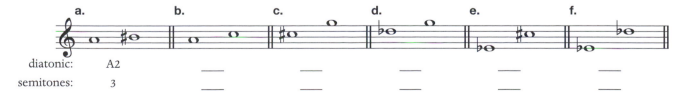

diatonic: A2   ___   ___   ___   ___   ___

semitones: 3   ___   ___   ___   ___   ___

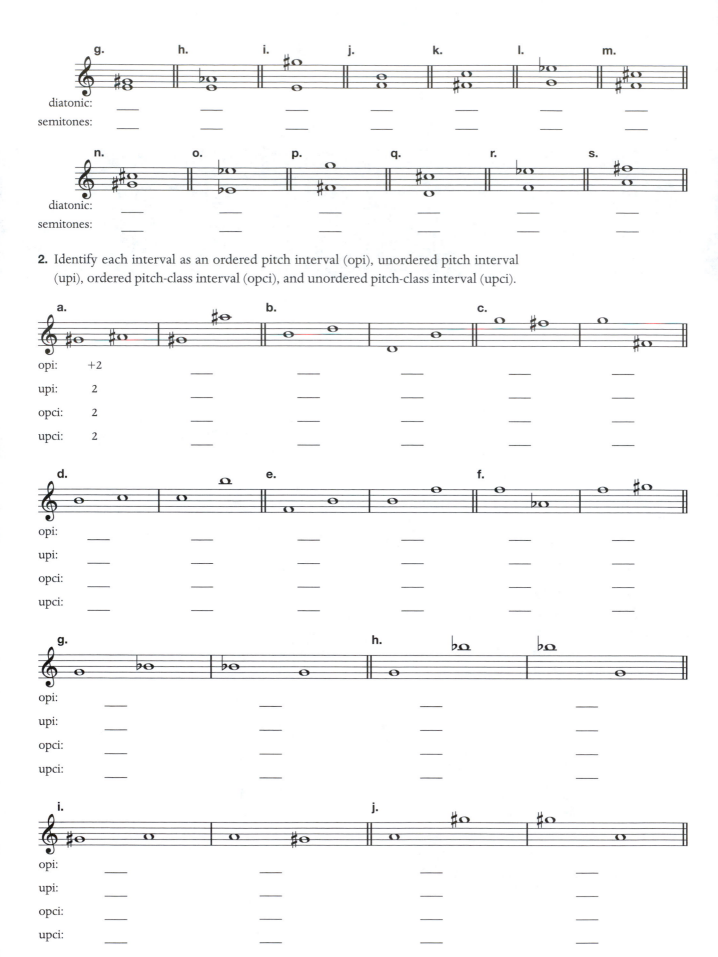

2. Identify each interval as an ordered pitch interval (opi), unordered pitch interval (upi), ordered pitch-class interval (opci), and unordered pitch-class interval (upci).

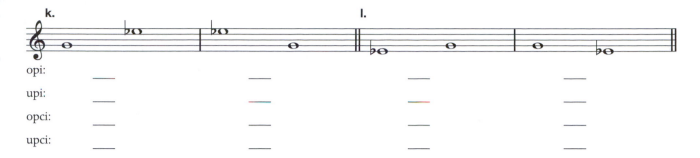

opi: _____ _____ _____ _____

upi: _____ _____ _____ _____

opci: _____ _____ _____ _____

upci: _____ _____ _____ _____

3. Identify each of the melodic intervals as an ordered pitch interval (opi), unordered pitch interval (upi), ordered pitch-class interval (opci), and unordered pitch-class interval (upci).

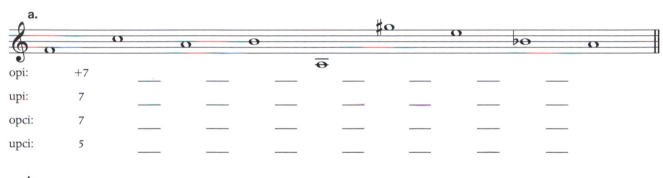

opi: +7 ___ ___ ___ ___ ___ ___ ___

upi: 7 ___ ___ ___ ___ ___ ___ ___

opci: 7 ___ ___ ___ ___ ___ ___ ___

upci: 5 ___ ___ ___ ___ ___ ___ ___

opi: _____ _____ _____ _____ _____ _____ _____

upi: _____ _____ _____ _____ _____ _____ _____

opci: _____ _____ _____ _____ _____ _____ _____

upci: _____ _____ _____ _____ _____ _____ _____

C. WRITING INTERVALS

1. Write each ordered pitch interval on the staff as indicated.

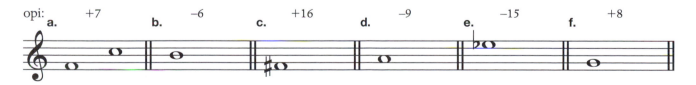

2. For each of the notes given, write two unordered pitch intervals: one below the note and one above it.

3. Complete each ordered pitch-class interval by writing the note in the right column.

	opci	
G	4	
A	9	
B♭	11	
F♯	3	
E♭	5	
D	7	

4. Complete each unordered pitch-class interval with two notes, above and below the given note.

	upci	above	below
F	4		
G	3		
A♭	5		
C♯	1		
B	2		
C	6		

5. For each given ordered pitch interval, fill in the chart by supplying the associated ordered and unordered pitch-class intervals, as well as the diatonic name.

Ordered pitch interval (opi)	Ordered pitch-class interval (opci)	Unordered pitch-class interval (upci)	Diatonic name
−3	9	3	minor third
−11			
−13			
+7			
+10			
+1			
−17			

D. COMPOSITION

1. Compose a short piece (6–8 measures) for a melody instrument of your choice in which every pitch interval is either a 1 or a 4 (or the octave equivalents of these).

- Provide clef and time signature.
- Add tempo and articulations.
- Above each staff, label the ordered pitch intervals between each pair of pitches (using numbers with + and − signs) and the ordered pitch-class intervals (using numbers).

opi:
opci:

opi:
opci:

opi:
opci:

2. Compose a short piece (6–8 measures) for a melody instrument of your choice in which every interval is either a 2 or a 6 (or the octave equivalents of these).

- Provide clef and time signature.
- Add tempo and articulations.
- Above each staff label the ordered pitch intervals (using numbers with + and − sign) and the ordered pitch-class intervals (using numbers).

opi:
opci:

opi:
opci:

opi:
opci:

E. ANALYSIS

1. Béla Bartók, String Quartet No. 3

- Identify all the ordered pitch intervals below the score using numbers with + or − signs.

- Circle adjacent combinations of pitch intervals 2 and 3 (some of your circles will overlap).

opi: ____ ____ ____ ____ ____ ____ ____ ____ ____ ____ ____

- The three most emphasized notes in the passage are A, B, and G♯ (in that order). What ordered pitch intervals connect them? _____

- The combination of pitch intervals 2 and 3 (moving in the same or opposite direction) acts as a unifying motive. Write one or two sentences in which you describe its use. Tell a brief story about the motive's journey through the music.

2. Ruth Crawford Seeger, Diaphonic Suite No. 1, i

- Identify all occurrences of pitch intervals 1, 2, and 11 below the score, with + and − signs for direction.

- An important motive features pitch intervals 1 and 2 moving in opposite directions (<+1, −2>, <−1, +2>, <+2, −1>, or <−2, +1>). Below each staff, use numbers and plus or minus signs to identify each occurrence of pitch intervals 1 or 2 or their octave equivalents (13 or 14) or inversions (11 or 10). Then circle each occurrence off the motive (motives may overlap).

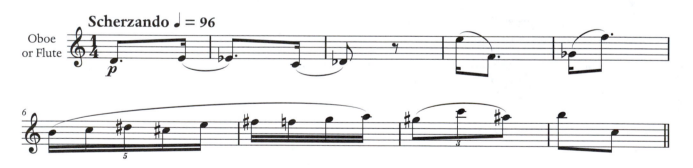

- Looking more closely at the first three measures, what are the notes on the three downbeats, and what are the opi between them? _____

- What are the lowest three notes in the first three measures, and what are the opi between them? _____

- Write one or two sentences describing how the motive that you identified is used in this passage.

- How is pitch-interval 11 used in this excerpt? How does it relate to phrase beginnings or endings? How does it relate to the frequently heard pitch-interval 1?

3. Edgard Varèse, *Octandre*

- This excerpt contains a motive that consists of pitch intervals 1 and 2, moving in the same direction (<+1, +2>, <−1, −2>, <+2, +1>, and <−2, −1>). Some instances of the motive may involve nonadjacent notes separated by pitches in a different register. The motives may also overlap. Label the ordered pitch intervals of the motive *above* the staff with numbers and + and − signs.

- The excerpt contains a number of large leaps. Label these opi *below* the staff with number and + or − sign.

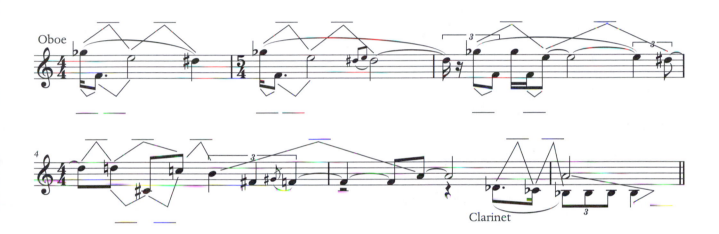

- What two large pitch intervals appear throughout this excerpt? _____

- What is the relationship between these intervals and 1s? _____

  _____

- Write a sentence or two tracing the statements of the three-note motive throughout the passage. What story do they tell, and how do the large pitch intervals contribute to the story?

4. Thomas Adès, First Mazurka

- Label the melodic (ordered) pitch intervals above the staff.

- Do you see any patterns in the series of labeled intervals? Is there a particular note on which patterns start or end? One interval does not quite conform to the pattern; circle it. How can you account for this interval?

5. Igor Stravinsky, "Music to hear" from *Three Shakespeare Songs*

Note: This passage was discussed several times in the textbook for this chapter.

- Considering the pitch classes used in this 24-note melody, circle any successions of four pitch classes that occur more than once in the same order.

- Fill in the table beneath the score, identifying all ordered and unordered pitch and pitch-class intervals.

- Looking at the unordered pitch-class intervals (upci) first, circle each occurrence of <4, 2, 1>.

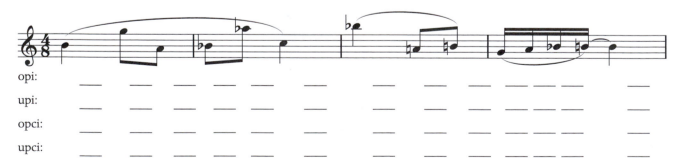

opi: ___ ___ ___ ___ ___ ___ ___ ___ ___ ___ ___

upi: ___ ___ ___ ___ ___ ___ ___ ___ ___ ___ ___

opci: ___ ___ ___ ___ ___ ___ ___ ___ ___ ___ ___

upci: ___ ___ ___ ___ ___ ___ ___ ___ ___ ___ ___

opi: ___ ___ ___ ___ ___ ___ ___ ___

upi: ___ ___ ___ ___ ___ ___ ___ ___

opci: ___ ___ ___ ___ ___ ___ ___ ___

upci: ___ ___ ___ ___ ___ ___ ___ ___

- Looking at the ordered pitch-class intervals (opci), the upci <4, 2, 1> in the lowest row of the chart are represented by two different strings of opci in the second-lowest row of the chart. What are those two strings of opci, and how are they related to each other? _____

  _____

  _____

- How do the patterns of pitch-class intervals (both ordered and unordered) work in this melody? Are the patterns clarified or concealed by the pitch intervals? If concealed, in what way and for what artistic purpose?

6. Milton Babbitt, Composition for Four Instruments

Note: Clarinet sounds as written.

- Under the score, write the ordered pitch-class intervals formed by the adjacent notes of this twelve-note melody.

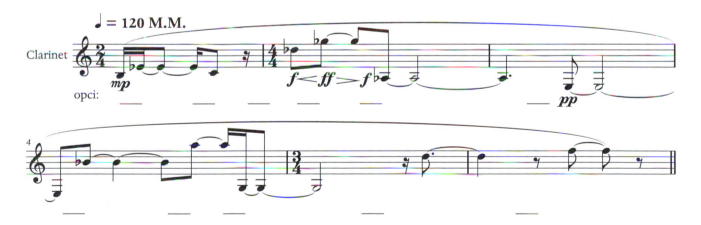

- How many opci are used in the melody? Are any repeated? _____

  _____

- What are the highest three melody notes? What are the ordered pitch intervals between them? _____

- What are the next highest three melody notes, and the opi between them?

  _____

- What are the lowest three melody notes, and the opi between them?

  _____

- What are the next lowest three melody notes, and the opi between them?

  _____

- What do the ordered pitch intervals in each of these three-note groups have in common? What distinguishes them from each other? _____

  _____

  _____

  _____

  _____

7. Sofia Gubaidulina, Ten Preludes for Solo Cello, No. 1 (Staccato—Legato)

- Identify all instances of pitch intervals 1 or 2, and label them below the staff using + and − signs to show direction.

- Circle every three-note motive that contains pitch intervals 1 and 2 moving in opposite directions. The four possibilities are <+1, −2>, <−1, +2>, <+2, −1>, and <−2, +1>. Note that the groups may overlap, and they may span across rests.

- How do the forms of the three-note motive relate to each other? How do they participate in the overall ascent of the line?

8. Anton Webern, Symphony, Op. 21, ii

- This melody contains twelve notes. Ignoring the immediate repetition of a note, identify the ordered and unordered pitch and pitch-class intervals in this melody and write them in the table beneath the staff.

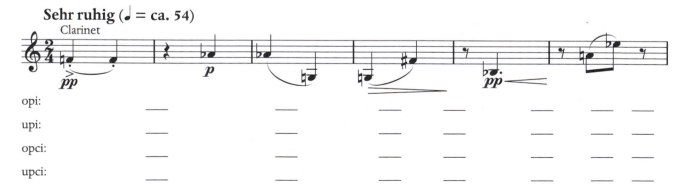

opi: _____   _____   _____   _____   _____   _____

upi: _____   _____   _____   _____   _____   _____

opci: _____   _____   _____   _____   _____   _____

upci: _____   _____   _____   _____   _____   _____

opi: ___ ___ ___ ___

upi: ___ ___ ___ ___

opci: ___ ___ ___ ___

upci: ___ ___ ___ ___

- Looking first at the unordered pitch-class intervals, what pattern do you see?

  _____

- Now also consider the ordered pitch-class intervals: how do the intervals before the 6 compare to the intervals after the 6? _____

  _____

  _____

- Finally, compare the pitch intervals: is the pattern maintained by them? Concealed by them? _____

  _____

  _____

  _____

9. Milton Babbitt, "The Widow's Lament in Springtime"

- This melody contains twelve notes. Ignoring the immediate repetition of a note, identify the ordered pitch intervals as well as the ordered and unordered pitch-class intervals and write them in the table beneath the staff.

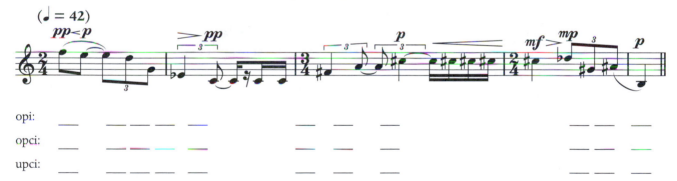

opi: ___ ___ ___ ___ ___ ___ ___ ___

opci: ___ ___ ___ ___ ___ ___ ___ ___

upci: ___ ___ ___ ___ ___ ___ ___ ___

- Looking first at the unordered pitch-class intervals, what pattern do you see?

  _____

- Of the six different interval classes, how many times does each one occur in the melody? Where do they occur?

  _____

  _____

  _____

- Now also consider the ordered pitch-class intervals: how do the intervals before the 6 compare to the intervals after the 6? _____

  _____

  _____

- Finally, compare the pitch intervals: is the pattern maintained by them? Concealed by them? _____
_____
_____
_____
_____

10. Elisabeth Lutyens, Bagatelle, Op. 48, No. 1

- Draw a line between any pair of adjacent or simultaneous notes related by interval class 1.

- Identify the unordered pitch interval for each and write it next to the interval.

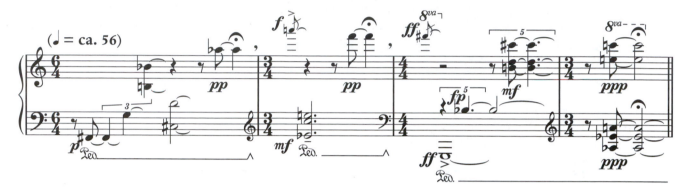

- What pairs of notes occur more than once? _____
- What pairs occur only once? _____
- Among the pairs of notes that recur, which are presented with the same pitch interval? _____

11. Elliott Carter, *Riconoscenza per Goffredo Petrassi* (for solo violin)

- On the score, draw a line between every pair of adjacent pitches related by interval classes 3 or 6 and then write the unordered pitch interval next to the line.

- Circle diminished triads and diminished seventh chords (these chords contain only interval classes 3 and 6).

Quasi improvvisando ♩ = ca. 92

Are there any notes in the melody that are not connected to at least one adjacent note by either 3 or 6? _____

Are there any notes in the melody that do not belong to a diminished triad? Which ones? _____
_____

chapter 44 Pitch-Class Sets: Trichords

A. QUESTIONS FOR REVIEW

1. What is a pitch-class set? What is a trichord?

2. What is a normal form? How do you find it?

3. How do you transpose a set? How do you tell if two sets are related by transposition? How do you figure out the interval of transposition?

4. How do you invert a set? How do you tell if two sets are related by inversion? How do you figure out the index of inversion?

5. What is a set class? How many trichord classes are there?

6. What is a prime form? How do you find it?

B. NORMAL FORM

- Write each trichord ascending within an octave, starting in turn on each of the three notes.

- Above the staff write the number of semitones from the lowest to the highest pitches.

- Circle the normal form (with the smallest interval from lowest to highest), and write its letter names in the blank beneath the staff.

- If there is more than one normal form (that is, more than one arrangement shares the smallest interval from lowest to highest note), list the letter names of every possible normal form.

1.

normal form: [F, G, B♭]

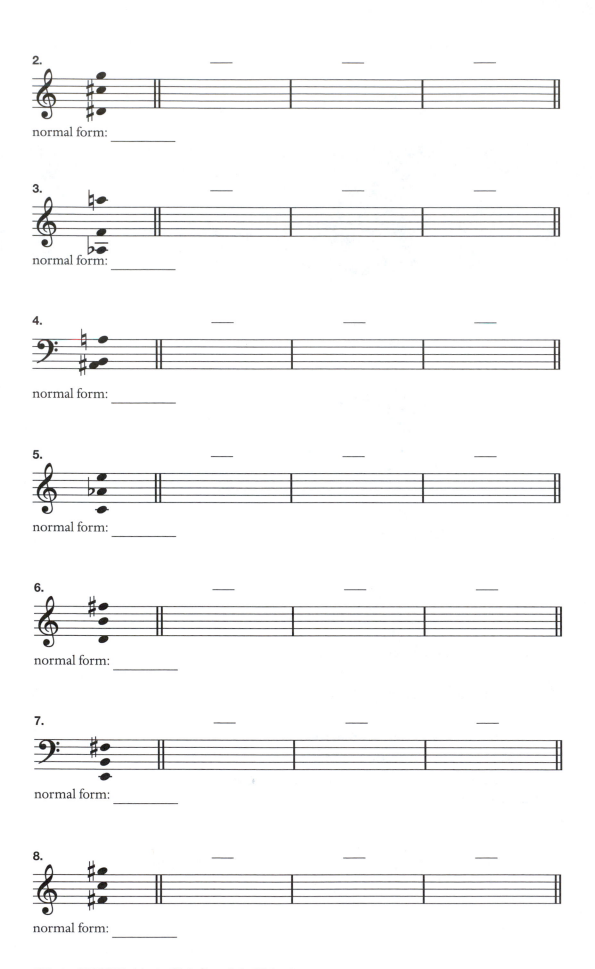

2.

normal form: _____

3.

normal form: _____

4.

normal form: _____

5.

normal form: _____

6.

normal form: _____

7.

normal form: _____

8.

normal form: _____

9.

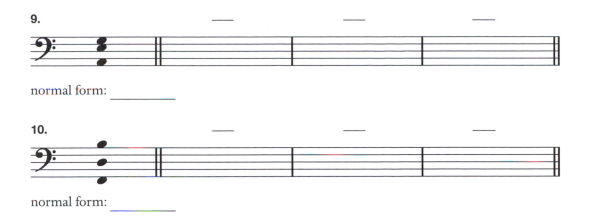

normal form: _____

10.

normal form: _____

C. TRANSPOSITION

1. Transpose these sets as indicated, writing your answer on the staff.

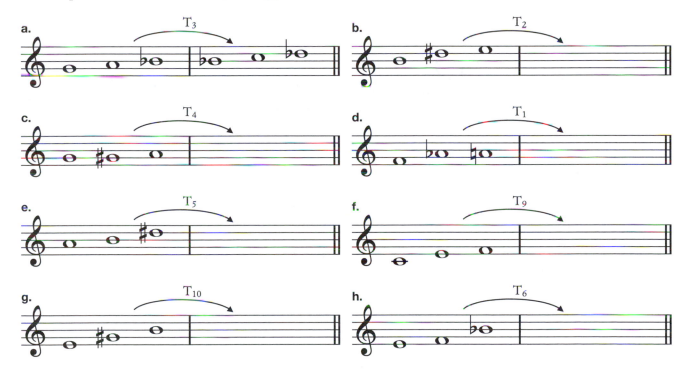

2. Transpose these sets as indicated, writing your answer on the staff and giving the note names of the trichord below it.

a.

[C, D, F] T_5 _____

b.

[F♯, B, C] T_6 _____

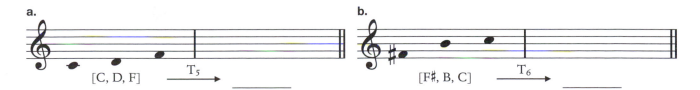

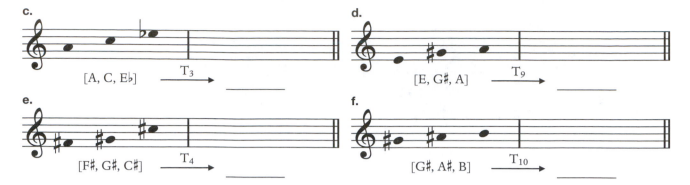

c. [A, C, E♭] $\xrightarrow{T_3}$ _____

d. [E, G♯, A] $\xrightarrow{T_9}$ _____

e. [F♯, G♯, C♯] $\xrightarrow{T_4}$ _____

f. [G♯, A♯, B] $\xrightarrow{T_{10}}$ _____

3. Identify these transpositions as follows:

- The following pairs of sets are related by transposition (T_n). Verify that by writing the intervals.

- Then write the letter names of the pitch classes in normal form beneath the staff and identify the interval of transposition.

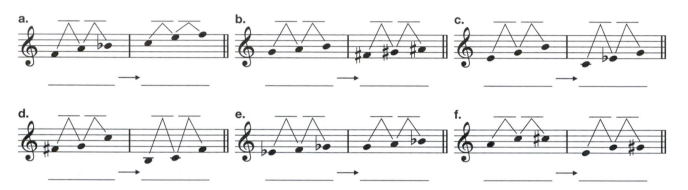

D. INVERSION

1. Invert the trichords by T_0I.

- In the first column, you will find trichords in normal form. Circle the notes of the trichord on the left-hand clockface.

- Then, circle the notes of the inversion on the right-hand clockface.

- In the last column, write the notes of the inverted set in normal form.

Trichords   Inversions

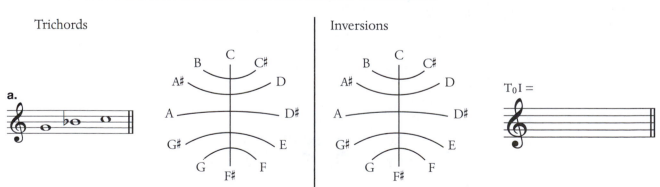

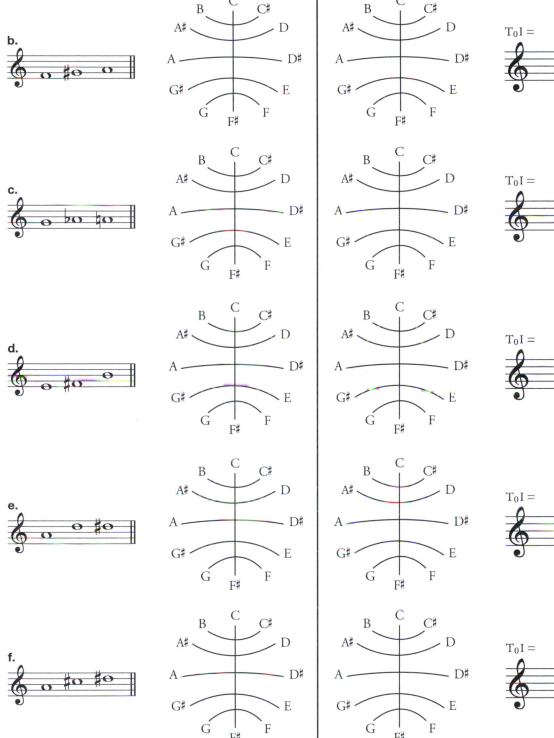

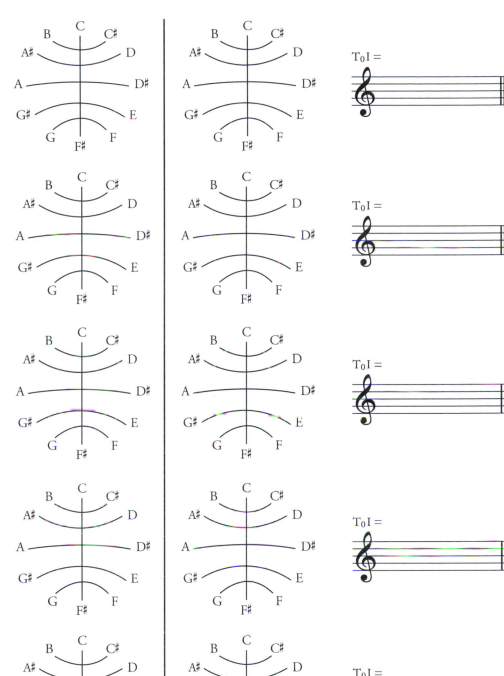

2. Invert these sets as indicated. Write your answers both on the staff and in letter names below the staff. Indicate intervals above the staff.

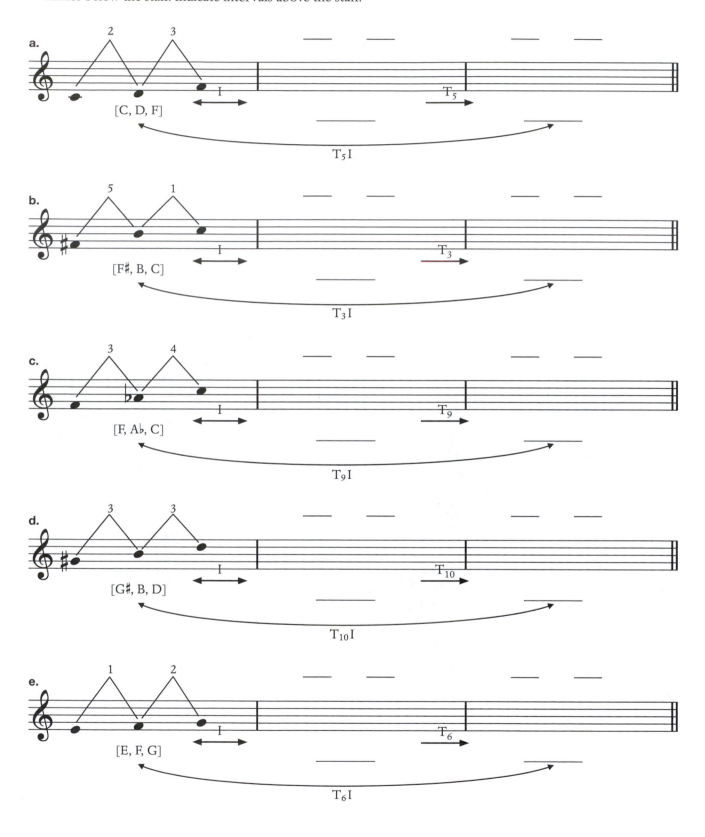

3. Identifying inversion
- The following pairs of sets are related by inversion (T_nI). Verify by writing the intervals over the staff.
- On the staff in the space between the two sets, write out the inversion of the left-hand set, with the intervals indicated above the staff.
- Determine the transposition (T_n).
- Identify the inversion that connects the two sets.

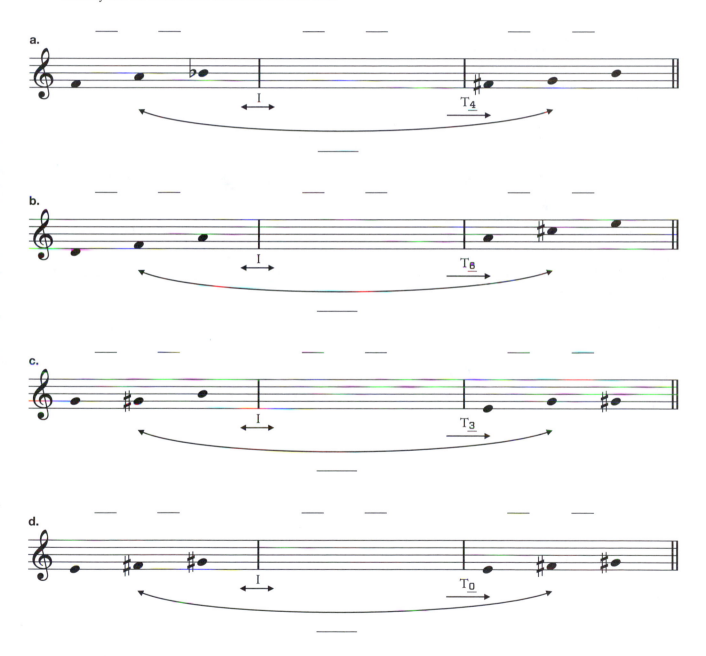

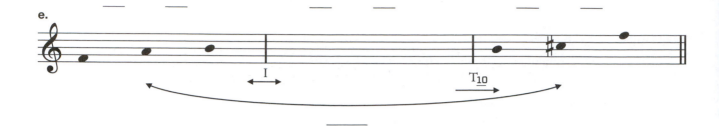

e.

E. TRANSPOSITION AND INVERSION

Below are pairs of trichords written in normal form. Write the intervals over the staff, then identify whether the sets are related by transposition, by inversion, by both transposition and inversion, or by neither.

a. T_n, T_nI, both, neither **b.** T_n, T_nI, both, neither **c.** T_n, T_nI, both, neither

d. T_n, T_nI, both, neither **e.** T_n, T_nI, both, neither **f.** T_n, T_nI, both, neither

g. T_n, T_nI, both, neither **h.** T_n, T_nI, both, neither **i.** T_n, T_nI, both, neither

j. T_n, T_nI, both, neither

F. PRIME FORM

1. The following sets are in normal form. Put them into in prime form.

- Start by extracting the succession of intervals.
- Then, if necessary, rearrange the intervals so the smaller interval is on the left.
- Finally, replicate that interval succession starting on pitch-class 0.

	NORMAL FORM	NORMAL FORM WITH INTERVALS	INTERVALS ARRANGED WITH SMALLER ON THE LEFT	INTERVAL SUCCESSION STARTING ON PITCH-CLASS 0	PRIME FORM
a.	[G, B, D]	4 3 [G, B, D]	3 4	3 4 0 3 7	(037)
b.	[A, C, E♭]	— — _____	— —	— — — — —	_____
c.	[F♯, B, C♯]	— — _____	— —	— — — — —	_____
d.	[F, A, B♭]	— — _____	— —	— — — — —	_____
e.	[D♭, F, A]	— — _____	— —	— — — — —	_____
f.	[E♭, F♭, G♭]	— — _____	— —	— — — — —	_____
g.	[G, A, C♯]	— — _____	— —	— — — — —	_____
h.	[A♭, C♯, D]	— — _____	— —	— — — — —	_____
i.	[C♯, E, F♯]	— — _____	— —	— — — — —	_____

2. Put the following sets into normal form and then into prime form.

		NORMAL FORM	PRIME FORM
a.	C♯–G–A		
b.	B♭–A–F		
c.	G♯–C♯–E		
d.	F–F♯–E		
e.	G–D–A		

G. COMPOSITION

1. Continue and complete a melody 8–12 measures in length in which most or all of the three-note groups represent set-classes (014) or (015).

   • Before you begin, think about the intervals that will be available to you within these set classes.

   • When you are done, analyze your melody by identifying the normal and prime forms of the sets you have used.

2. Write a six-measure progression and melody.

   • Continue and complete a progression of six chords for the left-hand part.

   • All chords should contain three different notes and lie within an octave, and all should be members of set-class (025).

   • Then add a melody in the right hand that either arpeggiates the chords or elaborates them with passing or neighboring notes.

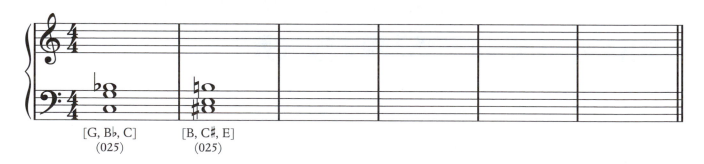

H. ANALYSIS

1. Anton Webern, Pieces for String Quartet, Op. 5, No. 2

- Determine the normal form for each circled set and write it in the blank provided.

- Label the arrows with the appropriate T_n and T_nI between sets.

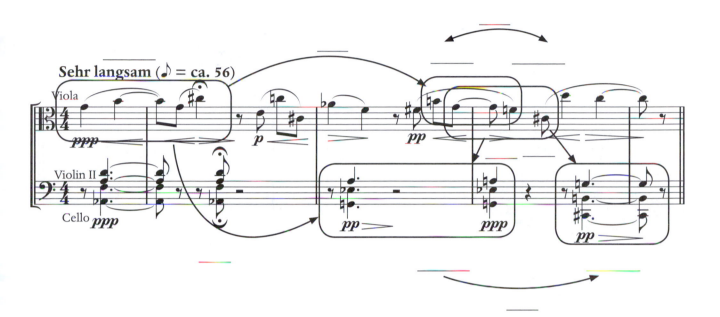

- The circled sets all belong to the same set class. What is its prime form?

  _____

- Do all five circled sets share a note in common? If so, what note? _____

- Looking at the transpositions, what tone(s) does each transposition in the example hold in common? _____

  _____

- Can you relate the intervals of transposition to the intervals in the set?

  _____

  _____

- Is there a larger collection that these sets combine to form? If so, what?

  _____

2. Arnold Schoenberg, *Piano Pieces*, Op. 11, No. 1

- Determine the normal form for each set, and write it in the blank provided.
- Label the arrows with the appropriate T_n and T_nI between sets.

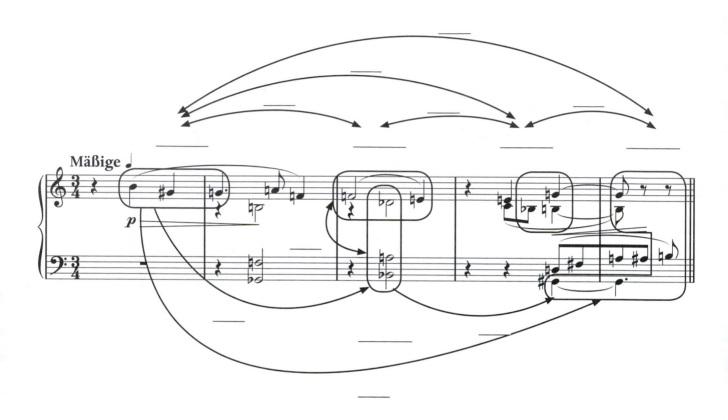

The circled sets all belong to the same set class. What is its prime form? _____

What is the common-tone relationship between the sets in m. 3? _____

Between the sets in mm. 4–5? _____

Between the first set and the last set? _____

3. Anton Webern, *Movements for String Quartet*, Op. 5, No. 3

- Determine the normal form for each circled set, and write it in lettered blank provided.

- Label the arrows with the appropriate T_n and T_nI between sets.

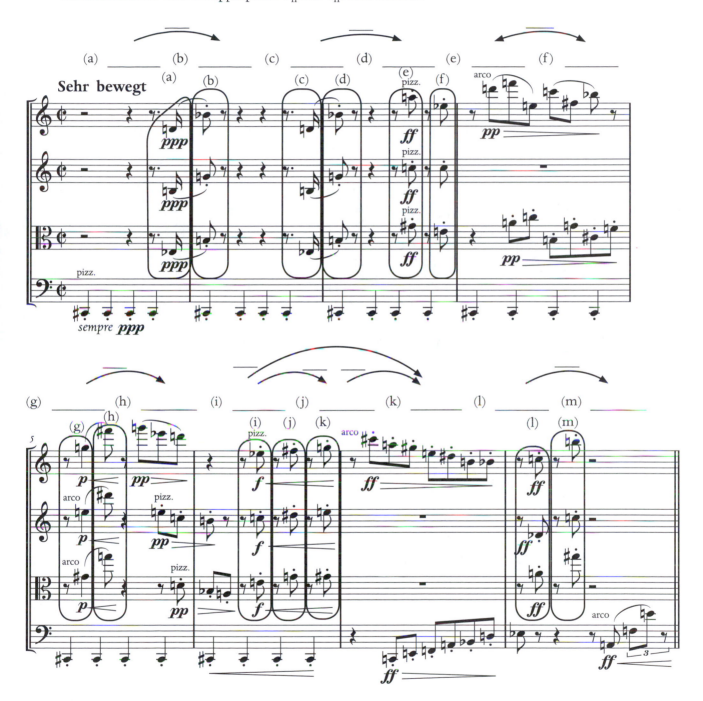

- The circled sets all belong to the same set class. What is its prime form?

_____

- Discuss intervals of transposition and common tones for the pairs of chords in mm. 1–5 and 8, as well as for the three chords in m. 6. What might have motivated the choice of intervals of transposition between the chords?

4. Anton Webern, Concerto for Nine Instruments, ii

- The melody of this example (in the treble staff) can be segmented into trichords, each consisting of three consecutive notes. The first note of each trichord is labeled with a letter.

- Then, identify the normal form for each circled trichord and label it in the corresponding lettered blank below the staff.

- Label the arrows with the appropriate T_n and T_nI between sets.

- Identify the larger collections formed by the bracketed pairs of chords.

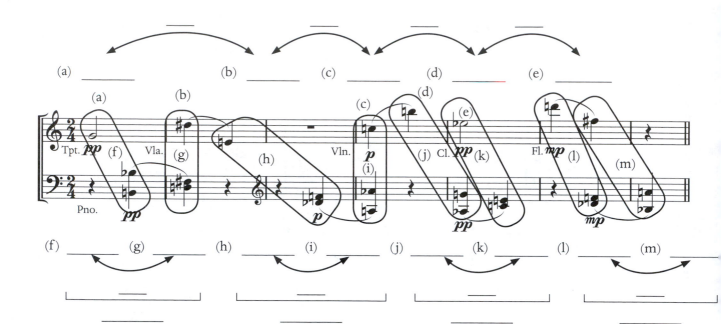

- The circled sets all belong to the same set class. What is its prime form?

  _____

- How are the sets in the melody linked? _____

  _____

- What larger collections are created by combining two melody notes with four piano notes, as indicated by the brackets beneath the score. _____

  _____

5. Sofia Gubaidulina, *Reflections on the Theme B-A-C-H*

- Determine the normal form for each circled set, and write it in the lettered blank provided.

- Label the arrows with the appropriate T_n and T_nI between sets.

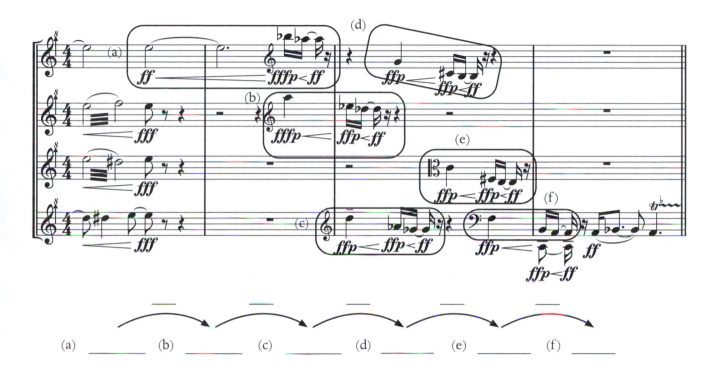

- The circled sets all belong to the same set class. What is its prime form?

  _____

- How do the circled sets relate to one another through the excerpt?

6. Sofia Gubaidulina, String Trio, ii

- Determine the normal form for each circled set, and write it in the lettered blank provided.

- Label the arrows with the appropriate T_n and T_nI between sets.

- Identify the larger collection formed by the first three sets, and label it under the bracket.

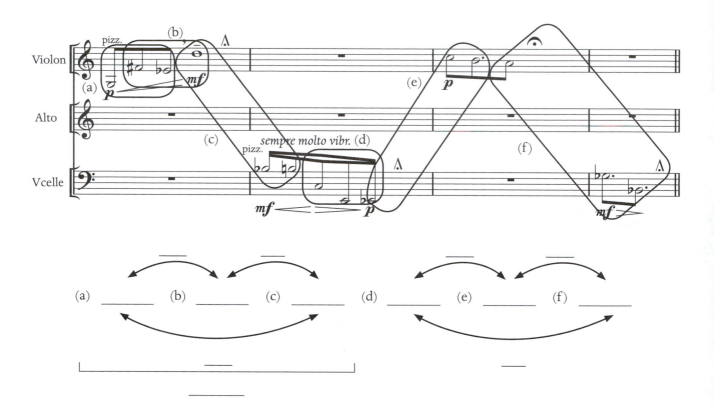

- The circled sets all belong to the same set class. What is its prime form?

_____

- What is the role of common tones in the first three sets? Compare the progression of the last three sets to the first three.

7. Milton Babbitt, String Quartet No. 2

- Determine the normal form for each circled set, and write it in the lettered blank provided.
- Label the arrows with the appropriate T_n or T_nI between sets.

- The circled sets all belong to the same set class. What is its prime form?

  _____

- Within each instrumental part, what T_n or T_nI connects the two sets?

  _____

- What larger collection is found in the instrumental parts? _____

  _____

- What is the relationship between the collection in first violin and viola compared to the collection in second violin and cello? _____

  _____

8. Tan Dun, *Intercourse of Fire and Water* (for solo cello)

- Determine the normal form for each trichord consisting of three consecutive notes and write it in the blank provided.

- Label the arrows with the appropriate T_n or T_nI between sets.

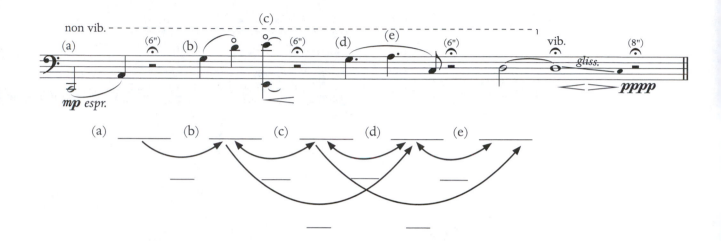

- The trichords all belong to the same set class. What is its prime form?

  _____

- What larger collection is formed collectively by all of these sets? _____

  _____

- Describe the network of common tones that connects these sets.

45   Inversional Symmetry

A. QUESTIONS FOR REVIEW

1. What is a wedge progression? What is an expanding wedge progression? A contracting wedge progression?

2. What is an axis of pitch inversion? What must be true about the pitches that lie above the axis in relation to the pitches that lie below it? What is the relationship between the pitch intervals from bottom to top and the pitch intervals from top to bottom?

3. What is an axis of pitch-class inversion? What must be true about the pitch classes that lie on either side of the axis?

B. WEDGE PROGRESSIONS

1. Continue these expanding wedges until you get back to the pitch class(es) you started on. Identify the intervals formed between the two lines (ordered pitch-class interval from lower to higher note), and write them beneath the staff.

a.

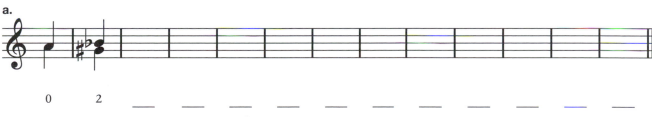

     0   2   ——   ——   ——   ——   ——   ——   ——

b.

     1   3   ——   ——   ——   ——   ——   ——   ——

2. Continue these contracting wedges until they reach the central pitch or pitches. Identify the intervals formed between the two lines (ordered pitch-class interval from lower to higher note).

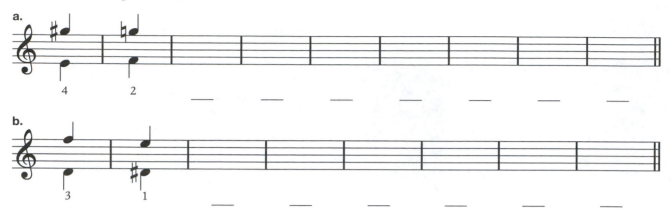

C. INVERSIONAL SYMMETRY IN PITCH

1. Find the axis of symmetry in the following collection of pitches.

- Arrange the pitches in registral order from lowest to highest.
- Identify the intervals between adjacent pitches.
- Circle the pitch (or pair of pitches) that serve as the axis of symmetry.
- Slur each note to its inversional partner around the axis.

2. Write four pairs of notes that are inversionally symmetrical around the given axis. Use a slur to connect each note to its inversional partner.

b.

D. SYMMETRICAL PITCH-CLASS SETS

- Circle the notes of the given symmetrical sets on the pitch-class clockface, and draw the axis of inversion.

- On the clockface, connect each note in the set to its inversional partner (which may be itself).

- Name the index of inversion (T_nI) that maps the set onto itself.

SET	CLOCKFACE	T_nI
[F, G, A]		——
[C♯, D, E♭]		——
[G♯, B, D]		——
[F♯, G♯, C♯]		——

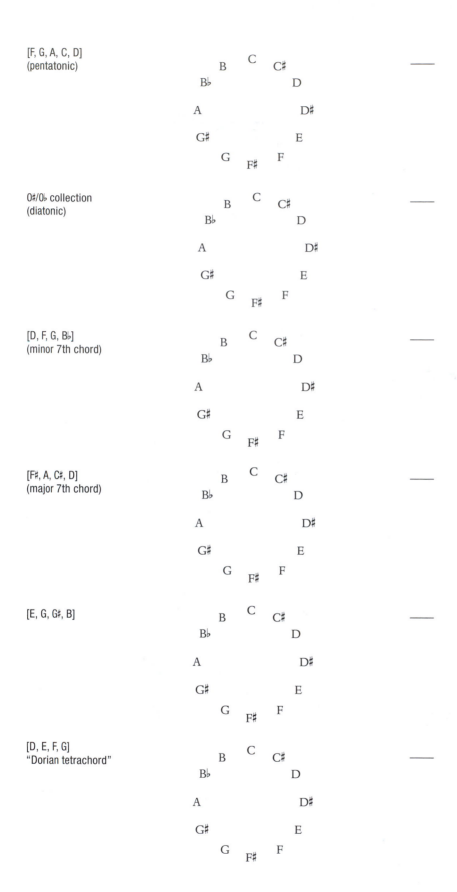

[F, G, A, C, D]
(pentatonic)

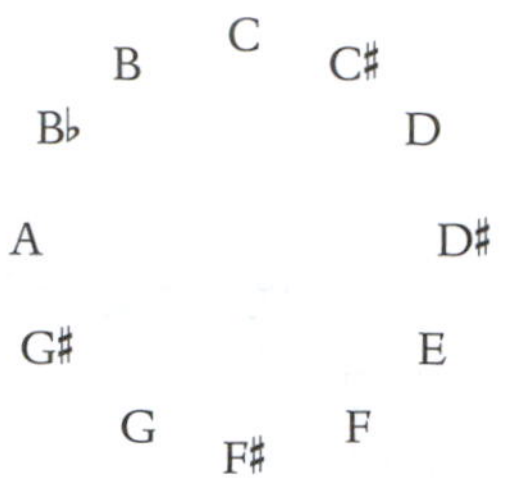

___

0♯/0♭ collection
(diatonic)

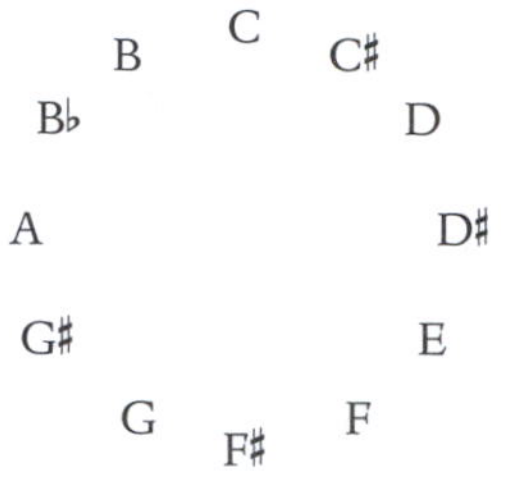

___

[D, F, G, B♭]
(minor 7th chord)

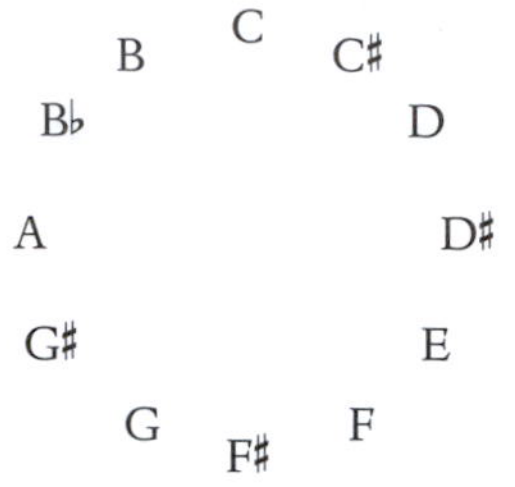

___

[F♯, A, C♯, D]
(major 7th chord)

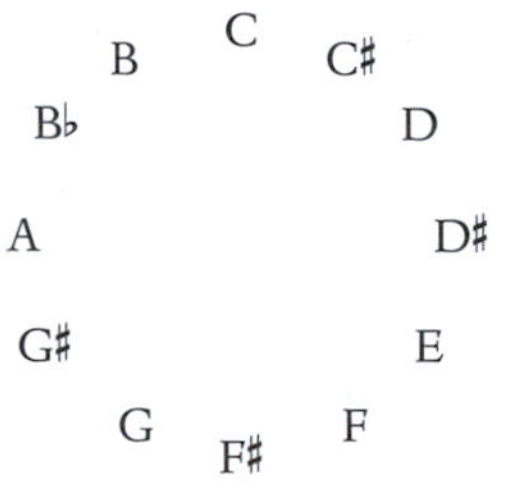

___

[E, G, G♯, B]

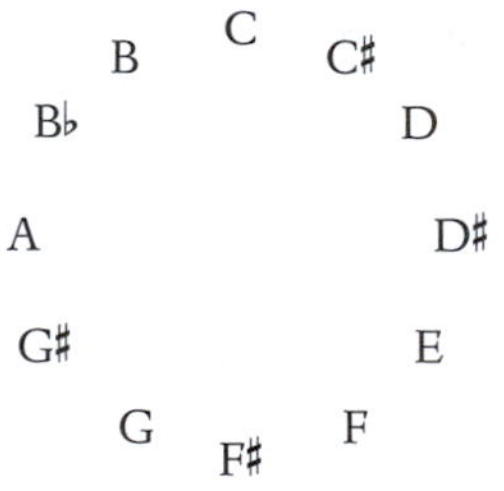

___

[D, E, F, G]
"Dorian tetrachord"

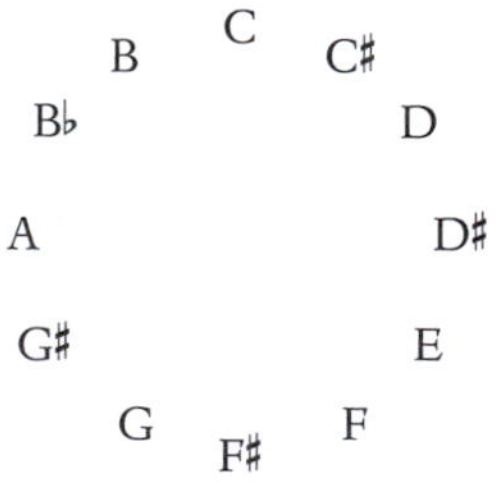

___

[B♭, C, E♭, F]

```
                          C
                   B          C♯
              B♭                  D
          A                           D♯
       G♯                               E
          G                         F
             F♯
```

E. COMPOSITION

1. Complete this duet by filling in measures 2–9 using whole notes only.

- Every harmonic interval should be pitch-symmetrical around the A in the first and last measures.

- Between the staves, write the interval between the melodies (counted in semitones).

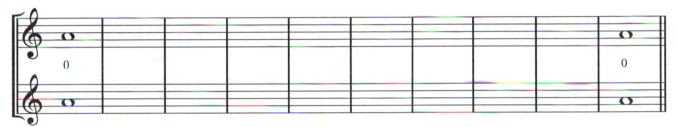

2. Complete this progression of four-note chords where all of the chords are symmetrical around middle C.

- The two notes in the treble should be the same intervals above middle C as the two notes in the bass are below middle C.

- There may be octave doubling.

- Label the intervals in each chord.

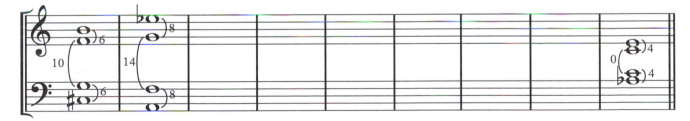

3. Write a melody 8–12 measures in length that is symmetrically balanced around the B above middle C.

- Each note should be heard in close proximity to, but not necessarily adjacent to, its inversional partner.

- End the melody with a wedge-like convergence on B.

F. ANALYSIS

1. Anton Webern, Piano Variations, Op. 27, ii

- On the staff below the excerpt, write the notes used in this passage in registral order, from lowest to highest.

- Use slurs to connect the pitches that are inversional partners.

- Draw a line through the axis of inversion.

- All parts are notated at pitch.

- Directly on the score, use slurs to connect the notes that are inversional partners.

- Among these many pairs of pitches, there are only seven different pairs of pitch classes. What are they? _____

- What is the role that pitch symmetry plays in this piece's organization?

2. Anton Webern, Quartet, Op. 22, i

Beneath the score you will find a simplified version dividing the music into two voices in note-against-note counterpoint. Each harmonic interval consists of a pair of inversional partners.

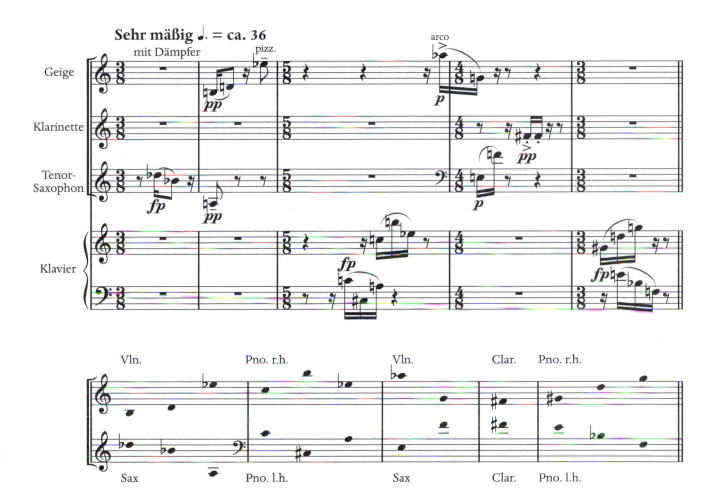

- Each harmonic interval is symmetrical around which pitch? _____

  _____

- On the score itself, use slurs to connect the inversional partners with respect to that central pitch axis.

- What is the role of inversional symmetry in organizing this piece?

3. Morton Feldman, *Crippled Symmetry*

Beneath the score, write out the notes of the flute and vibraphone melodies in registral order from lowest to highest, identify the intervals between adjacent notes, and determine the axis of pitch symmetry.

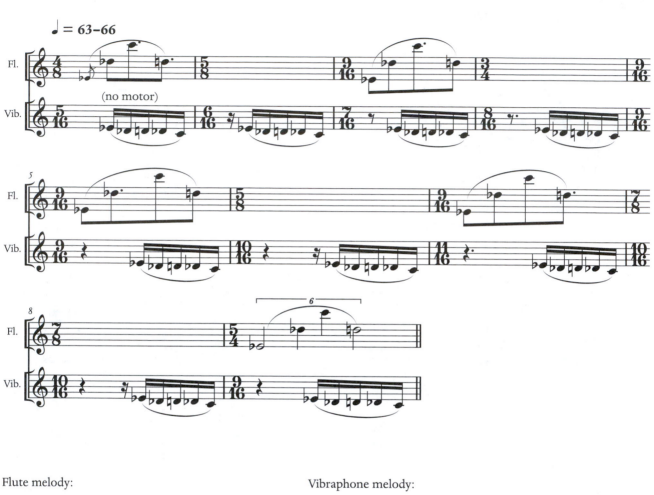

Flute melody: Vibraphone melody:

Intervals: Intervals:

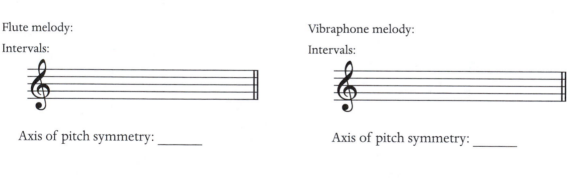

Axis of pitch symmetry: _____   Axis of pitch symmetry: _____

- What is the relationship between these two pitch axes? _____

_____

_____

4. Alfred Schnittke, *Stille Musik*

- Assume that C and G are inversional partners. Connect them on the pitch-class clockface below the score.

- Identify the inversional axis and draw a line through the clockface, then connect all of the remaining inversional partners.

- Draw lines connecting these pairs of notes on the score.

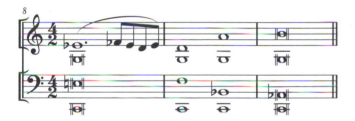

Is there a centric pitch or pitches, and if so, how do they function?

Are the chords inversionally symmertrical? In pitch or pitch class? What inversion (T_nI) would relate these chords to themselves?

5. Anton Webern, Six Bagatelles, Op. 9, No. 5

- Assume that E and C, the first two notes in viola and cello, are inversional partners. Connect them on the pitch clockface below the score.

- Identify the inversional axis and draw a line through the clockface, then connect the remaining inversional partners.

- Draw lines connecting the inversional partners directly on the score. Note that some inversional partners may be nonadjacent in the music, and that not all of the pairs need be present.

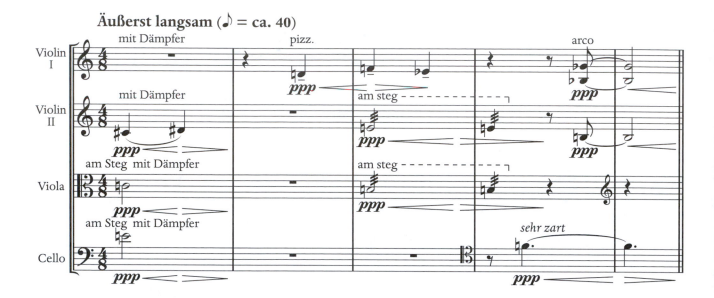

- How does symmetry around D shape this passage?

6. Edgard Varèse, *Hyperprism*

The C♯ above middle C is heard almost continuously in this passage. In what ways does it function as an axis of pitch symmetry? To what extent are pitches balanced around this axis? _____

_____

_____

_____

_____

_____

7. Sofia Gubaidulina, String Quartet No. 2

Answer the questions beneath the score.

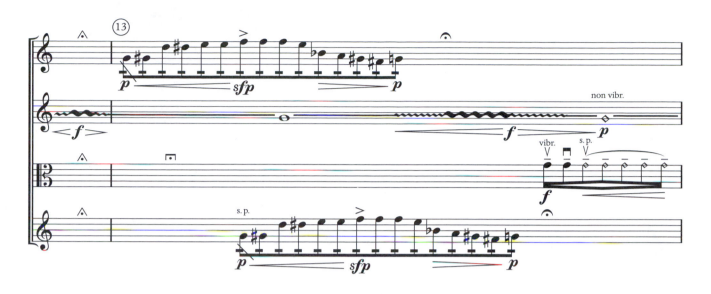

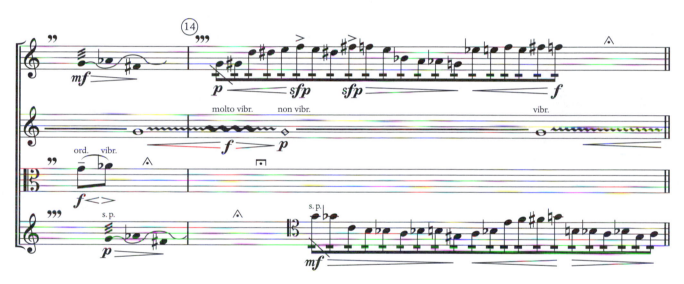

- Which pitch functions as an inversional axis and centric tone in this passage?

  _____

- How is this centric tone established? _____

  _____

  _____

  _____

- How does inversional symmetry around the centric tone shape the melodies
  in first violin and cello? _____

  _____

  _____

NAME: ....

46   Twelve-Tone Serialism

A. QUESTIONS FOR REVIEW

1. What is a twelve-tone series? What is twelve-tone music?

2. What are the four orderings of a twelve-tone series? How do they compare to each other in pitch? in interval?

3. How many different row forms are there, counting all possible transpositions?

4. What is a 12x12 matrix and how is it constructed?

5. What is a "twelve-count"?

6. What is a subset? What is a two-note subset called? What is a three-note subset called? What happens to the subset-types when the series is transformed by transposition or inversion or their retrogrades?

7. What is invariance?

B. SERIES FORMS

1. Write series forms as indicated.

   a.

$P_{B\flat}$	B♭	A	C	B	E♭	E	C♯	D	F♯	F	A♭	G
P_G	___	___	___	___	___	___	___	___	___	___	___	___
I_D	___	___	___	___	___	___	___	___	___	___	___	___
RI_D	___	___	___	___	___	___	___	___	___	___	___	___

b.

$P_{B\flat}$	B♭	F	C	B	A	F♯	C♯	E♭	G	A♭	D	E
RP_A	___	___	___	___	___	___	___	___	___	___	___	___
I_G	___	___	___	___	___	___	___	___	___	___	___	___
$RI_{A\flat}$	___	___	___	___	___	___	___	___	___	___	___	___

c.

P_E	E	F	G	D♭	G♭	E♭	A♭	D	B	C	A	B♭
$P_{B\flat}$	___	___	___	___	___	___	___	___	___	___	___	___
RP_F	___	___	___	___	___	___	___	___	___	___	___	___
I_D	___	___	___	___	___	___	___	___	___	___	___	___

2. Identify the relationship (transposition or inversion) between the following series forms, expressed as T_n or T_nI.

a.

I_G	G	A♭	C	E♭	F	B	B♭	D	E	A	G♭	C♯
P_F	F	E	C	A	G	C♯	D	B♭	A♭	E♭	G♭	B

Relationship: ____

b.

$I_{B\flat}$	B♭	B	E♭	G♭	A♭	D	C♯	F	G	C	A	E
$P_{A\flat}$	A♭	G	E♭	C	B♭	E	F	C♯	B	F♯	A	D

Relationship: ____

c.

$P_{A\sharp}$	A♯	A	B	C♯	D	C	D♯	F	E	F♯	G♯	G
I_E	E	F	D♯	C♯	C	D	B	A	A♯	G♯	F♯	G

Relationship: ____

d.

$P_{G\sharp}$	G♯	C♯	D♯	A♯	F♯	B	F	C	E	A	G	D
$P_{C\sharp}$	C♯	F♯	G♯	D♯	B	E	B♭	F	A	D	C	G

Relationship: ____

3. Complete 12×12 matrices. Then write out the indicated series forms.

a.

G#	A	G	F	B	E	D	D	A	C#	C	F#

$P_{F\#}$ ___ ___ ___ ___ ___ ___ ___ ___ ___ ___ ___ ___

RI_{G} ___ ___ ___ ___ ___ ___ ___ ___ ___ ___ ___ ___

b.

F#	C#	A#	F	D	A	E	D#	C	B	G#	G

RP_{E} ___ ___ ___ ___ ___ ___ ___ ___ ___ ___ ___ ___

RI_{E} ___ ___ ___ ___ ___ ___ ___ ___ ___ ___ ___ ___

P_{A} ___ ___ ___ ___ ___ ___ ___ ___ ___ ___ ___ ___

C. COMPOSITION

1. Complete these twelve-tone series as instructed.

   a. The first six notes and the last six are complementary hexatonic collections. The four trichords are all consonant triads (two minor and two major).

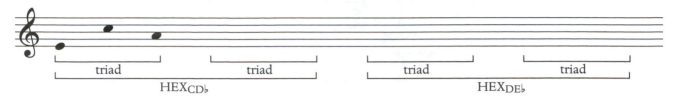

   b. Each of the eleven ordered pitch-class intervals (1–11) occurs once.

   c. As many trichordal subsets as possible are members of set-class (014). Trichords may overlap (share one or two notes in common).

   d. Every other interval is a member of interval-class 1.

2. Using one of the series you composed in the previous exercise, or one discussed in Chapter 46 of the textbook, write a melody using a Prime followed by its Retrograde. Before you compose your melody, write out the two series forms. In your melody, feel free to repeat notes or groups of notes.

Prime:

Retrograde:

Melody:

3. Using one of the series you composed in the previous exercise, or one discussed in Chapter 46 of the textbook, write a duet for violin and cello that has a Prime in one instrument and a Retrograde-Inversion in the other. Before you compose your duet, write out the two series forms. Within each part, feel free to repeat notes or groups of notes.

Prime:

Retrograde-Inversion:

Duet:

4. Using one of the series you composed in the previous exercise, or one discussed in Chapter 46 of the textbook, write a short piano piece where the melody is the Prime ordering and the accompanying chords are subsets of the Prime. Before you compose your piece, write out the series form and, in close position, the chords you plan to use.

Prime:

Chords:

Piano Piece:

D. ANALYSIS

For each of the following passages, the series is provided. Answer questions about the structure of the series and its use in the music.

1. Anton Webern, String Quartet, Op. 28, i

There are two series forms in this passage: $P_{B\flat}$, which begins in violin 1 in m. 1, and P_G, which begins in the viola in m. 2.

$P_{B\flat}$	B♭	A	C	B	E♭	E	C♯	D	F♯	F	A♭	G
P_G	G	F♯	A	G♯	C	C♯	B♭	B	E♭	D	F	E

- Complete a twelve count of the passage by labeling the beginnings of series forms and numbering the pitches. Use lines connecting pitch numbers to show how the series moves from one instrument to the next.

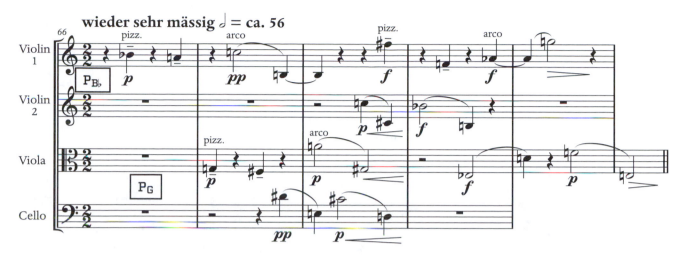

- Below, write the ordered and unordered pitch class intervals. Are there any patterns?

| P$_{B\flat}$ | B♭ | A | C | B | E♭ | E | C♯ | D | F♯ | F | A♭ | G |

- What interval class appears most frequently in the row? what does the composer do to articulate it? _____

  _____

  _____

- The first four notes of the series, B♭–A–C–B, spell Bach's name (in German, B is called B♭, and H is called B♮). Fill in the chart below showing how the other four-note groups are related to B♭–A–C–B by transposition and inversion.

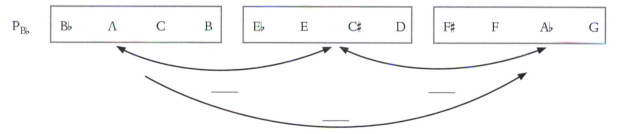

- There are three forms of this four-note motive in P$_{B\flat}$ and three more in P$_G$. Circle them on the score. What has the composer done to articulate them?

2. Arnold Schoenberg, Piano Piece, Op. 33a

There are three series forms in this passage: $P_{B\flat}$, $RP_{B\flat}$, and $RI_{E\flat}$.

$P_{B\flat}$	B♭	F	C	B	A	F♯	C♯	E♭	G	A♭	D	E	$RP_{B\flat}$
	E♭	A♭	C♯	D	E	G	C	B♭	F♯	F	B	A	$RI_{E\flat}$

- On the score, complete a twelve count by labeling each row form and numbering the pitches. Remember that within chords, the order of notes from lowest to highest does not necessarily follow the order within the series.

- The music is mostly organized into four-note subsets, PX, PY, PZ, IX, IY, and IZ. Circle and label these subsets on the score. What T_nI connects corresponding four-note subsets? _____

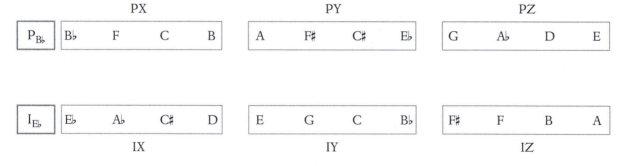

	PX				PY				PZ			
$P_{B\flat}$	B♭	F	C	B	A	F♯	C♯	E♭	G	A♭	D	E

	IX				IY				IZ			
$I_{E\flat}$	E♭	A♭	C♯	D	E	G	C	B♭	F♯	F	B	A

- How does inversional balance help to shape the six chords in measures 1–2? The two melodies in measures 3–5? _____

_____

_____

_____

- There is little or no invariance of dyads or trichords between these two series forms. But there is a special sort of invariance that affects the six-note groups (hexachords). How do the two hexachords of $P_{B\flat}$ relate to the two hexachords of $I_{E\flat}$ (in content, not order)? _____

   _____

3. Anton Webern, Quartet, Op. 22, i

Provide a twelve-count of the passage. The music is based on row forms $P_{D\flat}$ and I_B:

$P_{D\flat}$	D♭	B♭	A	C	B	E♭	E	F	F♯	G♯	D	G
I_B	B	D	E♭	C	D♭	A	A♭	G	F♯	E	B♭	F

- Label the beginning of each form and number the pitches within each row form. Note that the series move among instrumental parts.

- Describe the role of imitation between the two serial melodies. _____

   _____

   _____

   _____

- What is the T_nI that relates these two series forms? _____. What is the axis of symmetry? _____

- How does this inversional relationship shape the music? Is the inversion one of pitch or pitch class? _____

   _____

   _____

   _____

4. Arnold Schoenberg, Suite for Piano, Op. 25, Gavotte

- Provide a twelve count of the passage, which is based on these series forms:

P_E	E	F	G	D♭	G♭	E♭	A♭	D	B	C	A	B♭
$I_{B♭}$	B♭	A	G	D♭	A♭	B	G♭	C	E♭	D	F	E
$P_{B♭}$	B♭	B	D♭	G	C	A	D	A♭	F	G♭	E♭	E
I_E	E	E♭	D♭	G	D	F	C	G♭	A	A♭	B	B♭

- On the score, label the beginning of each form and number the pitches within each row form. Note that a single note may be both the end of one series and the beginning of another.

- How are the notes of the series distributed between the voices?

  - Presentation of P_E. _____
    _____
    _____

  - Presentation of $I_{B♭}$. _____
    _____
    _____

  - Presentation of $P_{B♭}$. _____
    _____
    _____

- Presentation of I_E. _____
  _____
  _____

- How many tritones are there within the series? _____
  List the tritones in each of the following series forms:

  P_E: _____

  $I_{B\flat}$: _____

  $P_{B\flat}$: _____

  I_E: _____

- Circle these tritones on the score. How do they shape the music?

- All four series forms begin and end on E and Bb, another tritone at this higher level. Circle those two notes on the score. How do they shape the music?

5. Luigi Dallapiccola, *Quaderno musicale di Annalibera*, Contrapunctus secundus (canon contrario motu)

The series for the piece is P_F.

P_F	F	E	C	A	G	C♯	D	Bb	Ab	Eb	Gb	B

- Construct a 12x12 matrix with P_F as the first row.

F	E	C	A	G	Db	D	Bb	Ab	Eb	Gb	B

- On the score, label the beginning of each series form and give a complete 12-count.

Poco allegretto; "alla Serenata" ($\downarrow$ = 69–72)

- The piece uses four pairs of simultaneously sounding series forms. Each pair consists of two forms related by inversion. What are the pairs? What are the T_nI that connect them?

Measures	Row in top voice	Row in bottom voice	T_nI
1–3			
3–4			
5–7			
7–8			

- The two halves of the piece have different axes of inversional symmetry: T_0I and T_6I. Draw those axes on these pitch-class clockfaces. How are the axes of symmetry manifested in the music? Do they receive any special treatment?

T_0I

```
        C
   B        C#
Bb               D
A                 D#
  G#           E
    G       F
      F#
```

T_6I

```
        C
   B        C#
Bb               D
A                 D#
  G#           E
    G       F
      F#
```

- The series is notable for its inclusion of traditional tonal harmonies, including two seventh chords and a triad with an added semitone. Complete the table below with the triads and seventh chords that are featured in each row form. What is the musical effect of these triads and seventh chords? _____

_____

_____

Row form	First four notes	Middle four notes	Last four notes
I_G	A♭M7	B♭M	F♯m7
P_F			
RI_E			
RP_A			
I_B			
P_A			
RI_F			
RP_C			

6. Luigi Dallapiccola, *Goethe Lieder*, No. 2, "Die Sonne kommt!"

- Provide a twelve-count of the passage. The music is based on two series forms
  ($P_{G\sharp}$ and I_A) and their retrogrades ($RP_{G\sharp}$ and RI_A).

$P_{G\sharp}$	G♯	A	G	F	B	E	D	E♭	B♭	D♭	C	F♯	$RP_{G\sharp}$
I_A	A	G♯	B♭	C	G♭	D♭	E♭	D	G	E	F	B	RI_A

Translation: The sun comes! A shining splendor! The crescent moon embraces it. Who could unite such a pair? This riddle, how can it be explained? How?

- Identify the ordered pitch-class intervals in $P_{G\sharp}$. Circle and label (with normal and prime forms) any trichord-types that occur more than once in the row (bearing in mind the possibility that trichords may overlap).

opci   —   —   —   —   —   —   —   —   —   —   —

$P_{G\sharp}$ G♯   A   G   F   B   E   D   E♭   B♭   D♭   C   F♯

Trichords

Prime forms

- Describe the intervallic and trichordal organization of the series and its realization in the vocal melody.
- $P_{G\sharp}$, I_A, and their retrogrades are the only series forms used in the piece. Fill in the chart below, showing where and in which part the series appear.

Measures	1–5	6–9	9–12	13–17
Voice				
Clarinet				

- How do the row forms organize the vocal line? What is the relationship between the clarinet melody and the vocal melody in their row forms? Their pitches? Their rhythms?
- Compare the two series forms and look for invariant dyads and trichords (groups of two or three notes that are the same in both series). Circle them and connect them with lines. Circle these invariants in mm. 9–17 of the score, and connect them with lines. What is the musical effect of these invariants?

$P_{G\sharp}$ G♯   A   G   F   B   E   D   E♭   B♭   D♭   C   F♯

I_A A   G♯   B♭   C   G♭   D♭   E♭   D   G   E   F   B

7. Igor Stravinsky, *Fanfare for a New Theatre*

This piece uses four series forms: $P_{A\sharp}$, its retrograde ($RP_{A\sharp}$), the inversion that starts on A♯ ($I_{A\sharp}$), its retrograde ($RI_{A\sharp}$), and the retrograde of the inversion that ends on G, which is the last note of $P_{A\sharp}$ (RI_E).

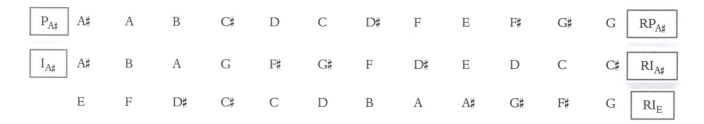

$P_{A\sharp}$	A♯	A	B	C♯	D	C	D♯	F	E	F♯	G♯	G	$RP_{A\sharp}$
$I_{A\sharp}$	A♯	B	A	G	F♯	G♯	F	D♯	E	D	C	C♯	$RI_{A\sharp}$
	E	F	D♯	C♯	C	D	B	A	A♯	G♯	F♯	G	RI_E

- Do a twelve-count (label the series forms and number the pitches within each series form 1–12, or in the case of R and RI, 12–1). Note that the last note of one series is frequently the first note of the next.

- On P$_{A\sharp}$, identify the ordered pitch-class, intervals. How would you describe them? _____

P$_{A\sharp}$	A♯	A	B	C♯	D	C	D♯	F	E	F♯	G♯	G

opci ___ ___ ___ ___ ___ ___ ___ ___ ___ ___ ___

- The row can be divided into four trichords, as shown below. Identify the ordered pitch-class intervals in each trichord, and label each trichord with its normal order and prime form. How many trichord classes appear in the row?

_____

P$_{A\sharp}$		A♯ A B		C♯ D C		D♯ F E		F♯ G♯ G

opci   __ __   __ __   __ __   __ __

normal order   _____   _____   _____   _____

prime form   _____   _____   _____   _____

- There is extensive invariance among the series forms. Label the normal forms of the trichords directly on the score. What is the musical effect of all of this invariance? _____

  _____

  _____

- Describe the ways in which A♯ functions as a centric tone in this piece. _____

  _____

  _____

  _____

8. Charles Wuorinen, Twelve Pieces, No. 3

This short piece uses a pair of inversionally related series forms:

P_E	E	C	F	D	G	E♭	A♭	G♭	A	B♭	D♭	B
I_A	A	C♯	G♯	B	F♯	A♯	F	G	E	E♭	C	D

- Provide a twelve-count directly on the score, noting series forms and numbering the pitches in each series.

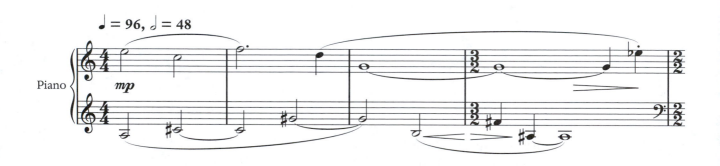

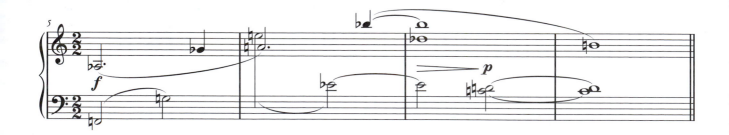

- Write the ordered pitch-class intervals between adjacent pitch classes in P_E. Are there any patterns among the intervals formed by the first six notes of the series? Among the intervals formed by the last six notes of the series? _____

_____

_____

OPCI

P_E E   C   F   D   G   E♭   A♭   G♭   A   B♭   D♭   B

- The interval pattern suggests that each six-note group is related to itself by inversion. Identify the TnI that inverts each six-note group onto itself, and slur together the inversional partners. _____

P_E E   C   F   D   G   E♭   A♭   G♭   A   B♭   D♭   B

_____   _____

- The row can be divided into four trichords. Label them below with their normal order and prime form. Then label the trichords on the score.

Prime forms: _____   _____   _____   _____

Normal forms: _____   _____   _____   _____

P_E	E	C	F		D	G	E♭		A♭	G♭	A		B♭	D♭	B
I_A	A	C♯	G♯		B	F♯	A♯		F	G	E		E♭	C	D

Normal forms: _____   _____   _____   _____

Prime forms: _____   _____   _____   _____

- When P_E and I_A are combined, the combined trichords form familiar six-note collections, either hexatonic or chromatic (a string of six adjacent notes in the chromatic scale). Label them on the chart below, and in the score.

P_E	E	C	F	D	G	E♭	A♭	G♭	A	B♭	D♭	B

I_A	A	C♯	G♯	B	F♯	A♯	F	G	E	E♭	C	D

Collection   _____   _____   _____   _____

- How do the series, trichords, and collections work together to organize the piece?

9. Thomas Adès, Third Mazurka

The melody expresses a twelve-tone series, first in Prime and then in Retrograde ordering:

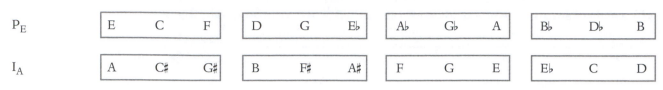

$P_{G♯}$	G♯	C♯	D♯	A♯	F♯	B	F	C	E	A	G	D	$RP_{G♯}$

- Provide a twelve-count of just the melody on the score, labeling the series forms and numbering each pitch in the series.

- Identify the ordered pitch-class intervals in the series, and write them below. Are there any recurring intervals or patterns? _____

_____

_____

_____

opci   __   __   __   __   __   __   __   __   __   __   __

$P_{G\#}$ G#   C#   D#   A#   F#   B   F   C   E   A   G   D

$P_{G\#}$ G#   C#   D#   A#   F#   B   __   F   C   E   A   G   D

(arrows connecting symmetric note pairs, with blank lines in the center)

- Identify the interval formed from the first note to the last, the second note to the second-to-last, and so on. What did you find? _____

_____

- The bass line relates to the melody as T_5 or $P_{C\#}$. Write out the series.

$P_{C\#}$ __   __   __   __   __   __   __   __   __   __   __   __

- Give a twelve-count of the bass line with reference to $P_{C\#}$. In what order are the notes of $P_{C\#}$ presented? _____

_____

_____

_____

- In the accompanying inner part that starts in measure 8, circle the minor triads and identify each triad root. How does that sequence of roots relate to $P_{C\#}$? How does the sequence relate to the actual bass line? To the perfect fifths formed between melody and bass on each downbeat? _____

_____

_____

_____

_____

_____

_____

10. Ursula Mamlok, *Panta Rhei*, iii

This passage is based on two inversionally related series forms:

P$_{F\sharp}$	F♯	C♯	A♯	F	D	A	E	D♯	C	B	G♯	G
I$_{D\sharp}$	D♯	G♯	B	E	G	C	F	F♯	A	A♯	C♯	D

- Provide a twelve-count of the passage, indicating row forms on the score and numbering the pitches of each series. Note that the ostinatos (violin and piano in the first half, cello and piano in the second half) contribute the first and fifth notes to each series.

- The six-note groups within the series are hexatonic collections. Identity them here and label them on the score.

Row form	First hexatonic collection	Second hexatonic collection
P~F♯~		
I~D♯~		

- Label the ordered pitch-class intervals in P~F♯~. Are there any patterns?

opci   __   __   __   __   __   __   __   __   __   __   __

P~F♯~   F♯   C♯   A♯   F   D   A   E   D♯   C   B   G♯   G

- Find the normal form and prime form of the trichords in the first half of P~F♯~ and I~D♯~, labeling every group of three adjacent notes. What trichord class appears in the first half of the rows? _____

P~F♯~

Normal form	Prime form
[F♯, A♯, C♯]	(037)

I~D♯~

Normal form	Prime form
[G♯, B, D♯]	(037)

- Now find the normal order and prime form of the trichords in the second half of P~F♯~ and I~D♯~, labeling every group of three adjacent notes. What trichord class appears in the second half of the rows? _____

P~F♯~

Normal form	Prime form

I~D♯~

Normal form	Prime form

chapter 47 — Form

A. QUESTIONS FOR REVIEW

1. What is a traditional tonal sentence? How are post-tonal sentences different from tonal sentences? What is a dissolving sentence? An immobilized sentence?

2. What is a traditional tonal period? Which aspects of a traditional period are maintained in post-tonal practice? Which may be changed?

3. Which features of traditional sonata form are maintained in post-tonal practice? Which may be changed?

4. What is moment form?

5. What is collage form?

6. What does it mean to say that form is process?

B. ANALYSIS: SENTENCES

- Identify the sentence type of these examples (sentence, dissolving sentence, immobilized sentence) or note "no sentence."

- Use brackets and labels to identify the presentation (basic idea, basic idea repeats) and the continuation and cadence.

1. Alban Berg, *Wozzeck,* Act 1, scene iii ("Marie's Lullaby")

sentence type: _____

2. Arnold Schoenberg, Little Piano Pieces, Op. 19, No. 6

sentence type: _____

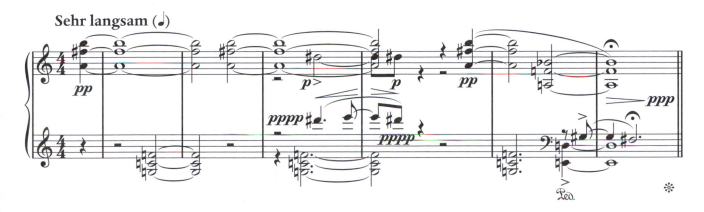

3. Anton Webern, Movements for String Quartet, Op. 5, No. 4

sentence type: _____

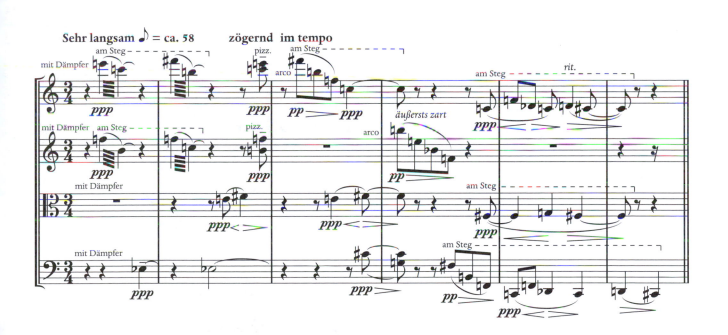

4. Igor Stravinsky, *Petrushka,* Second Tableau, "Petrushka's Curses"

sentence type: _____

5. Igor Stravinsky, Serenade in A, i

sentence type: _____

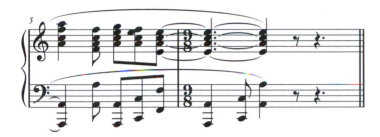

6. Kaija Saariaho, *Sept papillons* (for solo cello), iii

sentence type: _____

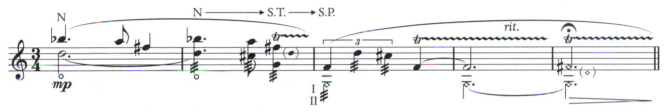

* In this excerpt, S.P. indicates *sul ponticello* bowing; S.T., *sul tasto;* and N., *normal*.

C. ANALYSIS: PERIODS

- Note whether these passages should be analyzed as periods.
- Use brackets and labels as appropriate to identify the antecedent and its relatively weak cadence (labeled HC, even without all of the attributes of a tonal HC) and the consequent and its relatively strong cadence (labeled PAC, even without all of the attributes of a tonal PAC).

1. Alban Berg, *Wozzeck,* Act 2, scene i

The composer identified this passage as a period with an antecedent and a consequent. Can you figure out what he had in mind? Hint: Focus on the instrumental accompaniment—the vocal melody cuts across the phrase boundaries.

Is this a period? _____

Why or why not? _____

_____

_____

2. Dmitri Shostakovich, String Quartet No. 3, i

Is this a period? _____

Why or why not? _____

_____

_____

3. Francis Poulenc, Sonata for Flute and Piano, i

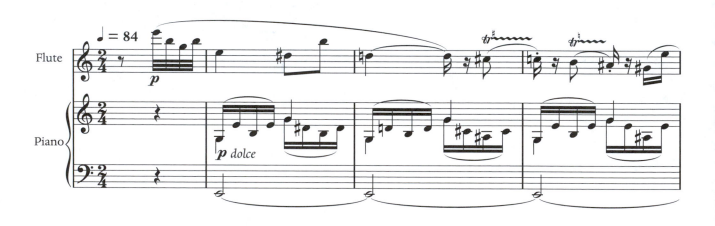

Is this a period? _____

Why or why not? _____

_____

_____

D. ANALYSIS: SONATA FORM

Answer the questions following each example.

1. Maurice Ravel, *Sonatine,* i

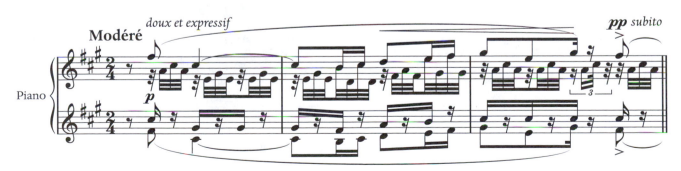

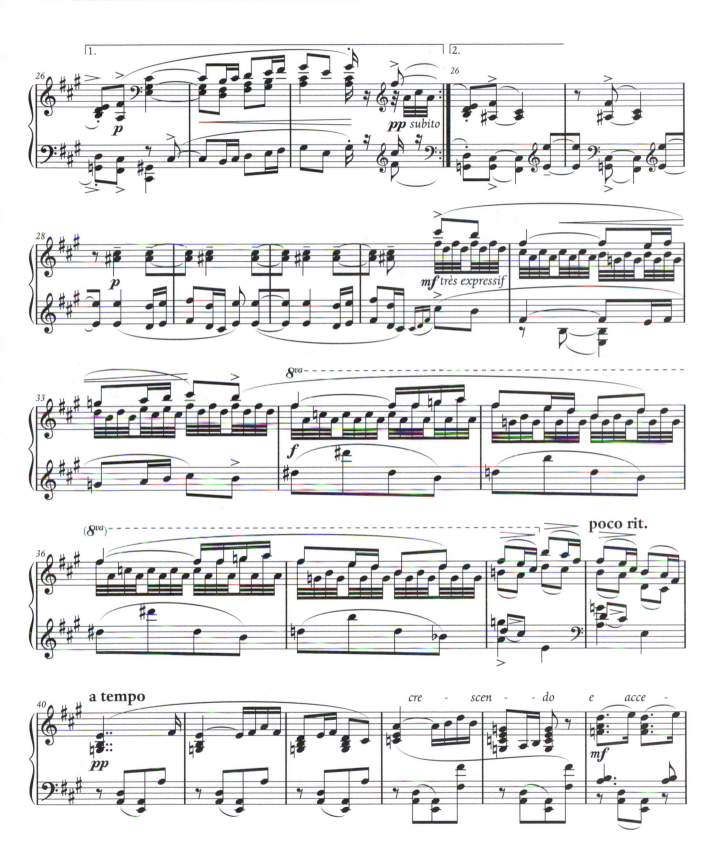

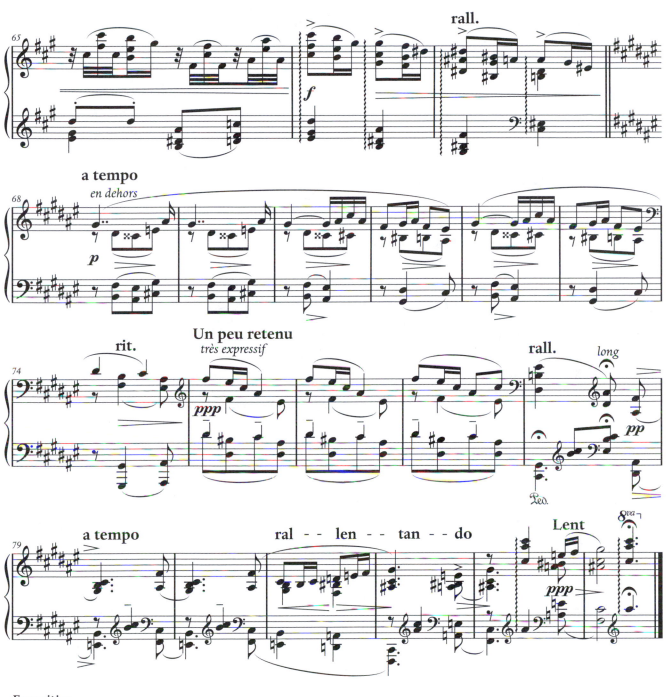

Exposition

- The primary theme begins in measure _____. In what key, and how can you tell? _____

  _____

- The transition begins in measure _____ and ends in measure _____ with a half cadence in the key of _____.

- The secondary theme begins in measure _____. In what key(s) is it in?

  _____

- The closing section begins in measure _____. How is it distinguished
  from the secondary theme? _____

Development

- The development begins in measure _____.
- Which theme returns in measure 31 and in what key? _____
  _____ Transposed from its occur-
  rence in the exposition by what interval? _____
- Which theme returns in measure 40, and in what key does it begin?
  _____ Transposed from its occurrence in the
  exposition by what interval? _____
- The theme that begins in measure 40 is rapidly transposed upward. Name
  the measures in which it is transposed, identify the starting melodic note, and
  name the interval of transposition. _____

  _____

Recapitulation

- The recapitulation begins in measure _____. Which theme? _____
  _____ In what key? _____
- The secondary theme begins in measure _____. In what key? _____
  How does the key compare to the secondary theme in the exposition?

  _____

- The closing section begins in measure _____.
- What key does the movement end in? _____ How does this key compare
  to the key of the exposition? _____ What is the final chord of the
  movement? _____

2. Dmitri Shostakovich, String Quartet No. 1, i

NAME: ....

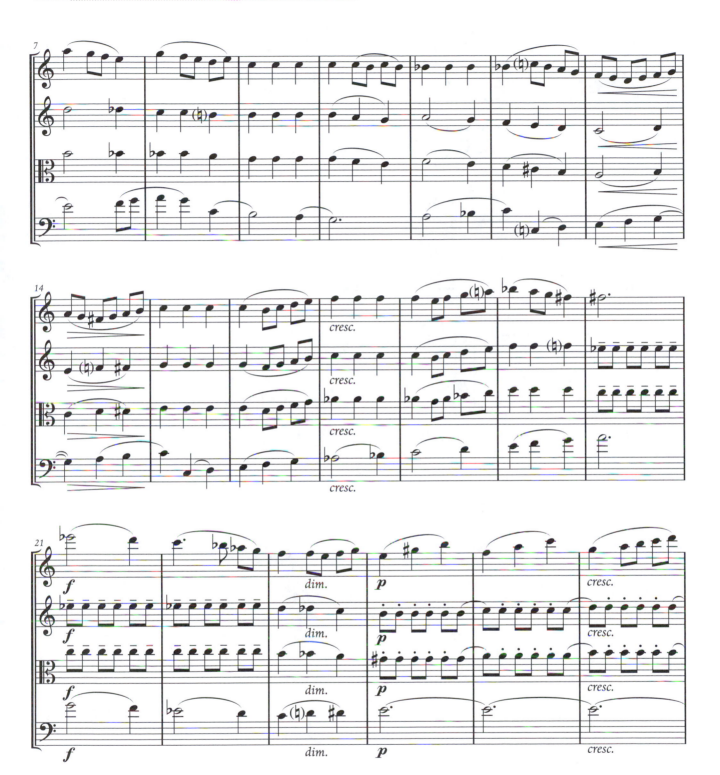

NAME: ....

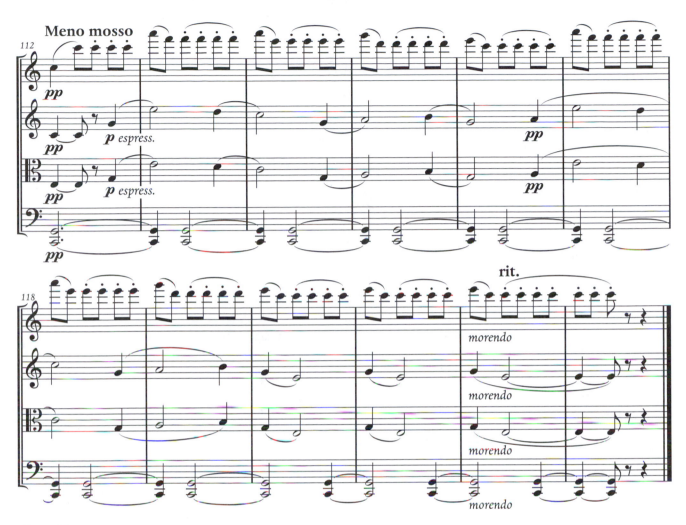

Exposition

- The primary theme lasts for eight measures, and is followed by a modified repeat lasting _____ measures and a more complete repeat lasting _____ measures. It is generally in what key? _____

- The transition is in two parts. The first begins in measure _____ and starts on what harmony? _____ The second begins in measure _____ and starts on what harmony? _____

- The secondary theme begins in measure _____ and is mostly in what key? _____ It repeats with different instrumentation starting in measure _____ and is still in what key? _____ It repeats for a third time starting in measure _____, and still in what key? _____

Development

- The development begins in measure _____. Which theme is the source of the material? _____ What is the initial harmony of the development? _____ How does it relate to the key of the secondary theme?

  _____

Recapitulation

- The recapitulation begins in measure _____. In what key? _____
  What harmony does this nine-measure statement of the principal theme end
  on? _____ What is the relationship between this harmony and the key of
  the principal theme? _____

- The secondary theme begins in measure _____. In what key? _____
  After an eight-measure statement of the secondary theme, what harmony
  do we arrive on? _____ What is the relationship between this harmony
  and the key of the secondary theme? _____
  _____

- The coda begins in measure _____ and derives its material from which
  theme? _____

E. ANALYSIS: MOMENT FORM

Igor Stravinsky, *Symphonies of Wind Instruments*, opening

This passage features seven distinct units that return throughout the example. Label
them A–G as they occur, then complete the table below with a brief description of
each unit.

NAME: ....

UNIT LABEL	DESCRIPTION
A	
B	
C	
D	
E	
F	
G	

Choose three pairs of consecutive blocks, and write a few sentences about what distinguishes them from each other and what they share in common.

F. ANALYSIS: COLLAGE FORM

Charles Ives, String Quartet No. 2, i

This passage makes reference to the following tunes, all popular at the time the piece was written: "Columbia, the Gem of the Ocean," "Dixie," "Marching through Georgia," "Turkey in the Straw," and "Hail, Columbia."

- Listen to these tunes (widely available on YouTube and other web sources) to get familiar with them.

- Label them on the score.

- Write a few sentences about them. In what ways are they similar? In what ways are they different? How do they relate to the surrounding musical material?

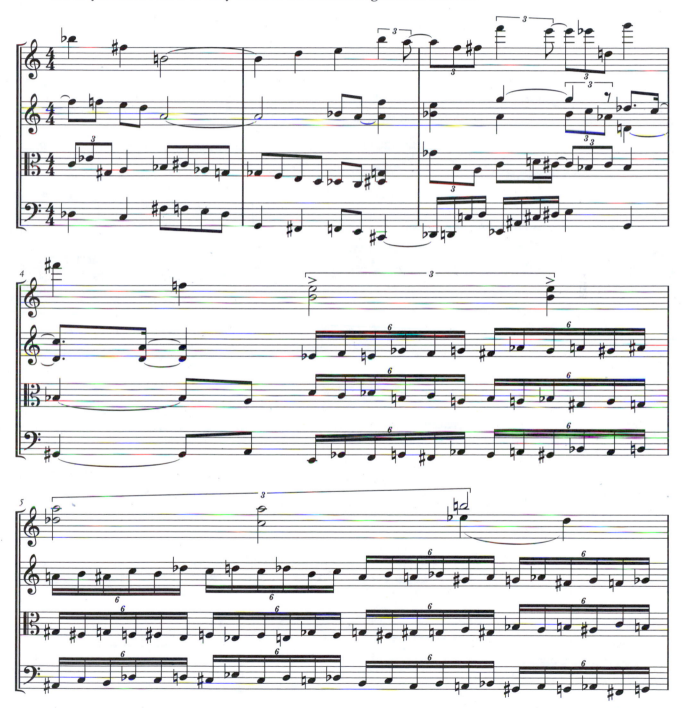

G. ANALYSIS: FORM AS PROCESS

1. Ruth Crawford, *Diaphonic Suite* No. 1 for oboe, iii

- The piece uses a seven-note series: G–A–G#–B–C–F–C#. Label it P_G in measure 1 of the score and number its notes 1–7.

- In measures 2–8, number all of the notes according to their position in P_G.

- Then answer the questions at the end of the score.

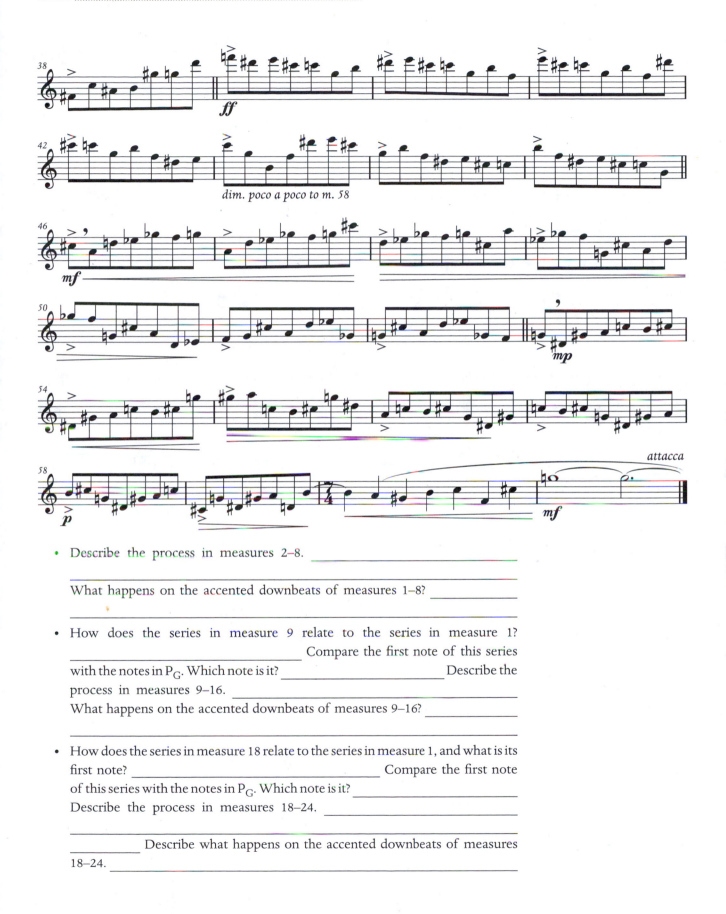

- Describe the process in measures 2–8. _____

  _____

  What happens on the accented downbeats of measures 1–8? _____

  _____

- How does the series in measure 9 relate to the series in measure 1? _____ Compare the first note of this series with the notes in P$_G$. Which note is it? _____ Describe the process in measures 9–16. _____

  What happens on the accented downbeats of measures 9–16? _____

  _____

- How does the series in measure 18 relate to the series in measure 1, and what is its first note? _____ Compare the first note of this series with the notes in P$_G$. Which note is it? _____

  Describe the process in measures 18–24. _____

  _____

  _____ Describe what happens on the accented downbeats of measures 18–24. _____

- Identify the series forms in measures 1, 9, 18, 25, 32, 39, 46, 53, and 60–61. _____ what are the starting pitches of each series form, and how do these compare with the notes of P_G? _____

  _____ Describe the process within each section of the piece. _____

  _____ Describe what happens on the accented downbeats within each section of the piece.

  _____

2. Steve Reich, *Clapping Music* (for two performers), first six phases

♩ = 160-184 Repeat each bar 12 times

- The piece is arranged in thirteen "phases." Describe the rhythmic pattern used by both players in Phase 1. _____

  _____

- What does each player do in Phase 2? _____

  _____

- What does each player do in Phase 3? _____

  _____

- Continue this process by writing out additional phases until the music returns to Phrase 1.

- Describe the process for the work as a whole. Why does it require thirteen phases to bring the two performers back into sync? _____

_____

_____

_____

Credits

40.E.8: *L'Amour De Loin*. **Libretto by Amin Maalouf. Music by Kaija Saariaho and Amin Maalouf.** Copyright © 2000 Chester Music Limited. This arrangement copyright © 2019 Chester Music Limited. International copyright secured. All rights reserved. Reprinted by permission of Hal Leonard LLC.

41.F.2: "From the Island of Bali," *Mikrokosmos SZ. 107, No. 109* **by Bela Bartok.** © 1940 by Hawkes & Son (London) Ltd. [Definitive corrected edition © 1987 by Hawkes & Son Ltd.] International copyright secured. Used with permission. All rights reserved.

41.F.3: "Diminished Fifth," *Mikrokosmos Sz. 107, No. 101* **by Bela Bartok.** © 1940 by Hawkes & Son (London) Ltd. [Definitive corrected edition © 1987 by Hawkes & Son Ltd.] International copyright secured. Used with permission. All rights reserved.

41.F.6: "Sept Papillons." **Music by Kaija Saariaho.** Copyright © 2000 Chester Music Limited. This arrangement copyright © 2019 Chester Music Limited. International copyright secured. All rights reserved. Reprinted by permission of Hal Leonard LLC.

41.F.8: "Harvest Song," *Forty-Four Duos for Two Violins*, No. 33 **by Bela Bartok.** © 1933 Boosey & Hawkes Inc. Copyright renewed. International copyright secured. Used with permission. All rights reserved.

41.F.9: "String Quartet No. 2" **by Ellen Taaffe Zwilich.** Copyright © 1989 by Merion Music, Inc. Theodore Presser Company authorized representative. Used with permission. All rights reserved.

41.F.10: IN MEMORY (for STRING QUARTET) **by Joan Tower.** Copyright © 2002 by Associated Music Publishers, Inc. All rights reserved. International copyright secured. Reprinted by permission.

42.F.1c: STRING QUARTET NO. 4 IN D MAJOR, OP. 83 **by Dmitri Shostakovich.** Copyright © 1954 (renewed) by G. Schirmer, Inc. (ASCAP). International copyright secured. All rights reserved. Reprinted by permission.

42.F.2a: "Piano Quintet in Five Movements" **by Alfred Schnittke.** © 1976 Anglo-Soviet Music Press Ltd, rights only in UK. Copyright © 1976 by C.F. Peters Corporation. All rights reserved. Used with permission.

42.F.3e: *Makrokosmos,* Vol. I, "Primeval Sounds (Genesis I)" **by George Crumb.** Copyright © 1974 by C.F. Peters Corporation. All rights reserved. Used with permission.

Index of Music Examples